From Bash to Z Shell: Conquering the Command Line

OLIVER KIDDLE, JERRY PEEK, AND PETER STEPHENSON

Apress®

From Bash to Z Shell: Conquering the Command Line

Copyright © 2005 by Oliver Kiddle, Jerry Peek, and Peter Stephenson

ISBN (pbk): 1-59059-376-6

Printed and bound in the United States of America 9 8 7 6 5 4 3 2 1

Trademarked names may appear in this book. Rather than use a trademark symbol with every occurrence of a trademarked name, we use the names only in an editorial fashion and to the benefit of the trademark owner, with no intention of infringement of the trademark.

Lead Editor: Jason Gilmore

Technical Reviewers: Bart Schaefer and Ed Schaefer

Editorial Board: Steve Anglin, Dan Appleman, Ewan Buckingham, Gary Cornell, Tony Davis, John Franklin, Jason Gilmore, Chris Mills, Dominic Shakeshaft, Jim Sumser

Project Manager: Beth Christmas

Copy Edit Manager: Nicole LeClerc

Copy Editor: Liz Welch

Production Manager: Kari Brooks-Copony

Production Editor: Laura Cheu

Compositor: Susan Glinert

Proofreader: Linda Seifert

Indexer: Kevin Broccoli

Artist: Kinetic Publishing Services, LLC

Cover Designer: Kurt Krames

Manufacturing Manager: Tom Debolski

Distributed to the book trade in the United States by Springer-Verlag New York, Inc., 233 Spring Street, 6th Floor, New York, NY 10013, and outside the United States by Springer-Verlag GmbH & Co. KG, Tiergartenstr. 17, 69112 Heidelberg, Germany.

In the United States: phone 1-800-SPRINGER, fax 201-348-4505, e-mail orders@springer-ny.com, or visit http://www.springer-ny.com. Outside the United States: fax +49 6221 345229, e-mail orders@springer.de, or visit http://www.springer.de.

For information on translations, please contact Apress directly at 2560 Ninth Street, Suite 219, Berkeley, CA 94710. Phone 510-549-5930, fax 510-549-5939, e-mail info@apress.com, or visit http://www.apress.com.

The information in this book is distributed on an "as is" basis, without warranty. Although every precaution has been taken in the preparation of this work, neither the author(s) nor Apress shall have any liability to any person or entity with respect to any loss or damage caused or alleged to be caused directly or indirectly by the information contained in this work.

Contents at a Glance

Contents

PART 1 ■■■ Introducing the Shell

PART 2 ■■■ Using bash and zsh

PART 3 ■■■ Extending the Shell

About the Authors

 **OLIVER KIDDLE** was first introduced to Unix systems while studying at the University of York. Since graduating in 1998, Oliver has worked as a software developer and system administrator. Over the past five years, Oliver has been actively involved with the development of the Z shell.

 **JERRY PEEK** is a freelance writer and instructor. He has used shells extensively and has taught users about them for over 20 years. Peek is the "Power Tools" columnist for *Linux Magazine* and coauthored the book *Unix Power Tools* (O'Reilly Media).

 **PETER STEPHENSON** grew up in northeast England and studied physics at Oxford. After nine years as a researcher in computational physics, he became a software engineer with Cambridge Silicon Radio, where he now works on short-range digital radio. He has been involved with zsh since the early 1990s and currently coordinates its development.

About the Technical Reviewers

BART SCHAEFER has served as a key architect and senior developer of e-mail systems for more than 15 years, creating flexible and scalable solutions with an emphasis on open standards. Before cofounding iPost he was a founder of Z-Code Software, whose groundbreaking multiplatform e-mail application, Z-Mail, won numerous awards. Dr. Schaefer contributes regularly to open software projects, including SpamAssassin and zsh. He holds a PhD in computer science from the Oregon Graduate Institute, focusing on automated process distribution and scheduling for massively parallel computer systems, and a BSS in computer science from Cornell College.

ED SCHAEFER is an ex-paratrooper, an ex-military intelligence officer, and an ex-oil field service engineer. He's not a total has-been. Presently, he's a software developer and DBA for a Fortune 50 company—a Unix island in a sea of Windows. He's also a contributing editor to *Sys Admin, the Journal for UNIX and Linux Systems Administrators*, and edits *Unix Review*'s monthly "Shell Corner" column at http://www.unixreview.com.

Acknowledgments

The authors would like to thank Martin Streicher for the initial concept behind this book and for bringing us together at the start of the project. Thanks also to the Apress staff and our technical reviewers who've done so much work "behind the scenes" to bring this book to you. We authors did only a small part of the job.

Jerry Peek's portrait is by Meredith Hayes.

Preface

A shell is a sophisticated way to control your computer—Unix, Linux, Microsoft Windows, Mac OS X, and others. If you do more than the most basic operations, you can do many of them more powerfully and quickly with a shell and your keyboard than by using a mouse.

The history of shells goes back some 30 years. In the early days of the Unix operating system, choosing and customizing your interface to a computer was a new idea. (It still *is* new to many people today, users of "one-size-fits-all" window systems that can be changed only superficially.) Before windows and a mouse were common, programmers began developing an interface that used the keyboard: typing one or a few words to run programs, then reading results from the same screen. As time went on, more shells were developed, giving users more choices.

New features have been added continually over the years, making the modern shell an incredibly rich environment that saves power users hours of time and frustration. Tasks that take lots of repetitive work with a mouse can be automated. For example, shell features such as *completion* let you accomplish a lot with little typing.

A shell can work in two ways. You can use it interactively to do things by hand. You can also automate a task by packaging those same operations into a *script* or *function*. Learning shell features lets you do both of those because a shell is a user interface and a programming language in one.

The shells we discuss run on many operating systems. What you learn about shells will let you use all of these operating systems in the same way. If you use more than one operating system, a shell gives you a powerful and familiar interface to all of them.

There are several major shells. Because each has its differences, covering all of the shells could make a book that's both confusing and unwieldy. We've concentrated on bash and zsh, two of the most modern and powerful shells. Both are freely available; in fact, they're installed on many of the systems we've listed and can be downloaded from the Internet for the rest.

- bash is the de facto standard shell on Linux. bash runs most scripts written for other Bourne-type shells, including the original Unix shell sh, and it has a growing list of features.

- zsh, also called Z shell, is an extremely powerful shell that's not as well known as bash. zsh combines most of the best features of several shells, including C-type shells such as tcsh. However, its basic usage is similar to bash.

  This book provides the first comprehensive Z shell coverage that we know of. If you consider yourself a power user (or if, after reading what shells can do, you want to *become* a power user!), you owe it to yourself to get familiar with all that zsh can do to make your work easier.

Covering both bash and zsh shows you what features the two shells have in common as well as their different approaches to the same tasks.

How This Book Is Structured

This book is divided into three parts consisting of 15 chapters. Part 1, *Introducing the Shell*, contains Chapters 1 through 3. Part 2, *Using bash and zsh*, is made up of Chapters 4 through 11. Part 3, *Extending the Shell*, includes Chapters 12 through 15. The book also has three appendices: a list of Unix-like commands, a list of resources, and a glossary. In this section we offer a brief introduction of each chapter.

Chapter 1: Introduction to Shells

This chapter covers the highlights of shells. Topics include: what a shell is, how to start one, the parts of a command line, running simple Unix commands and getting help with them, an introduction to the filesystem and how to use files by typing only part of their names, how the shell finds the programs you need, how the shell processes command lines, and recalling and editing command lines.

Chapter 2: Using Shell Features Together

Here we introduce several important features, including rerouting a program's input and output, using utility programs to edit text automatically, running loops (repeating a series of commands), handy command-line techniques, and more. The emphasis, though, is on one of the capabilities that make shells so useful: that you can combine programs, together with features of the shell, to do completely new things.

Chapter 3: More Shell Features

This chapter moves more slowly through several other major shell topics: passing information between programs, managing processes, using quoting to control how the shell interprets a command line, and a time-saving technique for moving through the filesystem.

Chapter 4: Entering and Editing the Command Line

When you use a shell interactively, you tell it what to do by typing commands on its command line. (When programming the shell, as we'll discuss in Chapter 13, you put those same commands into a shell function or a file.) Chapter 4 covers the command line in depth—including how to fix errors and how to save time by reusing previous command lines. This chapter also covers the interaction of a shell with its window (a terminal).

Chapter 5: Starting the Shell

A shell can be customized to work the way you want it to by setting its options and variables, by installing your own commands, and more. You can do this interactively (from the command line) after the shell has started. You can also customize the shell automatically each time it starts. Chapter 5 shows how.

Chapter 6: More About Shell History

Chapter 4 introduced shell history—a remembered list of previous command lines. Chapter 6 describes how to save, recall, and share history between shells. It also covers a way to let you reuse parts of previous command lines in later ones.

Chapter 7: Prompts

When the shell needs to ask you something (for instance, "Do you want to change the spelling of this word?") or tell you something (such as "You can enter a command line now"), it prompts you. Like almost everything about the shells, the prompt can be customized to show information you want, as you want it. This chapter shows you how.

Chapter 8: Files and Directories

One of a shell's greatest strengths is the power and control it gives you for working with files. This chapter highlights some useful information about files on a Unix-type system such as Linux and Mac OS X (also under Microsoft Windows, with Cygwin). Next it discusses how to refer to and use files from the shell.

Chapter 9: Pattern Matching

This chapter carries on from Chapter 8, showing one of the most useful and work-saving techniques in a shell: finding one or many files by their names and other characteristics. After seeing these powerful techniques, you might wish that the file-handling menus on your graphical applications (word processors, for instance) had a shell built in.

Chapter 10: Completion

One handy shell feature that *is* available on some graphical file-handling menus is filename completion: the ability to type the first few characters of a filename and have the remaining characters completed for you. As this chapter shows, modern shells have extended this basic idea in many ways. This chapter covers the many aspects of bash's and zsh's completion systems and the ways in which their behavior can be configured.

Chapter 11: Jobs and Processes

Shells let you control multiple programs (multiple processes) from a single terminal: starting them, suspending them, ending them early, and more. The shell lets you control some of the resources that a process uses—the amount of memory, for example. And, shells being the flexible tools that they are, there's more.

Chapter 12: Variables

Variables are places to store information within the shell and to pass information between the shell and other programs (processes). Variables are used to customize the shell and to keep something you want to reuse later (like a filename), and they are especially useful if you're programming.

Chapter 12 shows how data stored in variables can be manipulated. In addition, Chapter 12 shows how to use the shell's built-in math facilities.

Chapter 13: Scripting and Functions

The shell implements a full programming language. Chapter 13 covers features like loops and condition tests, which allow powerful things to be done just from the command line. Often, however, it can be useful to save a set of commands for later reuse—including some commands you just ran from the command line.

This "dual-use" ability of the shell—how it lets you use the same language for controlling your system interactively as for writing programs (to do things automatically)—is, as we've said, one of the great things about shells. The focus of Chapter 13 is on how you can write programs with the shell and how you can use these programs to extend the basic functionality of the shell.

Chapter 14: Writing Editor Commands

The Z shell has a completely configurable editor built in. This chapter explains how you can add new commands to your zsh editor.

Chapter 15: Writing Completion Functions

Chapter 10 shows how completion works "out of the box." If that's not enough for you, both bash and zsh also let you write your own custom completion definitions. Chapter 15 explains how.

Who Should Read This Book

Although shells are sophisticated, they aren't just for experts. For those of you without considerable shell experience, we've carefully chosen topics and a manner of instruction that will enable you to immediately begin using shells at a new level of proficiency. In particular, Part 1 of this book will help prepare you for some of the more advanced topics that follow throughout the remainder of the book.

Expert users interested in maximizing their already efficient use of the command line will find the hundreds of tips, tricks, and hidden gems that we present throughout this book quite useful. Based on our years of experience immersed in command-line interaction, we're well aware of the features that can even further improve your shell proficiency, and condense that knowledge into this book.

Prerequisites

This book covers bash version 3.0 and zsh version 4.2. Most of this material applies to other versions of these two shells—especially to bash 2.04 and zsh 4.0—and the concepts apply to other shells as well.

You can download the latest versions of both of these shells—as well as the Cygwin package you'll need for Microsoft Windows—for free on the Internet. (If you haven't used freely available software before, don't be concerned: this software is the highest quality, maintained by groups of professional programmers who want the very best software for their own use.)

There's more information about the software and where to get it in Appendix B.

Tips for Reading Technical Material

If you've found that reading technical topics can be a challenge, here are tips that may help:

- **Reading technical material is different than reading a novel:** In technical writing, the authors aren't trying to disguise secrets or surprise you. They're giving you information as clearly as they can. Instead of trying to obscure the clues to the "mystery," they're laying them out in front of you. But even words spelled out clearly don't always mean that a concept will be obvious at first.

- **Put on your detective's cap:** If the puzzle doesn't seem to be coming together, go back and see what the missing parts are. This can take some time and effort: learning something new isn't always easy! But, like reading a good mystery novel, finding the answer— putting the puzzle together—is well worth the time you spend.

- **If something's missing, find it:** Read each paragraph, or each group of a few paragraphs, then be sure the new concepts make sense before you go on. Sometimes they just won't make sense; there might be a missing piece to the puzzle. If that happens, try going back and reviewing what you've read before.

- **Check for understanding as you go:** Most sentences aren't "fillers"; we're trying to make a point, either to introduce a new idea or to tie some ideas together. For instance, after you've read a while and learned some new concepts, you might see a sentence like this:

  ```
  The list of directories comes from the standard output of tr.
  ```

  It's best not to just say "Oh, umm-hmm" and keep reading. Instead, you should ask yourself a question like "On the basis of what I've read before, does that sentence make sense?" or "Do I agree with what the sentence says?" You could also ask yourself about each part of the sentence, like "What list?" or "What's a directory?" or "What's the standard output again?" or "What does tr do and why does it write to its standard output?" If you aren't sure, don't read too much more before you go back to hunt for the missing clues.

- **Talk it over:** If you have some questions, and you have some computer-literate friends, talk it over with them. Discuss the problem—and, if you'd like to learn more than just the answer, discuss the topic in general. Explaining a problem to someone else, and being sure that each of you understands the other, is a great way to increase understanding.

  This is true even if your friends don't know about shells. We'll bet that they won't only be impressed at what you're doing. Soon your friends will be studying shells, too (and possibly asking *you* for advice!).

- **Please experiment:** Experimenting on your system is a great way to learn and to check your understanding—if, that is, you're careful about programs that could do damage— like rm, a program that removes files. For instance, as you read through a section, take some of the previous examples and change them slightly to see how that affects the results... then be sure you understand why.

We don't assign formal exercises in this book, but you could come up with a practical problem and see how to handle it. As an example, after you've learned how to remove many files at once by using a wildcard, create a lot of dummy files and try to remove them.

Contacting the Authors

You can send e-mail to the authors at shellbook@jpeek.com. While we can't promise to answer every message, we will do our best, and you can be sure that we *will* read every one. Thanks in advance for your messages.

We've listed some good places to get more information in Appendix B.

PART 1

■ ■ ■

Introducing the Shell

This introductory part of the book is a quick tour through some of the most useful features of all shells. We also describe features of Unix-like operating systems that shells take advantage of.

Unlike the rest of the book, the chapters in Part 1 are not intended to be exhaustive in detail. They're here to give you a flavor of how much you can do with a shell. Even if you've used shells for years, we suggest that you at least skim through this part to spot hints and tips you might not know about.

CHAPTER 1

■■■

Introduction to Shells

What's a Shell?

A *shell* is a program that runs other programs. It's full of features that make your computer easier to use. Shells can find programs and files quickly, remember what you've done before, and store information that you use over and over.

There are various definitions of the term *shell*. When we say "shell," we're talking about an interface between the user and the computer's operating system.[1] You can think of a shell as a "wrapper" around the operating system, one that protects you from the system (and the system from you!). It lets you use the computer without needing to understand the low-level details that programmers do. Figure 1-1 shows someone using a shell to tell the computer to copy some files. The figure also shows some of the layers of complexity that the shell hides from the user.

In early operating systems, users couldn't choose how to interact with the computer. There was no mouse and no windows: commands were typed on a keyboard and the computer's response was also in text. Shells grew out of this environment. Unix did things differently: shells were separated from the operating system. The shell is a stand-alone program, and users can choose their own shell. (When Unix appeared on the scene, there were only one or two shells to choose from.) As mice and graphical displays became popular, computer professionals kept using shells—and improving them to work better and faster.

Several popular modern shells are available, and all of them work in the same basic way. (We'll see a list of shells later in this chapter, and explore some of their main differences throughout Part 1.) The shells we cover in this book use a keyboard to send commands to a computer, as well as a screen full of text that shows what you've told the computer and what its answers are.

Once you learn some basics, you can save even more work by "teaching" the shell to execute a series of tasks for you. Here's an example.

At the start of each workday, you need to make a copy of every file you've been working on; each copy's name should start with *old*. The previous day's copies are removed. Doing that by hand is tedious, but there's a faster way! Instead of copying the files one by one, you can package those same steps into a *shell script* or *shell function*. Then, each day, with a few keystrokes, you simply "replay" those commands to do the job in a flash.

---

1. Programmers: On Unix/Linux systems, a shell basically prints a prompt, reads a command you enter there, converts it to an argument list for the operating system's exec function, starts a new process, and helps the user manage that process.

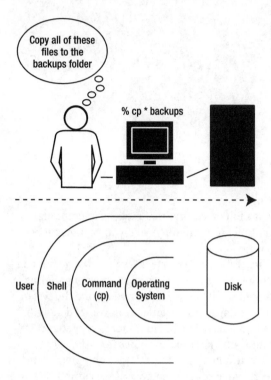

Figure 1-1. *The shell interface*

That's a small example of the power of a shell. There's much, much more. Shells are sophisticated programs developed for more than 30 years by people who use computers constantly, day in and day out. They're packed with features that make interaction with a computer faster and easier. For instance, a shell (working in conjunction with utility programs) can

- Do most of the typing for you by completing commands automatically.

- Locate files all through your computer's filesystem by their characteristics, then perform a number of operations on them.

- Remember and redo a command, or a series of commands, that you've done before.

- Let you quickly jump between two or more "memorized" locations in the filesystem.

- Create a series of filenames or decide how often to perform a task.

(If you've written computer programs before, it might help you to think of the shell as a programming language interpreter. The shell's language is designed for running other programs.)

Are you fairly new to computers? Or do you do most of your computer work using a mouse, buttons, and menus? In either case, learning to use a shell will be a new experience: a new way of thinking and working. A shell won't replace your mouse. Instead, it will *supplement* the way you've worked before. You'll learn when the shell is faster and easier, and when a mouse is better.

We'll bet that the shell will become one of your new tools—a very powerful tool that will change the way you work.

It doesn't take long to learn the basics of using a shell. But that's not where the power lies. The best shells have literally *hundreds* of powerful features. You don't need to learn all of them, and they'll take time to learn. In this part of the book, we'll introduce many of those features and show examples that you can try right away. The details are in later parts.

TYPING COMMANDS? WHY?

To use a shell, you'll be using the keyboard. If you're accustomed to giving commands by pointing to menus and buttons with a mouse, you might wonder why shells use a keyboard instead of a mouse.

One obvious reason is that computers had keyboards (and shells!) long before they had windows and mice. Shells developed to let you control your system from a keyboard.

"But," you might ask, "can't they just put those commands on some menus and buttons?" There *have* been some graphical shells—and there will certainly be more. So far, though, graphical interfaces aren't nearly as fast or powerful as standard shells. Here's why:

- Unix systems have hundreds of programs, and many of those programs have multiple options. (Other systems, like Microsoft Windows, have a lot of programs too.) You don't need to know or use all of those programs, of course. But try to imagine a menu system that would let an expert choose from all of those programs. It could have hundreds of menu entries, many with their own submenus for setting options. It would be a nightmare to use!

- Many Unix programs are like building blocks. They can work together to do something that one program can't do alone. As we'll see, it's easy to tell the shell how to build this big set of programs into an almost-infinite number of combinations. But—so far, at least—graphical systems are slower to set up and clumsier too. (Think about how a language like English has many thousands of words, which you can combine in an infinite number of ways to make an infinite number of different sentences—and thoughts. That's a lot like the power that a shell gives you for controlling your computer.)

- Moving a mouse around a screen takes time. If you have a system handy, try it now. Move the mouse to one corner of the screen, then take your hands away. Now reach for the mouse, move it to another part of the screen, point to a menu. and drag it down to a command that opens a dialog box (where, for instance, you could enter a filename). Depending on what you're doing, that probably took you a few seconds and a fair amount of wrist motion. What if you could have done all of that by keeping your hands on the keyboard—typing, say, five keys plus a filename? Unless you're a very slow typist, you'll probably find that (after some practice) the keyboard is faster. Over the space of days and weeks at your computer, the few seconds you save on each command can add up to hours of saved time. Most experienced shell users agree that leaving your hands on the keyboard will let you accomplish more in less time.

- One of the most powerful reasons to use a shell is *automation*. You can package a series of command lines so they'll all run when you simply type one word (or a few words). You'll learn how in Chapter 2.

Getting Started

If you used computers years ago, you didn't have a choice: the way you interacted with your system was through a shell. Now, most computers have a graphical user interface (GUI), with a mouse and windows, so you don't need a shell—at least not until you see how much it can do. (By the way, a GUI and a shell can work together: controlling parts of your window system, opening new windows and checking their status, and so on.)

You can recognize that you're working with a shell because its window (or your terminal screen, if you don't have windows) will have a shell prompt at its left edge. See Figure 1-2.

■**Definition** A shell prompt is the shell's signal to the user that it is ready for your instructions (it's ready to accept a command that you type next to the prompt). The prompt varies: most Unix systems have several kinds of shells available, and users can also customize their shells (as we'll see later). A typical prompt is $ or %, and it often has some other information too, such as the computer's name or your Unix username.

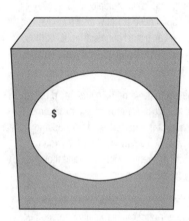

Figure 1-2. *The simplest shell interface*

How you get a shell depends on your local setup. Here are three possibilities:

- With a Unix or Linux window system, or with Macintosh OS X, you'll have menus or icons for starting programs. Look for an icon that looks like a terminal screen (it probably resembles a TV) or a menu item like xterm, *GNOME terminal*, konsole, or *terminal window*. (The section "Terminals and Shells" in Chapter 4 has more information.) When you choose that item, a new window should open and display a prompt.

- Under Microsoft Windows, you'll need a package like Cygwin (see the section "Getting Started with Cygwin" in Chapter 5) or the MKS Toolkit that provides Unix-like tools for Microsoft Windows. There's more information in Appendix B.

- If you're using a terminal (no windows or pointing device such as a mouse) that doesn't display a shell prompt, try pressing the Return key. If that doesn't help, ask your system staff—or the person sitting next to you.

The first thing to do is to press your Return or Enter key. (From now on, we'll call it Return. Use whichever key you have.) If all's well, you should get a new shell prompt that looks the same (or almost the same) as the first one. Pressing Return tells the shell to execute the command you typed—although, in this case, you haven't typed a command yet.

Simple Commands

Let's try a couple of simple commands. Most Unix commands have a short name; you type the command name just after the prompt. Type date—which is the name of a program that shows the current date and time—then press Return. The shell should find that command, run it, and then give you another prompt. Here's what your screen should look like; we'll show the part you type in boldface and the computer's response as plain text:

```
$ date
Sat Nov 20 09:05:19 MST 2004
$
```

If you make a typing mistake, what happens? The answer is: it depends on what you type and which shell you're using. Give it a try: type dtae and press Return. In general, if the shell can't find your command, it will output a message like command not found. Some shells have automatic spelling correction, though, like this example from the Z shell (zsh):

```
zsh% date
Sat Nov 20 09:09:11 MST 2004
zsh% dtae
zsh: correct 'dtae' to 'date' [nyae]? y
Sat Nov 20 09:09:27 MST 2004
```

(The [nyae] tells you that your answer can be one of the four single-letter choices: n for "no," y for "yes," a for "abort," and e to let you edit the command.) You'll find that shells are terse: they don't say much more than they need to. This is partly because many shell users are experienced, and they don't need much explanation to help them find out what's wrong. Some shells—like zsh—let you customize most of the shell's messages to say almost anything you want. You'll learn more about all of this in Chapter 7.

One thing that makes Unix commands so flexible is that you can modify the way they work. For instance, you can change their output format or the information they show. On many Unix systems, for example, date will output UTC (universal, or Greenwich Mean Time) if you add -u after the command name, separated by a space. The -u is an *option*; we'll cover options soon:

```
$ date
Sat Nov 20 09:11:13 MST 2004
$ date -u
Sat Nov 20 16:11:24 UTC 2004
$
```

■Warning Shells let you do things quickly; they're powerful tools that don't ask "Are you sure?" as often as graphical systems do. To avoid problems, take a moment to review what you typed before you press Return.

Command Lines

What you type at a prompt is called a *command line*. As you'll see, learning to use the command line is a bit like learning to speak a new language: you need to learn what words you can use and where, the punctuation, and so on. It's easier than a language, though, because you don't have to remember all of the things that can go on a command line. Once you've learned how to put together a command line, the documentation for Unix commands will show you what you can use there. There are many quick-reference guides and books with more detailed information. Your system probably also has manual pages (also called *manpages*), which provide brief summaries of what a program does and what you can put on its command line.

■Note We're introducing features here, showing what the shell can do. Don't be concerned about learning every detail.

■Definition Unix-like systems have a program named man that displays manual pages—manpages for short. Each program, such as date, has its own manual page, and so does each shell. Commands that are built into a shell, which we'll see later—cd, for instance—are covered in the shell's manpage.

Another man-like program is named info. If man doesn't show a manpage, try info instead.

If you're just getting started with Unix, you may want more information than you can get from some manual pages. Still, they can be helpful as a quick introduction or reminder. Let's try reading the manual page for date by typing man date at a prompt. You should see something like this:

```
$ man date
DATE(1)                  FREE SOFTWARE FOUNDATION                 DATE(1)

NAME
       date - print or set the system date and time

SYNOPSIS
       date [OPTION]... [+FORMAT]
       date [OPTION] [MMDDhhmm[[CC]YY][.ss]]

DESCRIPTION
       Display the current time in the given FORMAT, or set the
       system date.

   ...parts omitted...

       -u, --utc, --universal
              print or set Coordinated Universal Time

       --help display this help and exit

--More--(15%) q
$
```

The command line that you typed told your shell to run a program called man; it also told man that you want information about the date program. This is a lot like going to the menu with a mouse, selecting Programs, then System Accessories, choosing manuals to start the manuals program, pulling down the program's File menu, choosing the Open Manual page entry, moving the mouse to the dialog box, choosing date from a series of drop-down lists (because there are literally hundreds of manual pages), and then clicking the OK button. This is a simple example of how much faster a shell can be to use than a window system—once you've learned the basics of shells, that is.

Back to our example. As we've just shown, when man starts, your screen will probably fill with text, and then pause. The last line of your screen will have a prompt like a colon (:) character—or, as we've shown here, the word "More". What's happening? The man program (actually, another program called a pager) is pausing and prompting you to give a command. At the pager's prompt, you can press the spacebar (or maybe Return) for the next page, q to quit, and probably (depending on your system) commands that scroll back, search, and more.

■**Definition** A pager is a program that displays text page by page—or, actually, screenful by screenful. Three common pagers are named more, less, and pg.

After you look over this first part of the date manpage, type q to quit the pager program. When man sees the pager program exit, man will exit too. Your shell has been waiting for man to finish; now that it's done, you should see another shell prompt.

Let's take a closer look at the command-line syntax of Unix programs. *Syntax* means the formal properties of a language, or what you can put on a command line and where.

- The first component of a command line (after the prompt) is typically the name of a program or command. (As the section "Where the Commands Are Located" in this chapter explains, the shell can run programs both from external files and from built-in commands that are part of the shell.) The first program we've used was date. The second program was man, which we we're using to show the manpage for date. (The man program actually started a pager program, but the shell doesn't know that.)

- The rest of the command line varies. We won't try to cover all of the possibilities here; this is part of what gives Unix and the shells so much flexibility. In general, though, after the program or command name you can add *arguments*. (This term comes from mathematics and is similar to the arguments to an equation.) These tell the program how to work or what to work on—basically, they control the overall operation of the program. For instance, in the command line man date, the program name is man, and *date* is its only argument.

- The SYNOPSIS section of a program's manual page gives a very brief syntax summary.

- One important type of argument is an *option*. It changes the way that a command works. An option usually starts with one or two dash (-) characters. (One example is the -u option that we gave to the date program earlier.) Options usually come first on a command line, before other arguments. You'll find a list of a program's options in its manpage, often near the top. The date manpage, for example, lists -u (which starts with a single dash) and another common option, --help (which starts with two dashes).

Let's wrap this section up by typing date --help at a prompt. If it works, you can bet that many other programs on your system probably also accept the --help option:

```
$ date --help
Usage: date [OPTION]... [+FORMAT]
  or:  date [OPTION] [MMDDhhmm[[CC]YY][.ss]]
Display the current time in the given FORMAT, or set the system date.

...omitted...

-u, --utc, --universal   print or set Coordinated Universal Time
        --help           display this help and exit
        --version        output version information and exit

FORMAT controls the output.  The only valid option for the second form
specifies Coordinated Universal Time.  Interpreted sequences are:

%a   locale's abbreviated weekday name (Sun..Sat)

...omitted...
```

If you didn't see the first part of the date --help output, and if your terminal or window can scroll through previous output, you may be able to scroll back to the start. You can also view long output with a pager (as we saw in the section "Command Lines" in this chapter).

As the help message showed, your version of date may accept a format argument. This is a shorthand way to tell the date command exactly what to show. Here's an example; be sure to type it carefully:

```
% date "+Today is %x, day number %j of %Y."
Today is 11/20/04, day number 325 of 2004.
```

If that looks cryptic, don't worry: most Unix commands aren't that messy. (date's format was designed for programmers.) And, if you like to check the date that way, you don't have to type that long command every time. Almost all shells provide *aliases* or *functions*, which let you abbreviate one or more command lines to a single word.

■**Definition** The shell's alias is a single word that the shell expands into a complete command line. A shell function can contain one or many commands; like an alias, it's called by a one-word name.

For instance, you can make an alias called mydate to run the long command line above. The ways you can do this vary from shell to shell, as we'll see in the section the section "Shell Types and Versions," later in this chapter. Some shells use an equal sign (=) after the alias name (as shown in the first example that follows), and others use a space (as shown in the second example). If the first way doesn't work, try the second. Note that the outer quotes are apostrophes (' or *accents aigus*), often called *single* quotes by shell users, but ***not*** backquotes (` or *accents graves*):

```
$ alias mydate='date "+Today is %x, day number %j of %Y."'
$ mydate
Today is 11/20/04, day number 325 of 2004.
$
```

```
% alias mydate 'date "+Today is %x, day number %j of %Y."'
% mydate
Today is 11/20/04, day number 325 of 2004.
%
```

We've jumped ahead to advanced topics without explaining much about them. (We do that in these introductory chapters to introduce a lot of shell features in a short time.) You'll learn more about aliases in the section "Command Lines" in this chapter and about quoting (the " and ' marks) in the section "Control Shell Interpretation with Quoting" in Chapter 3.

Aliases are one of the many ways a shell can save you time by storing shortcuts and simplifying complex commands. Keep in mind, however, that the shell will forget many of its settings when you close the shell (close its window, shut down your system, and so on). If you want to use the `mydate` alias every time you use a shell, store the alias in your shell startup file; see the section "Startup Files, Login and Interactive Shells" in Chapter 5.

Let's try one more Unix program. The `cal` program prints a calendar for any month or year between 1 and 9999 AD (CE). With no argument, it prints this month's calendar. To see how it works, run the next three examples. In the second example, substitute the month and year you were born, and be sure to use all four digits of the year:

```
cal
cal 5 1973
cal 1752
```

If you're wondering why the calendar for September 1752 is short, it's because that's when many countries switched to the Gregorian calendar.

WHAT'S HAPPENING: PROCESSES

To get the most from a shell, it's important to understand what's happening—what the shell and the system do as you use the shell.

One of the most important concepts to understand about a Unix system is that a program is run ("executed") in a *process*. A process is a program that's running in memory. (The program comes from an executable file—which typically is stored on a hard disk.) A process keeps track of the state of a program: whether it's running or stopped, its current directory (in the filesystem tree, which we'll see later), its environment variables (a list of names and values), and more.

Each process has a unique identifying number called its *PID* (process identifier). When a program starts, the system gives a PID to the process. That PID stays the same until the process exits. You can use the PID to get information about the process and to control it.

All PIDs are between 1 and 30,000 or so. PIDs are assigned in order, depending on when a process starts. Once the top PID (like 30000) has been assigned, the system starts over at low numbers, reusing PIDs from old processes that have since finished. Some "system" processes start when your system starts and keep running until you shut it down. For example, PID 1 is the program called `init`.

A process (called the *parent process*) can start one or more other process (called *child processes*, or *subprocesses*). The `init` process is the ancestor of all other processes—its children, their children, and so on.

The shell can start its own child processes. In fact, this is what happens when you type most command lines: the shell starts a child process, waits for it to finish, then outputs another prompt.

The following graphic shows what happened when you ran the `cal` program a moment ago. The diagram shows a Z shell and some PIDs that we made up, but the basic idea is the same for all shells. The shell waits for you to type a command line. When you press Return, the shell finds the `cal` program and runs it as a child process. When `cal` finishes, its process terminates; the `zsh` process is still there, waiting for you to type another command line.

What's Happening: Processes

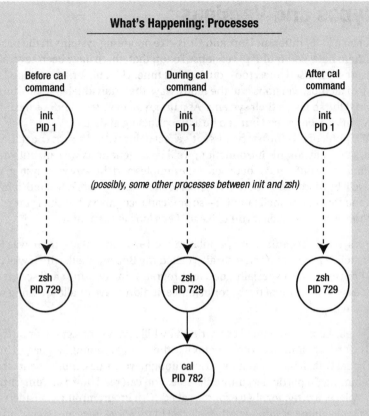

To see a listing of some of your processes, type the command ps -l. (The option is a lowercase letter "L"; it means "long format".) Here's an example:

```
$ ps -l
... PID PPID ...    TIME COMMAND
... 729    1 ... 0:03.10 zsh
... 793  729 ... 0:00.09 ps
```

We've left out most of the information. This listing shows two processes: zsh has PID 729 and PPID (parent's PID) of 1 (which, as we know, is the init process). In this case, ps is also showing itself (after all, it's a process too!): its PID is 793 and its PPID is 729, which is assigned to the shell that started ps (where you typed its name at a shell prompt).

In the section "Starting and Stopping Processes: Signals, Job Control" in Chapter 3, we'll explore what you can do with all of this information: controlling processes, putting them in the background, and more. We'll also cover *jobs*, which is a term for one or more processes that can be controlled as a unit. For now, remember that most (but not all) command lines start one (or more) new processes.

Shell Types and Versions

There have been a lot of different Unix and Unix-like operating systems in the past 35 years, and most of them have had multiple versions. To top that, there have been several major shells—and some less-used ones, too—during that time. Unix historians stay up late nights keeping track of all those versions and the many ways that individual system administrators have configured the shells on their systems. As a user, you have tremendous flexibility—which is good once you're experienced but can be a bit confusing at first.

What's the point of this (hi-)story? First, it's a fact of life with Unix that not all systems work in exactly the same way. In this introduction, we'll be as generic as we can, but you should be prepared to find some differences between our examples and the way your system works. Later in the book, we'll be more exact about how specific shell features work. Second, it helps to know something about the major shell families—so you can recognize what shell you're using, and so you can choose another shell if you'd like to. Let's look at them now:

- As Unix systems became more popular in the 1970s and 1980s, there was just one major shell: a program named sh, also called the Bourne shell, which was designed by Steve Bourne. It was especially good for programming (writing shell scripts), but it wasn't easy to use interactively: for instance, it didn't save or allow editing of previous command lines.

- The C shell, a program named csh, written by Bill Joy, was designed for interactive use—and also for programming, with a syntax like the C programming language. Unfortunately, the original C shell had what many users thought were bugs: quirky behavior that made programming (in particular) unpredictable. You can read more in Tom Christiansen's famous piece, written for shell experts, called "Csh Programming Considered Harmful." It's available online at (among other places) http://www.faqs.org/faqs/unix-faq/shell/csh-whynot/.

- Later in the 1980s, the Korn shell, ksh, by David Korn, extended sh scripting and added interactive features like command history. You'll find versions named ksh88 (from 1988, a version available on many commercial systems) and ksh93 (still actively maintained and available for free). Another shell that's similar, but different in many places, is pdksh, the "public domain ksh." In general, every sh command works on ksh, but there are some significant differences between the various kshs.

- The program tcsh, also called the T shell, was inspired by the TENEX operating system. Written to fix problems with the original csh, it also has many more interactive features. We don't encourage programming with tcsh because some systems don't have it and because sh-type shells are generally more flexible.

- The Bourne-again shell, bash (named with a bit of punny humor), is another extended Bourne shell that's the default shell on many Linux systems (where you'll often find it named sh because it has a superset of the original Bourne syntax). Currently maintained by Chet Ramey, bash shares most of its extended features with ksh and/or zsh. We cover bash version 3 in this book.

- You'll hear the term "POSIX shell" to describe a standardized Bourne-type shell with some features from ksh and bash. POSIX stands for Portable Operating System Interface. It's a standard intended to help make programming and user interfaces more uniform across the various Unix-like operating systems. Another shell you may run across is ash, a reimplementation of the Bourne shell that's designed to be small. And rc is a shell that's somewhat like sh but with a significantly different design.

- Last, but certainly not least, is the Z shell, zsh. Primarily based on the Bourne-like ksh, it also understands a lot of C shell syntax and has a large number of other new features. Paul Falstad wrote the original Z shell; now a different group of people maintain zsh as an open-source project. We cover zsh version 4.2 in this book.

Although Unix-type operating systems vary from machine to machine, the syntax of a particular shell version is about the same no matter where you find it. (You'll also find shells on Microsoft Windows machines—in Cygwin and MKS, for instance, which we mentioned at the end of the section "Getting Started" in this chapter. Once you've discovered the power of a Unix shell, we bet you'll want to use it on a Windows machine in place of the standard Windows shells named COMMAND and CMD.)

Which shell are you using? If you aren't sure, here are three command lines to try:

```
% echo $0
zsh
% echo $SHELL
/bin/zsh
% ps -p $$
  PID TTY          TIME CMD
21309 pts/0    00:00:00 zsh
```

(If the ps command complains about the -p, omit it.) Here, all of the commands show that we're using the Z shell, zsh. A shell may have more than one name, and the name the shell was called with is typically available in the parameter $0. (For instance, zsh can be invoked as sh or ksh; when it is, it will act like those shells instead of like the standard zsh.) There's more about this in the section "Positional Parameters" in Chapter 13. The setting of $SHELL is passed from process to process as an environment variable (see the section "Passing Info to Processes with Environment Variables" in Chapter 3), so it may be wrong. The shell replaces $$ with the shell's current PID (process ID number, explained in the sidebar "What's Happening: Processes").

The Filesystem: Directories, Pathnames

In the previous example, the answer /bin/zsh doesn't just show the shell's name. It's actually the program's *pathname*—it was a good lead-in to how you locate Unix files (including programs).

The *filesystem* holds groups of files, called *directories*, in a structure you can draw like an upside-down tree. (Other operating systems call these directories *folders*—which is a good way to visualize them, as we do in Figure 1-3.) The topmost directory, which holds all of the other directories and their files, is called the *root directory*; its name is / (a forward slash).

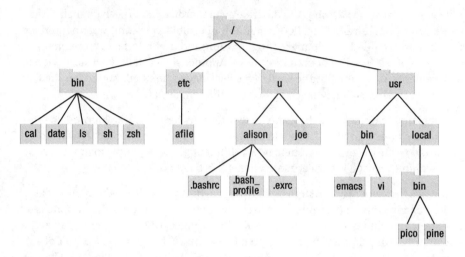

Figure 1-3. *Parts of a Unix filesystem, from the root directory down*

With a graphical file browser, you can see this structure—although your browser may show only one level at a time. On a command line, how can you tell the shell (or another Unix program) which file or directory you want to use? You enter its pathname. For instance, /bin/zsh is the location of the Z shell's program file in many Unix filesystems. If you compare that pathname to Figure 1-3, you'll see that a pathname starts with a / for the root directory; you give the name of each directory as you go down until you reach the directory or file you're specifying.

A pathname starting from the root directory (starting with a /) is called an *absolute pathname*. Absolute pathnames for objects deep in the tree can be long. To deal with this, you can also locate something in the filesystem using its *relative pathname*, which starts from your *current directory*.

Every process on a Unix system, including your shell, has a current directory. The path from that directory to the object—in other words, the pathname relative to the directory where the process is running—will often be shorter than the absolute pathname. Of course, relative paths to the same object vary depending on which directory the paths start from.

Let's take a look around your filesystem. It's probably similar to Figure 1-3. The Unix ls program is handy for this. If you give ls the pathname to a directory, it lists what's in that directory. With the pathname to a file, it lists that file (which isn't too useful unless you add options, as we'll do later). With no pathnames, ls lists the contents of your current directory. (Note that ls can't change your current directory; it only lists.)

Try the two commands that follow, then compare your results to Figure 1-3. The first command lists the root directory, and the second lists the bin directory under the root. (We're using absolute pathnames in both cases.)

```
% ls /
bin     etc     u       usr
% ls /bin
cal     date    ls      sh      zsh
```

Some of the program names in /bin should look familiar. That's because they're shells and other programs we've mentioned or used: cal, sh, and others.

Where the Commands Are Located

A Unix filesystem has lots of directories, and some of them contain program files. When you type a program name at a prompt, how does the shell find that program file? The shell has a list of directories to look in. It's stored in the environment variable (see the section "Passing Info to Processes with Environment Variables" in Chapter 3) named PATH. Let's use the echo command to see what's in PATH, the same way we saw SHELL in the section "Shell Types and Versions" earlier:

```
% echo $PATH
/bin:/usr/bin:/usr/local/bin:......
```

If you type the name of a program at a prompt but the shell can't find that program file in the directories /bin, /usr/bin, /usr/local/bin, and so on (and the command isn't built into the shell, as we'll explain next), the shell outputs the error "not found" (as it did earlier, when we typed *dtae*).

Most command lines run a program from a file, but some commands are *built into* the shell. This means that the shell doesn't need to search for a program file or start a new process. Although some commands are built in for efficiency (see the sidebar "Why Aren't All Commands Built Into the Shell?"), others *must* be built in because they affect the shell itself. (As you'll see in the sidebar "Inheritance" in Chapter 2, a child process started by the shell can't affect its parent process—which is the shell.) For instance, the alias command stores an alias within the currently running shell process, so alias must be built in. Another command that affects the shell is cd, which changes the shell's current directory. (Without cd, relative pathnames would be mostly useless.)

WHY AREN'T ALL COMMANDS BUILT INTO THE SHELL?

As we said, the shell has a few commands built in; these aren't in separate program files and don't start a separate process. For instance, most shells have the echo command built in—although you'll also see an echo program file in the /bin directory.

You might be wondering why all commands aren't built in. That's mainly because building lots of commands into the shell would make the shell's program file bigger—and the shell could need more memory to run. Thirty-some years ago, when Unix began, computers had very little memory, so almost every command was stored in a separate program file—except for commands like cd that absolutely had to be built into the shell. Modern systems have more memory and disk space, so often-used commands like echo are built in to make the shell run faster.

Relative Pathnames and Your Current Directory

If you give a relative or absolute pathname as an argument to cd, that directory becomes the shell's current directory. (This only changes the shell where you typed cd, not other shell processes.) Many Unix users simply say that cd "changes to" a directory.

With no argument, cd sets the current directory to your home directory.

■**Definition** Each Unix user has a directory, somewhere in the filesystem, that belongs to that user. This is the user's home directory. Many programs look for their setup and control files in a user's home directory—and so does the shell, as we'll see in the section "Startup Files, Login and Interactive Shells" in Chapter 5.

Here are some examples of cd and pathnames. You can follow along, looking back at Figure 1-3 as we go:

```
$ cd /bin
$ pwd
/bin
$ ls
cal     date    ls      sh    zsh
$ cd
$ pwd
/u/alison
$ ls
$ ls -a
.    ..   .bashrc    .bash_profile    .exrc
$ cd ..
$ pwd
/u
```

As you might have guessed, the pwd command shows the absolute pathname of the shell's current directory. (pwd stands for "print working directory.") The first cd changed the current directory to /bin. Running ls shows that directory's contents. Running cd with no arguments changes to this user's home directory, which happens to be (on this system) at the absolute path /u/alison. We mentioned that many programs' startup files are stored here. Most startup files' names start with a dot (.), which tells ls that these files are "boring" and to "hide" them unless you give the -a ("all") option to ls. Because Alison has only startup files in her home directory, plain ls outputs no names.

Here, the home directory is /u/alison; therefore, typing cd .. makes the current directory */u*. The name .. (two dots) always refers to the parent directory. (In this case, it would have been as quick to use the absolute pathname and type cd /u—but, in most cases, cd .. will be easier.)

You'll see two of the "hidden" entries in *every* directory: . (a single dot) and .. (two dots). Figure 1-4 shows this: a directory tree with these special entries. The dashed lines in the figure show where each special entry in each of these directories will take you. The . (dot) is used as an argument for commands that need to refer to the current directory. (There's an example in the section "Command History," later in this chapter.) We used .. (two dots) with the previous example; it's the relative pathname of the parent directory.

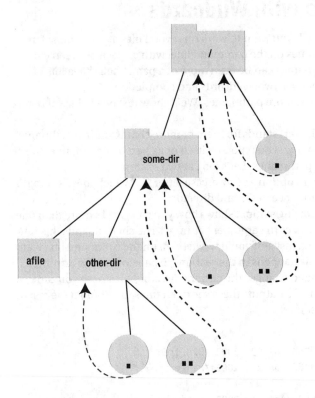

Figure 1-4. *Directories' . and .. entries, and where they point*

You can use these special entries just as you'd use any other directory entry. For instance, if your current directory is *other-dir* and you'd like to refer to the file *afile* in the parent directory, you can use the relative pathname ../afile. (You could also use the absolute pathname /some-dir/afile, but the relative pathname is easier to type.)

■**Note** One common mistake is trying to make a relative pathname to the parent directory by using the parent directory's name. For instance, if your current directory is other-dir and you want to refer to afile in the parent directory, you can't use some-dir/afile. This doesn't work because a relative pathname always starts with an entry in the current directory. (The pathname some-dir/afile would refer to a subdirectory named some-dir. But, in this case, there is no subdirectory by that name!)

Although the rules for pathnames are simple, it often takes new users a while to get really comfortable with writing them. Some practice at the start—hunting around the filesystem, trying various relative and absolute pathnames, and understanding why they work (or don't work)—will repay you many times later as you're using the system.

Building Pathnames with Wildcards

Typing long pathnames can be a pain. If you want to work on several files at once, most Unix programs will accept multiple pathnames on the command line, with a space between each pathname—but typing multiple pathnames can be even more of a pain. Shells have lots of ways to save you work and typing. Let's see two: wildcards and completion.

Wildcards let you abbreviate one or more pathnames. We'll show just one wildcard here; for the rest, see Chapter 9.

The wildcard character * (asterisk, star) stands for "zero or more characters in a pathname, in any combination," except slashes. When you type * by itself or as part of a pathname, the shell will replace it with all matching pathnames. Let's look at two examples.

In the first example, we'll use the ls option -l (lowercase letter "L," which means "long format"). It offers extra information about each file and directory.

The first command line in the following snippet shows how you can give ls more than one pathname. The second command line uses the argument /bin/g*. The shell expands this into all the pathnames that start with /bin/g, just as if you'd typed them on the command line yourself. (You can read more about how this happens in the section "Expansion and Substitution," later in this chapter.) The third command changes the current directory to /bin so you can use shorter pathnames; notice that the final ls outputs these shorter names too (though the rest of each file's listing is the same, of course):

```
% ls -l /bin/grep /bin/gzip
-rwxr-xr-x   1 root    root     116264 Jul 19  2002 /bin/grep
-rwxr-xr-x   3 root    root      63488 Jun 23  2002 /bin/gzip
% ls -l /bin/g*
-rwxr-xr-x   1 root    root     316530 Aug 11  2002 /bin/gawk
-rwxr-xr-x   1 root    root      36920 Aug 28  2002 /bin/gettext
-rwxr-xr-x   1 root    root     116264 Jul 19  2002 /bin/grep
lrwxrwxrwx   1 root    root          3 Sep 22  2002 /bin/gtar -> tar
-rwxr-xr-x   3 root    root      63488 Jun 23  2002 /bin/gunzip
-rwxr-xr-x   3 root    root      63488 Jun 23  2002 /bin/gzip
% cd /bin
% ls -l g*
-rwxr-xr-x   1 root    root     316530 Aug 11  2002 gawk
-rwxr-xr-x   1 root    root      36920 Aug 28  2002 gettext
-rwxr-xr-x   1 root    root     116264 Jul 19  2002 grep
lrwxrwxrwx   1 root    root          3 Sep 22  2002 gtar -> tar
-rwxr-xr-x   3 root    root      63488 Jun 23  2002 gunzip
-rwxr-xr-x   3 root    root      63488 Jun 23  2002 gzip
```

You can use one or more wildcards anywhere in a pathname. Table 1-1 shows several examples.

Table 1-1. *Wildcard Examples*

PATTERN	DESCRIPTION
*-old	All names that end with *-old*
*-old *-new	All names that end with *-old* or *-new*
m*.txt	All names that start with *m* and end with *.txt*
FIX	All names that start with, end with, or contain *FIX*

To match "hidden" names that start with a dot, you have to type the dot explicitly, like `ls .bash*` to list all filenames starting with *.bash*.[1]

Expansion and Substitution

Shells handle wildcards by *expansion*. You'll also see the term *substitution* used for the same type of operation. If you need to use a term precisely, check your shell's manpage. Otherwise, remember that these terms both mean "replacing something with something else."

Before we look at other kinds of expansion, let's see a few examples of wildcard expansion. The echo command is handy here because it simply outputs whatever arguments the shell gives it, with a space between each argument; this lets you see what the shell's expansion did:

```
$ echo great grape goop
great grape goop
$ echo great          grape        goop
great grape goop
$ echo /bin/g*
/bin/gawk /bin/gettext /bin/grep /bin/gtar /bin/gunzip /bin/gzip
$ cd /bin
$ echo g*
gawk gettext grep gtar gunzip gzip
```

The first two command lines had nothing to expand; those arguments were passed to echo as-is. In the second case, notice that the shell ignores multiple spaces. Whether you separate arguments by a single space or multiple spaces, the shell still passes only the arguments to the program—without the space. Then echo outputs the arguments with a single space between each. (You can pass spaces in an argument by using quoting. See the section "Control Shell

---

1. This isn't true if you've typed `shopt -s dotglob` in bash, `setopt glob_dots` in zsh, or the corresponding command in some other shells. But we don't recommend it! See the section "Basic Globbing" in Chapter 9.

Interpretation with Quoting" in Chapter 3.) The third and last command lines use wildcard expansion to build pathnames.

Most wildcards don't match the slashes (/) in pathnames; you have to type each slash for each "level" of a pathname. For example, echo /b* outputs /bin /boot, but doesn't output things like /bin/gawk or /boot/grub. To match those, you'd need to include the slashes, like echo /b*/*. Try those, if you'd like. (The Z shell has two wildcards that match slashes: ** and ***, explained in the section "Recursive Searching Like find" in Chapter 9.)

Shells can expand more than wildcards. For instance, when you ran echo $SHELL a while ago, the shell replaced $SHELL with the value of the environment variable named SHELL; when you typed ps -p $$, the shell replaced $$ with its own PID (the shell's).

In general, shells give special meaning to characters like $, *, and SPACE that aren't letters or digits. So it's a good idea not to use those characters in filenames (although you can if you *quote* them).

There's one more important question here: what happens if expansion fails? For instance, what if you type a wildcard pattern that doesn't match? The answer is: it depends. Shells have different ways to handle this; some can be configured, and others just use their default behavior. For instance, if a wildcarded argument doesn't match any pathname, Bourne-type shells generally pass that unexpanded argument on to the program. On C-type shells, if no argument matches, they print an error and won't run the command line at all. (Try it if you'd like to: type ls zz*zz on your shell, and see if the error seems to come from your shell or from ls.) In C-type shells, if *some* of the arguments expand and others don't, unmatched arguments are removed:

```
% echo zz*zz
echo: No match.
% echo *conf zz*zz
fsconf linuxconf netconf userconf
```

You may not want to worry about this level of detail. We're only mentioning it to give you a better appreciation of what shells do.

Building Pathnames by Completion

Many shells can finish parts of the command line after you type the first part. For instance, you can type the first few letters of a filename and press the Tab key once. (In ksh, press Esc twice; in the original csh, press Esc once.) If the shell can find only one filename that starts with the letters you typed, it fills in the rest of the name. This is called *completion*, and it's a very handy tool. Different shells have different types of completion. We'll explain filename completion and mention program name completion; Chapter 10 describes these and other kinds of completion.

In your home directory, you can create any files and directories you want. Let's go there (change the current directory to your home directory) and create an empty file named *this_is_a_long_filename.* (Use underscores instead of spaces because, as we've already seen, shells use space characters to separate command-line arguments. We'll see how to use spaces in filenames when we cover quoting in the section "Control Shell Interpretation with Quoting" in Chapter 3.) Among other things, the touch program creates empty files:

```
$ cd
$ touch this_is_a_long_filename
```

Next, let's list the file by typing a little of its name and pressing Tab (or use Esc, as we explained, for the original csh and ksh). If there's no other filename starting with *this*, the shell should output the rest of the name, add a space, and put your cursor after that:

```
$ ls -l thi<tab>
$ ls -l this_is_a_long_filename <return>
-rw-rw-r--    1 alison    users      0 Nov  7 11:09 this_is_a_long_filename
```

You can type more (another filename, for instance; and you can use completion on it too)—or simply press Return to execute the command. On the other hand, if the shell beeps or seems to do nothing after you try to complete a name, here are two things to try:

- On bash and ksh, press Escape followed by the Equals key.

- On zsh and tcsh, press Ctrl-d (hold down the Ctrl key, then press the d key).

In those cases, the shell should list all possible matches. You can type a bit more of the name—enough to make it unique—then press Tab again to complete it. For instance, maybe there's also a file called *thinking.txt*. You would see this:

```
$ ls -l thi<tab>
 ...terminal beeps...
$ ls -l thi<tab><tab>
thinking.txt   this_is_a_long_filename
$ ls -l this<tab>
$ ls -l this_is_a_long_filename
```

If filename completion doesn't work at all, you may need to configure your shell. To learn more, read Chapter 10 or your shell's manual page.

By the way, filename completion doesn't replace wildcards. For instance, it can only expand a single pathname at once. It also can't expand the first few characters of a pathname after you've entered the last few. If you learn both wildcards and completion, you'll be able to choose.

■**Tip** Filename completion works in the File dialogs of some GUI Unix applications. For instance, the Open File dialog of the GIMP image editor lets you type the first few characters of an image filename and press Tab to complete it. Try it with your graphical programs!

Your shell may also be able to complete command and program names. For instance, if you want to run gunzip (which we saw in the listing of /bin earlier), try typing gu or gun from a prompt, then pressing Tab. (You can cancel that command line by pressing Ctrl-c or backspacing over it. See the next section for more information about command-line editing.)

Command-Line Editing

All shells let you fix mistakes in a command line by "backspacing," with a key like Backspace or Delete, then retyping the incorrect part of the command line (and everything after it). On a long command line with a mistake at the beginning, though, doing this can be a pain.

Many shells also have built-in command-line editing. This lets you move the cursor back to a previous part of the current command line and make a change or insertion. You also can recall a previous command line (or several), possibly make a change, and rerun it.

Shells use basically the same editing commands as two sophisticated Unix text editors named vi and Emacs. If you know how to use those editors, you can get started with editing shell command lines by reading the section "Line Editing Basics" in Chapter 4. Otherwise, you can probably also do basic editing with your keyboard's arrow keys and the Delete key.

For example, let's say you type cd smoedir and get the error "smoedir: No such file or directory." (You meant to type cd somedir.) Try pressing the up-arrow key; if it works, you should see a copy of that command line; your cursor (where the text you type appears) will probably be at the end. Use the left-pointing arrow key to move backward, delete the letter m, then add a new m after the o. When you press Return, the edited command line will run; you don't have to move the cursor to the end of the command line first.

Command-line editing uses the shell's "history" list of commands—a shell feature that's been around much longer than command-line editing.

Command History

Thirty-some years ago, a typical Unix system didn't have a mouse and a graphical terminal. In fact, it didn't have a terminal at all. Many users used a teletype—that clattering machine, with a big keyboard and a roll of paper, used to send and receive telegrams. (It's amazing, isn't it, that Unix has scaled so well into the 21st century?)

Back then, if you wanted to repeat all or part of a previous command line, or if you made a mistake that you needed to fix, the C shell (but not the original Bourne shell) let you rerun previous command lines, and edit them too, using *history substitution*.

Modern shells with terminals and GUIs have more-sophisticated command-line editing, as the previous section explains. But the shell's remembered history, and history substitution, are still so useful that almost every modern shell supports them. Let's take a quick look.

When you enter a command line, the shell saves it in memory or in a disk file. Each line is assigned a number. To recall a previous command line, type the history expansion character ! (an exclamation point, also called "bang") followed by the history number or the first few letters of the command name. There are other shortcuts too—including ! ! to recall all of the previous command line, and ^x to recall the previous command line and remove *x*.

Let's see a few examples. For these examples, we've configured the shell to put a blank line before prompts and to start each prompt with its history number. (If you want your shell set up this way, read Chapter 7.) First we'll type a few command lines, then recall all or parts of them. After the shell does history substitution, it shows you the command line before running it. Each command is explained at the end of the examples; look for the boldfaced numbers.

```
33$ cal 1222 1995
cal: illegal month value: use 1-12

34$ ^22
cal 12 1995
   December 1995
Su Mo Tu We Th Fr Sa
 ...calendar appears...

35$ pwd
/u/alison

36$ ls /usr/local/src
 ...listing of /usr/local/src appears...

37$ !!/bigproj
ls /usr/local/src/bigproj
 ...listing of /usr/local/src/bigproj appears...

38$ cp !$/somefile .
cp /usr/local/src/bigproj/somefile .

39$ !ca
cal 12 1995
   December 1995
Su Mo Tu We Th Fr Sa
 ...calendar appears...

40$ ls -l !37:$
ls -l /usr/local/src/bigproj
 ...listing of /usr/local/src/bigproj appears...
```

There was a mistake in **command 33**: two extra 2s in the month. **Command 34** used the shortcut ^22 to remove *22* and rerun the command; the shell shows the corrected command line. (You could have used command-line editing—pressed the up-arrow key, used the back-arrow key for a while, then pressed the Delete key twice. But history substitution takes fewer keystrokes in this case.)

Next, we look for a file in another directory that we need to copy. **Command 36** shows a listing of the /usr/local/src directory, and there's a subdirectory we want to look at. Instead of retyping the whole pathname, we ask the shell to replay the previous command line by typing !!—and we follow it with the rest of the pathname (a slash and the subdirectory name *bigproj*). The shell echoes the new, longer command line, then runs it.

The file we want to copy is in this directory /usr/local/src/bigproj. We want to run the cp program instead of ls. The directory's pathname is the last argument on the ls command line, and we can grab it by using the operator !$, which means "last argument on previous command line." So, in **command 38**, the shell expands !$/somefile into the pathname /usr/local/src/bigproj/somefile before running cp to copy the file. (We've added the last argument to cp, which tells cp where to put the copy: here, a dot (.), the pathname to the current directory, as explained in the section "Relative Pathnames and Your Current Directory" earlier in this chapter.)

In **command 39** we rerun the previous cal command line (the corrected one, because it's the most recent) by typing ! followed by enough letters from the command name to make it unique. (!c wouldn't be enough because that would match the cp command line.) Finally, in **command 40**, we run ls -l with the last argument from command line 37.

These may seem cryptic, but the most common history substitutions are quick to learn: they follow a pattern of expressions (like the $ character, which often means "end") used in many Unix commands. These little gems can sometimes (but not always) be much faster to type than the equivalent command-line editing we showed in the previous section. We suggest learning a few (from the section "'Bang' History: The Use of Exclamation Marks" in Chapter 6) and keeping them in mind.

More Unix Programs

This book is about shells, not about Unix in general. So we can't go into detail about the literally hundreds of standard Unix programs available on a command line; for that, you'll need a good introduction to Unix. Still, to use the power of a shell, you need to run programs! With that in mind, see Appendix A for a brief look at some common Unix programs, also called Unix *utilities*.

Summary

In this chapter, we've introduced the major shells by giving examples that work on all of them. A shell is a text-based interface between you and the operating system (Linux, Unix, or other systems). Shells save time by letting you perform a wide variety of operations using just a few keystrokes. You give instructions to a shell by typing commands on its command line (which comes after a shell prompt), possibly editing the commands or recalling them from a previous command line.

The shell runs programs for you. For detailed information about a program, read its online manual page (manpage). Most programs accept command-line options to control how they work and arguments to specify what the program should work on. You can shorten command lines by storing them in an alias; a function can store multiple command lines. Most commands are files stored in program directories like /bin, but some are built into the shell.

On Unix-type systems, files are organized into a tree of directories. To locate something in the filesystem, you specify its pathname. A pathname can be absolute (from the root directory, and starting with /) or relative (starting from the current directory, with no leading /). The cd command changes the shell's current directory. To save typing, you can use wildcards, which the shell expands into one or more matching pathnames (or tells you if it can't). You can also use completion to build pathnames interactively: type the first few characters and press Tab.

The shell "remembers" previous command lines. You can reuse all or parts of them with shell history and command-line editing.

In the next chapter, we'll look at another strength of shells. They let you use programs as "building blocks," together with the shells' built-in programming features (and features you've seen in this chapter), to create your own customized programs. This lets you work even more quickly, and make fewer mistakes, than you might by working manually.

CHAPTER 2

■■■

Using Shell Features Together

In this chapter, we'll cover several important shell features. We'll focus on some of the things that make shells different from most graphical interfaces: the way that you can combine programs, together with advanced features of the shell, to do completely new things.

As with other chapters in Part 1, this chapter doesn't cover every detail of each one of these shell features. It's more of a narrative. If you'd rather read complete details in order, you'll find them in Parts 2 and 3.

Still, we do explain the concepts and go into some detail. If you aren't interested in the details right now, or you don't have time to try the examples, you can skim through this chapter and watch the shell features we use as we develop our application.

We'll build a complete, searchable list of all of the programs that you can run. The list is impressive on its own: your system probably has hundreds or even thousands of programs available—many more than a typical graphical system has on its menus, and even more possibilities when you combine these programs in the ways we'll show you. (So, by learning about both the shell and your GUI, you'll have two powerful ways to do the work you need to do!) The program list isn't *that* useful on its own, though. The main point of this chapter's tutorial is to give you a taste of the programs and shell features you'll be able to use once you've mastered the shell. These features include

- Redirecting (diverting) the output or input of programs to or from programs and files. Redirection also lets you build files, and streams of data, from the outputs of multiple programs.

- Searching for text with grep, paging through text with a pager program, sorting text with sort, making text into columns automatically, editing text on the fly, and more.

- Handling long command lines, and typing multiline commands and loops (a shell feature that lets you repeat a series of commands).

- Modifying command lines using a powerful method called *command substitution*.

- Testing files to see if they're a program, as well as other tests.

- Making and running a shell script file: a series of commands that you can reuse; making a bin directory for your shell scripts.

- Using shell aliases and functions (which are related to shell scripts).

Writing Output to Files: Redirection

Standard Unix input typically comes from the keyboard, while the terminal window receives commands' standard output and any error messages. The shell lets you change this using a feature known as redirection. In this section we'll introduce you to this feature.

■Note Redirection works with programs that work within your terminal, writing text there—and, sometimes, reading text from your keyboard. (Many of these are the original Unix programs that were designed before Unix "did windows.") Redirection doesn't affect the windows that graphical programs open.

A Unix process can read and write text from many places, but three of them are especially important: the standard output (abbreviated *stdout*, also called *file descriptor 1*), standard error (*stderr* or f.d. 2), and standard input (*stdin*, f.d. 0). When a shell runs a program, by default the standard output and standard error of that process are routed to your terminal screen, and the standard input is taken from your keyboard.

So, for instance, if you run cal (the calendar program we met in the section "Command Lines" in Chapter 1) from the command line, its output (its *stdout*) appears in the terminal. If there was an error, cal will write a message to *stderr*, which also goes to your terminal. In fact, the shell itself writes its prompt to *stdout*—and reads the commands you type from *stdin*. This isn't true in every situation, with every program—but it's generally true with standard nongraphical Unix programs. Figure 2-1 shows this.

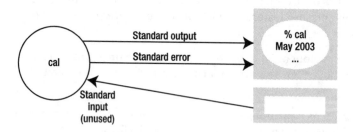

Figure 2-1. *A process's usual input and outputs, without redirection*

Why is this significant? Because you can tell the shell to reroute the output or input of a process. This is called *redirection*, and it's a powerful shell feature.

For instance, if you want to save the calendar for the month you were born, the shell can redirect cal's output to a file. Let's first run cal without redirection—so you'll see its standard output on your terminal, as always. Then we'll redirect its output to a file named birthcal. Running ls shows that the file is there, and running the cat program displays what's in the file—which, as we'd expect, has the output of cal:

```
% cal 10 1973
     October 1973
Su Mo Tu We Th Fr Sa
    1  2  3  4  5  6
 7  8  9 10 11 12 13
14 15 16 17 18 19 20
21 22 23 24 25 26 27
28 29 30 31
% cal 10 1973 > birthcal
% ls
birthcal     prog.pl     somefile
% cat birthcal
     October 1973
Su Mo Tu We Th Fr Sa
    1  2  3  4  5  6
 7  8  9 10 11 12 13
14 15 16 17 18 19 20
21 22 23 24 25 26 27
28 29 30 31
%
```

The shell's > (greater-than) operator tells it to redirect the standard output of a process (the program named at the left side of the >) into a file (named at the right side of the >). As you can see, when we redirected cal's output, there was no output on the terminal; it all went into the file. Figure 2-2 shows cal with its standard output redirected to a file named afile.

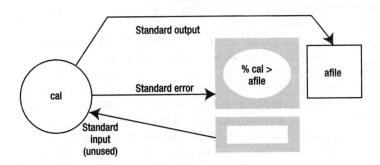

Figure 2-2. *A process's standard output redirected to a file*

PERMISSIONS

Unix-like systems are *multiuser,* which means they let many users share the same filesystem. The filesystem has access controls, often called simply *permissions,* that help you choose who can do what to your files and directories. Permissions include the permission to run a file as a program, known as *execute permission.* You'll typically use the chmod command to set the proper access modes.

We can't cover permissions in detail here. To find out more, see a good introductory book about your operating system or your emulation package (such as Cygwin).

To redirect program output to a new file, the user must have write permission for the *directory* where this file is created. If the file already exists, though, the user must have write permission on the *file* instead.

What if there had been an error? Would the error message have gone into the birthcal file? If cal is a properly designed Unix program (which it is!), its errors will go to *stderr*. The errors will appear on the terminal because > only redirects *stdout*, not *stderr*. Let's try it:

```
% cal 100 1973 > birthcal
cal: illegal month value: use 1-12
% ls
birthcal    prog.pl    somefile
% cat birthcal
%
```

The error didn't go into the birthcal file. (This is good—if the error had been written to *stdout*, you wouldn't have known that something went wrong unless you happened to look in the birthcal file.) In this case, *nothing* went into the birthcal file; cat shows that it's now empty.

This brings up an important point: by default, redirection to a file will overwrite whatever is in that file, no questions asked. This follows the shells' design philosophy that, in general, you know what you're doing. (And it *is* good to be able to replace a file easily when you need to.) If you want the shells to prevent overwriting when you use >, you can set the "no clobber" option, which we explain in the section "Preventing Files from Being Clobbered" in Chapter 8.

The shells also have a >> redirection operator that appends text to an existing file (adds text to the end). Let's try it to build a birthcals file with calendars for you and someone else. We'll also use echo to add a title above each calendar. (You'll need the double quote marks around echo's command-line arguments. The section "Control Shell Interpretation with Quoting" in Chapter 3 explains why.) Notice that we first use > to create the file, then >> to append other programs' output to it:

```
% echo "*** MY BIRTH MONTH ***" > birthcals
% cal 10 1973 >> birthcals
% echo "*** ZOE'S BIRTH MONTH ***" >> birthcals
% cal 6 1975 >> birthcals
% cat birthcals
```

```
*** MY BIRTH MONTH ***
     October 1973
Su Mo Tu We Th Fr Sa
    1  2  3  4  5  6
 7  8  9 10 11 12 13
14 15 16 17 18 19 20
21 22 23 24 25 26 27
28 29 30 31
*** ZOE'S BIRTH MONTH ***
     June 1975
Su Mo Tu We Th Fr Sa
 1  2  3  4  5  6  7
 8  9 10 11 12 13 14
15 16 17 18 19 20 21
22 23 24 25 26 27 28
29 30
%
```

By the way, what is the cat program doing here? As always, it's reading the files you name on its command line and writing their contents to standard output—in this case, the terminal.

Unix programs that write to standard output don't have to know how to write to a file or how to write to the terminal. They simply output that text to stdout, and the shell directs the output.

A program *can* tell whether its input and output are connected to a terminal or from a text file, and the ls program does that. Without redirection—when its output is a terminal—most versions of ls write output in columns, to fit more names onto your screen. When you redirect output away from the terminal, ls writes in a single column. This is handy for several reasons, as we'll see. Let's try it: list the contents of the /bin and /usr/bin directories on your screen first, then redirect them into a file named proglist:

```
$ ls /bin /usr/bin
/bin:
arch          df          igawk     nice           su
ash           dmesg       ipcalc    nisdomainname  sync
...

/usr/bin:
X11           gasp                  kmail          p2c
[             gawk                  kmedia         packf
...
$ ls /bin /usr/bin > proglist
$
```

Next, let's look through the proglist file. A good way to do that is with your favorite pager program (introduced in the section "Command Lines" in Chapter 1): more, less, or pg. (Type more proglist, less proglist, or pg proglist.) The file should look something like this, with the ls output in a single column:

```
/bin:
arch
ash
awk
...
zcat
zsh

/usr/bin:
X11
[
 ...
```

If the file has other characters in it—for instance, if names end with / or *, or there are sequences of strange characters like ^[[31m around the names—then your shell (or your system) has replaced the standard ls command with something else. (You might have an alias that adds some ls options every time you run ls.) In that case, try telling the shell to use the "real" ls by typing the command's absolute pathname, like this:

```
$ /bin/ls /bin /usr/bin > proglist
```

Using a pathname to a program file, like /bin/ls, tells the shell exactly where to find the program you want. (That way, the shell won't search for the program in the PATH.) This also tells the shell not to use any shell alias or function named ls.

CONFUSING PROGRAM NAMES

We suggest you don't "redefine" programs by using aliases. Instead, name the alias something different than the program. That way, when you type the program name—or when a friend is using your Unix account—there will be no question what should happen. This is especially important with programs like rm that do something that can be dangerous. Making "safety" aliases—so, for instance, when you type rm you actually get rm -i, which prompts before removing each file—can cause you grief if you use another shell or another system with no "safety" alias. It's better to learn what the "real" version of each program does. If you always want to use rm -i, make an alias named (say) rmi, and train your fingers to use that alias instead. Whatever name you choose, just be sure that it isn't overriding some other program that already exists. The which program can tell you this: which rmi will tell you whether there's already a program named rmi somewhere in your shell's PATH.

Using Programs Together: Pipes

Unix programs can work on their own, without help from other programs. But many of them are also designed to be "building blocks" that can be combined, from a command line, to do even more. In this section and the next, we'll look into the very handy feature called *pipelines*.

As we said earlier, the two directories /bin and /usr/bin have many of the standard program files. Wouldn't it be nice to have a list of all of the programs available on your system? There probably are programs in other directories, but let's start with these two.

As we saw in the previous section, the output of ls /bin /usr/bin isn't perfect. It has the directory names (with a colon after each) and a blank line between the directories' listings. But we can use other programs to fix that. Let's look into the wonderful world of pipelines: combining Unix programs to get just the output you want.

We'll need the handy Unix program named grep. It searches through text, looking for lines that match a pattern you give. If you don't give any filenames on its command line, then grep (like any well-behaved Unix program) reads from its standard input.

■**Definition** grep is one of a family of programs for searching through text. (The other two standard programs are egrep and fgrep. You'll see others with similar names.) This odd name can be thought of as "globally search for a regular expression and print." There's more about these search patterns—*regular expressions*—in the section "Quoting Pattern Characters" in Chapter 9.

Let's start by searching for program names that end with sh. Most of these are shells, like bash and ksh. We mentioned earlier (in the section "History" in Chapter 1) that Unix patterns often use a $ character to mean "end of line." Let's tell grep to search the proglist files for lines ending with sh. The first argument is the pattern to search for; put it inside single quotes:

```
$ grep 'sh$' proglist
ash
bash
csh
  ...
```

That list might be long and scroll off your screen. The cure for that is a pager program like less. (As before, if you don't have less, use more or pg instead.) You've read a file with less by giving the filename as an argument. But what we want to page with less here is not a file: we want to page through the standard output of another process.

How? There's one clue above: like most Unix programs, if you don't give less a filename, it reads its standard input. The missing piece of this puzzle is the shell's "pipe" operator, which is made with the vertical-bar key: | (which may be a broken bar on your keyboard). Use a pipe on the command line to send the standard output of one process to the standard input of the next process. We'll pipe grep's stdout to the stdin of less:

```
$ grep 'sh$' proglist | less
ash
bash
csh
  ...
```

You should see a prompt from less at the bottom of the screen. (If you're using more, and grep outputs less than a screenful of text, more won't prompt.) As before, you can press the spacebar to see the next screenful (if any) or q to quit less (and get another shell prompt).

What's happening here? The process diagram in Figure 2-3 shows the two processes, grep and less, that the shell started. The less process reads what grep writes and feeds it to your terminal, page by page. When you press q to quit less, its process exits. The system sees that the less process is gone—so, if grep hasn't also finished by this time, the system kills the grep process (and the shell often outputs a message like Broken pipe). Then the shell outputs another prompt.

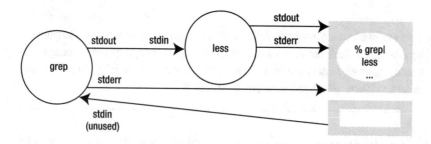

Figure 2-3. *grep's output piped to less*

This invisible "plumbing" may seem hard to visualize at first, but it's a fundamental part of why shells are so powerful. Take a few moments to review Figure 2-3, compare it to what you did on the command line, and look back at the earlier grep and less examples until it's clear what's happening. We'll have more practice with pipes soon, but the concept is so useful that it's worth some careful study.

Joining Forces

Let's start to make a much more useful proglist file, step by step. The first step is to use grep to remove the lines of ls output that aren't program names. The -v option tells grep to output all lines that don't match the pattern. To get a list of the program names only, we want to remove the lines with the directory names—which, in this case, both end with the string /bin:. So let's overwrite the old proglist file with a new one, piping the standard output of ls to the standard input of grep, and redirecting the standard output of grep to the proglist file. (If you haven't seen many shell command lines before, this one may look complicated. Think of it in pieces: two programs, each with its own arguments, connected by a pipe.) Before you start to type this, remember that you can probably use command-line editing to recall a previous ls command line, then insert the pipe symbol and the grep before the > character:

```
$ ls /bin /usr/bin | grep -v '/bin:$' > proglist
$ less proglist
 ...
```

Look through the file with your favorite pager—less or more, for instance. The lines /bin: and /usr/bin: should be gone (because grep "ate" them and output the other lines). But there's still an empty line between the directory listings. We can remove it too. One way to do that is by piping the output of the first grep to another grep—this one with the pattern ^$, which matches empty lines, and the option -v to omit those lines. Alternatively, you may be able to use a single invocation of grep if your grep accepts multiple patterns, each preceded by the option -e. (You could also use egrep—"extended grep"—which always allows multiple patterns.) Here goes:

```
$ ls /bin /usr/bin | grep -v '/bin:$' | grep -v '^$' > proglist
```

Let's review. The ls process is writing a listing of two directories to its standard output. A pipe sends that text to the standard input of the first grep -v, which removes the lines with the directory names /bin: and /usr/bin:. A second grep -v removes the blank line. Now proglist has a list of the programs. (Check the proglist file, if you want, with less proglist.)

Warning Don't try to read a file early in a command line, then use redirection to write a modified version of the same file back to itself, like this:

```
$ xyz proglist | ... > proglist
```

Why can't you do that? *Before* the shell runs the command line, it *empties* (removes all of the data from) the file you've redirected output to. (Here, that's the proglist file.) What can you do instead? Write output to a temporary file, then overwrite the original file with it: [1]

```
$ xyz proglist | ... > temp
```

```
$ cat temp > proglist
```

Our program list still isn't optimal: all of the programs from /bin are listed before the programs from /usr/bin. So let's sort the listing before writing it to the file. The Unix sort program reads files or standard input, then sorts it into, by default, alphabetical order. How can we add sort? It's simple: pipe the output of the second grep into sort. Recall the previous command line and edit it:

```
$ ls /bin /usr/bin | grep -v '/bin:$' | grep -v '^$' | sort > proglist
```

That example might seem a bit tedious. "After all," you might say, "couldn't I do that with a text editor?" You could do some of it with a text editor—what the grep -v processes are doing, at least—but the sorting could be more difficult. Anyway, this is meant more to demonstrate piping and redirection than as a rule that pipelines are "the only way" to do things with a shell. Shells give you the choice of lots of tools—so, if the best tool is a text editor, just use it!

---

1. You can also use the mv command to replace proglist with temp. This may break any hard links to the destination file (proglist), though. Redirection, as we've shown here, doesn't break hard links. There's more about hard links in the section "Hard Links" in Chapter 8.

Editing Data, Continuing Command Lines

The proglist file contains a single-column list of program names. Assuming that none of those names are very long, it might be nice to have a file with the names in columns. That's probably hard to manage with most text editors, but it's simple on Unix. There are several utilities for putting text into columns. Not all systems have the column utility, but it's so simple to use that we'll choose it. Let's pipe the output of sort through column.

If your system doesn't have column—if the shell gives you an error like column: command not found—then try the command pr -t -l1 -4 or pr -t -l1 --columns=4 instead. This asks pr to print four input lines on each output line—that is, in four columns. The second option is a lowercase letter l followed by the digit 1.

The command line is starting to get long. We'll continue the command line by putting a backslash (\) at the end of it. This is one way to tell the shell "I'm not finished yet." (Note that Bourne-type shells will automatically continue a command line that ends with a pipe symbol. In C shells, though, you have to type the backslash—and you can do that in Bourne shells, too, if you'd like.)

■**Note** The backslash (\) must be the very last character on the command line, just before you press Return. Don't accidentally put a space or other character after the backslash.

Depending on your shell, it may be hard to recall a previous command line and add a backslash in the middle of it—so, for this demonstration, you retype the whole command line instead of editing a previous one. After you type the backslash and press Return, the shell will probably prompt you at the start of the next line with its secondary prompt—which is something like > for Bourne-type shells, or ? for C-type shells, or pipe pipe pipe> on Z shell. You can also just keep typing when your cursor gets to the right-hand edge of the screen; it may not look tidy, but the command line should work as well:

```
% ls /bin /usr/bin | grep -v '/bin:$' | grep -v '^$' | \
? sort | column > proglist
%
```

Read the file with a pager to see how column worked. If one of the program names was long, then column probably made only a few widely spaced columns.

The columns show a problem here. Sometimes you might want to see the program list in columns. Other times, you might want to use the program list as a data source—for instance, searching it to find certain program names—and having the output already in columns could make that tough. Let's restore the single-column proglist file, then use it as a base for other commands. Rerun the earlier command line that didn't use the column program, then read proglist (with a pager) to be sure it's in a single column.

Like other Unix programs, column can read from a file. We'll have column read the proglist file, then pipe the column output directly into less (or your favorite pager program):

```
$ column proglist | less
```

The output should look like it did the previous time you used column. Maybe it has just a few widely spaced columns. Let's add a command to truncate (shorten) the long filenames. Then column should make more columns. (Of course, if you really wanted to see the complete names, you wouldn't do this. But we want to see more columns—and demonstrate more Unix programs.)

The cut program reads a file or stdin, removes some characters from each line, and writes the result to stdout. We want the -c option to remove certain character positions from each line. For instance, cut -c 1-15 will output the first 15 characters from each line, ignoring the rest. (Your system might need cut -c1-15, without the space after the -c.)

So (review): how can you make cut read the program file? Give the filename as an argument. And how can you send the output of cut to column, which will make it into columns? Right, use a pipe. Let's do it:

```
$ cut -c 1-20 proglist | column | less
```

Note that we haven't created any files here; all of the data flows through the pipe to less, which displays it on your terminal.

Let's make more columns by changing the 20 to 10. (Each line of cut output will have 10 characters or less—making more, narrower columns across the screen.) You can use the history substitution operator ^2^1 to change 20 to 10, if you want; it'll take fewer keystrokes than using your arrow keys to move up and over. To make that clearer, we'll start by showing the previous command line. After you type the history substitution, the shell quickly shows the new command line, then executes it:

```
$ cut -c 1-20 proglist | column | less
  ...output...
$ ^2^1
cut -c 1-10 proglist | column | less
  ...output...
```

Because the proglist file isn't in columns, we can also search it with a program like grep. Let's repeat the earlier search to find all lines ending with sh (which will give a list of shells). Please figure out the command line yourself.

Got it? Good.[2]

How could you put the list of shells into columns? Here's how to solve the problem: think "What Unix utility makes columns?" Right; it's column (or another program you've used instead of column). Next, think how to get the data into the column-making program: the grep utility does searches and writes the results to its stdout. Finally, think how to get data from one program's stdout to another program: use a pipe, and let the second program read from its stdin. (That's all review, but it's an important series of steps that you'll want to get familiar with doing.) So, let's do it. You probably won't need less to paginate the column output unless you have a lot of shells:

```
$ grep 'sh$' proglist | column
ash           bash          csh
  ...
```

---

2. The answer is: grep 'sh$' proglist.

If that command shows lots of non-shells—for instance, a shell script like lesspipe.sh—you can use the egrep program, which accepts extended regular expressions. This longer regular expression will match either the shell sh or any other name that doesn't have a dot (.) before the final sh. Here's an example. In an extended regular expression, the vertical bar (|) means "or":

```
$ egrep '(^sh|[^.]sh)$' proglist | column
```

Let's wrap this up: to do a lot of useful things, you need to learn what programs are on your system—and how shell redirection works, so you can connect those programs. If you're accustomed to using windowing systems, with a mouse and menus, you may also have to break an old mental habit that "each program should have everything you'd ever want to do somewhere on one of its menus." (A shell and pipes let you make a huge number of combinations.)

Command Substitution

We aren't done—our list has programs from only two directories, /bin and /usr/bin. Most systems have several other important program directories. Your shell looks for programs in every directory listed in your PATH environment variable. So let's build our proglist list from all of the directories in your PATH.

As we've seen, shells separate arguments with space characters.[3] Directory names in PATH are separated by colon (:) characters. Unix has several ways to translate characters, one of which is the tr program. The tr program reads text from its standard input, makes the translations you list on its command line, and writes the result to standard output. First let's show PATH with echo. Then we'll feed echo's stdout to tr, translating the colons to spaces:

```
$ echo "$PATH"
/bin:/usr/bin:/usr/local/bin:/proj/bin
$ echo "$PATH" | tr ':' ' '
/bin /usr/bin /usr/local/bin /proj/bin
```

Now that we have a list of directory names, we're ready to run ls to list the programs in them. There are a couple of ways to do the job. First, let's use the method we did before: a pipeline of commands. Then, in the following section, we'll see a better way.

The list of directories comes from the standard output of tr. We need to get it onto an ls command line. You could simply retype the list onto a command line. Or, if your terminal or window system has a copy-and-paste function, you could use that. But the shell also has a way to read a command's standard output and put it onto the command line of another command. It's called *command substitution*, and it's another unique and powerful shell feature. Here's how it works.

If you surround one or more commands with a pair of backquote characters (*accents graves*), like `command`, the shell will run the command line, then replace it with its standard output. (In newer Bourne-type shells, you can also use the operators $(*command*), as explained in the section "Command Substitution and Command Arguments" in Chapter 11. But the backquotes work

---

3. Bourne-type shells actually use the separator characters listed in the IFS shell variable. (IFS is explained in the section "Reading Input" in Chapter 13.) We could change IFS to split the PATH at colons, but that would add even more things to learn here!

in *all* shells.) This is harder to describe than to see, so let's try another example. First we'll show the previous command line again—to see the directory pathnames that tr outputs. Next, type those directory names onto an ls command line yourself (or use copy and paste). Finally, use command substitution to do the same thing you did by hand: pass the list of directories onto an ls command line. The output in the last two cases should be identical:

```
$ echo "$PATH" | tr ':' ' '
/bin /usr/bin /usr/local/bin /proj/bin
$ ls /bin /usr/bin /usr/local/bin /proj/bin
/bin:
 ...
/usr/bin:
 ...
/usr/local/bin:
 ...
/proj/bin:
 ...
$ ls `echo "$PATH" | tr ':' ' '`
/bin:
 ...
/usr/bin:
 ...
/usr/local/bin:
 ...
/proj/bin:
 ...
```

Take a careful look at what we've just done: we made a list of directories on the standard output of tr, and then passed that list as command-line arguments to ls—just as if you had typed the list on the ls command line yourself. Note that, as before, ls makes multicolumn output when its output is to a terminal (as we're doing here)—but it will make single-column output when we redirect its output (as we'll do later).

for and foreach Loops

If you want to, you can tack on the rest of the command line that you used before—the two greps and so on—to build a proglist file from all directories in your PATH list. But this is a good place to start looking at another way to do operations on a series of directories (or files—or, actually, *any* words). The shell's *loops* let you repeat a set of commands over and over.

Let's review: we want to make a list of the programs in each directory in the PATH. The Bourne shell's for loop, and the C shell's foreach loop, were designed for this kind of job. They accept a list of words (for example, directory pathnames) and a series of commands to perform on each of those words.

(Another kind of loop, described in the section "More Looping" in Chapter 13, is the while loop. It runs a command line, tests for success, and then, if the command succeeded, runs the commands from the loop body.)

Here's a simple example. Let's say you want to make a copy of all files in the current directory. The copy should have the same filename, but with "OLD-" added to the start. You could type these commands on a command line. (Or, as we'll see later, you could save them as a script or function so they're easier to repeat.) First let's see the loops in action. Then we'll explain:

```
$ ls
afile        bfile       cfile       dfile
$ for f in *
> do
>    echo "copying ${f} to OLD-${f}"
>    cp -i "${f}" "OLD-${f}"
> done
copying afile to OLD-afile
copying bfile to OLD-bfile
copying cfile to OLD-cfile
copying dfile to OLD-dfile
$ ls
OLD-afile    OLD-bfile   OLD-cfile   OLD-dfile
afile        bfile       cfile       dfile
```

Here's the same loop written for C-type shells (like tcsh):

```
% foreach f (*)
?    echo "copying ${f} to OLD-${f}"
?    cp -i "${f}" "OLD-${f}"
? end
copying afile to OLD-afile
copying bfile to OLD-bfile
copying cfile to OLD-cfile
copying dfile to OLD-dfile
```

Let's look at the Bourne-type for loop step by step:

1. The first line starts with the command for, the name of a *shell variable* (here we've picked f), and the word in.

2. End the first line with one or more words. For this example, we've used the wildcard *— which, as we saw in the section "Building Pathnames with Wildcards" in Chapter 1, the shell replaces with a list of all names in the current directory. (You can also type the words yourself; for instance, if you'd only wanted to copy afile and dfile, you could have typed for f in afile dfile instead of using the wildcard.) Press Return.

3. The shell will print a secondary prompt, >. Type do, and press Return again. (Pressing Return after the do is optional; you can type a command on the same line as do, separated by a space. We've used Return for neatness.)

4. Type the command lines you want to run, pressing Return after each one. The shell will run this set of commands, over and over, once for each of the words on the first line. Anywhere you want to use the word in one of these commands, type $ followed by the name of the shell variable. (It's safest to put curly braces around the variable's name, as we have here—but it's usually only required if there are other letters or numbers directly

after the variable name. It's also usually safest to put double quotes around the variable name; see the section "Control Shell Interpretation with Quoting" in Chapter 3 for more.) We've indented each command line to make it stand out, but you don't need to do this.

5. Finally, type done on a line by itself. This tells the shell that you've finished the loop; it will start to execute the commands in order from do to done, once for each word.

■**Note** Some programmers prefer to put both the for and do on the same line, separated by a semicolon (;), like this:

```
$ for f in * ; do
>    echo "copying ${f} to OLD-${f}"
>    cp -i "${f}" "OLD-${f}"
> done
```

You'll see that syntax in Parts 2 and 3 of this book. The note in the section "Control Flow" in Chapter 13 explains further.

The C shell's foreach loop, shown in the previous code snippet, follows the same pattern, but it's a little easier to type than a for loop. There's no word in; put the words inside the parentheses instead. Instead of done, use end.

Let's get back to our program-list example. We'll give the list of directory names to a for loop, and we'll use command substitution, as we did earlier. (The command line with echo and tr should look familiar.) Let's start by simply echoing the directory names:

```
$ for dir in `echo "$PATH" | tr ':' ' '`
> do
>    echo "I got the name $dir"
> done
I got the name /bin
I got the name /usr/bin
I got the name /usr/local/bin
I got the name /proj/bin
$
```

The loop is running a single command, echo, which is writing lines of text to its standard output.

More About for Loops

Let's extend the example from the previous section by saving the lines of output into a file. In a later section, we'll process this saved output.

■Note Programmers tend to use Bourne shells instead of `tcsh` or `csh`. One reason is the technique we'll demonstrate in this section: redirecting the input or output of all commands in a loop. So we'll show only Bourne shell syntax for the remainder of this chapter. You can start a Bourne shell temporarily, for the rest of this chapter, as we start to build a shell program. Simply type the shell's name (like `sh`) at a prompt. At the end of the chapter, type `exit` to end the Bourne shell and return to your original shell.

Just as you can redirect the standard output of a command to a file, you can redirect the standard output of a `for` loop to a file. Simply add the redirection after the word `done`. This collects the standard output of every command, from every pass through the loop:

```
$ for dir in `echo "$PATH" | tr ':' ' '`
> do
>    echo "I got the name $dir"
> done > testfile
$ cat testfile
I got the name /bin
I got the name /usr/bin
I got the name /usr/local/bin
I got the name /proj/bin
```

Now let's do something more useful. We'll replace `echo` with `ls`—which will list the directories' contents, one by one, instead of just outputting the directory names.

When `ls` lists a single directory, it doesn't output the directory name or a blank line before it lists what's in the directory. So our `testfile` should get a list of all program names in all directories in the PATH, without needing the `grep` filters we used before.

(If you don't want to retype the whole loop, check the section "Command-Line Editing" in Chapter 1. Your shell may support editing entire loops at once. If it doesn't, you can put the loop in a file, as we'll do soon, and edit that file.) Here's the loop and its output; Figure 2-4 has a diagram showing the series of `ls` outputs being collected in `testfile`:

```
$ for dir in `echo "$PATH" | tr ':' ' '`
> do
>    ls $dir
> done > testfile
$ less testfile
arch
ash
awk
  ...
X11
[
  ...
```

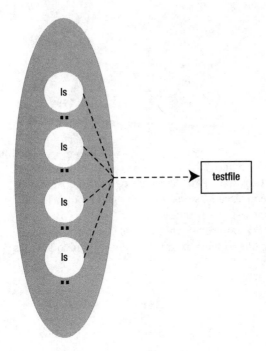

Figure 2-4. *Loop running multiple ls processes, their outputs redirected to a file*

We're almost there. We need to sort all of the ls outputs. Where does the sort command fit? It needs to read all of the program names that ls writes. So we'll pipe the output of the for loop to sort, then redirect the sort output to the proglist file:

```
$ for dir in `echo "$PATH" | tr ':' ' '`
> do
>    ls $dir
> done | sort > proglist
```

(Read the proglist file if you want to check it.)

We've got a pretty good system here, but it could be better. The directories listed in PATH don't necessarily have only programs in them. They may also have subdirectories and text files. (For instance, if you look back at our /usr/bin listings, you'll see *X11*. It's a subdirectory, not a program.) That's not a big problem, but let's look at a way to solve it.

Building Our Script

We want to loop through each directory and test each directory entry to see if it's a program file. Our code will look something like this:

```
for dir in `echo "$PATH" | tr ':' ' '`
do
  cd "$dir"

  ...test each entry in $dir and
  output its name if it's a program...

done | sort > proglist
```

What goes in the gap in the middle of the loop body?

We want to test every entry in every directory in the PATH. We'll use two for loops, one inside the other. The first loop, which we've seen already, steps through the directories in the PATH. Inside that, another loop steps through every entry in a directory.

After entering each directory with cd, the for loop for file in * will step through each entry in that directory—just as we did with the file-copying example earlier. So our code looks like this:

```
for dir in `echo "$PATH" | tr ':' ' '`
do
  cd "$dir"

  for file in *
  do
    ...test each $file in this $dir and
    output its name if it's a program...
  done

done | sort > proglist
```

Let's fill in the missing part. Bourne shells also have an if command that's designed to work with test—and, actually, with many Unix programs. if lets the shell make decisions based on the results of other commands. (By the way, the C shells' if works differently.) The if command runs a program and tests its exit status. If the status is zero (which means "success"), if executes the command lines after the word then. Otherwise, for a nonzero ("failure") status, if will execute the commands after the word else (if any). Our code will look like this:

```
if some-command-line
then
  commands to run if some-command-line returns "true" status
else (optional)
  optional commands to run if some-command-line returns "false" status
fi
```

The exit status isn't displayed on the screen (unless your shell is configured that way). The exit status of the previous command line is available from $? in Bourne-type shells and $status in C shells. You can see it by using echo. (If you aren't sure what the status of a command will be and its manual page doesn't tell you, this is a good way to find out!) As an example, let's use test to test the existence of file foo (which does exist) and file oof (which doesn't):

```
$ test -f foo
$ echo $?
0
$ test -f oof
$ echo $?
1
```

Now, back to our program. We'll use an if statement to check each directory entry and output its name only if it's an executable program file (but not a directory or a nonexecutable file). The *some-command-line* we'll use is a Unix program named [. Yes, that's an opening square bracket; you might have spotted it in the listing of the /usr/bin directory earlier. (That program is actually also named test. Unix programs can have multiple names.) It's designed to make tests on files, directories, strings of characters, and more. If the test succeeds, [returns a status of "true"; otherwise it returns "false."

■**Definition** The test and [commands test a file or an expression. They return a result that shows whether the test succeeded. They're typically used with the Bourne shells' if statement. Some shells have a built-in test operator, double brackets ([[...]]), with better features. You'll find details of all of this in the section "Condition Tests" in Chapter 13.

The test and [commands accept a series of command-line arguments. (To get a complete list, use man test.) The arguments are mostly mnemonic: for instance, the -x test is true if a file is executable, and -d is true if the file is a *d*irectory. (Directories are actually a special type of file.) The command name [requires a closing bracket (]) as its last command-line argument. Here's the test we'll use:

```
[ -x filename -a ! -d filename ]
```

Our test says: if the file *filename* is executable (-x), and (-a) if the file is not (!) a directory (-d), then return a status of "true." In other words, this test has two parts joined by the -a ("and") operator: -x *filename* and ! -d *filename*.

If the test is true, the shell will run echo to output the filename. The if statement will look like this:

```
if [ -x "$file" -a ! -d "$file" ]
then
   echo "$file"
fi
```

Finally, where does $file come from? It's set to each filename, in turn, by the inner for loop.

It's good programming practice to declare the output filename (which is proglist) at the beginning of the code instead of hiding it at the end. We'll create a shell variable named outfile for that. To set a shell variable, use the command name='*value*' or name="*value*". (Which quoting you use depends on whether you want the shell to expand *value* before storing it in the shell variable. See the section "Control Shell Interpretation with Quoting" in Chapter 3.)

Let's improve this by choosing an absolute pathname for the proglist file: instead of just proglist, we'll use $HOME/proglist. This means that, no matter what your current directory is when you run the code, the list of programs will always be written to the same place. On many systems, the HOME environment variable contains the absolute pathname of your home directory. (A few old systems use LOGDIR instead of HOME. To find out, type the commands echo $HOME and echo $LOGDIR at a prompt. Use HOME if it gives the right answer, or LOGDIR otherwise.)

(Here are two more "Unix-like" choices for data and configuration files like proglist. One is to name the file with a leading dot, like $HOME/.proglist, which "hides" it from commands like ls (see the section "Relative Pathnames and Your Current Directory" in Chapter 1). The other is to make a subdirectory named etc, and use the pathname $HOME/etc/proglist.

Making a Script File

If you want to try running this example code, you should probably use a Unix text editor—consider using a basic editor like pico or xedit, or a more sophisticated editor like vi or Emacs. Choose a filename for the program; this is the name you'll type at a shell prompt when you want to run the code. Just don't choose a name that's already used for another program. To check that, run type if you use the bash or ksh shells; otherwise use which. You're looking for an answer something like one of the following, which means your name hasn't been taken yet:

```
$ type make_prog_list
bash: type: make_prog_list: not found
$
```

```
% which make_prog_list
which: no make_prog_list in /bin:/usr/bin:/usr/local/bin:/proj/bin
```

To make this code work no matter what shell you normally use on your terminal (Bourne-type or C-type), put the code into an executable *shell script* file. You can choose the shell that reads the code by putting its absolute pathname in a special format, starting at the left edge (the beginning of) the first line of the file. The first two characters must be #!; this tells Unix that the pathname of an interpreter program (often a shell, but not always) is coming next on the line. Because this is Bourne shell code and all Unix systems have a Bourne-type shell at the absolute pathname /bin/sh, the first line should be #!/bin/sh.

A comment line starts with a # (hash or sharp sign).[4] It's a good idea to start a program with comment lines that explain what it does and how to use it. You can fill in whatever you like (including nothing).

Ready? Here's the file with the finished code:

---

4. This isn't true for all Unix program interpreters—but almost all. That it's usually true is part of why the special two-character sequence #! was chosen: that line is interpreted by the Unix kernel, but shells and other program interpreters ignore it as a comment.

```
#!/bin/sh
# put comments here, one or many lines,
# to describe this program and how to run it

outfile="$HOME/proglist"

for dir in `echo "$PATH" | tr ':' ' '`
do
  cd "$dir"

  for file in *
  do
    if [ -x "$file" -a ! -d "$file" ]
    then
      echo "$file"
    fi
  done

done | sort > $outfile
```

Once you have the script file ready, make it executable. For example, if the filename is make_proglist:

```
% chmod +x make_proglist
```

Running the Script

Now, if all's well, you should be able to run the script and rebuild your proglist file. If the script is in your current directory, the safest way to run it is by giving its relative pathname, starting with a dot (as the section "Relative Pathnames and Your Current Directory" in Chapter 1 explains, the relative pathname to the current directory is always .).

If it works right, the script should be silent: no output except to the proglist file in your home directory. (For more about this, see the sidebar "Making Error and Progress Messages".)

To be sure the script updates the file, use ls -l to check its size and last-modification time before and after you run the script. Here goes:

```
% ls -l $HOME/proglist
-rw-r--r--   1 zoe     users     6182 Dec  6 14:18 /home/zoe/proglist
% ./make_proglist
% !l
ls -l $HOME/proglist
-rw-r--r--   1 zoe     users     6129 Dec  6 16:44 /home/zoe/proglist
```

The program shouldn't take very long to run. If it takes much longer than a few seconds, terminate the program by typing (typically) Ctrl-c or Delete; you should get another shell prompt. Then look in the proglist file to see if there's output and try to track down what's wrong.

Compare it carefully to the example code we've shown here. If that doesn't help, you can ask the shell for debugging output while the program runs by changing the program's first line to

```
#!/bin/sh -xv
```

The options -xv tell the shell to list each command line it reads and show each command name as it's run. Watch carefully to see if you can tell what's wrong. We won't cover program debugging in detail here, but it's basically a matter of comparing what the program should do to what it actually does. For more about debugging, see the section "Debugging Scripts" in Chapter 13.

INHERITANCE

Inheritance? Well, yes—but we aren't talking money or genetics here. We're talking about Unix processes. When one process (the parent process) starts a new process (a child process), the child inherits many attributes from its parent. (The sidebar "What's Happening: Processes" in Chapter 1 introduces parent and child processes.) For instance, the parent's environment variables, like PATH, are copied to the child. The child starts in the same current directory where its parent was. And so on.

But once the child has started, its environment is separate from its parent's. Also, a child process can't change its parent's environment (unless both processes are set up to cooperate).

So: a child process can change any of its attributes, and the parent is safe from unanticipated changes in itself. In other words, the processes start nearly identical to each other, but they run basically independent of each other.

Why is this important? A child process can reset its PATH to a list that's right for it, to be sure it will find commands in the directories it needs to— but that won't affect the parent's PATH. The child can create and change shell and environment variables, but the parent's variable settings stay the same. A child process can cd all over the filesystem, but its parent's current directory won't change. We've taken advantage of this in our shell script.

This script cds all over the filesystem, then it exits. Beginners often think that the script has to save its starting directory pathname, then cd back to that directory before it exits. No—not if the code is running as a script, that is. (Keep reading, though, for a note about shell functions.) Because a shell script is run in a separate shell—a separate process—it does *not* need to save its starting directory. When it's done, it simply exits; other processes' current directories (and the rest of their environments) aren't affected by it.

A shell *function*—as opposed to a shell script—usually runs within the same shell process. (There's more about functions in Chapter 13.) So, if you wrote make_proglist as a shell function, you *would* need to remember the starting current directory and to restore it when the function exits.

Let's close with something obscure that's still worth a mention. We said that a shell function "usually" runs within the same shell process, but it doesn't when the directory-changing happens within a loop that has a pipe (|) on its output or its input. Remember that a pipe routes the output of one process to the input of another process. Typically, when a loop has input or output redirected with a pipe, the shell starts a new process to run the loop commands. An important consequence of this: variables you add or reset in a "redirected" loop may not take effect outside of that loop. (In zsh, a redirected-input loop runs in the same shell process, but a redirected-output loop requires a new process.) This obscure part of Unix is an example of why it helps to understand how processes work "under the hood" ("under the bonnet", if you prefer).

Programs and the Path

Every time you want to run your script to rebuild the `proglist` file, do you have to `cd` to the directory where the script file is stored? No—not if you put your script file in one of the directories in your `PATH` environment variable. You can change the directory list in your `PATH`.

Let's put the new script in a standard place, a directory you can use for all of your personal programs.

1. The most common setup is to have a directory named `bin` that's under (a subdirectory of) your home directory. To make this subdirectory, go to your home directory first:

   ```
   % cd
   % mkdir bin
   ```

2. The first time you create your `bin` directory, you need to add it to the `PATH` variable so the shell will search it for programs. See the section "Startup Files, Login and Interactive Shells" in Chapter 5 for details on editing the correct shell startup file. Until you log in next, or start using new terminals, you'll also need to change the `PATH` in all shells you're running at the moment. Here are the commands to type for C-type and Bourne-type shells:

   ```
   % set path = ($path ~/bin)
   $ PATH=$PATH:$HOME/bin
   ```

   (In Bourne shells, you may need to use `$LOGDIR` instead of `$HOME`. To check, type the command `echo $HOME`. If there's no output, that variable may not be defined; in that case, try `echo $LOGDIR`.)

3. Change to your new `bin` directory by typing `cd bin`.

4. You can create any new scripts, from now on, in this directory. To move your existing script into your `bin`, use the Unix `mv` (move) program. An `mv` command line can have two arguments, or more than two arguments. If there are just two arguments, the first is the file's current pathname and the last is the pathname you want the file to have after you move it; the last argument can also be the pathname of a directory. If there are more than two arguments, the last argument is the pathname of the directory where you want to move the files, and the first arguments are the pathnames of the files you want to move to that place. So if you created the script file in your home directory and you're now in your `bin`, you could type *one* of the following commands:

   ```
   $ mv -i ../scriptname .
       -- or --
   $ mv -i $HOME/scriptname .
       -- or --
   $ mv -i $HOME/scriptname $HOME/bin
   ```

The first, using relative pathnames, is easiest to type, of course, but you have to know where the script file is now. (The .. and . are explained at the section "Relative Pathnames and Your Current Directory" in Chapter 1.) Your shell may also understand a tilde (~) instead of $HOME, as in

```
$ mv -i ~/scriptname .
    -- or --
$ mv -i ~/scriptname ~/bin
```

The -i option makes mv ask before it overwrites (replaces) any destination file.

5. If you use a C shell, you may need to type the command rehash once. This tells the shell to search its PATH and rebuild its program lookup table (called a *hash table*, which is a special kind of table designed to be searched quickly).

Now, if all's well, you can change to any directory and type the program name at a shell prompt, and it should run.

MAKING ERROR AND PROGRESS MESSAGES

Unix utility programs run from the command line usually don't output status messages to tell you what they're doing. They simply do the job. Their only output is text, written to the standard output.

Part of the reason for this is that, as we explained earlier, you can redirect a program's output to a file or pipe it to another program. If status messages were written to the standard output, along with the good data, you might not see the messages and/or the messages could mix with the data you want to save.

Still, status messages can be useful in long-running programs. There are two important things to know about making a status message or an error message:

1. The message should start with the program's name. This is very helpful when you're using a pipeline with several programs because you can tell which of those programs the message comes from.

2. The message should be written on the standard error. To do this in Bourne-type shells, use echo and add the shell operator 1>&2 to the end of the command line. This redirects the standard output (which is file descriptor number 1) onto the standard error (which is file descriptor number 2). There's no easy way to do this under tcsh and csh, which is another reason programmers often prefer Bourne shells.

So the following command line would output an error message:

```
echo "make_proglist: blah blah blah" 1>&2
```

Because you might rename the make_proglist program some day, it's better to store the program name in a shell variable at the start of the file—where you're more likely to see it—like this:

```
myname=make_proglist
    ...
echo "$myname: blah blah blah" 1>&2
```

(Even better, have the program find its own name. You can get it from the shell parameter $0. Using command substitution, let's capture the output of the Unix basename program, which will remove any pathname from the front of the program's filename:

```
myname=`basename $0`
   ...
echo "$myname: blah blah blah" 1>&2
```

That's also handy for another reason: a single file can actually have multiple names—so a program can do multiple things by testing its name, which we've stored in the variable myname.)

Using the Results (via Aliases and Functions)

Finally, here are a couple of ways to use the proglist file. Let's make a shell function (for Bourne shells) and an alias (for C shells) named findpgm ("find program") that searches for program names containing a particular string of characters. We'll search with the grep program, but you might choose to use another search program—for instance, a "soundex" search program to find words that "sound like" the program name you enter. This is Unix, so there are lots of choices, and most programs' command lines will simply "drop in" to replace grep.

Assuming that your data file is in your home directory, an alias like this should do the job on tcsh and csh:

```
alias findpgm 'grep "\!^" ~/proglist | column'
```

(We introduced aliases in the section "Command Lines" in Chapter 1.) This alias takes advantage of the C shell tilde abbreviation (~) for your home directory. The bizarre-looking string \!^ is actually a history reference (see the section "History" in Chapter 1) that expands into the first argument on the command line when you use the alias. If you don't have column, you can use whatever other column-making program you used earlier.

Next, let's see the corresponding Bourne shell function. (The $1 expands into the first argument you give when you use the function. For instance, when you run findpgm edit, $1 from your function code would expand into edit. See the section "Positional Parameters" in Chapter 13.) Here's the function:

```
findpgm()
{
  grep "$1" $HOME/proglist | column
}
```

You can type the alias or function at your shell prompt to test it. If you want to keep it, add it to the appropriate shell startup file in your home directory. Let's see this work:

```
% findpgm edit
gedit           gnome-edit-properties-capplet    kedit        kmenuedit
gnome-edit      gxedit                           kiconedit    mcedit
```

We've covered a lot of material in this chapter. The point here isn't to show you everything there is to know about writing loops and tests in the shell. It's to show that, with some simple shell commands and features—many you also might use sometimes at a command line—you can write a series of commands that automates some tedious work.

Summary

In summary, here's what we've covered:

- A process (a program) has three places (standard output, standard error, and standard input) that you can redirect to or from a file. Redirecting output to an existing file erases the file first, but you can also append output to a file. A pipe redirects the *stdout* of one process to the *stdin* of another.

- We searched for text with grep and egrep, paged through text with a pager program like more or less, sorted text with sort, made text into columns with column and pr, edited text on the fly with cut and tr, and more.

- You can continue a long command line by ending each line (except the last) with a backslash (\).

- The for and foreach loops step through a list of arguments one by one, putting each into a shell variable and then running a series of commands.

- Command substitution runs a command line, then replaces the command line with its standard output. This lets you make a command line that modifies itself.

- The test and [commands test a file or an expression. They're typically used with the if statement for a "true or false" decision.

- To make a shell script, store a series of command lines in a file and give the file execute permission. To make a shell function, type its name followed by a series of commands inside curly braces. Then you can run the script or function by typing its name. If you have many shell scripts, making a bin directory and adding it to your shell's PATH gives you a central storage place.

In the next chapter, we'll wrap up this introduction by looking at a variety of useful shell features.

CHAPTER 3

■ ■ ■

More Shell Features

Chapter 1 introduced some related shell features and Unix concepts. Chapter 2 showed how to combine programs using redirection and shell programming features. In this chapter, we'll round out the book's introduction by digging into a grab bag of more advanced shell and Unix features, including

- Passing information from process to process, such as the current time zone or the name of your favorite text editor, with environment variables

- Controlling processes: getting their status, stopping and starting them with job control, and sending signals to them

- Using quoting to control how the shell interprets a command line

- Changing your current directory by giving just the end of its pathname using the CDPATH

Passing Info to Processes with Environment Variables

Every process on a Unix system has its own environment—attributes and settings that track the process information and maintain its state. One important part of a Unix process environment is its list of *environment variables*.

Environment variables hold information—strings of text that are designed to be passed from process to process, information that processes need to share with each other. For instance, the environment variable named SHELL contains the pathname of a shell you want to use, and HOME (also called LOGDIR on some systems) contains the pathname of your home directory. Some environment variables, like SHELL and HOME, are standard, and every process expects them to have been set. But you can also set any other environment variables that you wish—for instance, to communicate information from a parent process to its children.

When a parent process starts a child process, the parent's environment variables are copied to the child. Then the child can do whatever it wants to with those values. A simple example is the Unix program printenv. (If you don't have printenv, you can use env in some cases and echo in others, as we'll explain soon.) It simply outputs a list of all the environment variables that it received from its parent process. Typically, that parent process is your shell. Let's try it:

```
$ printenv
PAGER=less
MANPATH=/u/jpeek/.man:/usr/local/man:/usr/man:/usr/share/man:/usr/X11R6/man
VISUAL=vi
LESS=emqc
USER=jpeek
MAIL=/var/spool/mail/jpeek
EDITOR=vi
DISPLAY=:0.0
LOGNAME=jpeek
SHELL=/bin/bash
TERM=xterm
TZ=US/Arizona
HOME=/u/jpeek
PATH=/u/jpeek/.bin:/u/jpeek/mh/show:/usr/local/bin:/bin:/usr/bin:/usr/X11R6/bin
...
```

We've seen some standard variables, ones that certain Unix programs (or most Unix programs) expect. For instance, the man program looks for manual-page files in the directories listed in MANPATH, and it also could use the program named in PAGER to show those files screen by screen. When a program needs a text editor, it may use the editor named in VISUAL or in EDITOR.

As we saw in the previous chapter, the shell handles two types of variables: shell variables and environment variables. Shell variables (sometimes also called *parameters*) stay in the process where you set them; they aren't copied to child processes as environment variables are.

Some Unix users—especially C shell users—name shell variables in lowercase, like myvariable, and environment variables in uppercase, like MYVARIABLE. The two names are different because variable names are case sensitive in all shells. (In fact, the C and Z shells' path has the same list of names as the PATH, but in a different format.) That lower-versus-uppercase naming scheme is a convention, though, not a rule.

To see the value of a particular environment variable, you can pass its name to printenv as an argument. (This won't work with env, though.) You also can give echo the variable name preceded by a currency sign ($) and surrounded by double quotes; the shell expands this into the variable's value. Consider this example:

```
$ printenv TZ
US/Arizona
$ echo "$TZ"
US/Arizona
```

The TZ environment variable tells you what time zone you're in. The time zone name can be in a variety of formats. (Your system has a default time zone. If you use it, you don't need to set TZ.) You may want to change the value of TZ that the system gave you. For instance:

- You might have a portable computer that you've taken on a trip; you want to set the shell (and any child processes it starts) to understand your new time zone. You can change the TZ environment variable within your shell in each terminal window where you want to use the new time zone.

- You may be doing a remote login, via the Internet, to a system in a time zone other than yours. You can set TZ in your shell startup file on that remote system to your local time zone. That way, each time you log in to that remote system, TZ will be set for you.

- Maybe your company has an office in Tokyo and you'd like to know what the time is there. On Bourne-type shells, including zsh, it's easy to set an environment variable *temporarily*, just for a single process. (That's harder to do in C shells.)

Here's a Bourne shell example with numbered prompts. Read through it to get an idea of what's happening, and we'll explain at the end:

```
1$ printenv TZ
US/Arizona
2$ date
Tue Jul 15 09:26:03 MST 2003
3$ TZ="Japan" date
Wed Jul 16 01:26:08 JST 2003
4$ printenv TZ
US/Arizona
5$ export TZ=GMT
6$ date
Tue Jul 15 16:26:36 GMT 2003
7$ printenv TZ
GMT
```

Command 1 shows that TZ contains US/Arizona, and **command 2** uses that value when it shows the date in that time zone. In **command 3**, we're using the Bourne shell's way to set a variable temporarily, for just a single command: put *Name="value"* before the command. You can see that the date command is giving the date in Japan (where it happens to be tomorrow!). After command 3 runs, **command 4** shows that the value of TZ in the shell hasn't changed. But **command 5** does change TZ in the shell, as you can see by what date outputs in **command 6** and what printenv shows in **command 7**. From now on in this shell, the time zone is set to GMT.

In csh and tcsh, replace command 3 with

```
(setenv TZ "Japan"; date)
```

and command 5 with

```
setenv TZ "Japan"
```

both of which have the same effect. On older Bourne-type shells, replace command 5 with

```
 TZ=GMT; export TZ
```

because the original sh version of export can't set an environment variable's value.

We've used environment variables in other places. One was in the section "Building Our Script" in Chapter 2, and later in that chapter, where the shell expanded $HOME/proglist into the pathname of your home directory followed by /proglist.

You can use environment variables to store information you want to make available in all of your shells and subprocesses. In this example, we'll use the C shell syntax for setting environment variables. For instance, you could put this line in your shell's .login startup file:

```
setenv COPIES /var/tmp/joanna/backup-copies
```

Then, when you're using the vi editor and you want to save the file you're editing into that directory, you could give a file-writing command like this:

```
:w $COPIES/filename
```

and the file would be written to /var/tmp/joanna/backup-copies/filename.

QUIZ

Let's say you're using a portable computer that shows a graphical clock in the corner of your screen. You change the TZ environment variable from your shell by typing, say, setenv TZ CET.

Q: Why doesn't the graphical clock change?

A: You changed the environment variable *in your shell process*. As we saw earlier, one Unix process can't change the environment of another process that's already running. The graphical clock process has nothing to do with your shell process. You'll need to use your system's special tool for changing the graphical clock—possibly by changing the master system clock.

(Note that changing a clock on a running system is tricky because Unix systems do so much based on the number of seconds since the Epoch, which is the number of seconds since 00:00:00 on January 1, 1970. If your system clock uses UTC (GMT, Zulu) time, then changing the time zone isn't a problem—but changing the clock time can disrupt processes that are counting seconds. It may be safest to reboot your system and change the time while Unix isn't running—from the BIOS setup routine on a PC, for instance.

Starting and Stopping Processes: Signals, Job Control

When you start a Unix process, it runs until its program finishes, then it exits. (Actually, Unix may start and stop the process often as it juggles the computer's resources, giving small chunks of time to each of the processes on the system. The ps command, which we'll soon describe in the section "Finding Processes with ps," shows what each process is doing—or, as the case may be, is *not* doing.) By default, the shell waits for the process to finish before printing another prompt.

■**Note** This section describes features that may not work on some non-Unix operating systems.

You might want to do something else while the process is running, though. For instance, you might start the Mozilla web browser from your shell, like this:

```
% mozilla
...nothing happens in this window, no prompt...
```

Mozilla opens a new window, and you can work with Mozilla until you use its Quit command (on its File menu); at that point, the `mozilla` process finishes and the shell prints another prompt. But what if you wanted to run the `cal` command, from the shell, to check this month's calendar—while Mozilla is still running? You wouldn't have a shell prompt, so you couldn't type the `cal` command. (You actually could type the command, but the shell wouldn't run it until `mozilla` finished.)

To make the shell prompt available to you while Mozilla is running, you can run Mozilla in the background.

Background Processing

The shell has a handy feature called *background processing* for programs that you don't need to interact with in the terminal. Background processes are actually a feature of Unix, not just of shells. The shells just make them easy to use.

If you want to start a program and get another shell prompt right away, put the program into the background. The easiest way to do that is by adding an ampersand (&) to the end of the command line. The shell will start the process, output a job number (explained later) and the PID, then give you another prompt right away, like this:

```
% mozilla &
[1] 9989
%
```

Now you have two processes running simultaneously: the shell and Mozilla. If you also want to do some editing with the `xemacs` editor (which opens its own window), you could also start it in the background:

```
% xemacs &
[2] 10023
%
```

To view a list of the background jobs you've run from this shell, use the shell's built-in `jobs` command:

```
% jobs
[1]    Running              mozilla
[2]    Running              xemacs
%
```

Background processing is great for a program that makes its own window, like Mozilla or `xemacs`, because the shell can do something else for you while it waits for the process to finish. If the program writes any output to the terminal (to its standard output or standard error, as explained in the section "Writing Output to Files: Redirection" in Chapter 2), that output still typically goes to the terminal, so you'll see it there. (Background output can make a confusing jumble on the screen if you're doing something else in the foreground at the same time. The

Unix command `stty tostop` can prevent this jumble, but it's an advanced command that you probably shouldn't use unless you understand the shell's job control features. The section "Resuming Stopped and Background Jobs" in Chapter 11 has more information.)

It doesn't make sense to run a program in the background if it needs to read from the terminal (or terminal window) where it's running. Only one process can read from the keyboard (or whatever the standard input is) at a time.

Stopping a Job

Your Unix system is good at managing multiple processes, giving them time to run when they have something to do and letting them sleep (so other processes can run) when they're idle. It's possible, however, to have so many processes running that the system runs low on memory or CPU cycles. When that happens, system response can get sluggish. You can stop a background job completely to let the system do something else. Later, you can restart the job from where it left off; you won't lose your place. If the job has opened windows of its own, you should minimize (iconify) those windows before you stop the job; otherwise, they'll probably "freeze" when you stop the job, and you won't be able to do anything with them until you've restarted the job.

On the C shells, you can stop a job using the `stop` command and a job number. Job numbers start with a percent sign (%). For instance, to stop Mozilla, first minimize its window, then stop it—and, if you want to, check its status:

```
% stop %1
% jobs
[1]  + Suspended (signal)     mozilla
[2]    Running                xemacs
%
```

Most Bourne-type shells don't have a `stop` command, but you can use `kill` instead. The kill command doesn't necessarily "kill" a job; it sends a *signal* to the process(es) in the job. The basic idea is that `kill` lets you control a job or an individual process.

The first argument to `kill` is a signal name or signal number, preceded by a dash (like an option). The other argument(s) to `kill` are the job numbers or PIDs that should get the signal.

Most of the signals are useful for programmers, but a few are handy for all users. One signal, SIGTSTP, sends a "stop from terminal" signal to a process. SIGTSTP gives a process time to organize itself and stop gracefully, so it's the right signal to send when you can. But a program also can ignore SIGTSTP. A "stronger" stop signal, SIGSTOP, can't be ignored and will take effect immediately—but it may leave a process in an inconsistent state, so only use it when you have to stop a process and SIGTSTP doesn't work. Let's assume that you started Mozilla from the Z shell. To stop it, you'd do the following:

```
zsh% kill -TSTP %1
zsh%
zsh% jobs
[1]  + suspended (signal)  mozilla
[2]    running             xemacs
```

If you'd like to add a `stop` command to your non-C shell, an alias (see the section "Command Lines" in Chapter 1) should do the trick:

```
alias stop='kill -TSTP'
```

You might also want to send a signal to a job that's not in the background—that is, a job that's running in a terminal and you don't have a shell prompt (so you can't use the `stop` or `kill` command with the job number). Years ago, when most users had only a single terminal (and no windows), being able to stop what you were doing—get a shell prompt, run another command, then resume the job where you left off—was revolutionary. These days, many users with windows will simply leave one window where it is and open another window. But opening a new window has some disadvantages:

- The new window won't have any changes you've made to the existing window (its command history, current directory, shell and environment variables you've reset, and so on). However, you can save and restore history entries through shell variables like `HISTFILE`, as Chapter 6 explains.

- Opening a new window probably requires you to move the mouse, open menus or click a button, move to the new window and click on it, and so on: it takes some time. But getting a new shell prompt in your current window takes just two keystrokes: Ctrl-z.

- A new window takes some system resources (especially memory) to open. On the other hand, stopping the job in your current window takes no resources; in fact, it can free system resources. That may be important on an overloaded system.

Signals from the Keyboard

To send signals to a "foreground" process—one that's in control of your terminal, when you don't have a shell prompt there—you typically use the Ctrl key plus one other key. The key combinations are configurable, but Table 3-1 lists some typical values:

Table 3-1. *Keys Set by* `stty`

Key Combo	Sends Signal	Effect
Ctrl-z	SIGTSTP	Stop process (you can restart with the `fg` command)
Ctrl-c	SIGINT	Terminate (interrupt) process
Ctrl-\	IGQUIT	Terminate process, make debugging file ("core dump")

To restart a stopped job and put it into the background, use the shell's `bg` command; the arguments are job numbers. (You can also type `kill -CONT` followed by the PID of a job you've previously stopped with `kill -TSTP` or `kill -STOP`.) For instance, to restart our suspended Mozilla job:

```
% bg %1
[1]    mozilla &
%
```

The main use of signals, though, is to terminate jobs that are taking too long or that have other problems: for instance, if something goes wrong and the program won't respond. You'll have a few choices, all of which send signals, but in different ways:

- If the job is in the background and you started it from a shell prompt, you can kill it by job number, like kill %2.

- If the job is in the foreground, use a key combination like Ctrl-c (listed in Table 3.1).

- Otherwise, open (or go to) another terminal (if one terminal is frozen or unavailable). Get the job's PID number, and kill it by PID, such as kill 12345. This is handy for jobs that you didn't start from a shell—such as jobs started from a menu or button on your desktop.

We'll see examples of those in a minute. But first: If you didn't start a process from the shell where you have a prompt—or if you don't have a prompt in this shell and can't get one (because the foreground job is stalled for some reason)—you'll probably need to get the PID of the process. How can you find the PID of a process if the shell didn't tell you? (Many systems have a program like killall that tries to kill a process by the name of the program running in that process. But those can make mistakes or miss some processes. On some systems, killall actually tries to kill *all* processes. So be careful!) Our technique is more thorough—and it also shows you a lot about what's happening in your Unix system.) The answer is the ps (process status) program that we mentioned briefly in the sidebar "What's Happening: Processes" in Chapter 1.

Finding Processes with ps

The ps utility displays a list of processes. Unfortunately, different systems have very different versions of ps. Some will show all of your processes on all terminals, some show only your current terminal (unless you add options), some hide "uninteresting" processes, and so on. Explaining all of the versions, and how to use them, is beyond the scope of this book, but let's look at an example. Try the command ps l (a lowercase letter "L") or, if that doesn't work, ps -f. You'll get a listing something like this:

```
$ ps -f
UID        PID  PPID  C STIME TTY          TIME CMD
jpeek      673   666  0 Nov21 pts/1     00:00:04 bash
jpeek     2224   673  0 Nov24 pts/1     00:00:19 vim p1c1.xml p1c2.xml
jpeek     2514   673  0 10:36 pts/1     00:00:00 ps -f
```

Each line shows information about a process of yours. The format varies from system to system; we'll discuss the example that's shown here. Some of the most important columns are

- The name of each process is in the rightmost column, followed, in some versions of ps, by its command-line arguments.

- The second column shows the PID (process ID) number.

- The third column shows the PPID, the parent PID. It's the PID of the process that started this process.

- The TTY column shows the terminal (actually, *teletype*) where the process is running. Each terminal, or terminal window, has its own name. If you have several open, you can find which is which by running the command tty from a shell prompt inside the window.

- The TIME column shows how much CPU time the process has used. A runaway process often accumulates a lot of CPU time.

Comparing the PID and PPID columns tells you which process started which. The first process, the bash shell, has PID 673. (It was started by a process owned by another user, *root*. By default, you won't see other users' processes in your ps list.) The other two processes have 673 as their PPID—which shows that the shell started vi and ps. This means that you should be able to see these processes in the listing from that shell's jobs command.

A process might have a PPID of 1. Process number 1 is init, the parent (or grandparent, or...) of all processes, as we mentioned in Chapter 1. These processes won't be in your shell's jobs list. (One way to get a process with a PPID of 1 is to log out without ending your background jobs. If the shell doesn't kill those jobs, they'll be "inherited" by init.)

Once you've found the process you need to terminate (for which you may need to use other ps options), the simplest command is kill followed by the PID. For instance, if you started Mozilla from a menu (not from your shell) and it's now frozen, you might find that there are actually several mozilla processes. It might be best to kill them one by one, the highest-numbered first; the others may go away by themselves. Or you can give all the PIDs at once, on a single command line:

```
$ ps
    ...
  773 pts/4  S    0:00 sh /usr/local/bin/mozilla
  774 pts/4  S    0:00 sh /usr/local/mozilla/run-mozilla.sh ./mozilla-bin
  783 pts/4  S   12:05 ./mozilla-bin
  785 pts/4  S    0:00 ./mozilla-bin
  786 pts/4  S    0:01 ./mozilla-bin
  787 pts/4  S    0:03 ./mozilla-bin
    ...
$ kill 787
    ...
```

After you kill a process, check again to be sure it's gone. By itself (with no signal name or number), kill sends SIGTERM. You may need to send a different signal to "hard-to-kill" processes. Try kill -HUP, then (if that doesn't work), kill -KILL (which is often written kill -9). The SIGKILL signal, signal number 9, is a last resort because it doesn't give a process a chance to clean up after itself (handle open files, and so on).

A Bourne shell script can use the shell's trap command to do something before the script terminates. For example, when the shell receives a signal, the script could remove its temporary files and close an open network connection, then exit. See the section "Traps and Special Functions" in Chapter 13 for details.

Tip To kill windowing programs, you can also try xkill.

Control Shell Interpretation with Quoting

When the shell reads a command line, it interprets special characters. Those special characters include spaces to separate arguments from each other, $ characters that tell the shell to expand a variable name, * characters that expand into pathnames, and more. There are times you want special characters to be taken literally. For instance, you might have a filename with spaces in it; you want the shell to include the spaces and not treat the filename as several separate files.

To control the shell's handling of special characters, use quoting. Quoting works a little differently in different shells, but the basics are about the same everywhere. The idea is that *quoting disables the meaning of special characters.* Here are some examples with a wildcard:

```
$ echo a*
afile.txt      apple_tarts     azimuth
$ echo 'a*'
a*
$ ls -l a*
-rw-------    1 jpeek    users       623 Jan 23 09:17 afile.txt
-rw-r--r--    1 jpeek    users      1739 Jul  3  2003 apple_tarts
-rw-r--r--    1 jpeek    users      8462 Jul  2  2003 azimuth
$ ls -l 'a*'
ls: a*: No such file or directory
```

When the wildcard * has been quoted, the shell doesn't expand it into matching filenames. Instead, the shell removes the quotes and passes the remaining characters on to the program. So echo outputs the literal string a* because that's the argument that the shell passed to it. In the same way, the ls program says that it can't find a file named a* (which is true: there isn't one!).

Of course, trying to list a nonexistent file named a* (by quoting the wildcard) doesn't make sense. (You'd only do that to access a file with the literal two-character name a*.) You want to use unquoted wildcards on an ls command line so the shell will expand the wildcard into the correct filenames. We've shown that example so you'll see what the shell normally does, and how quoting a wildcard changes that.

In general, Unix programs depend on the shell to handle special characters. But some Unix programs have their own special characters, and you want the shell to leave those characters alone—that is, not to interpret them, and to pass them to the program as they are. That's one time you'll need to use quoting.

For instance, many Unix programs use *regular expressions* (sometimes shortened to *regex* or *regexps*). The grep program, which we saw in the section "Using Programs Together: Pipes" in Chapter 2, is one of those. Its first command-line argument is a regular expression; other arguments (if any) are files to search. One handy file to search, available on many Unix systems, is the dictionary file named something like /usr/dict/words, /usr/share/dict/linux.words or /usr/share/dict/web2. This is a great place to search for crossword-puzzle words. For example, you could make a regular expression to search for any word containing *ei*, followed by two or more characters, followed by *le*, like this:

```
$ grep 'ei...*le' /usr/dict/words
conceivable
imperceivable
inconceivable
perceivable
receivable
reimbursable
Weissmuller
```

If we hadn't put quotes around the regular expression, the shell would have tried to turn ei...*le into a list of matching filenames! (To the shell, * is a wildcard character. The shell doesn't know what grep does.) But, with quotes, the shell passed the expression onto grep literally (after stripping off the quotes, that is).

Note We suggest that, unless you need to do something special, simply put single quotes around any argument containing a character that isn't a letter, number, dot (.) or underscore (_). That's usually safe.

The newline character (which you get by pressing the Return key) is also special to the shell. Why? (Think back on what the shell does when you press that key.) It's a command-line separator; when the shell sees a newline character, it knows that the command line has ended. If you want to include a newline as part of a command line, you have to quote it. Let's store a multiline address in a Bourne shell variable. (The previous chapter introduced shell variables.)

```
$ addr='Jerry Peek
> 1234 Main Street
> Flagstaff, AZ   56789'
$
```

When the shell sees the opening quote, it keeps looking for the next matching quote—that is, the closing quote. Since the newlines were inside quotes, they weren't command separators; they're simply included in the variable. The shell prints secondary prompts—which, for Bourne shells, is usually >—until you complete the command line.

C shells do this differently. That's the main difference between Bourne- and C-type shell quoting. You have to put a backslash (\) before each newline character. If you don't, you'll get an error message:

```
% set addr = 'Jerry Peek
Unmatched '.
% set addr = 'Jerry Peek\
? 1234 Main Street\
? Flagstaff, AZ   56789'
%
```

The C shells' secondary prompt is ?. In general, all shells have three kinds of quoting—three different quote marks:

1. When you put \ (backslash) before a character, that always disables the character's special meaning. (So, how can you echo a backslash? Put a backslash before it: echo \\ does the trick.)

2. When you surround a string of characters with a pair of ' (single quote) characters, that disables the special meaning of almost all special characters inside the string. (In most shells, single quotes allow history substitution—with the ! character. And, in C shells, single quotes also don't disable newlines. In both of those cases, you have to put a backslash before each ! and newline.)

3. When you surround a string of characters with a pair of " (double quote) characters, that disables the special meaning of most characters inside the string. It allows variable substitution (the $ character) and command substitution (the ` or $() operator). Again, in many shells, it also does not disable history substitution or newlines, as we explained earlier.

In a lot of cases, the sort of quoting you use doesn't matter. For instance, the grep command we saw previously works with any sort of quoting because all kinds of quoting disable wildcards. Use whichever you like best:

```
grep 'ei...*le' /usr/dict/words
grep "ei...*le" /usr/dict/words
grep ei...\*le /usr/dict/words
```

(The dot (.) is a special character to grep, but not to the shell. Because you use quoting to control the shell, there's no need to quote the dots.)

Most shells treat spaces and newlines as argument separators inside shell variables and command substitution. That is, if the value of your shell variable or the output of your command has spaces or newlines in it, most shells will break the text into separate arguments there.

For example, let's look back at the address we stored earlier in the addr shell variable. When you give that value without quotes, most shells will break it into separate arguments at the spaces and newlines. The echo command outputs its arguments with a single space between each of them. See what happens when you echo the variable's value on Bourne shells: the shell breaks it into arguments and echo adds a space between each:

```
$ echo $addr
Jerry Peek 1234 Main Street Flagstaff, AZ 56789
```

(The C shell does something similar, but it treats a newline as a separate, empty argument, so you get two spaces between each of the original lines.) Notice that we lost the three spaces that we'd stored between AZ and 56789; the shell used them as an argument separator.

In Bourne and C shells, you have to tell the shell not to break the line into words. To do that, quote the value so the shell will ignore the special meaning of spaces and newlines. Do we want single quotes or double quotes? We want double quotes because they don't disable the $ character:

```
$ echo '$addr'
$addr
$ echo "$addr"
Jerry Peek
1234 Main Street
Flagstaff, AZ   56789
```

Here's one area that Z shell is different from other shells. By default (unless you configure it to work like a Bourne shell), zsh won't break expanded variables and command substitution at spaces and newlines. So, in the Z shell, there's no need for double quotes in this case—though you can use them if you want to:

```
zsh% echo $addr
Jerry Peek
1234 Main Street
Flagstaff, AZ   56789
zsh% echo "$addr"
Jerry Peek
1234 Main Street
Flagstaff, AZ   56789
```

Here again, the C shells do things that some people consider quirky. To quote a newline from a shell variable, you have to use some special C shell-only quoting:

```
% echo "$addr"
Unmatched ".
% echo ${addr:q}
Jerry Peek
1234 Main Street
Flagstaff, AZ   56789
```

Here we're getting into some of the twisty, bizarre corners of the differences between shells. Unless you want to be an expert—or you're just interested—this sort of arcane detail isn't very important, but you can find all of it in the latter parts of this book (along with lots of much more practical information).

Let's finish quoting by reminding you of the three types of quoting—", ', and \—and the general rule that, if you don't need to do anything special, use a pair of single quotes (') around an argument; you'll probably be fine.

Quick Directory Changes with cdpath

In these first three chapters, we've covered only a few of the most useful shell features. There are many more in this book's next two parts. Let's finish with a simple feature that's also very handy: changing your current directory somewhere without typing a long pathname.

Many users, and sites, have "top-level" directories that group a collection of subdirectories into one place. For instance, a team of software developers might have a series of projects under the directory /local/work, each subdirectory named for the individual project:

/local/work/annie for the project code-named "annie", /local/work/bennie for the "bennie" project, and so on. Each of those projects may have their own subdirectories named bin for programs, src for source code, and so on.

A programmer working in her home directory (say, /u/jill) may not want to type cd /local/work/bennie (or, worse, cd /local/work/bennie/src) each time she needs to work in one of the project directories. As we saw in the section "Building Pathnames by Completion" in Chapter 1, shells have filename completion to let you type parts of pathnames and complete them by pressing Tab. But shells also have cdpaths: lists of common parent directories that the shell will check to find a subdirectory by name. For instance, if Jill has told her shell that she often wants to go to /local/work/bennie, she may not need to type cd /local/work/bennie/src; instead, she simply types the end of the pathname: cd src, or maybe cd bennie/src; the shell finds the first matching pathname, tells her what it is, and takes her there.

To set this up, she needs to set the CDPATH shell variable on Bourne shells or the cdpath variable on C shells. This is a list of the parent directories where she works a lot of the time.

■**Note** In Bourne-type shells, be sure to include your current directory in your CDPATH (as we'll explain). Otherwise, you won't be able to cd to subdirectories of your current directory. C shells automatically try the current directory before the cdpath, so you don't need to include the current directory in your list.

For instance, if Jill often works under /local/work/bennie and also under /u/jill/logs, she could set this CDPATH in her Bourne-type or C-type shells:

```
CDPATH=:/local/work/bennie:/u/jill/logs
```

```
set cdpath = (/local/work/bennie /u/jill/logs)
```

Then, if she types cd foo, the shell will first try to change to the subdirectory foo under the current directory. If there's no such directory, it will try cd /local/work/bennie/foo and cd /u/jill/logs/foo. If the shell finds foo under some other directory (not the current directory), it will show the pathname; otherwise it will print an error.

The C shells' cdpath list is separated by spaces. The Bourne shells' CDPATH is separated by colons (:). In Bourne-type shells, you include the current directory by using either an empty pair of colons (like : :) or by using a single colon at the start or end of the CDPATH string. (There's a leading colon on our sample CDPATH.)

Although you can set CDPATH or cdpath from a shell prompt, you'll usually set it in a shell startup file (explained in the section "Startup Files, Login and Interactive Shells" in Chapter 5). That makes it available to all shells, in all windows, each time you log in. Another way to get to an often-used directory is through a named directory, described in the section "The Directory Stack" in Chapter 8.

Summary

In this grab bag of a chapter, we've looked at a few more of the many features that make shells a great working environment for users and programmers:

- Environment variables are similar to shell variables, but they're copied from a parent process to its child. This lets environment variables spread data throughout all or part of a system. However, you can't change environment variables in processes that are already started (unless the process makes the change itself).

- You can send signals to a process—usually to terminate it, but also to start and stop it— with `kill`. Most shells will also simplify that job—and also allow handy manipulation of groups of processes—with their job control features. The `ps` command shows the status of processes.

- Background processing is related to job control, but it's available on all shells, even very old ones. It lets you start a process from the shell; then the shell outputs another prompt so you can keep working from the same terminal.

- Quoting controls the shell's interpretation of special characters such as spaces, newlines, asterisks, and more.

- The `CDPATH` shell variable is a list of directories where `cd` should look for subdirectories to change to. This lets you avoid typing complete pathnames to often-used directories.

PART 2

■ ■ ■

Using bash and zsh

In the second part of this book, we will not try to cover all the Unix shells, as we did in Part 1. Instead, we will look at two powerful shells, bash and zsh, in a bit more detail. They are both freely available on all the most common operating systems. We will show you how to configure both shells and make them do more for you, expanding on many of the points in Part 1 as well as introducing some new ways of controlling the shell from the command line. Later, in Part 3, we will start to string things together to make programs (which in shell language are called *scripts* and *functions*). For now, most of what we tell you will be in short chunks, making it easy for you to try things out.

CHAPTER 4

■ ■ ■

Entering and Editing the Command Line

In this chapter, we'll introduce you to a wide array of nuances concerning command-line manipulation. We'll start with some basic concepts, showing you how to choose a shell, and how to copy and paste commands. We'll then introduce line-editing basics using both vi and Emacs bindings, followed by a discussion of command history and navigation. We'll conclude this chapter with a series of discussions about advanced line manipulation and editing. By its conclusion, you'll be quite familiar with command-line navigation and best practices, knowledge that will undoubtedly save you considerable time and inconvenience as you interact with the shell. To begin, let's review the options and procedures involved when choosing a shell.

Terminals and Shells

If you're interacting with a shell, it can be running in one of two places:

- Occupying a full screen. If you used MS-DOS in the past, this will be what you remember. However, this way of using a computer is now rather old-fashioned.

- Sitting in a window in part of a screen, which may have lots of windows. This is much more common now. The window running the shell is a *terminal emulator*.

We'll now spend a little while explaining some of the features of a terminal emulator—how to start one, how to copy text from one to another, and so on.

Opening a Terminal and Choosing the Shell

Normally when you open a terminal emulator it starts your shell. By default, it uses the shell defined by you or your system administrator when your account was set up. (Cygwin is a little different. See the section "Getting Started with Cygwin" in Chapter 5.) This happens no matter which terminal emulator you use.

The other way of starting your shell is by going through a login procedure. That happens either from a login prompt at a console before the windowing system was started, or by logging in remotely to a system using one of the programs telnet, rlogin (you may be more familiar with the similar rsh or remsh), or ssh. We'll use the first approach. It's probably the more common, and it gives you more choices to make.

In the "old days," there was only one terminal emulator for the X Window System, xterm. It's still there, it still works, and it's still a good choice. In fact, at least one of the authors regularly uses xterm. Nowadays, there are plenty of other terminal emulators. The good news is that most others work pretty much like xterm as far as the user is concerned and, in fact, many of them are just enhancements to xterm.

To start a new xterm, execute the following:

```
% xterm &
```

Remember the & at the end. This lets your current terminal carry straight on, ignoring the new xterm. (This is further explained in the section "Starting and Stopping Processes: Signals, Job Control" in Chapter 3.) If the shell says it can't find xterm, try typing /usr/X11/bin/xterm or /usr/X11R6/bin/xterm or something similar; on a SunOS/Solaris system, there's probably an xterm in the directory /usr/openwin/bin. If it works, you'll get a new window looking more or less like the window you were in before.

You can run a different command (which will usually be a shell) using the -e option. For example, to start an xterm that is running bash, type the following:

```
% xterm -e bash &
```

Without the -e option, xterm consults the environment variable SHELL. This variable is typically set when you log in to the shell set up by the system administrator (which is specified in your system's password file). You can also set SHELL yourself. For example, if you want new xterms to start up a zsh that lives in /usr/local/bin/zsh, you can set

```
% export SHELL=/usr/local/bin/zsh
```

You need to include that in a startup file if you want it to be remembered. (See the section "Startup Files, Login and Interactive Shells" in Chapter 5 for more on this topic.) Otherwise it only works for the current shell and other programs you start from it. Unfortunately, these days it's not so easy to find out what startup files are run when you log in graphically to a computer that starts up a desktop for you. Finding what the desktop will start can be hard work; it's a lot more complicated than simply starting a shell. So the easiest way to be sure terminal emulators use the shell you want is to change your login shell. Usually this is done with the chsh command. You type the command name and follow the prompts to change your login shell. You will need to enter the full path to the shell, for example /usr/local/bin/zsh.

Here's how to start a new xterm so that it remembers the shell but doesn't affect any other xterms you start:

```
bash$ SHELL=/usr/local/bin/zsh xterm &
```

This sets the value of SHELL for this single xterm. Because it's immediately in front of that program, it's only set for that program. So if you echo $SHELL you'll find it hasn't changed locally, but the new xterm is using zsh instead of bash. (This is pointless if the value already was /usr/local/bin/zsh.)

Copy and Paste

Most terminal emulators have a copy-and-paste system based on xterm. They involve moving the mouse. The mouse position is completely separate from the cursor's current position. When you copy a chunk of text, it is done entirely with the mouse. Only when you paste it is the cursor position important—the text you paste begins at that point.

■Note Mouse-1, Mouse-2, and Mouse-2 typically refer to the left, middle, and right mouse buttons, respectively.

Let's highlight some of this feature's basic behavior:

- To select a region, hold and move the left mouse button. Or click the left mouse button once at the start of the region and click once with the right mouse button at the end.

- Rapidly clicking the left mouse button twice selects a word; clicking three times selects a line.

- To extend a region, click the right mouse button at the point to which you want the region to be extended. The shell remembers whether you originally selected characters, words, or lines and continues to use the appropriate type. In some terminal emulators, this doesn't work; instead it brings up a menu. You may still be able to extend a region by holding down Shift and clicking the left mouse button.

- There is no special cut or copy operation; the selected region is immediately ready to be pasted somewhere else, and there's no way of deleting it. To paste it, click the middle mouse button (or wheel if there is one). Clicking both of the outside mouse buttons at the same time has the same effect on many systems.

Not all terminal emulators' cut and paste works in quite the same way. If the instructions we've just given don't seem to work, read the documentation for your terminal emulator.

Choosing a Terminal Emulator

Do you use either KDE or Gnome (two of the most popular desktops for Unix and GNU/Linux systems)? If you do, opening a terminal window will probably retrieve either Konsole or gnome-terminal, respectively. These behave pretty much like xterm with a menu bar. Note that there's nothing to stop you from using gnome-terminal with Gnome or Konsole with KDE, except that they probably aren't in the menus. You can start the one you want in the same fashion as opening an xterm window, described earlier.

■Tip Old xterms don't handle colors. Newer versions, and most alternatives, do. You will find colors are very useful with zsh's completion listings to make different types of files stand out. The GNU ls command also supports colored file lists (try ls --color=auto).

We've summarized several key points concerning terminal emulators we've used in the past in the hopes that it will clear up some of the confusion as you begin your own experimentation. Keep in mind that the terminal emulator you choose is largely a matter of preference.

- Plain old xterm doesn't have menu buttons visible, but actually there are three menus that appear if you hold down the Ctrl key and then one of the mouse buttons. Two are quite useful. Holding Ctrl and clicking the middle mouse button gives you some options to change the look of the terminal, such as adding a scrollbar or turning on reverse video. Holding Ctrl and clicking the right mouse button lets you change the font to make it more (or less) readable. These also have command-line options, given in the xterm manual page.

  Saving options for future xterm sessions is trickier than setting shell options, though. It's done by the "X resources" mechanism, which is a bit out of the scope of this book. As an example, you can put the following lines in the file ~/.Xdefaults. (Some systems use ~/.Xresources instead, and some systems allow either file.)

  ```
  ! Change the font
  xterm*VT100*font: 10x20
  ! Turn on reverse video
  xterm*VT100*reverseVideo: true
  ```

  On most systems, those lines may automatically set the font and reverse video option for xterm when your desktop starts up. You also may need to load the values in the file by hand, which is done by the following command:

  ```
  % xrdb -merge ~/.Xdefaults
  ```

  (You will certainly need to do this to install the settings without logging in again.) Many traditional X Window programs like xterm will look for settings in this format in a file in your home directory. The name of the file is based on the program, for example xterm. (You can configure which directories are searched for such files by using the environment variable XUSERFILESEARCHPATH. Type man X and search for this variable for more information.) This is on the computer where the program is running, not necessarily the computer where the display is. The command xrdb is known as the "X server resource database utility." The -merge option tells xrdb not to remove existing resources. To find other things you can set in ~/.Xdefaults in the same way, see the list of "RESOURCES" in the xterm manual page.

- In the case of KDE's Konsole, settings are done much more simply via obvious menus. Konsole has the additional feature that you can have multiple sessions (in other words, different shells, or even other programs) handled by the same Konsole. You create a new one from the New menu at the bottom, and can then switch between them by clicking on the appropriate name, or by using Shift-Left Arrow and Shift-Right Arrow. I tend to get confused and prefer to start separate windows. Needless to say, there are many other features. I have not yet successfully persuaded Konsole to accept a Meta key; see the sidebar "The Meta Key" (later in this chapter) for what that means.

- Gnome's `gnome-terminal` behavior is fairly similar to KDE's Konsole. Its version of the multiple-session feature is called "tabs," because of the way you select them, as you do the tabs in newer versions of the Netscape and Mozilla web browsers; you create a new tab from the File menu. It also has "profiles," which means you can store different groups of settings, for example different combinations of foreground and background colors, and switch between them by selecting a completely new profile instead of changing the options separately. You may find that the Alt or Meta key on your keyboard sometimes gets hijacked by `gnome-terminal` when you expect it to perform some editing task; you can fix this by going to the Edit menu, selecting Keybindings, and checking the option "Disable all menu mnemonics" (this is for `gnome-terminal` 2.0.1; older versions may be different).

- The third of the three most common Unix desktops—there are plenty of others—is the Common Desktop Environment (CDE). It's found on many versions of Solaris, HP/UX, and AIX. If you ask for a terminal here, you're likely to get `dtterm`.

- There's a lightweight `xterm` look-alike called `rxvt`. Its main claim to fame is it has fewer features than `xterm`. This may seem more impressive if you know some of the really strange things `xterm` can do. It's most likely to interest you if you have an old PC or workstation that strains to start terminal windows. Otherwise, it looks pretty similar.

- The `aterm` terminal emulator is based on `rxvt`; it was designed for AfterStep, the desktop used by one of the authors, but like all the others it can be used with any desktop or window manager. One nice feature of `aterm` is the option `-tr` that makes it appear transparent, which actually means it copies the piece of the root window (wallpaper in Windows-speak) that is behind it into its own background.

  Neither `rxvt` nor `aterm` provides menus. Note that both will pick up many of the values in `~/.Xdefaults` for `xterm`, but in that case you should remove the string `VT100*` from wherever it occurs in the example I showed earlier. It's there because `xterm` has another, now very seldom used terminal emulator built into it that handles graphics, and I didn't want to affect that, only the normal VT100 mode. VT100 is the name of an extremely widespread terminal of the 1980s made by DEC; `xterm` and its friends have borrowed many of the VT100's features.

- The Enlightened terminal, `Eterm`, is another enhanced `xterm`. It has a readable manual page and flashy backgrounds, and can be configured via configuration files, a fact that should make it appealing to those who are real shell programmers at heart.

- Old SunOS/Solaris systems came with OpenWindows, which had `shelltool` and `commandtool` as the terminal emulators. If you are stuck with these you should go for `shelltool`, since `commandtool` swallows up the escape sequences that the editors in `bash` and `zsh` use for advanced editing. There's an option for disabling `commandtool`'s special features, which essentially turns it into a shelltool. OpenWindows also provides genuine `xterm`, though on some really old versions it's hidden in a demo directory. It's unlikely to support color in any version of OpenWindows.

There are various ways to connect to a Unix-style system from Windows. The most powerful is to get hold of one of the full X Window servers that essentially turn your PC into an X server. In addition to the commercial packages such as XWin-32 and eXceed, you can get an X Window server with Cygwin. We'll discuss Cygwin in the section "Getting Started with Cygwin" in Chapter 5.

If you don't want all of that complexity, there is a useful program called PuTTY that connects via the telnet or ssh protocol, among others. The administrator of the machine you are logging into will be able to tell you which one you should use. When PuTTY is connected, it behaves exactly like a color xterm, and even indicates to the Unix system that it is an xterm by setting the environment variable TERM to xterm. The emulation is very good, and we recommend this over other solutions.

The Command Line

Entering a key on the command line can have one of two effects:

1. Something appears on the screen. This is normal text.

2. The key has some special editing effect. Sometimes you can see what it is straight away, because some text was deleted or the cursor moved.

In the next few sections we'll introduce you to that second behavior. We'll also introduce the notion of command history and show you ways of referring to lines you've already typed, maybe at a previous session. There will be more on command history—including how to make sure it is saved and restored—in Chapter 6. (Some of the basics were already covered in the section "History" in Chapter 1.)

Line Editing Basics

Even if you're new to shells, you might well have found some of the simpler features of line editing already:

- We saw in the section "Editing Data, Continuing Command Lines" in Chapter 2 how you can break long lines. You can insert a backslash and a newline, and the shell will allow you to continue typing at the start of the next line. We also saw that Bourne-type shells (which include both bash and zsh) know that if there is something you need to finish typing, zsh will prompt you with a message saying what that is (in Chapter 2, you can see it produced the message pipe pipe pipe> to show that three pipelines are in progress). In that second case, you don't need a backslash.

- You can delete the previous character you typed with the Backspace or Erase key. (It's not always that simple, unfortunately; see the section "The Backspace and Erase Confusion" in this chapter.)

- You can move the cursor around the command line using the Left and Right Arrow keys. (This works on most terminals, but on sufficiently weird ones the cursor keys may result in strange effects; see the section "Finding the Key Sequences for Function Keys" in this chapter for what to do if you have problems.)

- The Up Arrow and Down Arrow keys allow you to go back and forth in the list of commands you've already entered.

These basic operations are similar in bash and zsh. In fact, some particularly simple operations can be carried out by the terminal itself, as we explain in the sidebar "The Terminal Driver," later in this chapter. However, the more complicated the operation, the more different the shells look.

Emacs and vi Modes

Both bash and zsh offer two editing modes based around the Emacs and vi editors. The emacs mode presents the more obvious operation for people who have no particular preference, whereas vi behavior can seem a bit strange at first. In vi mode, the keyboard can be in two different states, where the same keys are used either for entering text or for performing editing operations. There is no visual indication of whether you are in the insert or editing state. (These are usually known as "insert mode" and "command mode" by vi users.) Because Emacs is a little easier to pick up, we will spend most of this section talking about this editing mode. If you know Emacs's reputation for complexity, don't worry: the shell's editor is much simpler, and most editing is done just with a few keystrokes.

Setting the editing style is done differently in bash and zsh. In fact, virtually all the shell commands used to control editing are completely different in the two shells. In bash, to enter emacs or vi mode you can set options as follows:

```
bash$ set -o emacs
bash$ set -o vi
```

In zsh, almost all the commands that change the behavior of keys use the bindkey command. As we'll see in the section "Configuration and Key Binding: readline and zle" in this chapter, this command is normally used for associating a keystroke with an editor command. However, it's also used for putting the line editor into emacs or vi mode. The following shows the command to enter emacs mode, then the command to enter vi mode:

```
zsh% bindkey -e
zsh% bindkey -v
```

(From version 4.2, zsh understands set -o vi and set -o emacs. We suggest you learn about bindkey, however, since it is so useful in other ways.)

If you usually use vi —or your system administrator thinks you do—one or both of the environment variables EDITOR and VISUAL may be set to vi. Many commands use this variable to determine your preference when they need to start up an external editor. zsh will also examine these variables when it starts. If either contains vi (including names like elvis, which is an editor like vi), it will set the editing mode to vi. So if you are sure you want to use emacs mode, it is a good idea to include an explicit line bindkey -e in ~/.zshrc.

If you use other editors, a lot of things probably won't be set up quite how you want them. We'll talk about how to configure the shells later in the section "Configuration and Key Binding: readline and zle."

Conventions for Key Names

The shells inherit some conventions from Emacs. They are also used in vi mode, so you should know them. Here, we'll explain how the syntax used in describing keys is related to the keys you type.

The Ctrl Key

Where we write \C-x, you should hold down the Ctrl key and then press x. Do it in that order, or you will get an x on the screen. There are many other possibilities instead of x, although typically you will use a lowercase letter. When you use a zsh bindkey or bash bind command, that's the form you need to use. Elsewhere, when we're talking about what you type, we'll just say Ctrl-x. Don't type the hyphen; it just shows which keys are held down at once.

The Meta and Esc Keys

In \M-x the Meta key is used instead of the Ctrl key. We talk about the Meta key in the sidebar "The Meta Key." However, you can get the same behavior as \M-x by typing the Esc key, nearly always at the extreme top left of the keyboard, then pressing x (don't hold Esc down). (The Meta and Ctrl keys, and any others used similarly, are usually known as *modifiers*. The Shift key is a modifier, too, but you don't need a special symbol since Shifted characters are different from the un-Shifted ones.)

In bash, preceding a key with Esc and holding down Meta while you press a key do exactly the same thing. The shell uses \M-x for both purposes. You can combine the effects of modifiers, for example \M-\C-x. Using the Esc key, you get this by pressing Esc, then Ctrl-x. (You don't need Ctrl with the Esc key.)

In zsh, Meta and Esc aren't always tied together and it's often easier to use the Esc key alone. The Esc key is represented within zsh by \e, so we'll use that when we're referring to shell code. Note that zsh rather unhelpfully shows Esc in lists of keys as ^[. This means the same but isn't as obvious.

Key Sequences

Some more complicated operations use a *key sequence*, a set of keys pressed one after the other. We show these with a space in between when there is a special key like one of the two above. For example \M-xfoo means press Meta x or Esc x, then type the ordinary characters foo.

THE META KEY

Few keyboards now have a key marked Meta. It is intended to be a modifier, just like Shift or Ctrl. On some PC keyboards the Alt key functions identically to the Meta key. You can combine modifiers; for example, \M-\C-x is given by holding down both the Meta and Ctrl keys, followed by the x key.

bash and zsh have different approaches to key bindings with the \M- prefix. In bash, they are tied to the corresponding key bindings with Esc automatically. In zsh, however, the keys are actually different. There is no automatic link in zsh between what \M-x does and what Esc x does. You can force zsh to use equivalent bindings for both sets, so that, for example, pressing Meta x has the same effect as pressing Esc x. The following command has this effect on all the bindings that use the Esc key in emacs mode:

```
zsh% bindkey -me
```

For vi mode the equivalent command is the following:

```
zsh% bindkey -mv
```

The extra -m has the effect of copying bindings for Esc x to those for Meta x. Nothing happens if the key has already been bound. This means that you need to remember to add separate commands to bind \e and \M-, if you use both.

Actually, Esc is often a good deal more useful than any Meta key. This is not just because that may be hard to set up, but more importantly because of how Meta works. It makes the terminal produce the same character but with the eighth bit set. This is not what you want if those characters are actually part of the character set you are using. In particular, it is no use at all if you are using the increasingly popular UTF-8 representation of characters, since the eighth bit has a special effect. So from now on we'll assume you're using the Esc key. However, we'll still refer to bindings in the form \M-x for bash, since that's how the bash documentation describes them. When we're not showing the code you use for key binding we'll say Esc x.

Tour of emacs Mode

If you use Emacs, XEmacs, or some other editor with similar functions such as MicroEmacs, many of the keys you use will be very familiar. If you don't, many of them might seem a little obscure at first, but there is a theme you can get used to. Most of the keys in this section are common to zsh and bash. We won't give examples, but you can try everything very easily; just type a few characters, without pressing Return, and then the special keys we tell you.

A few terminal emulators won't let you use the Esc key in the shell editor because it's taken for the terminal's own purposes. If you find this annoying, you either have to look at the terminal's documentation to see how to change this, or use another type of terminal.

Basic Moving and Deleting

Simple move and delete keys for single characters are nearly all either special keys or keys with Ctrl held down. The most obvious are in Table 4-1.

Table 4-1. *Simple Move and Delete Keys*

Key	Purpose
Backspace or Erase	Delete previous character
Ctrl-d	Delete character under cursor
Left Arrow or Ctrl-b	Move to previous character
Right Arrow or Ctrl-f	Move to next character
Ctrl-t	Transpose the character with the previous one (see the sidebar "Transposing Characters")
Ctrl-v	Insert the next character literally (explained later)

Note that the Delete key on a full-size PC keyboard is not the same as Erase or Backspace. You might expect it to delete the next character, as it often does under Windows. See the section "Configuration and Key Binding: readline and zle" in this chapter for help with this. (We're describing the most common case on a PC-style keyboard. Some older Unix keyboards may behave differently.)

It's sometimes useful to remember Ctrl-b and Ctrl-f if you find yourself using an odd keyboard where the shell is confused by the cursor keys.

The key Ctrl-d is often rather overworked:

- If there are characters after the cursor, Ctrl-d deletes the first one, as we showed in Table 4-1.

- In zsh, if you press Ctrl-d at the end of a line, it will probably show you a list of files. This is part of the shell's completion facility, described in Chapter 10. (This is a feature taken from the C shell.)

- In both bash and zsh, typing Ctrl-d on an empty line may even cause the shell to exit! That's because traditionally Unix treats Ctrl-d as "end-of-file" (EOF), a message from the user that they have finished sending input. Both shells have mechanisms for suppressing this. Here, bash's is more powerful. If you set the following, then bash will only exit if you press Ctrl-d ten times in a row:

```
bash$ IGNOREEOF=10
```

In zsh, the equivalent effect is achieved by setting an option, as follows:

```
zsh% setopt ignore_eof
```

However, in zsh the value 10 is fixed. This needs to be a finite number so that the shell can exit if the terminal has completely gone away. In that case the shell will read EOF characters continuously, and it would be unfortunate if it kept on doing so forever.

TRANSPOSING CHARACTERS

It may not be obvious quite what Ctrl-t, bound to the command transpose-chars, is doing. If you type it at the end of the line, it transposes the previous two characters, so repeating it swaps them back and forth. However, if you do it early in the line, it swaps the character under the cursor with the one before it, then moves the cursor on. The point of this rather complicated behavior is that pressing Ctrl-t repeatedly has the effect of marching a character further and further up the line. This is useful if more than one character were out of place. Of course, in that case deleting it and inserting it somewhere else may be easier.

You use Ctrl-v to put onto the command line a character that would otherwise be an editing key. One common use for this is to insert a Tab character. On its own, Tab performs completion. If you want to insert a Tab character, you need to press Ctrl-v-Tab.

Moving Further: Words and Lines

Some more powerful motion keys that move the cursor further than a single character are shown in Table 4-2. The backward and forward keys are easy enough to remember, and Ctrl-e for end is also easy enough, but you'll just have to remember Ctrl-a, the start of the alphabet, meaning the start of the line.

Table 4-2. *More Powerful Motion Keys*

Key	Purpose
Esc-b	Move backward one word
Esc-f	Move forward one word
Ctrl-a	Move to the beginning of the line
Ctrl-e	Move to the end of the line

The keys Esc-b and Esc-f move the cursor backward and forward over *words*. There's some disagreement over what a "word" means. In particular, it doesn't mean a complete command-line argument. In bash, it's simple: only letters and digits (alphanumerics) are part of a word.

In zsh alphanumerics are part of a word, too. However, there is an additional set of characters that will be considered part of a word. These are given by the shell variable WORDCHARS, whose initial contents are the following:

```
*?_-.[]~=/&;!#$%^(){}<>
```

You can set WORDCHARS to any set of characters. In particular, if you always want the bash behavior, you can make it empty:

```
zsh% WORDCHARS=
```

There's no equivalent to WORDCHARS in bash; the notion of a word is fixed. In both shells, there are only two kinds of characters: word characters and the rest. That may sound rather stupid, but remembering it helps you to understand what Esc-b and Esc-f actually do:

- Esc-b skips backward over any number of nonword characters, and then any number of word characters before that.

- Esc-f skips forward over any number of word characters, and then over any number of nonword characters after that.

In each case "any number" may be zero if there aren't any characters of that type at that point. The reason for this behavior is so that repeated Esc-b or Esc-f keystrokes take you over as many words as necessary, without you having to move the cursor in between.

The Command History and Searching

The shells remember previous lines you've entered; you can scroll back or search in that list. How many previous lines it remembers, and whether they are saved between sessions, is discussed in Chapter 6. For now, just think of the history as a series of command lines in the order you typed them.

Two very useful keys you may already have found are given in Table 4-3.

Table 4-3. *The Simplest Keys for the Command History*

Key	Purpose
Up Arrow	Go back in the command history
Down Arrow	Go forward in the command history

The last few commands are waiting for you to scroll back through them with the Up Arrow key. Usually the command you're just typing is at the end of the command history, so Down Arrow is only useful after one or more presses of Up Arrow. However, both shells allow you to edit any line in the history, and all those edits are remembered until you press Return to execute the command. At that point the history returns to the actual history of executed commands.

Here's an example. Type the following:

```
% echo this is the first line
this is the first line
% echo and this is the second
and this is the second
```

Then press Up Arrow twice to see the first line again. Change it in some way, but don't press Return. Then press Down Arrow, and change that line. You'll find you can move up and down between the two changed lines. Let's suppose you change the first line and press Return:

```
% echo but this is no longer the first line
but this is no longer the first line
```

Now you'll find the history contains the three last lines I've shown you; the edits to the second line you made were lost, and the edited version of the first was added as a new line at the end.

Searching the Command History

One very common task involves searching backwards through the command history to find something you entered before. There are various shortcuts that let you avoid having to scroll up through the history until you see it.

First, there are easy ways to get to the very top and very bottom of the history, although they don't perform searches. These are shown in Table 4-4.

Table 4-4. *Moving to the Start and End of the History*

Key	Purpose
Esc<	Go to the start of the command history
Esc>	Go to the end of the command history

Next, there are real searches. You have various ways to tell the shell what to search for. The easiest to use are the "incremental" searches, shown in Table 4-5. These search for the nearest string in the history that matches everything you've typed. The whole line is searched.

Table 4-5. *Incremental Searches*

Key	Purpose
Ctrl-r	Search backward incrementally
Ctrl-s	Search forward incrementally (also Ctrl-x-s in zsh)

Normally, Ctrl-r is more useful since you start at the end of the history and want to search back through it.

THE NO_FLOW_CONTROL OPTION

We've offered Ctrl-x-s as an alternative version of Ctrl-s, which is made available in zsh. (So is Ctrl-x-r, but you don't need that so often.) The problem is that very often the terminal is set up so that Ctrl-s and Ctrl-q perform flow control: another feature provided by the terminal itself, not the shell. We talk about other such features in the sidebar "The Terminal Driver." When you press Ctrl-s, any output to the terminal, including anything you type, is stopped. When you press Ctrl-q, it starts up again and you can see what you typed. In zsh you can fix this by setting the shell option no_flow_control. This doesn't stop the use of Ctrl-s and Ctrl-q in external programs, to let you see something which is scrolling past quickly, so it's fairly safe. (You may find if your terminal output is very fast they don't have an instant effect even then.) There's another, clumsier way of getting control using the stty command, which we'll explain near the end of this chapter.

Let's consider an example depicting the effects of Ctrl-r. Suppose you've typed the three lines I used as an example earlier:

```
% echo this is the first line
this is the first line
% echo and this is the second
and this is the second
% echo but this is no longer the first line
but this is no longer the first line
```

Now you type the following:

```
<ctrl-r>this is
```

Both shells prompt you during searches, showing you what you've typed to find the line you have reached. In bash, you'll see the message (reverse-i-search) appear. If you've entered an incorrect character for the search, you can press Backspace to delete it.

You'll return to where that string occurs on the third line. Now continue so that the complete line looks like the following:

```
<ctrl-r>this is the
```

Now you'll find you're looking at the line before. Finally, continue with the following text:

```
<ctrl-r>this is the first
```

You've returned to the first line. If you type something other than a key that inserts itself or deletes backwards, the search ends and you stay on the line found. Be careful with Return, however, since it immediately executes the line. If you want a chance to edit the line first, press another key such as Left Arrow.

This is probably as good a point as any to tell you about Ctrl-g, which you can press to abort the current operation. If you were in the middle of a search, you will return to the line at the end of the history, quite likely still blank. If you were just doing normal editing, Ctrl-g would abort the current line and display an empty one.

You can resume searching from where you left off by pressing Ctrl-r twice, once to start the search and again to restore the string you were searching for before. If you abort with Ctrl-g, however, the shell doesn't remember what you are searching for on that occasion and keeps whatever was there before. In other words, it's best to get into the habit of exiting with a different key.

There are two other types of searching. First, there are nonincremental versions of the search commands, available in bash as Esc-p and Esc-n. (The p and n stand for previous and next. In fact, Ctrl-p and Ctrl-n are actually alternatives to the Up and Down Arrow keys, respectively.) If you press Esc-p, you will see a colon as a prompt. Type a string after it, then press Return. The shell searches back for that string.

Often there is no advantage to using the nonincremental instead of the incremental versions. Still, if you feel called to use the zsh versions, they can be borrowed from vi mode. The names of the commands are vi-history-search-backward and vi-history-search-forward; we'll see shortly how you can use this information to associate the command with a key.

A more useful alternative is to have the shell search backward for a line that begins with the same command word, or with the same string up to the cursor position, as the current line. Both forms are present in zsh, but only the second form in bash.

The first (zsh only) form is shown in Table 4-6.

Table 4-6. *Searching Lines for the First Word in* zsh

Key	Purpose
Esc-p	Go to the previous line starting with the same word
Esc-n	Go to the next line starting with the same word

This means that wherever the cursor is on the command line Esc-p will take you back to the previous line beginning with the same command word, ignoring any other text. There's an exception: If you are still typing the command word, Esc-p will take you back to any line beginning with the same characters. Note that in bash the same keys do nonincremental searching as described above.

The other form is called history-beginning-search-backward (or -forward) in zsh and history-search-backward (or -forward) in bash. In this case, the shell looks back for a line in which every character between the start of the line and the cursor position is the same, so the more you have already typed, the more precise the match. It's essentially a form of nonincremental search where you type the characters before you search for them. For those of us with limited foreknowledge of our own actions, this can be quite a blessing.

(As an extra piece of confusion, the bash names history-search-backward and -forward are what zsh calls the commands behind Esc-p and Esc-n.)

Deleting and Moving Chunks of Text

For deleting chunks of text larger than a single character, the shells use the word *killing*. This is more slang from Emacs. It means the shell has deleted the text, but has remembered it on something called the *kill ring*. Some keys for killing text are given in Table 4-7. (Editor commands exist for simply deleting text, but since remembering the deleted text is usually harmless, they're not often used.)

Table 4-7. *Keys for Killing Text*

Key	Purpose
Esc-Backspace or Esc-Erase	Kill the previous word
Esc-d	Kill the next word
Ctrl-k	Kill to the end of line
Ctrl-u	Kill to the beginning of the line (bash); kill the entire line (zsh)

Retrieving the text you killed is called *yanking*. You can do this after moving the cursor or even on a new command line. There are two basic commands, shown in Table 4-8.

Table 4-8. *Keys for Yanking Text*

Key	Purpose
Ctrl-y	Yank the last killed text
Esc-y	Remove the last yanked text and replace it with the previously killed text

Most of the time, you just want to pull back the last text using Ctrl-y. You can get back earlier text, though, as we explain in the sidebar "The Kill Ring."

THE KILL RING

The shell doesn't just remember the last text you killed; it remembers several of the previous strings as well. The place it stores them is called the "kill ring." After pressing Ctrl-y to bring back the last piece of text killed, you can press Esc-y one or more times. (Pressing Ctrl-y again has a different effect; it yanks back the same piece of text repeatedly.) Each time you press Esc-y, the text that was just yanked is taken away again, and the previous piece of killed text is inserted instead.

It's a "ring" because only a finite number of chunks of text are remembered. When you have reached the last one stored, pressing Esc-y cycles back to the start, which is the text that was last killed. The ring contains up to ten elements. Just keep typing Esc-y until you see what you want or you get back to the original.

The Region

The *region* is yet another concept originating from Emacs. You set a *mark* in one place and move the cursor somewhere else. The "region" is the set of characters between the cursor and the mark. To be more precise, the cursor defines a *point* just to its left. When you make a mark it remembers that point, and when you move the cursor, the region is between the new "point" and the "mark." Some keys for using the region are given in Table 4-9.

Table 4-9. *Keys for Using the Region*

Key	Purpose
Ctrl-Space	Set the mark at the current point. This is written \C-@ in both shells; if Ctrl-Space doesn't work, try Ctrl-2.
Ctrl-x Ctrl-x	In zsh, swap the mark and the point. Present in bash without a key defined.
Ctrl-w	In bash, kill the region for later yanking. Present in zsh without a key defined.
Esc-w	In zsh, copy the region for yanking, but don't actually delete the text. Present in bash without a key defined.

As you see, we're getting to the point where the behavior of bash and zsh start to diverge. So as to keep the information together, here are the commands to set up Ctrl-x Ctrl-x and Esc-w in bash:

```
bind '"\C-x\C-x": exchange-point-and-mark'
bind '"\M-w": copy-region-as-kill'
```

Here is how to set up Ctrl-w in zsh:

```
bindkey '\C-w' kill-region
```

Those are the first key bindings we've shown; there will be more. You need to type them at a prompt, or save them in your .bashrc for later use. For now, note that the long names with hyphens are *editor commands*, also known as *editor functions*, or known in zsh as *widgets*. There are many of these, and you can bind them to any set of keys the shell understands.

If you try Ctrl-w in zsh without this, you'll find it kills the previous word. For example, suppose you type the words echo this is a line. With the original binding of Ctrl-w, typing those keys would delete the word line. If you have rebound it to kill-region, however, it will probably delete the whole line. That's because by default the region starts at the beginning of the line.

A Few Miscellaneous Commands

Before we move on to more complicated matters, Table 4-10 gives a few commonly used commands available in both shells.

Table 4-10. *Miscellaneous Common Keys*

Key	Purpose
Esc-c	Capitalize the next word and move over it
Esc-u	Uppercase the next word and move over it
Esc-l	Lowercase the next word and move over it
Ctrl-l	Clear the screen and redraw it. In zsh this may preserve the list of possible completions.
Esc-. (period)	Insert the last argument of the previous command line. Repeat to retrieve arguments from earlier lines.

Beyond Keystrokes: Commands and Bindings

Every editor command has a name, whether or not there is a key associated with it. The names mostly have the form several-hyphenated-words. A few editor commands are just a single word with no hyphens. The name is useful when you come to attach a command to a key or set of keys. For a complete set of commands, consult the documentation for the shell.

Names and Extended Commands

In zsh you can execute a command simply by knowing its name. To do this, you press Esc x, then the name of the editing command. Completion is available—type as much as you like, then press Tab. If you haven't typed much, you may be overwhelmed with information when you press Tab and the shell will ask if you really want to see it all before showing it.

Configuration and Key Binding: readline and zle

It's time to talk a bit more about how to set up the line editor the way you want it. First, we'll offer some background about the way the shells' line editors work, which is a bit different between bash and zsh.

bash uses the GNU project's standard library, *readline*, which does exactly what its name suggests. Because it's a library, it is used as part of a lot of different programs. For example, if you use the GNU debugger, gdb, you will find it uses readline to handle command-line editing. readline has its own configuration file, from which you can configure a lot of different tools; the sidebar "readline Configuration" has more information on this. You can still configure readline settings from your ~/.bashrc. To keep things simple, we'll show you how to do everything from there.

READLINE CONFIGURATION

Configuration for the readline library goes in a file named ~/.inputrc. (A system-wide /etc/inputrc file also exists but you shouldn't need to be concerned with that.) Although the syntax of this file is different from the normal shell syntax, it is fairly simple. Each line takes the same form as an argument to the bind built in. So to bind a key you might, for example, use the following command:

```
"\C-u": kill-whole-line
```

A number of *readline variables* allow other aspects of readline's behavior to be configured. One example is mark-modified-lines. It makes readline warn you about lines in the history that have been modified since readline added them to the history. When you recall a modified line, an initial star ("*") will be displayed at the beginning of the line. To enable this feature, you can put the following line in your .inputrc file:

```
set mark-modified-lines on
```

You can see what the current settings for all the variables are by typing bind -v. You can also set readline variables direct from bash using the bind command:

```
bind 'set mark-modified-lines on'
```

We mention specific readline variables later in the book, particularly in Chapter 10. Be aware that many are new. They may not work if you don't have the latest version of bash.

---

zsh has its own "zsh line editor," or "zle" for short. Because it's always used within zsh, the only way to set up zle is with standard shell commands.

The most common action to configure the line editor is to attach a series of keystrokes to an editing command. This is described as "binding" the command. Both shells use this language, and it shows up in the name of the respective commands. The bash command is bind and the zsh command is bindkey; they have rather different syntaxes.

You can find out what commands are bound to keys already. Here's how to do that in bash:

```
bash$ bind -p
```

This produces a complete list of editor commands. Each line is in the form you can use for a later bind command to re-create the binding (although if you're just looking at the defaults, that's not so useful). Unbound commands are shown with a comment character (#) in front. Here is an example of a bound and an unbound command:

```
# vi-yank-to (not bound)
"\C-y": yank
```

The equivalent in zsh is the following:

```
zsh% bindkey -L
```

which is better than bind in one way—it generates a complete command that you simply paste into your ~/.zshrc—and worse in another—it doesn't show you unbound commands. Omitting -L produces a simpler list with the keys and bindings but not in a form you can cut and paste.

There is another command to generate a complete list of all editor commands that can be bound:

```
zsh% zle -la
```

It's just a simple list of names, one per line. The zle command is used for creating extensions to the editor; we'll meet it in Chapter 14. The -l option means list, and -la means list all. Without the a you just see user-defined commands. These are features you've added to the editor yourself; we'll see how to do this in Chapter 14.

In zsh, you are allowed to query individual bindings to see if they already do something. Here is an example:

```
zsh% bindkey '\C-y'
"^Y" yank
```

That's the binding for Ctrl-y. Don't put spaces in the argument to bindkey, since they count as characters. In bash you can use the grep command:

```
bash$ bind -p | grep '"\\C-y"'
"\C-y": yank
```

This produces comfortingly similar results. Note that extra backslash inside the quotes, since backslash is special to grep as well as to the shell.

Finally, you can always find out from zsh what a command is bound to on the fly by using the editor command where-is. This isn't itself bound by default, so you need to use Esc x where-is unless you have bound it. It then takes an editor command, just like Esc x itself, and will tell you what keys you need to type to get that command.

For example, I entered the where-is command, typed backward-char, and pressed Return, and zsh reported the following:

```
backward-char is on "^B" "^[OD" "^[[D"
```

The last two sets of characters are the two most common strings of characters sent by the Left Arrow key.

Note there is nothing stopping you from binding a command to a key sequence that is already in use; the shell will silently replace the old one.

Once you've picked the editor command and a key sequence, the commands to bind the two together are the following. For bash, let's bind history-search-backward to Esc-p:

```
bash$ bind '"\M-p": history-search-backward'
```

You do need to remember all those quotes. The rationale is that the single quotes surround a string that bash will pass to the readline library. That in turn expects the name of complex characters such as Esc-p to be quoted, hence the double quotes around the \M-p inside the single quotes.

For zsh, let's bind history-beginning-search-backward to Esc-p:

```
zsh% bindkey '\ep' history-beginning-search-backward
```

Here, the key and the command are separate arguments to bindkey. You still need the single quotes around \ep, though. Suppose you issue the following command:

```
zsh% bindkey \ep history-beginning-search-backward   # Wrong!
```

Because of the shell's quoting roles, the command-line processor uses the backslash to quote the e that follows, and bindkey sees only ep, which just means exactly those two characters—not what you meant. You need to be on your guard in this way any time you see "funny" characters being passed to a command. For bind and bindkey, "funny" characters are so common it's just as well to get into the habit of quoting any reference to keys.

The sequence \e for Esc is one of a set of special keys. Other useful sequences include \t for Tab (strictly a horizontal tab, since there's a rarely used vertical tab), \b for Backspace, and \\ for backslash itself. All need the extra quotes when used with bindkey.

■**Warning** You can't just use the characters Escape in a bind or bindkey command because they just mean exactly those characters: E, s, c, a, p, e. This is one of many places where the backslash is necessary to tell the shell that some special behavior is required.

You can bind any 8-bit character in this fashion if you know the character's number in the character set. The easiest way (in both bash and zsh) is to convert the number to two hexadecimal digits *HH*. The character is then represented as \x*HH*. For example, character \x7f (127 decimal) is the Delete key. This might look a little more memorable than the standard but obscure string \C-?.

Finding the Key Sequences for Function Keys

Your keyboard probably has a row of function keys at the top. If you are using a full-size PC keyboard there is also a group of six named keys above the cursor keys. The keys have names like F1 and Home. It's very useful to bind these to commands.

Unfortunately, you can't simply use the name on the key. Shells only have the ability to read strings of characters. The terminal emulator generates a string of characters (often called an *escape sequence*) for each special key. These bear no relation to the names on the keys. Luckily, it's easy to bind the escape sequences. The hard part is finding out what sequence of characters the function keys send. The simplest, most general way we know of is to type read, then press Return, then the key combination you want to investigate. You'll see the characters the terminal sends. Let's try the function key F1. On my system this has the following effect:

```
zsh% read
^[[11~
```

(If you press Return again, you've actually assigned that value to the variable REPLY. We'll meet read in the section "Reading Input" in Chapter 13.) The characters appear literally because neither shell currently uses the line editor for the read command.

The key sequence ^[[11~ shown above is the one most commonly produced by F1. It's not guaranteed to be the same in other terminal programs, if you use more than one, but there's a pretty good chance. However, it doesn't matter as long as you know what the string is.

The ^[represents an escape character. The shells know that as \e, which is a little more obvious. So here's how to make F1 perform the command forward-word in bash:

```
bash$ bind '"\e[11~": forward-word'
```

Here's the corresponding example in zsh:

```
zsh% bindkey '\e[11~' forward-word
```

Very often the key sequences sent by Shift-F1, Ctrl-F1, and Alt-F1 are different from the key sequence sent by F1 alone. I get \e[23~, \e[11^, and \e\e[11~, respectively; you can of course investigate and bind these in just the same way. You may also be able to combine the modifiers, for example Shift-Alt-F1, to get yet another key sequence.

Warning There is a good chance that one or more of the modified forms of the function keys are intercepted by the window manager for some special task. Usually it is possible to get round this by changing key bindings for the window manager, either in a startup file or interactively using the Gnome or KDE control panel or equivalent. Also, the terminal emulator itself may intercept keys; for example, often Shift-PageUp scrolls the terminal window.

The set of six keys—Insert, Delete, Home, End, PageUp, and PageDown—found on modern PC keyboards can be treated in the same way we just described for function keys. You may decide to make these do what their names suggest. (In modern graphical editors, they already will:

Home often moves the cursor to the beginning of the line. However, the shell doesn't have a binding until you give it one.)

For example, both shells have an overwrite-mode editor command that toggles the line editor between two states. In the normal state (insert), typing a character in the middle of a command line inserts the new character and pushes the existing text to the right. In the other state (overwrite), typing a character replaces the character that was there before and leaves the rest of the line where it was. It's quite useful to bind this to the Insert key. (If you like overwrite mode, in zsh you can use the command setopt overstrike to make it the default mode when the line editor starts.)

Also, you might want to bind Home and End to beginning-of-history and end-of-history, which take you to the first and last line in the history.

On my terminal, I can bind the keys as follows:

```
zsh% bindkey '\e[2~' overwrite-mode         # Insert
zsh% bindkey '\e[1~' beginning-of-history   # Home
zsh% bindkey '\e[4~' end-of-history         # End
```

As we just noted, \e[2~ has the same effect as ^[[2~, and so on. The \e for escape is just a little more readable. Note that the cursor keys, too, send escape sequences of this sort. The shells try to find out what the cursor keys send and bind them for you, but in any case you can use the read command to find out. What's more, the cursor keys with modifiers, such as Ctrl-Up Arrow, may send different key sequences from the Up and Down Arrow keys alone. So you can bind those, too.

If you use several terminal emulators where the function keys send different escapes, you can use the shell's case statement to choose the right binding for the terminal. We show an example of that in the section "Case Statement" in Chapter 13.

Binding Strings

Both shells have ways of binding a string instead of a command to a key sequence. This means that when you type the key sequence the string appears on the command line. What's more, the string can itself consist of special keys that have a meaning to the editor.

In bash, this is done by putting a quoted string in the place of the command when you use bind. Here's an example:

```
bash$ bind '"\C-xb": "bind"'
```

The quoted "bind" is treated as a string, so when you press Ctrl-x-b the shell acts as if you'd typed b, i, n, d. From now on, you can use this instead of typing the full name of the bind command.

The same thing in zsh is done by the -s (for string) option to bindkey:

```
zsh% bindkey -s '\C-xb' bindkey
```

If you include special characters, they have exactly the same form as they do in the part of the command where the keystrokes are defined:

```
zsh% bindkey -s '\C-xt' 'March 2004\eb'
```

This inserts the string March 2004 onto the command line, then emits the sequence \eb. If you are using normal Emacs bindings the cursor goes back a word to the 2 so you can insert the day of the month before the year. You can make these strings as complex as you like.

This only works with the normal key bindings for emacs mode. If you rebind \eb, that other command is called when the \eb is processed instead of the backward-word command. In Chapter 14 we show you how to write your own editor commands to avoid this problem.

In addition to \C-x, zsh accepts ^x (a caret followed by a letter) as a string for the key Ctrl-x, and similarly for other control keys. We recommended that you put it in quotes, since in some circumstances ^ can have a special meaning to zsh:

```
zsh% bindkey -s '^xf' foo
```

Executing Commands

Now you know about binding a named command to a keystroke, it's worth pointing out that the action of executing a command line uses an editor command. In both shells it's called accept-line and, as you will guess, it's bound to the Return key. There's usually no reason for changing this, except for special effects. In zsh, we'll see such effects in Chapter 14.

There are related and more sophisticated commands, however. Both shells have a handy function bound to Ctrl-o in emacs mode, though it has different names— accept-line-and-down-history in zsh and operate-and-get-next in bash.

An illustration shows this best. Let's suppose you're using the vi editor to edit a program, then the make command to compile it. (The make command reads instructions from a file, usually named Makefile or makefile.) Often, you need to look at the output from the compiler, then edit the program again to fix a problem. Suppose you've already issued the following commands:

```
% vi myprogram.c
% make
... error message from make ...
```

(If you want to try that straight away, just put "echo" at the start of both lines. Then you can see what the shell would execute if you were really writing a program.)

Now press the Up Arrow key twice to get back to the first of the two lines, then press Ctrl-o. The line is executed again, but this time when you get back to the line editor it puts up the second line again. This makes it very easy to recycle a complete set of history lines.

Press Ctrl-o again, and you see the first line again. (It was saved to the history the first time you pressed Ctrl-o.) If you keep pressing Ctrl-o, you keep re-executing those two lines, as many times as you like.

When you've finished editing and want to run the program, just delete the line the shell shows you and start a new one. When you press Return at the end it will be added at the end of the history as normal.

Multiple Key Sequences

We've referred to several keystrokes that consist of several keypresses chained together, such as Ctrl-x t for Ctrl-x followed by t. You may wonder what the rules are for constructing them. The answer is that you can do pretty much what you like. It's a convention that Esc and Ctrl-x are *prefixes*, in other words keystrokes that don't do anything on their own but wait for you to type something else. However, any keystroke can be a prefix, and you are not limited to two characters in a row. Suppose, for example, you decide to keep all the bindings to do deletion in sequences beginning with Ctrl-x-d. Here are bash and zsh bindings to make Ctrl-x-dd remove the next word:

```
zsh% bindkey '\C-xdd' kill-word
bash$ bind '"\C-xdd": kill-word'
```

Conflicts between Prefixes and Editor Commands

You can actually make a prefix, such as the sequence Ctrl-x-d in the previous example, into a keybinding in its own right. In bash, the required command is as follows:

```
bash$ bind '"\C-xd": backward-kill-word'
```

This binding conflicts with the example using kill-word at the end of the previous section: After Ctrl-x-d, the shell doesn't know whether you're going to type a *d* next, to get kill-word. bash resolves this simply by waiting to see what you type next, so if you don't type anything, nothing happens; if you then type a *d*, you get kill-word, and if you type anything else, the shell executes backward-kill-word, followed by the editor commands corresponding to whatever else you typed.

zsh works like bash if you type something immediately after the prefix. However, it has a bit of extra magic to avoid the shell waiting forever to see what character comes after the Ctrl-x-d. The shell variable KEYTIMEOUT specifies a value in hundredths of a second for which the shell will wait for the next key when the keys typed so far form a prefix. If none turns up in that time, and the keystrokes so far are themselves bound to a command, then that command is executed. So let's consider the following:

```
zsh% bindkey '\C-xdd' kill-word
zsh% bindkey '\C-xd' backward-kill-word
```

When you've entered those commands, go up to the previous line, position the cursor at the start of forward-word, press Ctrl-x-d, and wait. You'll find that after a short time the previous word is deleted. That's because the default value of $KEYTIMEOUT is 40 in units of 100ths of a second. Why hundredths of a second? When KEYTIMEOUT was introduced, the shell didn't handle numbers with a decimal point. The unit had to be small enough to be useful, and a second was too large, so hundredths of a second was chosen.

Choosing a value for KEYTIMEOUT is a bit of an art: It needs to be small enough that you're not annoyed by the wait, but large enough so you have time to type a complete key sequence. There is an extra factor when you are using a shell over the network; the various keys can be sent out at any old time the network feels like, so $KEYTIMEOUT has to be large enough to cope with the sort of delays you get. There's no real way of predicting this; you just have increase the value of KEYTIMEOUT until everything seems to work. You set it by the following assignment:

```
zsh% KEYTIMEOUT=60
```

Of course, you can set it to whatever value you please. To make this setting permanent put it in a startup file. Remember, there are no spaces around the =.

Cursor Keys and vi Insert Mode

In case you think the key timeout feature that we introduced in the previous section is a bit pointless and you never want to use that feature, there is one case that is very common; indeed, if you use vi mode you come across it all the time. As we said, the keys can do two completely different sets of things in vi mode. To begin with, they simply enter text ("insert mode"), but you can switch to a mode in which (for example) the cursor keys Up, Down, Left, and Right are replaced by *k, j, h, l,* respectively ("command mode").

The usual way of switching to command mode is by pressing the Esc key. (vi users are trained to do this without thinking.) Unfortunately, on most modern terminals, the real cursor keys are turned into a key sequence, which starts with Esc. Most commonly, for example, The Up Arrow key sends \e[A or possibly \eOA. Therefore, when you press Esc to switch from insert mode to command mode, the shell will wait for $KEYTIMEOUT hundredths of a second. You can enter an editing command, though, and the shell will respond immediately.

Partly for this reason, zsh used not to make the cursor keys available in vi insert mode at all. However, the developers decided that beginning users were more likely to need the cursor keys than to be worried about the delay pressing Esc.

Keymaps

The vi insert mode and command mode are examples of *keymaps*. A keymap is a complete set of key bindings in use at the same time. Looked at this way, emacs mode is simply another keymap. These are the three you will meet most often, but in special operations, particularly in zsh's completion system, you will come across others. Keymaps are completely independent; when you bind a key in a certain keymap, nothing happens to any other keymap.

There are two things you most often want to do with a keymap: switch to it, or bind keys in it. You've already seen how to switch to vi or emacs keymaps, but let's summarize the easiest ways in each case. These are shown in Table 4-11. (In the case of vi, you always start in the insert keymap.)

Table 4-11. *Command to Change between emacs and vi Keymaps*

	bash	zsh
emacs	set -o emacs	bindkey -e
vi	set -o vi	bindkey -v

To bind keys in a particular keymap, the clearest way is to use the keymap's name. In the case of emacs mode the name is just emacs. The two vi keymaps are called in bash, vi-insert and vi-command and in zsh, viins and vicmd. To bind a key in a keymap, use bind -m or bindkey -M followed by the keymap name, then the remaining arguments as normal.

For example, the commands below bind B to backward-word in the vi command keymap in each shell:

```
bash$ bind -m vi-command '"B": backward-word'
zsh% bindkey -M vicmd B backward-word
```

(Actually, *B* is already bound to something similar (a vi version of backward-word) in both shells already.) All keymaps in both shells are case-sensitive, so this is not the same as binding *b*. If you don't give a keymap, bind and bindkey always operate on the current one, which is usually emacs or vi-insert/viins. The shells never start up with vi-command/vicmd active. So to bind a key in the vi command keymap you need to specify the name of the keymap. There's a shortcut in zsh: bindkey -a works like bindkey -M vicmd. The vicmd keymap is also known as the *alternate* keymap. We've avoided this since it's less clear.

You can use the -m and -M options with other bind and bindkey commands. For example, you can list the vi command keymap with the following commands for bash and zsh, respectively:

```
bash$ bind -m vi-command -p
zsh% bindkey -M vicmd
```

You never lose information simply by switching keymaps. As you switch between bindkey -e and bindkey -v in zsh the bindings in each keymap are preserved, including any you added yourself. The commands simply switch between the sets—they don't perform any rebinding:

```
zsh% bindkey -e
zsh% bindkey '\C-xf' forward-word
zsh% bindkey -v
zsh% bindkey '\C-xf'
"^Xf" undefined-key
zsh% bindkey -e
zsh% bindkey '\C-xf'
"^Xf" forward-word
```

We bound the key sequence '\C-xf' in the emacs keymap. We switched to vi mode, and found it wasn't bound. Then we switched back to emacs mode, and found it was still there.

Creating Your Own Keymaps

In bash you are restricted to the existing keymaps. In zsh, however, you can create and use your own keymaps. You might use this for a special editing task where you intend to return to one of the standard keymaps such as emacs when you have finished. It's not completely obvious, but all you need to know can be summarized in a few sets of commands.

- You can create a new keymap by copying an existing one. This is usually more useful than creating one from scratch. The following example copies the keymap emacs into the new keymap my-keymap:

  ```
  zsh% bindkey -N my-keymap emacs
  ```

  Now you can treat my-keymap as your own private copy of the emacs map. Note it's a copy of the keymap in its current state, not with the default bindings.

- To create a new keymap from scratch, omit the final argument from the previous example:

zsh% `bindkey -N my-keymap`

You can use pretty much any name you are likely to want. However, it overwrites any existing keymap of that name, which may be a bad thing, so be careful. The keymap you create has no bindings at all, not even standard alphanumerics; you have to fill it from scratch. You can bind ranges of characters. For example, the following command forces all the lowercase characters to insert themselves as they do in an ordinary keymap such as Emacs:

zsh% `bindkey -R -M my-keymap 'a-z' self-insert`

The order, with -R first, is because -M is a bit tricky. In versions of zsh up to 4.0, the my-keymap is not as you'd expect an argument to the -M option, but the first non-option argument to the command. In other words, -M doesn't take an argument; it swallows up the first argument left after the option processing. This changed in version 4.1, but the order we've shown here will always work.

- Now you need to switch to your new keymap. This is done in a slightly obscure way by giving the new keymap the name main as an alias:

zsh% `bindkey -A my-keymap main`

(Remember the order; main comes last.) This is basically what the `bindkey -v` and `bindkey -e` commands do for you. When I talked about "the current keymap" earlier, I could have talked about main instead. If you want to switch back to the original keymap, you issue another `bindkey` command. For example, you can return to the emacs keymap with the command `bindkey -e`.

Don't alias the vicmd keymap to main, as I just did. If you do that, both of the keymaps in use for vi-style editing are bound to vicmd. In that case you can't ever enter text! Instead, use viins. The effect of `bindkey -v` is to alias viins to main.

- To get rid of a keymap, you can delete it as follows:

zsh% `bindkey -D my-keymap`

but since the current keymap is lost when you leave the shell, you're unlikely to care enough to want to delete one.

■**Tip** There's one keymap in zsh you probably don't want to come across. If you delete the main keymap, zsh uses a keymap called .safe. This keymap is specially restrictive; most of the commands we showed earlier for use with keymaps won't work. The only bindings in the .safe keymap are the characters that usually insert themselves and the Return and Linefeed keys (Ctrl-j if there isn't one so marked). That's enough to let you type a command and execute it to put things back to normal. You should immediately type something like `bindkey -e` to return to a better keymap.

Options for Editing

The shells have various other options for choosing the behavior of the editor. There's not much in common between many of these, so this section will be something of a ragbag of possibilities.

Customization of readline from within bash needs the shell to pass a complete string down to the readline library (the readline variables we mentioned in the sidebar "readline Configuration"). Let's show an example to make this clear. You may have noticed that the shell makes a beeping noise when you make a mistake or try something the shell won't permit. Many users find this effect infuriating and want to turn it off. In bash, this is done by setting the readline variable bell-style to none. Options to readline are set using bind; in this case the command is as follows:

```
bash$ bind 'set bell-style none'
```

In contrast, options in zle are just ordinary shell options. We'll introduce options properly in the section "Setting zsh Options with setopt" in Chapter 5. You set options using the setopt command. To turn off the beeping noise you need to set the option nobeep as follows:

```
zsh% setopt nobeep
```

An alternative to turning off the audible warning is to tell the shell or the terminal emulator to use a visible bell. This makes the screen flash at you. It's a little less annoying than the noise. In bash, you can set the readline variable bell-style:

```
bash$ bind 'set bell-style visible'
```

There's no such variable in zsh, but you can make a terminal emulator derived from xterm use a visible indication instead of beeping. This is done with a line in the .Xdefaults file mentioned in the section "Choosing a Terminal Emulator" earlier in this chapter:

```
*visualBell:    true
```

Strictly, this turns on the visual bell for any application that has it, but that might be what you want. Put xterm in front of the * to restrict it to xterm-like programs, including rxvt and aterm. Alternatively, simply start xterm using

```
xterm -vb
```

Add & to the end of the line if you try this from the shell command line; otherwise your current shell will wait for the xterm to exit.

zsh has a separate option, hist_beep, to control whether it beeps (or otherwise signals) when you try to go past the end of the history.

Finally, there are two zsh options to start up the line editor in a different way. The option overstrike starts the editor so that each printable character overwrites the character that was there before. (Normally, it pushes the rest of the line to the right.) You can swap in and out of this mode by using the overwrite-mode editor command (the one we bound to Insert in the section "Finding the Key Sequences for Function Keys" earlier in this chapter).

How the shell retrieves its history is controlled by many options. These will be explained in Chapter 6, since there are several other ways of getting at the same information and all are affected. Also, options for completion will be discussed in Chapter 10 although they have a bearing on the line editor.

Multiline Editing and the zsh Editor Stack

In Chapter 2 we saw various examples of entering commands on multiple lines. The shell presents a special prompt to show that it is expecting more input. When the input is complete, the shell executes the command. In bash, if you scroll back in the command history to reedit such a line, you will find that the whole command has been put on a single line. When you execute the line, it still has the same effect as the original because bash inserts special characters to make sure the line you are editing has the same effect as the original one. There's no way of editing it in the original form, though.

However, zsh has powerful handling for editing commands that span more than one line. We already explained how the shell would prompt you if a command wasn't finished. In that case, you are effectively editing a new line. For example,

```
zsh% cp file1 file2 file3 file4 \
> /disk1/storage/pws/projects/utopia/data/run32
```

If you use the cursor keys on the second line, the editor behaves pretty much as if you were editing a separate command, with the previous line already in the history.

However, it's possible to edit two lines at once. In fact, that's how continuation lines are put into the history. If you press Return and then Up Arrow, you will find both lines appear, without the continuation prompt >. Go up once more, and you go from the bar to the foo line. (We're assuming you use the normal binding for the cursor keys, up-line-or-history. There's another possible binding, up-history, which always takes you back in the history, not through the set of lines displayed for editing.) Go up again, and you are taken to the previous command.

There are two ways of editing multiline commands without the continuation prompt:

1. Use Esc-Return where you would normally press Return on its own. It puts the cursor onto a new line with no prompt. You can add as many lines as you want this way, and they will go into the command history together. Be careful to note that unless you use a \ at the end of the previous line, the next line will be treated as a new command, even though the previous line hasn't yet been executed. For example,

   ```
   zsh% mv file1 old_file1<escape><return>
   mv file2 old_file2<return>
   ```

   There are two complete commands there. We executed both at once so that the two files were renamed at (almost) the same time. We could have put a semicolon between them (remember the semicolon connects a list of different commands on the same line), but this is a little easier to read.

2. The other way uses `push-line-or-edit`. We'll bind that to a key sequence, to avoid typing a very long command after Esc x:

```
zsh% bindkey '\eq' push-line-or-edit
```

Now go back and again type the following:

```
zsh% cp file1 file2 file3 file4 \
> /disk1/storage/pws/projects/utopia/data/run32
```

But this time press Esc q at the end instead of Return. You'll see the continuation prompt magically disappear and you will be editing the complete command.

The Buffer Stack

The `push-line-or-edit` command has two functions. In the previous section we showed the `-or-edit` part. Let's move on to the other one.

Suppose you have forgotten to do something you need to, and are halfway through typing the next command when you remember. For example, you are in the middle of a long `ls` command and forget what options you need:

```
ls -L here/there/everywhere
```

Or should that be `-l` instead of `-L`? Press Esc-q; this time the line completely disappears. Now execute the following command:

```
man ls
```

This confirms that you meant `-l` to list in the long format, not `-L`, which follows links. The point of the Esc-q becomes apparent when you quit reading the manual: The complete previous command magically reappears.

You are using `zsh`'s *buffer stack*. Every time you press Esc-q on a complete buffer, the buffer is pushed onto the end of the stack. Every time you press Return, the last piece of text pushed onto the end of the stack is popped off and loaded back into the line editor. (You can also summon the last value explicitly with Esc-g.) By the way, Esc-q has this `push-line` effect by default in emacs mode; however, it doesn't have the extra `-or-edit` function unless you bind that as described earlier.

A Quick Way of Getting Help on a Command

The use of `push-line` we explained is so common that there is a special command that does it all for you. You can look up the documentation for a command you are entering by simply pressing Esc-h, without clearing the command line. This pushes the line for you, then runs the command `run-help`, which by default is an alias for `man`. Afterwards, the command line appears from the buffer stack.

You can customize `run-help` to be even more helpful, as we describe in the sidebar "Customizing zsh's run-help Command."

CUSTOMIZING ZSH'S RUN-HELP COMMAND

You aren't stuck with the default behavior of `run-help`. The shell comes with a function you can use instead, which should be installed into your function search path. In that case you can use it by entering the following:

```
zsh% unalias run-help
zsh% autoload -U run-help
```

Now when you press Esc-h, you get more help. If you do this a lot with the commands that are part of the shell, you can get the `run-help` function to show you the documentation for the individual command, but you need to do some setting up first. Somewhere create a directory called `Help`, change into it, and run the Perl script `helpfiles` provided with the `zsh` distribution in the `Util` subdirectory. The script isn't installed with the shell, but you only need to run it once. There's some documentation at the top of the script (run `more` on the file to see it). To make it work, you need to pass the `zshbuiltins` manual into it. Here's an example that creates the help files in the directory `~/zsh-help`:

```
zsh% mkdir ~/zsh-help
zsh% cd ~/zsh-help
zsh% man zshbuiltins | col -bx | perl ~/src/zsh-4.2.0/Util/helpfiles
```

If you see error messages, make sure your `zsh` manual pages are installed properly. Sometimes you can replace `col -bx` with `colcrt` and get slightly better effects, depending on the system. Both commands strip the terminal control characters from the output of man to turn it into plain text. That's the bit you only need to do once. Then you need to tell the `run-help` function where to find those files; this goes in `~/.zshrc` (without the prompt, of course):

```
zsh% HELPDIR=~/zsh-help
```

along with the two-line setup for `run-help` shown previously. Now pressing Esc-h on a line starting with a shell built-in will show you the manual entry for the built-in.

Keyboard Macros

Many editors provide keyboard macros, where you record a set of keystrokes by typing them in, and they can be played back when you need them. bash offers this, but zsh doesn't; the nearest zsh has is the bindkey -s feature we described earlier. That will do everything a recorded macro can; you just have to remember the names for the keys instead of typing them. This is harder at first, but easier to edit if you make a mistake.

The readline keyboard macros available in bash work (surprise, surprise) much like those in Emacs. You start recording by pressing Ctrl-x (and after typing all the necessary keys end it by pressing Ctrl-x). You then play back the macro by pressing Ctrl-x-e. As a trivial example, find a command line and type the following keys:

```
<ctrl-x><(><escape><b><escape><b><ctrl-x><)>
```

Now every time you press Ctrl-x-e the cursor moves left two words.

Other Tips on Terminals

We'll finish the chapter with a few remarks regarding interaction between editing command lines and the terminal. Unix terminal drivers—the part of the system that handles input and output for a terminal or terminal emulator—are slightly weird things. We say a little about why in the sidebar "The Terminal Driver." We've already met some occasions where certain special keys are swallowed up. They were Ctrl-d at the start of the line, which meant end-of-file (EOF), Ctrl-s to stop output, and Ctrl-q to start it again.

There's a program called stty that controls these settings, as well as a lot of others, many of which, we can assure you, you will not want to know about. However, it is useful to know the basics of stty if you are interested in customizing your own environment. The following lists the settings:

```
% stty -a
speed 38400 baud; rows 24; columns 80; line = 4;
intr = ^C; quit = ^\; erase = ^?; kill = ^U; eof = ^D; eol = <undef>;
eol2 = <undef>; start = ^Q; stop = ^S; susp = ^Z; rprnt = ^R; werase = ^W;
lnext = ^V; flush = ^O; min = 1; time = 0;
-parenb -parodd cs8 -hupcl -cstopb cread -clocal -crtscts
-ignbrk brkint ignpar -parmrk -inpck -istrip -inlcr -igncr icrnl ixon -ixoff
-iuclc -ixany imaxbel
opost -olcuc -ocrnl onlcr -onocr -onlret -ofill -ofdel nl0 cr0 tab0 bs0 vt0 ff0
isig icanon iexten echo echoe echok -echonl -noflsh -xcase -tostop -echoprt
echoctl echoke
```

This is from a Linux system using the GNU tools. Your output could be completely different, since other versions of Unix can have very different setups. However, stty is a program provided by the system, so it doesn't matter if you're using bash or zsh or any other shell.

The settings we're most interested in here are the three lines starting with intr = ^C. This means that the interrupt character is set to Ctrl-c. We met this feature and used it to interrupt a running program in the section "Starting and Stopping Processes: Signals, Job Control" in Chapter 3, but we didn't say you could change the key. You can do so like this:

```
% stty intr '^t'
```

(The quotes are recommended, since zsh's extended_glob option makes ^ special. By the way, control characters are case insensitive; ^t and ^T are the same.) This makes Ctrl-t the interrupt character. You can try it by typing the following command:

```
% sleep 10
<ctrl-t>
```

The sleep 10 makes nothing happen for 10 seconds, unless you interrupt it early with Ctrl-t. Note you can only have one key doing each special task, so we freed Ctrl-c at the same time as we started using Ctrl-t. This is different from the way shells work: the shells remember what single function is assigned to each key, for every key, while the terminal driver remembers for each special function what key is assigned to it.

It's also possible to turn off special keys—that's what the `<undef>` after `eol` meant. The traditional way of doing this is with the sequence `^-`:

```
% stty intr '^-'
```

Yet some versions of `stty` understand the more logical `undef`, too. Obviously, doing this means you can't send an interrupt from the keyboard until you redefine `intr`.

As you'll see in the sidebar "The Terminal Driver," not all keys known to `stty` are special inside `zsh`. On my system, at least, you only need to worry about `intr`, `eof`, `start`, and `stop` inside the shell. This is probably just as well since some of the others are rather obscure. Hence you can bind an editing command, for example, to Ctrl-z, despite the fact that it is assigned to `susp` by `stty`. (This is one of the more useful special keys used for job control; see the section "Starting and Stopping Processes: Signals, Job Control" in Chapter 3.)

THE TERMINAL DRIVER

Why are there all these strange effects associated with terminals, and why do we need the `stty` command to control them?

In the early days of Unix, shells had no editing capabilities of their own, not even the basic ability to delete the previous character. However, a program existed that read the characters typed by the user, and sent them to the shell: the *terminal driver*. It gradually developed a few simple editing features of its own, until it grew to include all the features you can see from the output of `stty -a` in the main text.

By default, the terminal driver accepts input a line at a time; this is sometimes known as "canonical" input mode. For commands that don't know about terminals, such as simple shells without their own editors, the terminal driver usually runs in a mode sometimes known as "cooked." (This is Unix humor; when not in "cooked" mode, the terminal is in "raw" mode.) Here, all the special keys are used. This allows you some very primitive editing on a line of input. For these simple editing features, the command `stty` shown in the main text acts as a sort of `bind` or `bindkey` command.

For example, let's try `cat`, which simply copies input to output. Type the following:

```
% cat
this is a line<ctrl-u>
```

The line disappears; that's because of the `kill` stty setting. If it didn't work, try setting the following first:

```
% stty kill '^u'
```

This is handled entirely by the terminal driver; neither the program (`cat`) nor the shell knows anything about it. In "cooked" mode, the terminal passes a complete line to the program when you press Return. So `cat` never saw what you typed before the Ctrl-u.

Since not all programs want the terminal driver to handle their input, the terminal has other modes. The shell itself uses "cbreak" mode (not quite equivalent to "raw" mode), which means many of the characters which are special in "cooked" mode are passed straight through to the shell. Hence when you press Backspace in either `bash` or `zsh`, it's the shell, not the terminal driver, that deals with it.

Working Around Programs with Bad Terminal Handling

Every now and then, you may find a program that reacts badly to the terminal settings and needs you to issue an stty to fix things up. This is usually a bug in the program, but zsh provides you with a way to work around the problem: assigning a command line for stty to the environment variable STTY. In practice you would use it in a way similar to the following example:

```
zsh% STTY="intr '^-'" sleep 10
```

That turns off the keyboard interrupt character for the life of that one command. It's not worth remembering the details of this feature; just come back here to look if you suspect terminal problems with a program.

zsh has another way of dealing with programs that mess about with stty settings: the built-in command ttyctl. You use this to "freeze" or "unfreeze" the terminal settings:

```
zsh% ttyctl -f
```

After this command, the terminal is frozen, which means if an external program changes one of the settings that would show up in stty -a, the shell will immediately put it back so that any future programs won't see that change. The following command has the opposite effect:

```
zsh% ttyctl -u
```

Now the terminal is unfrozen, and changes from an external program will show up later. Note that "an external program" includes stty itself. Suppose you enter the following commands:

```
zsh% ttyctl -f
zsh% stty intr '^-'
```

Because the terminal settings are in their frozen state, the stty setting won't take effect. You need to unfreeze the terminal, then run stty, then freeze it again.

Variables That Affect the Terminal

Both shells handle resizes to the terminal window—if you extend your terminal emulator to the right, the shell will know it has extra columns on the display, and so on. For future reference, you might like to know that the width and height of the terminal are stored in the variables COLUMNS and LINES, respectively.

There's one other variable in zsh that's worth mentioning here. BAUD is set to the speed of the connection between your terminal and the actual computer in bits per second. Usually you don't need to set this, but there are two reasons why you might. First, if you have a really slow line, set BAUD to the proper speed; for example if your connection speed is 2400 bits per second, the setting

```
zsh% BAUD=2400
```

tells zsh that your terminal will be slow to respond. Conversely, if the terminal appears to be doing something very slowly, you may need to increase the value. The reason is that when BAUD has a low value, the shell tries to change the screen a little bit at a time, to keep it consistent.

When the value is larger, it will try to be more sophisticated, making more changes at once. Setting BAUD to 38400 as follows is usually good enough:

```
zsh% BAUD=38400
```

The number doesn't have to be set to the actual speed of the link between your keyboard and the shell.

When Unix Gets a Bit Confused about Keys

There are two occasions when the keys you type may look to the system like some other keys. If you're lucky enough never to have these problems, you can safely skip this section: the first of the two issues below isn't noticed by a lot of users, and the second depends on your system's settings as well as the way the system handles your keyboard.

The Carriage Return and Linefeed Confusion

There is rather a lot of confusion on Unix systems about the difference between Return (more properly, carriage return, sent by Ctrl-m or the Return key) and Linefeed (Ctrl-j, or possibly a special key on some Unix keyboards).

When the terminal is in "cooked" mode—in other words the shell or some intelligent interface is not running—the terminal actually turns an input Return into Linefeed. This is controlled by the setting stty icrnl, which is usually on (you can turn it off with stty -icrnl). The shell protects you from this, but it does make it difficult for *typeahead input* to distinguish the two characters. ("Typeahead input" is where you don't wait for a program to finish before typing a new command line.) If you have Return and Linefeed bound to different commands you might notice this. Luckily, they normally do the same thing.

The Backspace and Erase Confusion

You might have thought deleting the previous character using the Erase key was simple enough. However, this is not always the case. On traditional Unix keyboards, the key at the top right of the largest group of keys, marked as "delete" or "erase" or something similar, generates a certain character usually written as Ctrl-? (^? to stty) and described as "delete". However, on a PC keyboard the key at that position, often marked with a backward arrow or something similar, sends a backspace, which is the same as Ctrl-h. To make it worse, some systems where the key would normally send Ctrl-h intercept it and send Ctrl-? instead.

Luckily, both zsh and bash will delete the previous character when they receive either of those keys, so much of the time you don't need to know. The time you do need to know which is which is when you are entering input that is not under the control of the shell. As explained earlier, stty only handles one special character for any function, in this case the function named erase, so the other won't work in cooked mode—for example, when you are entering text to cat. The usual indication something has gone wrong is a series of ^H or ^? characters appearing when you try to delete. It is a strange fact about the universe that the erase value is almost always set incorrectly by default. However, putting it right is simple. One of the following will set the value you want:

```
% stty erase '^?'
```

or

```
% stty erase '^h'
```

As the final part of this confusion, the key on a PC keyboard marked Delete or Del is different again. On a full-sized keyboard you usually find it in the group of six over the cursor keys. It probably does nothing by default and you have to bind it yourself using the tricks in the section "Finding the Key Sequences for Function Keys" in this chapter.

Summary

In this chapter, you learned about

- Starting a terminal window with a shell running in it

- How continuation of command lines works

- The line editor, and its various modes of operation using different keystrokes

- Moving around the command line

- Finding previous command lines

- Deleting and restoring chunks of text

- Defining your own keystrokes for the editor's commands and setting options for the editor

- Using function keys, and other special keys, to execute commands

- How the various sets of keystrokes are arranged in keymaps

- The tricks you can use for handling multiline input

- Defining keyboard macros

- Avoiding problems caused by the part of the operating system that controls the terminal, known as the "terminal driver"

In the next chapter we will take a look at what happens when the shell starts. Knowing that will help you to customize the shell. We will also talk about shell options, the simplest way of changing the behavior. Also, we introduce Cygwin, a way of letting the shell work under Windows with a good deal of the Unix look and feel.

CHAPTER 5

■■■

Starting the Shell

In this chapter, we're going to talk about what happens when you start the shell. This may not sound very complicated, but you'll need to know how the shell starts in order to understand how you can change the shell's settings. We'll explain how you can configure the shell so that it starts up with the settings you want to use. We'll also show you how to influence the shell when you invoke it by name.

A large portion of this chapter deals with the shell's startup files, which is where you put commands to configure the shell. We'll show some of the things you put in there, and we'll introduce shell options, which are an important way of controlling the shell. Setting options is an essential use of startup files.

We'll assume a fairly plain Unix-style environment. If you are running Windows and using the Cygwin environment to provide Unix emulation, much of what we say will still apply. However, there might be a few surprises.

Starting Shells

If you're in front of the computer now, start a shell so you can use it to enter commands for listing files, changing the directory, editing files, and so on. Remember that the shell itself is just another command. You probably won't start it directly yourself, unless you're using it to run a script, but you can:

```
% zsh
hostname%
```

It may look like nothing happened, although possibly the prompt changed. (Prompts are highly configurable, as you'll see in Chapter 7, and your system may use a different prompt. The default in zsh is for the name of your computer to appear where we showed hostname.) Actually, however, you're in another shell, started from the first one. The first shell is waiting for that command to finish; it doesn't care that the other command is another instance of zsh. This is a bit more obvious if you start a different shell:

```
% bash
bash$
```

You'll almost certainly see a different prompt in the bash you've just started than in the zsh you were in before. To get back to the original shell, type

```
bash$ exit
zsh%
```

(If you followed both examples in sequence, you'll need to type exit once more to get back to your original shell.)

Startup Files, Login and Interactive Shells

If you know what a shell does when it starts, you can customize its behavior. Throughout the rest of the book, you will see short chunks of code that change the shell's behavior, and you'll think "That looks useful." If you put the code in a *startup file*, it will be executed every time the shell starts to run. These startup files are sets of commands entered into a file just as you would type them at a prompt—but with no prompts.

Startup files differ from normal text (typed at a prompt) in two ways:

1. The history mechanism with ! is not active, so you don't need to quote exclamation marks (as introduced in the section "History" in Chapter 1). That makes sense, since there's no reason why you'd ever use the history mechanism in a startup file.

2. A startup file is likely to have a lot of *comments*. The shell ignores these pieces of text; they're useful to you when you look at the file later. A comment, which starts with the character #, can occur at the start of a line or anywhere in a line preceded by a space.

Although you can type comments interactively (at a prompt) in bash—and in zsh, too, if you have the interactive_comments option turned on—there's usually not much point. However, adding comments to a file is entirely useful, in case you look at it months or years later and wonder why you did something.

Here's a simple chunk of text that sets an *environment* variable (see the section "Passing Info to Processes with Environment Variables" in Chapter 3) with a comment explaining what it's doing:

```
# Tell programs to pass output through 'less' instead of 'more'
export PAGER=less
```

We met pagers in the section "Using Programs Together: Pipes" in Chapter 2. Now you know how to tell the system which one to use. First, though, you need to know one thing more: which startup file to put that shell code into.

Which files a shell executes at startup depends on two things: whether it's a *login* shell, or an *interactive* shell. We'll introduce these two types of shells, and then show how the type influences the files that the shell executes.

Login Shells

First, is the shell a *login* shell? In the old days, that was simple to decide: when you logged into a computer on a dumb terminal, that was your login shell; if you decided to start another shell inside your login, it wasn't. Nowadays, your shell probably runs in a window. This means that it probably isn't a login shell—but it's not quite that simple. It's possible that the shell was started as a login shell anyway.

The shell actually has two ways of deciding whether to act as a login shell. One is if it's given an option, -1, or --login in bash. (This is a standard option, like the ones we saw back in the section "Command Lines" in Chapter 1; we'll discuss the shell's own options shortly. You can pass -1 or --login to a shell just as you'd give it any other option, should you want to.) The shell can also be started under a name that begins with a dash (-). This probably seems a bit odd; it's an old Unix convention. The Unix login program, which runs when you log into a Unix system, uses this convention to tell the shell that it should act like a login shell.

If you're wondering why this is useful, it's because of a slightly odd feature of Unix. At the lowest level, you start a Unix program by telling the system two things: the pathname to the file that contains the executable program and the name to give the program. This allows a single Unix program to have multiple names, and to change its behavior by checking its name. Although this may seem bizarre in today's world of gigabyte memories, it was very useful when systems had extremely limited memory and storage space.

Apart from determining which startup files the shell runs, as we mentioned, you can type logout to leave a login shell, whereas you need to use exit or bye to leave any other shell.

■Tip If you aren't worried whether you're in a login shell—and most of the time you won't be—use exit to leave the shell. That always works, and in a login shell the effect is the same as logout. So save yourself from worrying.

Interactive Shells

The shell also decides whether it's *interactive*. An interactive shell is for use at a *terminal*, that window where you're entering your commands. We discussed terminals in the section "Terminals and Shells" in Chapter 4.

In other words, the shell prompts you, you enter instructions into the shell, and the shell executes them and comes back with another prompt when it's finished. The existence of the prompt is a good sign that the shell is interactive. If it isn't, the shell is probably getting its input from somewhere else, like a file. It happens that you *can* start a noninteractive shell that reads input from the terminal but doesn't show you a prompt. However, there's no good reason for you to do that.

The -i option says a shell is interactive. You would only use this if the input or output of the shell you are starting is redirected so that the shell doesn't know it should use the terminal. Redirection is one of those ways of telling the shell to use different input or output; we met it in the section "Writing Output to Files: Redirection" in Chapter 2.

bash Startup Files

bash behaves differently according to which type of shell is running, for the types we just discussed. If it is a login shell, it executes the code in the following files, in this order:

1. /etc/profile, as set up by the system administrator (or maybe the person who wrote the shell package for your system).

2. ~/.bash_profile, and if that doesn't exist, bash executes the file ~/.bash_login instead, as long as that does exist. If *that* doesn't exist either, it looks for ~/.profile and executes that if it exists. All these are files beginning with a dot in your home directory. Note that ls won't show them; you need to use ls -a.

Be particularly careful with ~/.profile, if you use that file to contain bash code. It is executed by the Bourne shell and all its direct descendants such as ksh. Putting bash-specific code in ~/.profile can cause problems. On the other hand, if you use lots of different shells, it can be quite useful to put common code in this single file. For example, setting up your PATH or CDPATH variables here and marking them for export is a task common to all those shells.

If the shell isn't a login shell but is interactive, bash executes the single file ~/.bashrc. (It doesn't execute /etc/profile, .bash_profile, .bash_login, or .profile.)

Note that no startup file is read by both login and non-login shells. If you want all interactive bash shells to run ~/.bashrc, you can put an appropriate command in ~/.bash_profile. The following makes bash execute the commands in your .bashrc:

```
. ~/.bashrc
```

The first "." is actually a command that tells the shell to read the named file (here, the file is ~/.bashrc) like a startup file. That is, all code will be run inside the current shell instead of in a separate process. This is necessary for the shell to set options and variables. If the shell started a new process to read the file (as it would for a shell script), the current shell wouldn't get your new settings. We'll call this command "the dot command" to avoid too many cryptic punctuation marks in the text.

You can use the dot command to split your startup files, if you like to keep things neat. For example, some people like to keep all their aliases in a separate file. (We introduced aliases back in the section "Command Lines" in Chapter 1.) Let's call the file ~/.bash_aliases and insert the following lines into it:

```
alias l=less
alias ll='ls -l'
alias la='ls -a'
```

To execute those lines from ~/.bash_aliases, you can put the following in both .bashrc and .bash_profile:

```
. ~/.bash_aliases
```

That command executes all the lines in the file passed as the argument as if you'd typed them as input to the shell. We sometimes describe this as *sourcing* a file. That's really slang from the C shell, which has the command source instead of the dot command. The phrase "sourcing a file" is a bit more understandable than "dotting a file."

None of the startup files have to exist; the shell will silently carry on if one isn't there. Generally speaking, in fact, you will want to pick one file for all your commands. For most uses, it's probably best to stick with ~/.bashrc and run it from other files with the dot command if you need to. If you use a GNU/Linux distribution, the shell package may well be configured this way, so you may only need to edit `~/.bashrc`.

If the shell is not interactive, bash does not automatically read any of the files we just discussed. Instead, it looks for an environment variable called BASH_ENV. If it's set, that variable should contain the full path to the startup file (you'll see an example in couple of paragraphs).

As we said, shell scripts are typically run by a noninteractive shell. Often it's best to write scripts so that they don't depend on the settings from a particular startup file. Then it's easy for other people to run the script and to move it to other machines.

If you need a startup file for noninteractive shells, the simplest way is to have bash read your `~/.bashrc`:

```
export BASH_ENV=~/.bashrc
```

One more file needs mentioning for completeness: `~/.bash_logout` is run at the end of a login shell. There is no specific file run at the end of shells that aren't login shells, but you can make the shell run `~/.bash_logout` or any other file by putting the following in `~/.bashrc`:

```
trap '. ~/.bash_logout' EXIT
```

A *trap* specifies code, within the quotes, for the shell to execute when something happens. Here we've told the shell to source `~/.bash_logout` when it exits.

This trap actually isn't well designed. It makes a login shell read `~/.bash_logout` *twice*. That's because, as we said earlier, a login shell always reads `~/.bash_logout` automatically. However, a trap is run by all shells—both login and non-login. So a login shell will read `~/.bash_logout` once from the trap and again automatically.

The way to prevent the trap from being executed twice is only to execute the trap command if the shell isn't a login shell. Here's an example showing how to do that. The test itself is the command `shopt -q login_shell`, which tests whether the option login_shell is set:

```
if shopt -q login_shell; then
  # Put the code to be executed only if the shell is a login shell here.
else
  # Put the code to be executed only if the shell is not a login shell here.
fi
```

In this case, you should put the trap we showed in the previous example in place of the line after the `else`.

zsh Startup Files

The concepts behind zsh startup files are similar to those for bash, but the actual files are different. The syntax of zsh is sufficiently unlike that of bash that having different startup files is probably a good thing.

When zsh starts, it can execute up to eight different files. That's a lot, and you'll never need all of them. Many of the files correspond to those in bash, and so have similar names. The extra files are mostly because zsh allows more *global* startup files (startup files executed for all users). Also, the .login and .profile variants have come from different predecessors of zsh, csh, and sh. You probably won't need both variants. Here is a complete list (in order) in which the files are considered by the shell to see if they should be executing:

/etc/zshenv–This is the only file that is always executed. This is a file for all users, written by the system administrator, as are all the files stored in the directory /etc.

~/.zshenv–This is a file in your own home directory, abbreviated ~. (Type echo ~ to see the full name of the directory.) This is executed as long as the option rcs is turned on, which is true by default. The only purpose of this option is to tell the shell to execute startup files apart from /etc/zshenv. We'll describe what shell options are for, and how to turn them on or off, in the section "Shell Options" later in this chapter. This option is here for exactly the purpose of deciding whether startup files are executed. This is where you put stuff of your own to run at the start of all shells, interactive or not.

/etc/zprofile–This is executed if the options rcs, globalrcs, and login are set. The option globalrcs is normally turned on, like rcs. Its only purpose is to tell the shell to execute the startup files beginning with /etc, apart from /etc/zshenv, which is always executed. Note that old versions of zsh don't have the option globalrcs. The option login is turned on automatically by the shell if it is a login shell, otherwise it isn't; again, the option has no other purpose.

~/.zprofile–This is executed if the options login and rcs are turned on; in other words, the same as for /etc/zprofile, except the globalrcs isn't used.

/et/zshrc–This is executed if the options interactive, rcs, and globalrcs are turned on.

~/.zshrc–This is executed if the options interactive and rcs are turned on. This is probably the most commonly used startup file, since it's the normal user startup file for interactive shells.

/etc/zlogin–This is executed if the options login, rcs, and globalrcs are turned on.

~/.zlogin–This is executed if the options login and rcs are turned on. /etc/zlogin and ~/.zlogin are only different from /etc/zprofile and ~/.zprofile because of the execution order. It's up to you to decide if you want the script that runs at login to run before or after ~/.zshrc.

The options login and interactive are the same as the -l and -i options you can pass to the shell, the ones we described earlier, which are usually turned on automatically. Since you don't usually set these options yourself, you can think of them simply as a way of telling whether the shell is a login shell or an interactive shell.

As we said, the options rcs and globalrcs are usually turned on by default. If you want, you can turn them off by passing the options -f and -o noglobalrcs, respectively, to the shell. Note also you can even turn them on inside startup files. For example, suppose you issue the following command in the file ~/.zshenv:

```
setopt noglobalrcs
```

The result is that the files /etc/zprofile, /etc/zshrc, and /etc/zlogin would be skipped. You'd only do that if you've found there's some stuff there you don't want executed (for example it's too slow or sets aliases you don't want to use).

There is no way to skip /etc/zshenv (other than some of the tricks we'll discuss in the section "Porting Scripts" in Chapter 13 to convince zsh it's a different shell). That means that it's usually a good idea to put only things you really need every time anyone starts zsh. That's particularly important if your system is used by people other than you. (If you need, you can put tests in /etc/zshenv, like the one we showed for an interactive shell in the section "bash Startup Files" earlier in this chapter.)

By and large, you will probably put most startup commands in ~/.zshrc, and possibly transfer them to ~/.zshenv if you find that you need the settings in noninteractive shells. One case for putting things in ~/.zshenv is that it is used by zsh when started from within other programs to execute commands. For example, within the Emacs editor, you can search files using M-x grep; Emacs prompts you for a pattern and a list of files to search, and then passes the list to your shell for wildcards in it to be expanded. You can make sure zsh will use its advanced wildcard (globbing) features here by putting

```
setopt extended_glob
```

inside ~/.zshenv.

Here's a simple but fairly typical ~/.zshrc file. The code consists of things we'll cover in Part 2 of the book:

```
# Turn on some options.
setopt auto_cd          # Change directory by typing a directory name on its own.
setopt extended_glob  # Turn on the more powerful pattern matching features.

# Set some variables.
# Use 1000 history lines internally, save all of them
# to the file ~/.history
HISTSIZE=1000
SAVEHIST=1000
HISTFILE=~/.history

# Define some aliases.
alias ll='ls -l'
alias pu=pushd

# Load the function-based completion system.
autoload -U compinit
compinit
```

Shell Options

Most Unix programs take some sort of options, and the shells are no exception. Programs often take arguments, such as filenames, too; we aren't concerned with those here. Options control aspects of a program's behavior—and don't forget a shell is a program. Options are one of two main ways to control the shell; shell variables (including environment variables) are the other way. Shell variables are discussed in Chapter 12.

Almost all Unix programs accept options from the command line. Some shell options are set on the command line, as you start a shell. Some are set after the shell has started, either from a startup file or by hand from a shell prompt. Some can be set either way.

Setting Options with bash and zsh

Command-line options can start with a single or double dash (hyphen or minus sign) character, - or --, and sometimes a + (plus). We introduced command-line options in the section "Control Shell Interpretation with Quoting" in Chapter 3. Anything else that appears on the command line is an argument to the shell rather than an option; we will discuss arguments to the shell in Chapter 13.

For example, sometimes you'd like the shell to start up without running your startup files. Maybe one file has a bug that you need to fix. You might want to try a different setting, or think you've found something surprising in the shell and want to see how easy it is to reproduce. Both bash and zsh have options that let you skip the startup files, but unfortunately the options are different.

In bash, the option is --norc. You should read that as "no RC file." The name "RC file" is even older than Unix; apparently it originally meant "runcom file."

```
bash$ bash --norc
bash-3.00$
```

A new shell was started, using just the default settings. You may find the prompt changes when you do that, as we've shown. The prompt is usually set in one of your startup files, but here the shell might use its built-in default. (It will unless the prompt, the variable PS1, is in the environment; see the section "Passing Info to Processes with Environment Variables" in Chapter 3.) In bash, this shows you the name of the shell followed by the version number, a $, and a space.

In zsh, the corresponding option works like the following. Again, you may see a different prompt:

```
zsh% zsh -f
hostname%
```

Setting Options with set

Setting options on the command line isn't usually the most convenient method. There are lots of different settings, and you don't want to have to type them every time, particularly because the shell was probably started by your terminal emulator and you didn't get a chance to give any options. As a result, almost all shell users have some option settings in their startup files, and they can be enabled and disabled using set and unset, respectively. We'll discuss both commands in this section.

Both bash and zsh use the command set to turn on options. set accepts the same options you can give the shell at startup time (as in the previous section). Note, though, that bash doesn't let you set any of the options beginning with -- (two dashes) this way. Those "long options" are used only when you start the shell.

Let's pick another option, this time one common to both shells: -v, for "verbose." This option tells the shell to echo (show) what it's about to execute. We'll see two different ways to set this option. First, on the command line as you start the shell:

```
% zsh -v
% echo you will see this line twice
echo you will see this line twice
```

```
you will see this line twice
```

In this first case, you are very likely to see more output immediately after the zsh -v, before the shell prints its first prompt. That output will come from your startup files being executed, which is a useful way of seeing how things are being set up.

When the echo command is run, the shell first echoes the line. This isn't very useful when you've just typed the line, but it's handy if the line comes from somewhere else, such as a script or startup file. After echoing the command line, the shell runs it. Here we're running the echo command, which simply echoes its arguments. That's why you see the arguments twice (or three times, depending on how you count).

Second, we'll set the option after starting the shell:

```
% zsh
% set -v
% echo you will see this line twice
echo you will see this line twice
you will see this line twice
%
```

To turn the option off again, use +v instead of -v:

```
% set +v
set +v
% echo I will show this only once.
I will show this only once.
%
```

The set +v was echoed just before verbosity was turned off.

Single-letter options can be confusing: their short names (like v) don't offer much about the option's purpose. Both shells have a more obvious way to set those same options from inside the shell: by using names like verbose. Only a small set of these names are common to both shells; it so happens that the verbose option is one of them. The shell manual pages have complete lists of these; in zsh, the zshoptions manual page shows you the single-letter options that correspond to each name. (This means you should type man zshoptions to read it. See the section "Command Lines" in Chapter 1.)

All options have a descriptive name, but only some have a corresponding single letter. The single letters forms can be difficult to remember. It's highly recommended that you use the single-letter versions only when starting up the shell by name, following it with options; the difference in speed is unnoticeable, and the difference in readability is considerable.

Since set has other purposes as well as option setting, you need to tell the shell there is a named option coming up, which you do with a -o. To turn off that option you use +o instead. In the following example, note that the first echo command is repeated before it is executed, while the second isn't:

```
% set -o verbose
% echo This is a verbose demonstration of $SHELL
echo This is a verbose demonstration of $SHELL
This is a verbose demonstration of /usr/local/bin/zsh
% set +o verbose
set +o verbose
% echo This is a demonstration of $SHELL without the verbosity
This is a demonstration of /usr/local/bin/zsh without the verbosity
```

You can actually use this form when starting the shell, too:

```
% zsh -o verbose
(possible messages from startup files)
% echo verbose has been set
echo verbose has been set
verbose has been set
```

If you need to turn on more than one option, repeat the -o:

```
bash$ set -o verbose -o emacs
```

Be careful to include each -o, since there's no error message if you don't. (It just triggers one of the other uses of set. See the sidebar "The Many Uses of set" in Chapter 13.)

The -o has another use: if you type set -o on its own, not followed by anything, the shell will show which options are turned on. This didn't work in older versions of zsh; use setopt instead, which we discuss next.

Setting zsh Options with setopt

So far we've seen that bash and zsh are quite similar in a lot of ways. As is often the case, however, there's a bit more to be said about options in zsh. Since set -o and set +o aren't all that memorable, the commands setopt and unsetopt do the same things; this is what most zsh users use, since you can forget about all those annoying -o's and +o's and just string together named options on the same command line.

Tip Being able to set several options at once in a natural way is a good reason for using setopt in zsh instead of set -o. We'll use setopt below.

There is some freedom in zsh about how you spell named options. This can make options even more readable. It may not be obvious what histexpiredupsfirst means, but Hist_Expire_Dups_First is clearer. zsh ignores all the underscores as well as the string's case. In other words, yet another way of writing this option is hist_expire_dups_first. Note that single-letter options are sensitive to case—set -f and set -F, for example, do different things.

To invert a zsh option, you can place no (or NO, or No_, and so on) in front of the option name. So the following two lines of code have the same effect. The second line is a rather perverse way of achieving it, however:

```
zsh% setopt verify
zsh% unsetopt noverify
```

Let's start up a shell with -f and look at the options:

```
zsh% zsh -f
zsh% setopt
interactive
monitor
norcs
shinstdin
zle
```

Every option not listed has its default setting. Here, four options were turned on automatically by the shell—all of them except norcs. The interactive means you are typing commands at the command line, rather than reading scripts; it's the same as the -i option we mentioned earlier. The other three are also associated with interactive shells:

- monitor means you can do job control.

- shinstdin means the shell's input is standard input (which it isn't if it's reading a script).

- zle means the zsh line editor is in use for editing command lines.

The norcs corresponds to the -f given on the command line. By default, zsh sets the option rcs, which means it runs startup files. To show you that this option currently has a nondefault setting, norcs appears in the list.

If you prefer to see every option together with its setting, there is an option for this. Strangely, it's a shell option, not an option to the setopt command; type setopt ksh_option_print. Then zsh will use the same verbose option listing as ksh and bash—it shows whether every option is on or off.

bash has a command shopt that's a bit like setopt. You can turn options on with shopt -s and turn them off with shopt -u. The options are different from the ones you set with set -o, although you can use shopt -o to manipulate that other set. Unfortunately there's no easy way of deciding which of the two sets contains the bash option you want, apart from looking at the manual. (You can set shopt options when starting the shell by using -O to introduce it instead of -o. Once the shell has been started, you must use shopt.)

Getting Started with Cygwin

We've mentioned that you can run zsh on Windows in an environment called "Cygwin," for "Cygnus Windows." You can get the Cygwin installer from http://sources.redhat.com/cygwin/. A more memorable link to the same place is www.cygwin.com/. When you run it, choose the nearest location from which to pick up files, and select a set of files to pick. It's quite large, so you will need a fast network connection. The default set of files will be enough to get you going; bash is always installed, as it's the main shell in Cygwin.

The installer allows you to add or delete packages from the list it will install. If a package is marked as skip it won't be installed. If you want to use zsh you probably need to select that explicitly by clicking on the appropriate line until it says install. The installer doesn't show you all of the names at once; you may need to click on a plus sign (+) to make the section for shells visible.

When installed, Cygwin gives you a command you can run to start bash in a window.

■**Tip** Earlier versions of zsh exist that run directly under Windows, without Cygwin. This was a nice thing at the time, but nowadays we suggest using Cygwin instead. For one thing, the versions of zsh that don't run under Cygwin are old and lack many of the advanced features we'll be talking about, and there are no plans to upgrade them. For another, you will probably find yourself a bit lost without all the extra tools that come with Cygwin. Unix relies on lots of different parts working together, and a shell isn't much use without tools like the cat and grep commands.

Files in Cygwin

The most difficult part of getting used to Cygwin is the way you specify files. Many Unix utilities, including the shells, are tied to the usual way of specifying paths with slash (/) characters. This is rather different from the Windows form with a drive letter and backslash (\) characters.

Cygwin lets you use both Unix and Windows styles whenever possible. As a rule of thumb, if you are starting a Windows program that doesn't support Cygwin, you should use the normal Windows form, and if you are using a Cygwin program, you should use the Unix form.

There is a utility, cygpath, for converting filenames between Unix and Windows. The command cygpath -w converts to the Windows form, and cygpath -u converts to Unix. Be careful when specifying the Windows form, since all backslashes need to be quoted to prevent the shell from removing them. Windows filenames often have spaces in, too, so it's a good idea just to quote the whole thing:

```
% cygpath -u 'C:\Program Files\Mozilla'
/cygdrive/c/Program Files/Mozilla
```

Note the special notation to access drives such as `C:` from Cygwin with `/cygdrive/c`. This is handled specially by Cygwin to let any Unix-style utility refer to a file on any drive.

By the way, most old-style Windows paths that fit into the form of an eight-character name plus a three-character suffix are turned into lowercase by Cygwin. You can still refer to them without worrying about case sensitivity (both `config.sys` and `CONFIG.SYS`, for example). However, not all utilities know that, so it's best to stick to lowercase.

You can also use the `mount` command to tell Cygwin how to map between Windows and Unix paths. If you type the name on its own, it shows you what's already mounted, and you will see that Cygwin inserted one or more entries automatically. In particular, the Unix path / refers to wherever Cygwin was installed—for example, the Windows path `c:\cygwin`. You can easily add your own mount points:

```
mkdir /c
mount 'c:' /c
```

Note that a directory has to exist for it to be used in this way, hence the `mkdir` command. Now `/c` points at your `C:` drive and you can use it in any command that understands Unix-style paths, including, obviously, the shells.

Another point to do with filenames is that Windows requires that an executable program have the suffix `.exe`. Since this isn't necessary for Unix commands, Cygwin will automatically add the suffix if necessary. So you can refer to `cat` or `cat.exe`, and they have the same effect. If you really mean to refer to the file, not the command, you should use the full name with the suffix, since it's only when executing a file as a program that this mapping occurs. Other types of commands, such as shell built-ins and functions, behave exactly as they normally would. In particular, when we talk about autoloaded functions, exactly the same instructions will apply to Cygwin as to other systems; no suffix is necessary.

A good set of commands come with Cygwin, including a compiler and commonly used utilities like Perl, but it's not as comprehensive as a full Unix or GNU/Linux environment. So sometimes you will find there are things that don't quite work. Most of the time, however, the biggest problem you will come across is that Cygwin programs are a bit slower than native Windows and Unix programs, because the Cygwin system is effectively doing the work of both.

The Terminal in Cygwin

Under Cygwin, you do not usually use a terminal emulator like `xterm` as a separate program. Windows remembers which programs don't start with their own windows. It then uses its own built-in version of a terminal emulator whenever it finds a program of that kind. This includes shells and the "command prompt," Windows' own version of a shell. (Sometimes Windows people talk about a command prompt where Unix people might say "terminal emulator" or "shell window".) In Figure 5-1 we show how the Cygwin window looks when running `zsh`. It's quite similar to a Unix terminal emulator.

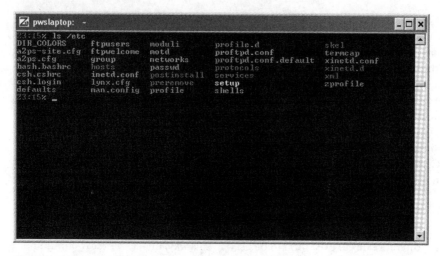

Figure 5-1. *The Cygwin window running a zsh session*

You can create a link to the shell to make it easier to start. Add an entry to the Start menu pointing to bash or zsh, or create a shortcut on your desktop. Then you can use that to start a new shell. This is typically done for bash when Cygwin is installed; in fact, you may start it under the name Cygwin rather than bash.

If you start a shell from inside a window, it works just as it does in Unix, running within the current window rather than creating a new one. This is the simplest way of starting a zsh.

To get zsh running by itself, create a new shortcut in the desktop:

1. Right-click on the desktop, then select the New menu and the item Shortcut. The target is simply the zsh executable. Remember that you need a Windows path here, not a Cygwin one: give the path to the Cygwin root directory, then the path down to zsh using backslashes. For example, if Cygwin was installed in C:\Cygwin, and inside Cygwin zsh is installed in /usr/local/bin, the path is C:\Cygwin\usr\local\bin\zsh.exe.

2. Make sure zsh can find the Cygwin library when it starts up. This library is the file cygwin1.dll.

- The library is usually in the main /bin directory, since Windows doesn't necessarily know about Cygwin's command search path.

- If zsh.exe is in the same directory as cygwin1.dll, there is no problem. Otherwise, you may need to edit the Windows path to include /bin, which in the example above is referred to as C:\Cygwin\bin.

- An easy trick is to copy cygwin1.dll into the directory where zsh is; however, you have to remember to keep this copy in sync with the original if you upgrade, so this isn't without its problems.

If everything worked, the desktop should now have an icon with the zsh logo, which you can see in the top left-hand corner of Figure 5-1. Double-clicking on the icon should start zsh in its own window. The icon appears because zsh recognizes when it is compiled under Cygwin and appends the icon to the executable in a way Windows recognizes. We apologize for the way it looks; it was designed by a graphical illiterate (one of the authors of this book). If Cygwin is properly installed, things inside the safe haven of this window should work pretty much as they do under Unix.

The obvious method for copy and paste is the normal Copy and Paste entries in the Edit menu. These are always available. (Of course, you can't copy text until you've selected some, and you can't paste it until you've copied it.)

There is also a shortcut that allows you to do copy and paste with the mouse alone, like xterm in Unix. Right-click the title bar, select Properties, go to the Options tab if it's not already there, and check the Quick Edit Mode box. On recent versions of Windows, you can then specify that this should apply to the icon that started this window, so you don't need to set it again.

When you have turned Quick Edit mode on, you can copy by selecting the start and end of the region with the left mouse button and clicking the right mouse button. Then you paste it by clicking the right mouse button again.

If you find your terminal appears to be stuck and won't accept input, it may be because it's waiting for you to finish selecting a region. Either another left-click or pressing the Return key will restore normal operation.

Summary

In this chapter we have learned the following:

- What bash and zsh do when they start

- How to control the shells by writing startup files

- How to make the shell execute commands in other files with the command ".".

- What login and interactive shells are

- How to control the shells with options; how to turn options on and off

In the next chapter we will further examine the command history. We showed in the last chapter how you can navigate through previous commands using the Up and Down Arrow keys. We'll explain how the history is saved and restored, show how you can see other information about the commands you've typed, and demonstrate other shortcuts for accessing it.

CHAPTER 6

■ ■ ■

More About Shell History

You've learned about using the shell history in Chapter 4, but there's a good deal more to learn. We start by discussing how to ensure that the shell saves the history when you exit and restores the history when you start a new shell. Later, we cover the method of referring to entries in the history using the ! character in more detail, and look at how you can share history between shell sessions running at the same time.

Setting Up Variables

In order to enable the shell history feature, you need to know how to arrange for the shell to save the lines you've typed and restore them for subsequent sessions. This is done by setting variables to indicate the size of the history in lines (every time you get a new prompt is a new line), how much to save, and in which file to save it. bash has this set up to work by default, but zsh doesn't. Here are the three crucial variables controlling history for each shell:

Variable in bash	Variable in zsh	Purpose
HISTSIZE	Same	Number of lines stored within the shell
HISTFILE	Same	File where history is saved for future use
HISTFILESIZE	SAVEHIST	Maximum number of lines in $HISTFILE

bash has defaults for all these: both sizes are set to 500, and the file is set to ~/.bash_history. This means the shell will remember up to 500 lines internally, and when you exit it will save all of them in the file .bash_history, located in your home directory. Then when you start up any other bash it will look in that file and read the history back.

zsh only sets HISTSIZE by default, and then to the rather small value of 30, so it will only remember 30 lines internally. The other two aren't assigned default values. You should assign only integer values to HISTSIZE and SAVEHIST.

You can use the same values as the bash defaults by adding the following to your .zshrc:

```
HISTFILE=~/.bash_history
HISTSIZE=500
SAVEHIST=500
```

This makes the shells share the same history. The shells have so much syntax in common that it often makes sense to do that. That assumes you use both shells sometimes, perhaps for their different features. Sharing history files usually works since the file just contains a list of the strings you typed. If you often use another shell, such as csh or tcsh, you might consider sharing history between them by using ~/.history. This is the most common name used by csh and tcsh. Many complex commands in those shells are very different from zsh or bash, so not all the history will be useful.

Sharing history between different shells doesn't work so well if you're using the extended_history option in zsh, which saves extra information. In that case, you'd better make zsh's HISTFILE a different file from any that you use for other shells.

It's normally reasonable to increase HISTSIZE (in either shell), SAVEHIST (zsh), or HISTFILESIZE (bash) to a number indicative of the total lines you'd like to store in the history. The shells were first written in an age when computers had much less disk space than they do now. Nowadays, a few hundred kilobytes of shell history is not considered a lot of space.

You might wonder what happens if HISTSIZE and SAVEHIST are different. There's no problem, in fact. If SAVEHIST is smaller, the shell won't save all the lines, and if HISTSIZE is smaller, the shell will write a truncated file. Keeping them the same is the obvious thing to do, but again, we detail some special cases below.

If your zsh came preinstalled on your computer, or you installed it from a package created by the suppliers of your operating system, you may well find there are default values for all three variables in the global /etc/zshrc file. In that case, the file given by HISTFILE probably already contains a lot of history. That's one reason for not changing it.

You can change the value of HISTSIZE from the command line in order to save more commands, if you like. The shell won't forget the ones you already have. If you reduce HISTSIZE, the shell will remove the ones at the start of the history, so the most recent ones are still there.

"Bang" History: The Use of Exclamation Marks

Both bash and zsh have a history mechanism inherited from the C shell that uses the ! character to retrieve history lines. We introduced this feature in the section "History," in Chapter 1; in this section we'll offer a little more detail.

When csh was written, this feature was the only way of using lines from the shell's history. There was no command-line editing except for the few simple operations configured with stty (which we discussed in the section "Other Tips on Terminals" in Chapter 4). You'll probably use the line editor to do many of the tasks represented by complex history substitutions like !1023:1:t.

However, there are plenty of simple and useful tricks. All the features here are introduced by an exclamation mark, or "bang" for short. The simplest feature is to repeat the last command.

```
% echo This is the last command.
This is the last command
% !!
echo This is the last command.
This is the last command.
```

Note that the shell showed you the result of the history command. Typing !! made it look in the history for the command immediately before and reexecute in whole. You don't have to have *only* !! on the line; you can put any other text around it. The !! will be replaced with the previous line at any point it occurs, even if it occurs more than once.

For commands before the last one, you can use a negative number. !! is the same as !-1, !-2 is the command immediately before that, and so on.

History entries also have an absolute number, starting from 1. If the shell has read history in from a file, those lines read back in will usually grab the first numbers, so you will find that the lines you type have numbers starting from 501, or 1001, or whatever. There are two ways of finding out what the number of the lines is. The foolproof method is to type history. This will produce output similar to the following:

```
1035   echo  \!\!
1036   man zshmisc
1037   man zshexpn
1039   less /etc/bashrc
1040   less ~/.history
```

In this list the numbers on the left give the history line number corresponding to the remaining text. So with that history, typing !1037 will execute the command man zshexpn. The same result can be achieved by pressing Up Arrow three times, then Return.

We've shown only the end of the output. bash will show you the entire history stored in the shell. zsh truncates it to the last 20 or so entries, but you can show the entire history with the command history 1. In zsh, giving a single number to the history command tells it the number to start from. If that is no longer in the shell's memory, the command starts from the first entry it has. Conversely, you can give it a negative number, just like after !, which tells the shell to start the list from that many entries ago. You can give a second number, which tells the command where to stop. So the following shows the 21 entries from the 40th ago to the 20th ago, counting inclusively:

```
zsh% history -40 -20
```

(The example assumes you have enough entries to have a history list of at least 40 entries.) bash, by contrast, takes only one positive number. This is how many lines back in the history to look. In bash, history 1 behaves like history -1 in zsh.

In zsh, you can set the option hist_no_store to prevent new history commands from being added to the history list. That's useful if you use the command a lot but don't need to retrieve it. The last command is always available for immediate use. Hence if you've just typed history, !! will always repeat that, even with the option set. Likewise, you can always use the Up Arrow key to edit the last line. (Related commands, such as fc-1, are also not added to the history when hist_no_store is in effect.)

Another way of picking a line in the history is by the text it starts with. Simply put the text after a single exclamation mark:

```
% echo This file was created on $(date) >file
% cat file
This file was created on Tue Jan 20 21:39:47 GMT 2004
% !echo
echo This file was created on $(date) >file
```

The shell searches back in the history for the nearest line that matches. zsh allows you to search for a line containing certain text by using !?:

```
zsh% ls -l ~pws
...contents of pws's home directory
zsh% ls -l ~csr
...contents of csr's home directory
zsh% !?pws
ls -l ~pws
...contents of pws's home directory, again
```

History Words

There are two more arguments you can have in a history expansion: one to select the word in the history, the next to modify the retrieved text in some way. Neither needs to be there, but you can have all three. The arguments are separated by colons.

To restrict the retrieved text to one or more words in the history line, you can use one of the following:

- Numbers, where 0 is the command name and 1 is its first argument.

- * for everything except the command name.

- $ for the last argument on the command line.

- Two numbers, or a number and a $, with a - in between. This selects a range.

Let's consider a few examples. The first line shows a simple echo command. Each of the other examples is to be typed immediately after that command line, so that in each case, !! refers to the same command line.

```
% echo History is bunk.
History is bunk.

% !!:0
echo
<empty line>

% !!:0-1
echo History
History

% echo I said !!:$
echo I said bunk.
I said bunk.

% echo The arguments were !!:*
echo The arguments were History is bunk.
The arguments were History is bunk.

% echo And once again: !!:1-$
echo And once again: History is bunk.
And once again: History is bunk.
```

You can shorten the !! to a single ! if it's followed by one of these forms, so the first one could be reformatted like so:

```
% !:0
echo
<empty line>
```

That only works with the colon after it. A ! on its own is never substituted.

In zsh, a single ! refers to the last line you referred to, if you had previous history substitutions on the line. In other words,

```
% perl -e 'printf "%c\n", 65;'
A
% perl -e 'printf "%c\n", 48;'
0
% perl !-2:* !:*
perl -e 'printf "%c\n", 65;' -e 'printf "%c\n", 65;'
A
A
```

The first set of arguments was inserted twice. (The example uses Perl to print out the characters corresponding to decimal numbers 65 and 48 in the ASCII character set.) You can turn this feature off by setting the shell option `csh_junkie_history`. It has that name because that's the way `csh` does substitutions. (It was requested by `csh` addicts suffering withdrawal symptoms.) `bash` does substitutions that way, too.

That example shows that "words" in history are really command arguments—here, a full quoted expression. That's true in all recent versions of `bash` and `zsh`. You need to use the line editor if you want to extract smaller pieces from a command line.

Modifiers

The third part of a history substitution is a "modifier" because it modifies the word you've picked out so far. This is particularly useful for extracting parts of filenames. The two most useful sorts of modifier are those that work on files and those that do substitutions. In `zsh`, these modifiers are useful in other places we'll discuss later in the section.

Modifiers that deal with filenames assume a standard Unix-style path. This means if you're working under Cygwin you won't get the right effect from Windows-style paths with backslashes. Let's assume we've just executed the line

```
% ls -l /home/pws/zsh/sourceforge/zsh/Src/Zle/zle_main.c
...file details...
```

Then we can get three effects on that second argument to `ls`, the head (directory part) of the filename:

```
% ls !:2:h
ls /home/pws/zsh/sourceforge/zsh/Src/Zle
...directory contents ...
```

Next we can get the tail (nondirectory part):

```
% echo !-2:2:t >>source_files.lis
echo zle_main.c >>source_files.lis
```

Then we can remove the suffix:

```
% echo !-3:2:r
echo /home/pws/zsh/sourceforge/zsh/Src/Zle/zle_main
/home/pws/zsh/sourceforge/zsh/Src/Zle/zle_main
```

Often you remove the suffix in order to replace it with another one. Here we strip `.c` and add `.o` to turn a C source file into the compiler output file:

```
% ls -l !-4:2:r.o
ls -l /home/pws/zsh/sourceforge/zsh/Src/Zle/zle_main
...file details for the .o file, if it exists
```

You can combine modifiers, but you need to repeat the colon each time:

```
% echo !-5:2:t:r.o >>object_files.lis
echo zle_main.o >>object_files.lis
```

The modifiers are evaluated from left to right. This is important to know when you have :h and :t in the same expression. Almost certainly any :t should come after any :h, since :t removes all the slashes. Two :h's in a row strip off two levels of path.

Substitutions are a bit hairier. If you know about sed or perl, or are a vi user who makes use of substitutions there, the form of a substitution will be familiar to you:

```
% echo There\'s no subsitute for hard work.
There's no substitute for hard work.
% !!:s/substitute/accounting/
echo There\'s no accounting for hard work.
There's no accounting for hard work.
```

The /'s delimit the text that is being replaced and the text it's being replaced with. As you can see in that example, you don't need to have a word selector before the modifier. The shell is smart enough to realize that if something that could be a word selector actually starts with s it must be a modifier instead. This is often useful with substitutions.

Once you've done one substitution, you can repeat it with the command &:

```
% echo There are substitutes for butter.
There are substitutes for butter.
% !!:&
echo There are accountings for butter.
There are accountings for butter.
```

The substitution—replacing "substitute" for "accounting"—was remembered. It is kept until the next :s, or until you exit the shell. Note that there is only one set of search and replace data for all use of modifiers, including those not from the history mechanism we describe later.

The delimiters after :s don't actually need to be slashes, just as long as they're the same character three times. This is useful if you're replacing chunks of a filename:

```
% pr -h "Study this carefully, ASAP" Src/main.c | lpr -Pink
-rw-r--r--    1 pws      users        1362 Aug  2 2000 Src/main.c
% !!:s'Src/main.c'Doc/zshexpn.1'
+pr -h "Study this carefully, ASAP" Doc/zshexpn.1 | lpr -Pink
```

(This formats a file for printing with the header shown and sends it to the printer called ink.) The quotes work here because history substitution occurs very early in processing, before the shell has looked for special characters.

Changing something in the last line is so common that there's a shorthand for it:

```
% echo There\'s no subsititute for hard work.
% ^hard work^taste
echo There\'s no substitute for taste.
There's no substitute for taste.
```

In full there would be three ^'s, just as you need three delimiters in a normal substitution. You can get away with two unless there's more text. In that case, you can even have more modifiers:

```
% echo There\'s no substitute for hard work.
There's no substitute for hard work.
% ^hard work^taste^:s/substitute/accounting/
echo There\'s no accounting for taste.
There's no accounting for taste.
```

Substitutions usually just substitute once in each line:

```
% echo this line is not a large line
this line is not a large line
% ^line^lion
echo this lion is not a large line
```

The way to do global replacements is to use :gs in place of :s:

```
% echo this line is not a large line
this line is not a large line
% !!:gs/line/lion/
echo this lion is not a large lion
```

Unfortunately, there's no way of doing this with the ^ form. Remember the g should be placed in front. This is different from, for example, substitutions in sed or Perl. These languages have a similar syntax, although they use regular expressions to match the text to be replaced. However, in sed and Perl the g comes at the end.

Other Uses of History Modifiers

Now, as promised, let's look at other uses of modifiers in zsh. These provide a consistent syntax for manipulating strings, particularly filenames, that you can use for shell variables and file patterns as well as history references. Thus, if you followed the previous section you'll be able to use the syntax we introduced right away. These uses of the modifier syntax don't work with bash. First, you can use modifiers with variable substitution, a subject we'll be dealing with in more detail in Chapter 12:

```
zsh% file=~/.zshrc
zsh% echo $file:t
.zshrc
```

You can also use modifiers for filename generation, although in that case the modifier must be surrounded by parentheses:

```
zsh% echo ~/.z*(:t)
.zcompdump .zfbkmarks .zlogout .zshenv .zshrc
```

You need the parentheses in that example. Otherwise, without the parentheses the :t would just be part of the word. This syntax is part of a feature called *glob qualifiers*, which will be fully explained in the section "Glob Qualifiers in zsh" in Chapter 9.

The last example shows a feature of modifiers when applied to a filename pattern with more than one expansion. The modifier is applied to each element separately. This gives us a good way of extracting just the base names of a group of files. This feature also works when applied to an array containing a list of filenames; we'll meet arrays in Chapter 12.

You need to be more careful about special characters—spaces, quotes, etc.—when using modifiers with variables or filename patterns. Although history itself is done so early that they don't matter, variable and filename modifiers are handled along with normal shell expansions. Here is an example:

```
zsh% foo='two words'
zsh% echo $foo:s/two\ words/oneword/
oneword
```

We had to quote a space in the substitution with a backslash. Without it, the substitution would see $foo:s/two, while word/oneword/ would be a different word. Alternatively, this would be a good place to use braces, which tell the shell where a parameter substitution starts and ends: ${foo:s/two words/oneword/} would work fine.

In the section "Patterns" in Chapter 12 we'll see a more powerful form of substitution on variables that works in both bash and zsh.

Verifying and Quoting History References

Both shells support a very useful option, histverify, which lets you check the line after modification. (In bash, set this with shopt -s histverify.) When the option is set, any history substitution involving !'s or ^'s causes the modified line to appear in the line editor. You can edit the line or simply press Return to execute it.

bash supports a relative of histverify, named histreedit. In this case, you are given a line to edit if the history modification failed. This can happen either because a modifier did nothing, or because you referred to a line or word that wasn't there. Since history expansion occurs so early in processing, a failed history expansion usually just disappears. It's not saved in the history because it was never executed.

zsh doesn't support histreedit. It also complains (more than bash) about failed modifiers. For example, it complains if you use a :h modifier on a word with no slash. bash just gives you the whole word.

If you want your exclamation marks to be treated normally, the simplest thing to do is put a \ in front. However, quoting an expression with single quotes also renders exclamation marks harmless. Hence, for example:

```
echo What a line that was'!!'  Full of interesting commands\!\!
What a line that was!! Full of interesting commands!!
```

Using double quotes does *not* have this effect; ! 's in double quotes are subject to history substitution:

```
% echo unrepeatable
unrepeatable
% echo "!:1"
echo "unrepeatable"
unrepeatable
% echo '!!'
!!
% echo \!\!
!!
```

It's also possible to turn off this form of history completely. In bash it's accomplished with the following command:

```
set +H
```

In zsh it's easiest to set the option by name:

```
setopt no_bang_hist
```

This disables both the ! (bang) forms and the substitution shortcut using ^. bash actually allows you to turn off all forms of history by set +o history. After this it won't store history lines at all. (There's no obvious reason for doing this.)

Note that noninteractive shells don't do any form of history at all. All lines are read one at a time and then forgotten, and ! is not a special character. This applies any time the input doesn't come from the keyboard. For example, ! characters aren't special in startup files.

In zsh, putting ! " on a line stops any ! 's after it from being substituted. Hence for example:

```
% echo Bang, you\'re dead.
Bang you're dead.
% echo !:1 Bang !"!!
echo Bang, Bang \!\!
Bang, Bang !!
```

The first ! was active. The ! " was removed from the line, but prevented the following ! ! from being used for history expansion. It doesn't take word identifiers or modifiers; a colon after it is a normal colon.

■**Tip** Both shells offer an editor command called `magic-space`, designed to be bound to the spacebar. It inserts a space into the current line, as the spacebar normally does. The "magic" part is that it also performs history expansion on the current line, resolving all uses of ! for history that are present. This makes the command line much easier to read. In `bash`, the command `bind '" ": magic-space'` turns on this effect. In `zsh`, use the command `bindkey ' ' magic-space` instead.

More Options for Manipulating History

`zsh` allows you to show the history in more detail with some extra options to `history`. It records internally the time when each command started. That's useful later on when you're trying to remember what you've just done. For example: How long did a certain command take? Did I run that program before I went for lunch as I meant to? You can show this with these options:

- `-d` for the time the command started.

- `-E` for the time and date in European format (day.month.year).

- `-i` for the time and date in international format (year-month-day).

- `-f` for the time and date in U.S. format (month/day/year).

- `-D` for the elapsed time of each command. You can combine this option with one of the others, or use it on its own; this prints the elapsed time of each command. The "elapsed" time is the time between the command starting and it stopping, not the amount of time running on the processor. It's not just the difference between the timestamps, though, since it does measure the actual execution time, not including any idle time while you were editing.

For example, here is the end of my command history. Each line shows the history line number, the time taken to execute the command, and the command executed:

```
zsh% history -D
 1067  0:00  grep PWS *.dtd
 1068  0:08  make chapters
 1069  0:14  cvs commit -m 'Final(?) changes for getting_started.xml'
 1070  0:00  make lint |& l
```

The extra information for the time options isn't saved unless you set the shell option `extended_history`. Setting the option changes the format of the history file, making it harder to share with other shells. Here is how the history lines shown previously were saved to the history file:

```
: 1087852429:0;grep PWS *.dtd
: 1087852683:0;make chapters
: 1087852731:0;cvs commit -m 'Final(?) changes for getting_started.xml'
: 1087854172:0;make lint |& 1
```

There is method to this madness. You can actually execute one of those lines. The part between the colon and the semicolon is ignored, and the command line after is executed. This works in bash, too, so if you happen to read in a zsh history file in this format into bash it will work. It will look rather bizarre on the command line, however.

Until recently, bash didn't handle timestamps in history. This was added in version 3 of bash. To enable it, you set the variable HISTTIMEFORMAT to a string that specifies the format for times. It's in the form used by the Unix strftime function, which we'll talk about in Chapter 7. That's all you need to do; there are no additional options to the history command.

bash has two slightly more obscure options for the format of history. If you execute shopt -s cmdhist, multiline commands appear in the same history entry—this happens in the current shell as well as in the output file. This is done by appending a semicolon and then the next line. This isn't necessary in zsh, which saves multiline commands complete, and in the form you entered them.

The second option is histlit; this is only useful if cmdhist is on. In this case, bash uses newlines instead of semicolons for multiline entries. This is what zsh normally does; its more powerful multiline editing features mean that it doesn't require an option to turn it off.

Appending to the History List

It can often happen that you have several shells, each running in a different window. When you log out, all the shells exit at once and they all try to save their history at the same time. The default behavior means that the last to exit will win, and will overwrite the output saved by the others. You can fix this in bash by using the following setting:

bash$ **shopt -s histappend**

The equivalent option in zsh is set like this:

zsh% **setopt append_history**

These settings cause lines to be appended to whatever is already in the history. The saved history has the same maximum size, however, so it's still possible for all output to come from one shell. This is one time where setting the variables HISTSIZE and HISTFILESIZE (bash) or SAVEHIST (zsh) to different values is useful. If the saved size is larger than the internal size, output from lots of different shells can fit in the file. The shell will still only read in a number of lines given by HISTSIZE, but the other values are still present in the history file if you need to search a long way back.

Sharing History

You may already have found that if you have two different shells running at once, they don't share the history. In other words, if you execute a line in one shell, going back up the history in the other shell doesn't show that line. In zsh you can set the option share_history to make this work. The mechanism is that each shell saves a line immediately to the history file when you execute it. Every time a shell accesses the history, it checks the history file to see if another shell has added something to it. The shell remembers whether the line has come from another shell. Without this, the history numbering would be completely messed up, because you would have additional lines inserted in the middle every time you executed a command in another shell. (The idea for this features comes from ksh, in which sharing history is the standard behavior.)

A compromise option, inc_append_history, saves the line to the history file immediately but doesn't attempt to read back lines from the history file. You can issue the command fc -R in another shell to read the history file.

In bash, explicitly writing and reading history is the only way to share history. We'll see the commands for doing this in both shells a bit later.

Pruning and Massaging the History List

Both shells have mechanisms that give you more control over what is saved in the history list. This avoids the frustration of having a large number of useless lines remembered while the line you actually want has already been forgotten. The shells do this in their own ways, so we'll consider them separately.

Most pruning is done on the history as it is stored in memory. However, some zsh options apply only when the history is written.

bash Features for Pruning History

bash provides two variables that you can set to prune lines that are added to the history.

The variable HISTCONTROL can take various values. From version 3 of bash you can give a list of the following values separated by colons:

ignorespace: Lines beginning with a space are not to be saved in the history. You have to remember to type a space by hand if you know you don't want a line to be saved. This can often be annoying if you are pasting text from a file, since code in files is very often indented, so this option is less useful than it may sound.

ignoredups: If the same line occurs twice in a row, only one instance is saved. Hence if you scroll back through the history list, every time you press the Up Arrow you see a different line. Lines that are the same but not together in the history are not pruned.

ignoreboth: Combines the effect of the two previous values.

erasedups: This is new in version 3 of bash. When a line is added to the history any duplicate of the line is erased from the history.

The other variable is HISTIGNORE. This requires a bit more thought. It is colon-separated list of patterns that are matched against the complete line. You can use the wildcard * to match any text. A matched line is not saved to the history file. There's one shortcut, which is that & matches the last line saved in the history before the one being considered. This means that setting

```
HISTIGNORE=" *:&"
```

is equivalent to setting HISTCONTROL to ignoreboth.

zsh Features for Pruning History

zsh doesn't have the general history control of bash's HISTIGNORE at the moment; everything is controlled by shell options.

There are a whole group of options controlling how the shell treats duplicate lines:

hist_ignore_dups: This is like bash's HISTCONTROL=ignoredups. Consecutive duplicates are not saved. Actually, the most recent version of the line is always kept. This means that if you look at the timestamps, you will see the values for the last line you executed.

hist_ignore_all_dups: This extends the meaning of the previous command so that all duplicates are removed from the history, whether they are consecutive or not. This is not a good option to set if you regularly reuse chunks of history lines in order, since there may be unexpected gaps.

hist_save_no_dups: When writing the history file, duplicates are not saved, but they are kept internally.

hist_expire_dups_first: This option comes into play when the internal history list reaches $HISTSIZE. At that point, the shell looks for duplicate lines anywhere in the history. It then removes the earliest occurrence. If it can't do that, it will simply remove the first item in the history list as normal.

There's a subtlety here. Suppose you save your entire history to the history file, i.e, $SAVEHIST and $HISTSIZE are the same number. The shell will gradually remove all duplicates from the history file. Eventually the effect is the same as if hist_ignore_all_dups were set. The way to get round this is to set HISTSIZE to be larger than SAVEHIST. The shell accumulates duplicates in memory to begin with using the extra space, then prunes them as the need arises.

hist_find_no_dups: When you search backward for history lines, each search will always produce a line different from the one you are currently on. However, the lines are not unique. You might find yourself searching back through a repeated pair of lines, for example. When this option is turned on, you only see each line exactly once, even if there were some other, different, lines in between.

Two other options control what lines are saved to the history (apart from `hist_no_store`, which we've already described):

`hist_ignore_space`: This is like `bash`'s `HISTCONTROL=ignorespace`. Lines beginning with a space character aren't saved to the history.

`hist_no_functions`: Function definitions aren't saved to the history. Most functions you use will probably be autoloaded rather than typed in, so this usually just refers to the few short functions you type by hand.

Remember you can always retrieve the immediately preceding command. It only becomes a candidate for pruning after the next command is executed.

There's one miscellaneous option: `hist_reduce_blanks`. Unlike the others we've listed, this works on individual lines. It removes any blank spaces that are not syntactically important—in other words, those that separate command arguments, but not those within quotes.

A Few More History Tricks

We'll round the chapter off with a few more history tricks. They are features you may not need all that regularly. However, every now and then they will make your life a little easier.

Forcing History to be Read or Written

Both shells have the ability to force the history to be read from the history file or written back to it. One reason for doing this is to make commands executed in one terminal window available in another. Save the history file from one window, switch to the other, and read it; the commands you typed in the first window are now available in the second.

In `bash`, reading and writing history is done with the commands `history -r` and `history -w`. Because `bash` doesn't have history sharing, these commands are probably more useful than the `zsh` counterparts.

In `zsh`, the command to read and write history is less memorable. Before all the line-editing and `!`-style history features appeared, the Korn shell had a command `fc` (standing for "fix command") that offered some primitive control over history. You could select lines from the history to pass to a text editor, or to be reexecuted immediately. `zsh` has taken this over, but nowadays it is a very clumsy way of using the shell history and we won't go into details.

In `zsh`, the options `fc -R` and `fc -W` read and write the history file, respectively. This is quite useful if you don't like the `share_history` option but sometimes need to share the history between shells. You can simply save it from one shell with `fc -W`, and then read it in the other shell with `fc -R`. Now the second shell's history looks like the first's. You can avoid ever using `fc -W` if you have the option `inc_append_history` set.

Running an Editor on a History Line

Every now and then, you might have a command line unwieldy enough that you want to run a full editor on it. There are various ways of doing this. zsh comes with an add-on editor command called edit-command-line, which you can use as follows:

```
autoload -U edit-command-line
zle -N edit-command-line
bindkey '\ee' edit-command-line
```

Now pressing Esc-e loads the line so far into the editor. (The editor is usually given by the environment variable EDITOR or maybe VISUAL.) When you leave the editor, the line is left in the shell's editor for you to press Return or abort.

It's also possible in zsh to run a command that executes the previous command line directly, without editing it. The command to do this is r, short for fc -e -. It usually has the same effect as typing !! and then pressing Return. However, r has the advantage that it still works if you set the option no_bang_history.

Finding the History Line Number

bash provides a variable HISTCMD, which contains the number of the current command. There's nothing so direct in zsh; if you need the number, you can find out by using prompt expansions:

```
zsh% print -P '%!'
1022
```

This tells print to treat the arguments as if they were in a prompt, as discussed in the next chapter.

Completing Words from Lines in the History

You can extract information from history lines in both bash and zsh. In bash, you can use the Meta-Tab key combination, which calls the editor command dynamic-complete-history. This looks back through recent history lines to find words that complete what you've typed already. For example, if you type super and then press Meta-Tab, the shell might complete superintendent or supernatural, if you'd typed them recently. If you'd typed both, it would beep and let you add more letters to make the word unambiguous. This works just like completion of files. You'll learn more about completion in Chapter 10.

In zsh, you need to have loaded the completion system, as described in the section "zsh's compinit" in Chapter 10. Then you can press Esc-/ after a partial word, and the shell will look back in the history for the remainder.

Summary

In this chapter we've met various features of command history. There's more to the subject than appears at first sight, and we've shown quite a lot of different aspects:

- Saving and restoring the history and controlling the history's size

- Using history with ! characters, selecting words, and modifying the words you've selected

- Referring to and displaying history lines by number

- Using history modifiers to pick bits out of shell variables and filenames

- Quoting history references

- Showing the times at which commands in the history were executed

- Automatically pruning the history to remove unwanted lines

- Various additional tips: reading and writing the history without leaving the shell; running an editor on a history line; finding the current history line number; completing a word from somewhere back in the history

In the next chapter we'll look at prompts, the short messages that appear at the start of each line when you're about to type. You can easily get them to give you a lot of information; we'll see how.

CHAPTER 7

■ ■ ■

Prompts

In this book, you've already seen lots of command lines. Throughout the previous chapters, you've probably noticed a short chunk of text at the beginning, located just to the left of the area where you type. This string is called a *prompt*. As an example, in the case of bash we show command lines that start like the following:

bash$

It is possible to change that string to show you information about your environment, such as the current directory, the username, or the time. In this chapter we show you how to make such changes. We also discuss a few operations the shell can carry out at about the time the prompt is printed, such as checking for mail or looking to see if other users have logged in or out. You can use these features to make the shell display information that you can't easily get from a prompt.

Basic Prompting

In Table 7-1 we show a list of prompts used by bash and zsh. The name in the first column is a shell variable that you need to set in order to change the prompt. We usually refer to the various prompts by the name of the variable. You will see that many start with the letters PS, which stands for "prompt string."

For this list we are using a fairly generous definition: a prompt is any string that you can configure that the shell uses to offer information about the present environment. This definition includes cases where the shell isn't prompting you for input. The shells are a bit more logical, and the names of variables that fall into that second class usually end in FORMAT (bash) or FMT (zsh).

Table 7-1. *Prompts in bash and zsh*

Prompt Name	bash or zsh	Purpose
PS1	Both	Normal command prompt
PS2	Both	Continuation command prompt. See the section "Editing Data, Continuing Command Lines" in Chapter 2.
PS3	Both	Prompt for select built-in
PS4	Both	Debugging with xtrace (-x) option
RPS1	zsh	Normal command prompt at right
RPS2	zsh 4.2	Continuation command prompt on the right
SPROMPT	zsh	Used when offering to correct spelling
TIMEFORMAT	bash	Output from time built-in
TIMEFMT	zsh	Output from time built-in
WATCHFMT	zsh	Information on logins and logouts

If you set prompts yourself, you will probably put the definitions in your .bashrc or .zshrc file. The startup scripts supplied with some packages export these as environment variables, using the built-in command export. This means that the values appear in any shell, even if you don't execute a startup file. (The startup file may override the definition, though.) For example, if your bash prompt is exported and you start a zsh, you might see the bash prompt string. This is usually not very useful, because of the differences between the shells; it probably looks like a mess of characters with backslashes in front. So if you use more than one shell, it's best not to export prompts. You can use the following command to tell the shell not to export a variable from .bashrc or .zshrc:

```
declare +x PS1
```

The command declare is also known as typeset.

The Four Main Prompts

As you see, the prompts referred to by the variables PS1 to PS4 are available in both bash and zsh. Let's briefly summarize here what they're for:

PS1: Appears at the start of lines where you type commands. You've already seen lots of these in this book.

PS2: Appears at the start of lines when the shell is waiting for more input. We showed you an example of this, too, in the section "Editing Data, Continuing Command Lines" in Chapter 2.

PS3: This is the most specialized. It is only used with the shell's `select` command, which is a simple way of generating a menu and making a user select one of the options. PS3 is printed to make the user pick an option. On the whole, `select` isn't used all that much, so we'll skip over this. However, it works exactly like all the other PS prompts.

PS4: This is not really a prompt; it appears when you have the `xtrace` option set to show what is being executed. This is used mostly for debugging so we describe it in more detail in the section "Debugging Scripts" in Chapter 13.

Values for Prompt Variables

A prompt variable can contain ordinary text, which will be output unchanged. You can have a newline in a prompt, too—this makes it easy to have a prompt spread over multiple lines. Many people do this so that they can have a lot of information on one line, and still keep plenty of space to type on the line below. Consider the following simple example of setting PS1:

```
bash$ PS1="Enter a new command line below.
? "
Enter a new command line below.
?
```

The cursor appears after the question mark and a space. Users of one of the C-shell family (`csh` and `tcsh`) should notice that in `bash` and `zsh` you can simply put a newline directly into a string like any other character.

Strings only give you the same information every time, however. They can't identify changes between two prompts, such as the current directory or the time. For this the shells have a system referred to as *prompt escapes* (or *escape sequences*). These give you a shorthand for telling the shell to substitute the information you want at a place in the string. Unfortunately, `bash` and `zsh` have different escape sequences, so we will discuss the shells separately. However, the escape sequences are the same in the prompts within each shell. (This is not true of the special variables TIMEFORMAT, TIMEFMT, and WATCHFMT shown in Table 7-1. We will discuss those separately.)

Prompts in bash

In bash an escape sequence consists of a backslash character followed by another character. We show a list of common sequences in Table 7-2. For your convenience, we've put the bash and zsh forms in the same table. In the rest of this section we'll explain the information conveyed by the bash prompts.

Table 7-2. *A Few Common bash and zsh Prompt Escapes*

bash Form	zsh Form	Expansion
\\$	%#	# if superuser, else $ (bash) or % (zsh)
\u	%n	Username
\h	%m	Host (machine) name
\W	%.	Last part of current directory
\w	%~	Full name of current directory
\A	%T	Time in the 24-hour format, such as 18:20
\@	%@ (or %t)	Time in the 12-hour format, such as 06:20
\t	%*	Time in the 24-hour format with seconds, such as 18:20:15
\T	%D{%l:%M:%S}	Time in the 12-hour format with seconds, such as 06:20:15
\d	%D{%a %b %d}	Date as Mon Jul 19
\D{%a %d}	%w	Date as Mon 19
\D{%m/%d/%Y}	%W	Date as 07/19/2004
\!	%!	Line number in shell history, for history substitution with !
\j	%j	The number of background jobs

Username and Hostname

The username is given by \u and the hostname by \h. The hostname is the computer you are logged into—if you use Telnet or some other remote access protocol, it may not be the computer right in front of you:

```
bash$ PS1='\u@\h \$ '
pws@pwstephenson $
```

Note the single quotes—you need those to make sure all the special characters aren't processed immediately by the shell. Even double quotes aren't good enough here, since \\$ in double quotes just gets turned into a $, which isn't what you want.

The prompt was followed by a space to separate it from what you're typing. The shell doesn't do that automatically, so we added it to the end of the string. Most users find it much clearer with the space.

The prompt that comes up shows you my username, and the name my PC is set to use. (If your system isn't set to use the network, it may not have a very distinctive name, possibly just localhost.) If your hostname includes dots, \h just shows up to the first one, but \H shows the whole thing.

Finding Out If You're the Root User

In the previous example, we used a \$, not just a $. This displays a $ for most users, but it displays a # for the user called root, the system administrator. This lets you use the same prompt for everyone, but still be warned when you are running as root—an important fact, given all the damage you can do there if you are not careful. When run as root, the example would become the following:

```
bash$ PS1='\u@\h \$ '
root@pwstephenson #
```

Directories

For the current directory, you can either output the last part of the directory path by using \W or the whole path using \w. Note, however, that your home directory is output by \w as ~, so your own directories are a bit shorter. One very common alternative is to put the name of the current directory into the title bar of the terminal window instead. We show how to do that in the section "Special Effects," later in this chapter.

Times and Dates

Times and dates are more difficult, because there are so many possible formats. Four standard escapes are available for the time; we show the same time in all four formats in Table 7-3.

Table 7-3. *The Built-in Escapes for Time in bash Prompts*

Escape	Sample Expansion
\A	18:20 (Not available in older versions of bash)
\@	06:20
\t	18:20:15
\T	06:20:15

There is just one escape for the date, \d, which is fairly verbose; a complete time and date using '\A \d' turns into, for example, 18:20 Sat Jul 12.

However, it's possible to roll your own date and time. There's a handy function in the Unix program library called strftime. The programmer passes a string to the function, which includes escape sequences similar to those used for prompts but introduced by a percent string. bash gives you direct access to this using its own escape \D{*format*}. The *format* is the string that is passed as an argument to strftime. We show examples of those strings together with a sample of the output they produce in Table 7-4. Type man strftime for a complete list of the escapes your system supports. These vary between operating systems and their different versions, so some of the examples we show may not work on your system.

Table 7-4. *Creating Your Own Date and Time Format in* bash

Escape Sequence	Sample Output
\D{%Y-%m-%d %H:%M}	2003-07-12 18:20
\D{%a %b %d %I:%M:%S}	Sat Jul 12 06:20:15
\D{%l:%m}	6:20

The History Line Number

You can get the current history line number with \!. (This may not work in older versions of bash.) This is useful if you make extensive use of history in the form !320, which refers to a particular line number, since it means you don't have to count the line numbers yourself.

Taking Advantage of Shell Variables and System Commands

If the shopt option promptvars is set, which it is by default, bash will do variable substitution on prompts. Take this example:

```
PS1='[$OLDPWD] \w\$ '
```

This puts the directory into the prompt, preceded by an indication of the directory you were in immediately before, which is stored in the shell variable OLDPWD. (Note that when you start the shell, OLDPWD isn't yet defined; you must change the directory at least once.) Once again, the single quotes are crucial here—if you had used double quotes, the shell would have substituted $OLDPWD at the point you created the variable. Then it would have been fixed for the lifetime of the shell instead of being expanded at each prompt.

In fact, within prompts bash does any form of substitution it would normally do in double quotes, including command substitution. This means you can get the prompt to show output from commands. Here's a way of making it show the last two pieces of the current directory:

```
bash$ PS1='$(pwd | sed -e "s%^.*/\(.*/.*\)%\1%")\$ '
projects/zshbook$
```

It's messy, but the important thing is the expression inside the outer parentheses. That pipes the output from the pwd command, which prints the current working directory, to the stream editor sed, which substitutes the path by just its last two components. We say a little more about sed in the sidebar "The Stream Editor, sed."

THE STREAM EDITOR, SED

Entire books have been written about sed; therefore we won't go into much detail here, although for new users the topic is worth a short introduction. The command is used to transform input lines into output lines by sets of instructions passed as arguments. Each instruction is applied to each input line. In the example in the main text, we used the option -e to pass an instruction to sed. The instruction that follows the –e is "s%^.*/\(.*/.*\)%\1%", where the double quotes are used to quote the special characters inside, in order to prevent the shell from interpreting them. The type of instruction is indicated by the first character. Here it is s, which shows that we want to substitute an occurrence of a pattern with some replacement text. This instruction has the form s%*pattern%replacement%. We used the character % because it does not occur in the pattern or the replacement text; it is more common to use /, but that would have caused confusion here since this character does occur in the pattern we want to match. The replacement text was \1; this is an instruction to sed to substitute the string that matched the part of the pattern between the first \(and the \). Substitution is the most common use of sed; there are also instructions to delete or add lines. In addition, the command has a rudimentary form of scripting language. For complicated operations we recommend a more powerful language like Perl, but for straightforward substitutions sed is useful because it is standard on all Unix systems.

The Special Prompt TIMEFORMAT

There's a shell command time that you will find useful if you care how long programs take to execute. If you preface a command (strictly a pipeline, in other words either one command or a set of commands joined by |) with time, the shell tells you how long it took, possibly together with some other information about the commands that ran. We mention this here since time works by printing out the time taken in a format given by the variable TIMEFORMAT. The format works in a similar way to prompt escapes: the variable contains a string, with various escape sequences for information to output. In this case, the escape sequences are introduced by percent signs. Here is an example:

```
bash$ TIMEFORMAT="real: %3lR; user %3lU; system %3lS"
bash$ time sleep 5
real: 0m5.003s; user 0m0.000s; system 0m0.002s
```

This shows that the command we used—an instruction to do nothing for 5 seconds—actually took slightly over 5 seconds of real time (the value after real:). It took very little processing time, as shown by the values after user: and system:. The difference between these two numbers is more useful in programs you write yourself in C or another language that is compiled; in that case, the user time is the time taken for the code you see, and the system for functions that call into the system. For more on TIMEFORMAT's behavior, see the bash manual (type man bash and search for TIMEFORMAT). Note this is a compilation option for bash, so is not always available inside the shell.

Special Effects

Many users like to make parts of their prompts stand out by using color, or to make the information that usually appears in prompts appear instead in the title bar of their terminal window.

As we'll see, zsh has a few functions that are supplied with the shell to allow tricks using prepackaged "themes." For bash, you need to search on the Web for that sort of thing. A good starting point is the "Bash Prompt HOWTO" available from the Linux Documentation Project, http://www.tldp.org/. If you're not on a GNU/Linux system, some of the more detailed information may not be relevant, but most of it will be. If you search with one of the well-known search engines such as Google, http://www.google.com/, with keywords such as bash prompt themes, you will find lots of suggestions; at the time of writing, however, there didn't seem to be a permanent home for these.

Many of the special effects are not performed by the shell, but by the terminal. To produce them you have to send special sequences to the terminal, another set of escape sequences different from the ones used in prompts. Detailed information on programming terminals is beyond the scope of this book, but we will introduce the subject, and how to make use of the terminal's features from inside prompts.

The possible effects include changing the appearance of the following piece of output text, for example, by emboldening it, underlining it, or coloring it. The effect lasts until it is reset by another escape sequence. Because this is handled by the terminal, the same effects are possible in both bash and zsh, and we'll show examples for both.

The sequences are usually introduced by an escape character. This sequence is produced by your keyboard's Esc key. When it's used as input, the terminal does not intercept the ESCAPE; only outputting it from the shell has the special effect we need here. Here's an example of a sequence you can output in bash or zsh:

```
% echo -e "\e[1mWHAM\e[0m"
WHAM
```

The "WHAM" should be in bold text. The -e option causes echo to turn the \e into escape characters. The sequence \e[1m turns bold on, and \e[0m turns it off again.

Although not all terminals understand these sequences, they are standardized. They are often referred to as "ANSI sequences" from the standards organization that promoted them, although the relevant international standard is ISO 6429. Recent terminal emulators have acquired the ability to do color using escape sequences. If this is supported on your terminal, the following will produce red text on a yellow background. (With some terminals, it may be brown, which is harder to see.) The \e[31m produces the red foreground, and the \e[43m produces the yellow background. We use \e[0m at the end to turn all effects off:

```
% echo -e "\e[31m\e[43mWHAM\e[0m"
WHAM
```

To use these in prompts, you must surround them with prompt escape sequences that tell the shell that the characters inside don't produce any output. (Remember, prompt escapes and terminal escapes are quite different things.) This is so that the shell knows that the escape sequences don't move the cursor, so it can keep track of the position on the command line. In bash, you need to put \[before the sequence and \] after it. Because we aren't using the echo command, we need another way of inserting escape characters. We can do this by using the special version of quotes introduced by $'. Here is an example:

```
bash$ PS1=$'\[\e[31m\e[43m\]\W\[\e[0m\]\$ '
book$
```

This puts the last word of the current directory (called book) in red on yellow, followed by a $ and a space. The actual colors vary a bit between terminals. In zsh, the escape sequence should be surrounded by %{ and %}:

```
zsh% PS1=$'%{\e[31m\e[43m%}%1~%{\e[0m%}%# '
book%
```

In many terminal emulators, terminal escape sequences exist for putting strings into the title bar. The following puts the complete current directory into the title bar of an xterm using bash:

```
bash$ PS1=$'\[\e]2;\]\w\[\a\]\$ '
$
```

Everything before the \$ refers to the title bar, so only the $ and the space are left on the command line. Translating this for zsh is left as an exercise for the reader.

In Table 7-5 we show numbers for standard colors understood by most terminals, both to use the color in the foreground and to use in the background. See our earlier examples for where you should place the number. Note that what is described as yellow may be brown on some terminals, whereas what is described as white may appear gray. In addition to the colors, there are various special codes. The code 0 restores the default colors (foreground and background), 1 produces brighter colors, 4 produces underlined text, and 5 produces flashing text. Often 5 doesn't work; however, many consider the effect to be distracting so this is really not an issue for most users. Also, keep in mind not all terminals are capable of underlining and as a result code 4 may produce some other effect.

Table 7-5. *Color Codes Used in Terminal Escapes*

Color	Code for Foreground	Code for Background
Black	30	40
Red	31	41
Green	32	42
Yellow	33	43
Blue	34	44
Purple	35	45
Cyan	36	46
White	37	47

You can find more information on terminal escape sequences in the zsh function colors. This function is installed with the prompt theme system described in the section "Prompt Themes," later in this chapter. The various functions for the zsh prompt themes also provide examples. The Linux Documentation Project has a description of xterm title bars at http://www.tldp.org/HOWTO/Xterm-Title.html.

Prompts in zsh

Basic prompts in zsh are quite similar to those in bash. The main difference is the way in which escape sequences are handled. Instead of a backslash, they are introduced by a percent sign. Earlier we saw other types of escape that use percent signs, so this isn't too surprising. It will also be familiar to you if you know about prompts in the shell tcsh.

For percent escapes to be replaced, the option prompt_percent has to be turned on, as it usually is. (You'd only turn it off if you needed compatibility with some other shell without these substitutions.)

To be able to include variables and other standard substitutions in your prompts, the option prompt_subst has to be turned on. This is *not* on by default, since very old versions of zsh didn't have the option. It's probably a good idea just to turn it on (with setopt prompt_subst) even if you don't use it; unless you have stray unquoted $'s in your prompt, which isn't likely, it's harmless. (zsh prompts traditionally end with a % rather than a $.) If you do, you can simply put a backslash in front of the $ in the prompt definition.

There are two other options to use with prompts. Many people have problems with the option prompt_cr. It is normally turned on, which makes zsh print a "carriage return" character before printing a prompt. This makes the prompt line up with the left edge of the terminal—even if there was something there. This looks a bit odd in something like the following:

```
zsh% echo -n 'No newline'
zsh%
```

The -n option to echo (and to print) stops it from printing a newline at the end. The text has vanished completely, however. That's because of the carriage return at the start of the next prompt. You can turn the option off:

```
zsh% setopt no_prompt_cr
zsh% print -n 'No newline'
No newlinezsh%
```

Why is this option turned on by default? It's similar to the reason we needed the \[and \] when we inserted escape sequences to change the color in bash. zsh keeps track of the print column so that it knows when the output wraps around to the next line. That information is also crucial for printing prompts on the right-hand side of the screen with RPS1, as discussed below. Most users don't need to print out a lot of things without newlines at the end; for these people, having the prompt_cr option set means the shell does the right thing most of the time. If you don't like it, try with the option not set and see what difference it makes.

Previewing zsh Prompts

Before we discuss zsh's prompt escapes, we'll tell you about how to preview prompts without setting them. We'll also mention a feature that allows you to abbreviate directory names. This can make the string that appears shorter, giving you more space to type.

zsh lets you preview prompts with print -P:

```
zsh% print -rP '%j%# '
0%
```

The %j is replaced by the number of background jobs; 0 appears to show there are none. Next, the % appears because the user is not logged in as root. If the user were root, a # would appear. Note the extra option -r (for raw), which tells print not to expand other sequences special to print, such as \n or \r, since those wouldn't be expanded in the prompt.

The shortening of the home directory is obviously useful, but zsh allows you to have names of your own choosing for any directory, as we'll discuss in the section "Shorthand for Referring to Directories" in Chapter 8. If you set up a name for a directory as we discuss there, it shows up in the prompt as a name, rather than the full directory path.

Prompt Escapes in zsh

All of the bash formats we've discussed thus far have corresponding zsh equivalents. They are shown in the second column next to the corresponding sequences for bash in Table 7-2. From the table you can see that zsh uses strftime just like bash except with a % instead of a \. zsh also has escapes that don't correspond to any in bash. We introduce several in this section; however, you might want to consult the shell's manual for a complete listing (type man zshmisc for the listing).

Directory Components and Full Directory Names

zsh gives you a way of extracting a given number of trailing path segments, without that long substitution with sed we needed in bash. You can put a number between the % and the ~ (or /) and you will get that number of trailing segments. Here is an example using my home directory, /home/pws:

```
zsh% print -rP '%1~%# '
~%
zsh% print -rP '%1/%# '
pws%
```

With the first form, a home directory (or, more generally, any directory for which there is an abbreviated reference) is considered just one segment, so the name isn't shortened. Using the full name of the directory produces the last segment of the path. The number 1 needs to come right after the %.

Showing Information About What the Shell Is Executing

You've already learned about the %_reference for inserting the name of the activity or activities the shell is performing. This is the magic in PS2 that makes the shell display what syntactical structure it's waiting to complete. The default $PS2 is %_>. Remember that PS2 is the continuation prompt; the shell outputs this when the first piece of output wasn't a complete command, so that it is waiting for more.

%_ is also useful in PS4. This prompt is printed out when the shell is executing a script or function and the option xtrace is turned on. We'll see examples of this option in action in the section "Debugging Scripts" in Chapter 13. In this case, %_ will output the names of shell constructs that are being executed, such as if commands and while or for loops. However, a construct may be just about any complex piece of shell programming: not just if blocks and loops, but also quotes and shell functions. %_ is not present in PS4 by default; the default value for PS4 is +%N:%i>. The %N gives you the name of the function or script being executed. It works in normal prompts, but you will usually just get "zsh", which isn't very interesting. The %i refers to the line in the function or script as it was read in. %i is also effective in normal prompts, but note that the number it outputs increases when every prompt is output, including continuations of unfinished lines, and it starts at 1 when the shell starts. It's not the same as the history number, which you can get with %!.

You will probably find it useful to change PS4 to the following, for example:

```
PS4='+%N:%i:%_>'
```

When the option xtrace is turned on (with setopt xtrace) inside a script or function, the value of PS4 is expanded. The value we have given it shows the name of that script or function, the line that is currently being executed, and a list of the types of any blocks of command that are currently being executed. For example:

```
header:30:case> print -n -P - '\e]2;%m:  %~\a'
```

This comes from a function called header, which puts the name of the computer and the current directory into an xterm title bar. The line number is 30, and the shell is in the middle of a case statement, a type of block that allows you to choose code to execute based on patterns (we'll meet the case statement properly in the section "Case Statement" in Chapter 13). After the >, the line being executed appears.

Like the directory escapes, %_ can take a number after the %, which here indicates the maximum number of constructs you want to know about. The number restricts the output to the most recent components.

Visual Effects

You can make the prompt stand out in bold or underline. There is also an effect called "standout," which may mean reverse video or some other striking effect depending on your terminal. Underline isn't always underline and may be a color code if the terminal prefers; my xterm produces a sort of purple. Each of these effects has an uppercase start code and a lowercase stop code:

- %B and %b start and stop bold mode.

- %S and %s start and stop standout mode.

- %U and %u start and stop underline mode.

Let's consider an example. The following command outputs a string with prompt escapes substituted, using %B and %b to activate and deactivate bold text:

```
zsh% print -rP 'show things in %Bbold%b.'
```

Executing this code produces the following result:

```
show things in bold.
```

We described other effects in the terminal in the section "Special Effects" in this chapter. Because these are properties of the terminal rather than the shell, they work the same in bash and zsh. The difference between the shells lies in the way of embedding them inside a prompt.

Advanced Examples

Here are a few more features of the zsh prompt system. They are mostly based around percent escapes but are a little more complicated than just a percent, an optional number, and a single letter code.

Tip If you're playing around with a prompt trying to get it right, an easy way of editing the prompt is to type vared PS1. Then you can edit the prompt and press Return to go back to the normal prompt with your modifications included.

Ternary Expressions

zsh supports a so-called *ternary operator*, which allows you to pick one of two alternatives. (The name "ternary operator" comes from the C programming language.) In the following example, the shell outputs one piece of text if the last command returned the status zero (true), and another if the last command returned a nonzero status (false):

```
zsh% true
zsh% print -rP 'The last status was %(?.zero.non-zero)'
The last status was zero
zsh% false
zsh% print -rP 'The last status was %(?.zero.non-zero)'
The last status was non-zero
```

The special expression is delimited by % at the string's conclusion. (If you need to put a real closing parenthesis inside the expression, you can use %).) Inside, the first character is ?; this behaves a bit like the code in a normal percent escape. (We'll call it the *condition character*.) In this case it indicates the shell should compare the status of the last command with zero. If the status was zero, the shell outputs the text between the dots; if the status was nonzero, the shell outputs the text between the second dot and the closing parenthesis. Hence the differing output based on whether we just executed true or false.

You can compare the command status against numbers other than zero by putting a number either after the % or after the (. (We recommend putting the number after the % since that's consistent with other prompt escapes.) Also, you can use pretty much any character as a separator, not just ., as long as the separator occurs in balanced pairs. (If you use anything that looks like an opening bracket or quote, you should finish with the corresponding closing bracket or quote.) So for example:

```
zsh% false
zsh% print -rP 'The last status was %(1?/one/not one)'
The last status was one
```

Here's how to use this feature to display the status for any command that didn't return success, that is, zero. There's a prompt escape, predictably %?, to display the status itself. A simple version is as follows. We then show a simple example:

```
zsh% PS1='%(?..(%?%))%# '
% false
(1)%
```

This makes use of the %) escape to display a closing parenthesis. The ternary expression shows nothing if the last status was zero, but the status appears in parentheses if it was nonzero. We've shown the new prompt below. Because the command to set the prompt executed successfully, no status was shown. We then executed false, which does nothing except return a nonzero status. This caused the text (1) to appear at the start of the next prompt. Another special effect imitates a feature found in time prompts in tcsh, where on the hour the time shows up as Ding! as if a clock were striking. The same effect in zsh results if you use a ternary expression with the condition character t. This compares the number given (or zero) against the minutes of the current hour. Hence, it's easy to do something special on the hour—in other words, when the minute count is zero. In the example that follows, it's 32 minutes past the hour, so the time shows up normally:

```
zsh% PS1='%(t.Ding!.%D{%L:%M})%# '
12:32%
```

By the way, %L is a zsh extension to strftime formatting. It gives you the hour in the 12-hour format, but if the hour is just a single digit, you only see that digit; there is no leading zero or space. You can do the same (inside %D{*fmt*}) with %K for the hour in 24-hour format, and with %f for the day of the month.

Another useful ternary form has the condition character #. This compares the user ID of the current process against the appropriate number. That allows you to do something different from normal if the shell is running as the superuser, who always has user ID zero. Thus %# is equivalent to %(#.#.%%), where the doubled %% produces a single percent sign in the output.

The final form we'll introduce is with the condition character L. The number here is compared against the variable SHLVL, an abbreviation for shell level. The first instance of the shell to start assigns the value 1 to SHLVL. If you start another shell, it looks at the existing value (assuming it's in the environment, which it usually is), and adds 1 to it, so this shell has SHLVL 2, and so on. You can actually get the raw variable as the percent escape %L, but since most people don't want that number in their prompts probably the ternary form is more interesting.

The easiest way to see how this works is to set the prompt in your .zshrc:

```
PS1='%(2L.+.)%# '
```

Next time you log in, you should see just the familiar "% ". If you don't, maybe you are already on a higher shell level—this can happen if the windowing system runs your shell to initialize, for example. Then SHLVL may already have the value 1 in the environment of windows when they start up. This shows that the shell doesn't need to inherit the value from its immediate parent; it just has to be passed down the process tree. If you're in that position, you should instead use

```
PS1='%(3L.+.)%# '
```

Add the line to your .zshrc. Then when you next log in, the prompt will appear as follows:

```
%
```

If you then start a new shell by typing zsh, the prompt changes, even though the value of PS1 is the same in the new shell:

```
% zsh
+%
```

The expression %(3L.+.) actually tests to see if $SHLVL is *at least* equal to 3, so neither SHLVL=1 or SHLVL=2 would trigger the + to appear.

It's possible to have ternary expressions as part of the text inside another ternary expression. Because all inner expressions are evaluated before the shell returns to look at the outer one, this works without any special quoting or escaping.

Truncating Prompts

The shell has a mechanism for truncating prompts if they get too long. This is useful, for example, if you include the full directory path in your prompt with %/, and that expands to a long path that uses up a lot of the area in which you are typing:

```
zsh% print -rP '%/'
/home/pws/zsh/sourceforge/zsh/Src
zsh% print -rP '%10<..<%/'
../zsh/Src
```

In the example, first we output the complete current directory using prompt syntax. Next, we printed it again, but preceded the directory escape %/ with an instruction to truncate the prompt on the left. A tip for remembering that this truncates on the left is that this the direction in which the < is pointing. The number before the first < gives the maximum length of the truncated string, here 10 characters. The string between the <'s is used when printing the remainder of the prompt would exceed the given length. As it does, the shell prints the two dots at the left, then whatever fits of the remainder of the prompt, here just eight characters. The rest of the prompt can contain any of the normal features of a prompt. Its length is examined only after all the substitutions have been done. The example therefore shows you how to limit the amount of a directory printed by the total number of characters rather than by the number of segments in the path. You can apply truncation only to a particular part of a prompt, too. Truncation is turned off when the length is given as zero, in other words using the expression %<<. Then the shell applies truncation only up to that point; everything after is printed in full. So the previous expression can be expanded to give

```
zsh% print -rP '%10<..<%/%<<%# '
../zshbook%
```

You have the same truncation for the directory path, but the final two characters are always printed in full.

The form %>> works in exactly the same way, but the prompt is truncated at the right-hand end, and the string between the >'s is printed there:

```
zsh% print -rP '%10>..>%/%>>%# '
/home/pw..%
```

Variables in Prompts

We have already mentioned that if you want variables or command substitutions to be expanded inside prompts you need to set the option prompt_subst. There's one special case that works without that option: the variable psvar. It's actually an array, so you assign to it in the form

```
psvar=(one two three four)
```

The shell can extract elements from the array into a prompt using the %v escape. You give this a number to tell it the element of $psvar you want. Hence:

```
zsh% print -rP '%1v and a %2v'
one and a two
```

This form works if you don't have prompt_subst turned on, though you do need the option prompt_percent turned on. However, note that the element of psvar inserted is not further changed when it is put in the prompt; it is exactly the string that was assigned to the array, even if it contains % characters.

Some of the more interesting variable substitutions you might want to consider putting into prompts for one reason or another are $SECONDS, which tells you how many seconds the shell has been running; $COLUMNS, which tells you the width of the terminal; and $RANDOM, which is just a random number. That's probably not all that useful on its own, but you can get some interesting fun effects by using it as part of an expression. This gives you a short random pattern at the start of a prompt (hit Return a few times to see it):

```
zsh% expr='%$(( RANDOM & 1 ))(?./.\\)'
zsh% PS1="$expr$expr$expr$expr%# "
//\\%
///\%
\\\/%
```

The key is the arithmetic expression $((*expr*)), which gets turned into either a one or zero with (roughly) equal probability. (We'll meet shell arithmetic in the section "Numeric Variables and Arithmetic" in Chapter 12.) This requires the prompt_subst option. Any expression substituted by virtue of that option may contain text for use in prompt escapes (this is different from the way psvar works). Here, the arithmetic expression produces either a one or a zero, which is used as an argument to the ? condition code. Hence the resulting expression expands to either the first or the second piece of text, depending on the status of the last command. The doubled backslash, \\, is necessary because backslashes are used for quoting when prompt_subst is turned on. (The rules for prompt_subst are a lot like those for double quotes.)

Prompt Themes

zsh supports a set of "prompt themes." A prompt theme is a complete prompt that has been designed by someone else and bundled with the shell containing many of the pieces of information we've talked about so far. If you like the look of it, you are saved the work of designing your own prompt from scratch. Using this system it takes just a single command to transform a prompt into a different one. This assumes your zsh was installed with all its usual functions. To initialize the prompt theme system, execute the following in either your .zshrc or the command line:

```
autoload -U promptinit
promptinit
```

This makes available the command prompt. Running it with the option -l lists all available prompts. You can then use any of them as an argument to prompt to install that theme. If you give the option -p before the argument, you will be shown a sample of what the prompt looks like; you can preview all themes by only giving the option -p. The preview gives you a hint of what it looks like with a command line by putting in a dummy one. Then you install the theme by giving its name as the only argument:

```
zsh% prompt -l
Currently available prompt themes:
adam1 adam2 bart clint elite2 elite fade fire off oliver redhat suse walters zefram
zsh% prompt -p suse

suse theme:
pws@pwstephenson:~zs/ > command arg1 arg2 ... argn

zsh% prompt suse
pws@pwstephenson:~zs/ >
```

The prompts tend to be long on verbose information and color, and short on conciseness. You can reuse the code that produces colored prompts for your own prompts. Examine the function colors, which is installed as part of the system. You can look at it by typing functions colors. If you receive a message saying the command isn't found, or a brief piece of output containing a line similar to builtin autoload -X, the function isn't loaded yet. You can force the shell to load it by typing autoload +XU colors, just as long as the function is properly installed on your system. Then run functions colors again, and it will show you what the function does.

Showing Prompts on the Right-hand Side

zsh provides a variant of PS1 named RPS1 that appears on the right-hand side of the screen. The most noticeable advantage of the right prompts is that the display is a bit less cluttered, since some of the text is shifted to the right. You can use all the features of the other prompts—the right prompts are processed identically.

Here's an example where we use a short string in PS1 and put the directory in RPS1. On the final line the cursor appears to the right of the ordinary PS1 prompt. Another advantage appears when your typing reaches the right prompt: it simply disappears. So you can use it for information that's handy to have but you don't always need. In the last line, the cursor appears after the first % and a space:

```
zsh% PS1='%# '
% RPS1='%/'
%                                                  /home/pws/src/zsh/Src/Modules
```

Although we're mostly discussing version 4.0 of zsh, a couple of features of 4.2 are worth mentioning. There is a new variable RPS2 to go with PS2, so you can have a continuation prompt on the right. You will probably want to use %^ inside it instead of the %_, to get the shell constructs in reverse order, which is more logical when the prompt is on the right.

Also in zsh 4.2, if you set the option transient_rprompt, the right prompt disappears not only temporarily when you type near it, but permanently when you hit Return on the line. This keeps your terminal window looking neat, highlights the current line, and also (the original intention) makes it much easier to copy text from the window using the mouse. So we recommend it.

One common use of right prompts is for a longer version of the current directory than fits in the main prompt. However, in the section "Special Effects" in this chapter we showed how to put the current directory in the title bar of the shell window, which is usually even neater. You can compromise and use RPS1 on a dumb terminal and the title bar in a window. However, even some dumb terminals allow you to have a status line.

Prompts for Spell Checking

We haven't yet mentioned zsh's ability to perform spell checking. The shell can correct the first word of the name of a command, if you misspell it, and it can correct words in the name of a file. This feature is taken from tcsh. It's fairly simple; there's a much more sophisticated way of performing spelling correction that is available as part of the function-based completion system, which we'll meet in the section "Approximate Completion" in Chapter 10.

You can activate spell checking in various ways:

1. By pressing Esc-s, which tells the line editor to correct the word. However, you are probably better off relying on the completion system. If you have it loaded, you can use Ctrl-x-c to correct the word. This is usually bound to the editor function _correct_word.

2. By setting the option correct. Then when you press Return the shell looks at the command word, and if it doesn't recognize it as a command it tries to find a correction, which it then offers to you.

3. By setting the option `correct_all`. This is like `correct`, but it checks arguments after the command. However, it simply assumes they are files, and tries to correct the words to filenames. Often this isn't what you want.

In the second and third cases, the shell prompts you for what to do using the variable `SPROMPT`, which is processed just as we've discussed earlier. However, there are two additional prompt escapes: `%R` turns into the original string, the one the shell wants to correct, and `%r` turns into what it wants to correct it to.

The default value is `zsh: correct '%R' to '%r' [nyae]?`. The letters in square brackets indicate the letters you can type. Your options are

n: Reject the correction and leave the word alone.

y: Accept the correction.

a: Abort the entire operation and start from scratch—this still causes the line to be added to the command history.

e: Return to edit the line again.

The last one is a good choice if you did make a spelling mistake but the correction offered isn't the right one.

The built-in spelling correction system's corrections are based on the layout of the keyboard; it will try to find nearby letters to correct the spelling. If your keyboard is not the standard English-language "qwerty" keyboard, this is less useful, though there is a shell option `dvorak` for users of the Dvorak layout.

Timing

Like `bash`, `zsh` has the command `time`, but the variable output to show times is `TIMEFMT`. This *doesn't* use the standard prompt escapes; it has its own. It's quite similar to the `bash` variable `TIMEFMT` described in the section "The Special Prompt TIMEFORMAT" in this chapter; see the `zshparam` manual page for details.

Watching Logins and Logouts

A long-standing `zsh` feature taken straight out of `tcsh` is the ability for the shell to tell you when other people log into or out of the computer. This is very useful in an environment such as a school or university where you want to know when your friends are there for you to contact. You set the array `watch` to a list of usernames. You can use the names `all` or `notme`, too, which watch for everyone or everyone except your own username, respectively.

If one of those users logs in or out, the shell then prompts you with the variable `WATCHFMT`, which has its own prompt escapes. This means that `WATCHFMT` does not understand the escapes we described for the PS strings. The default is `%n has %a %l from %m`, where the escapes get turned into a username (`%n`), "logged on" or "logged off" (`%a`), the terminal or possibly display (`%l`), and the host they logged in from, if it was a remote login (`%m`). This always happens right before a prompt is printed, and only if at least `$LOGCHECK` seconds (default is 60) have elapsed since the last check. You can set `LOGCHECK` to zero so it checks each time. There's a command `log` to show if the users requested are already logged in:

```
zsh% watch=(all)
zsh% log
pws has logged on :0 from .
pws has logged on pts/0 from .
```

This says I've started up a session on the main display (the only one, in fact), called :0 in normal X Window System notation. I also have a terminal emulator running, which is using the terminal device /dev/pts/0. The terminal is useful mostly for sending immediate messages to someone using the write or talk command.

You might want to make the message that is printed more or less verbose. Here we show how to customize WATCHFMT to change what the shell reports when it detects a user logging in or logging out. This uses ternary sequences similar to the ones used by the PS variables.

```
zsh% WATCHFMT="The %(a.eager beaver.lazy so-and-so) %n has \
dquote> %(a.appeared.vanished) at %t."
zsh%
The eager beaver pws has appeared at 12:25.
zsh%
The lazy so-and-so pws has vanished at 12:25.
```

To demonstrate this example, I logged in and out on a different terminal and pressed Return in the appropriate place to see the message.

More Special Output Formatting

We've demonstrated how you can incorporate special visual effects into your prompts using special escape sequences such as %B for bold, and also how to put colors in prompts. Two zsh commands allow you to send other sorts of output to the terminal resulting in special effects. The results you can obtain are similar to those we discussed in the section "Special Effects" earlier in this chapter, but they are independent of the terminal type. The effects can be quite powerful, but they are also quite inconvenient since you need to know at least a little of how Unix-style systems handle different terminals.

In the old days, there was *termcap*, a library of terminal capabilities. Everything the terminal could do was encoded as a set of two-character codes, some of which took numeric arguments. For example, the string RI means move right a given number of characters. In zsh you can use the command echotc to output one of these codes, with the arguments given if any:

```
zsh% print -n hello; echotc RI 32; print goodbye
hello                           goodbye
```

We used print -n to output a string without a newline, then made the cursor move right 32 characters, then printed a string, this time with a newline at the end. Table 7-6 shows some termcap codes you might find useful.

Table 7-6. *A Few of the More Useful* termcap *Codes*

Code	Function
Move to Absolute Position	
cl	Clears window and moves cursor to top left
ll	Moves cursor to lower left of window
ho	Moves cursor to top left of window
cm	Moves cursor to row *arg1*, column *arg2* from top left
cr	Carriage return: moves cursor to start of line
Delete and Insert Text	
cd	Clears from cursor to end of screen
ce	Clears from cursor to end of line
dc	Deletes one character, moving the remainder of the line left
DC	Deletes *arg* characters, moving the remainder of the line left
ec	Turns *arg* characters to spaces starting from cursor
ic	Inserts one character, moving the remainder of the line right
IC	Inserts *arg* characters, moving the remainder of the line right
Move Cursor to Relative Position	
up	Moves cursor up one line
UP	Moves cursor up *arg* lines
do	Moves cursor down one line
DO	Moves cursor down *arg* lines
le	Moves cursor left one character
LE	Moves cursor left *arg* characters
nd	Moves cursor right one character
RI	Moves cursor right *arg* characters
Enable and Disable Special Text Effects	
md	Starts bold mode for text
mr	Starts reverse mode for text
so	Starts standout mode for text
se	Ends standout mode for text

Table 7-6. *A Few of the More Useful* `termcap` *Codes (Continued)*

Code	Function
us	Starts underlining text
ue	Ends underlining text
me	Ends all special text modes, return to normal text

* *Where* arg *is shown, the code needs to be followed by a numeric argument; where* arg1 *and* arg2 *are shown, two numeric arguments are required.*

There are `termcap` codes for bold and reverse characters, for the strings sent by certain keys (useful on input), and for clearing bits of the display, as well as moving the cursor; anything you might want to do to the terminal other than simply outputting a character is probably there somewhere. We show a few of the sequences you are most likely to want in Table 7-6. However, different terminals have different sets of capabilities; there is no standard for things the terminal has to do, so the results will vary. `zsh` gives you an error message if the terminal doesn't have a particular capability. Further discussion of the things you can do with `termcap` are well outside the scope of this book. Have a look at the manual entry for `termcap` if you want to know more.

When `termcap` started to look a bit outmoded, it was replaced by a system called *terminfo*, whose derivation is obvious enough. `zsh` isn't always compiled with links to the `terminfo` database, but if it is then the command `echoti` is available, and you should consult the `terminfo` manual entry. The names of `terminfo` capabilities are often similar to `termcap` ones, but are not restricted to two characters. Your system will use one of the two. Quite often both are available.

Checking for Mail and Idle Terminals

We'll wind up this chapter with some things that happen just after a command has finished executing, and just before the shell prints the main prompt (`PS1`) for you to enter a new command. We've already dealt with one of these, the `watch` facility. We'll also discuss scheduled events in `zsh` and timeouts.

Checking for New Mail

The shell can be used to notify the user when new mail arrives. `bash` and `zsh` offer a similar mechanism for doing so. If mail arrives, the shell prints a message just above the prompt. In the following example all the output comes from the shell. The cursor is placed after the prompt:

```
You have new mail in /var/spool/mail/pws
bash$
```

First, you can set the variable `MAILCHECK` to how often you want it to check for mail, in seconds. Since the shell will in any case only check before the display of each new prompt, it's perfectly reasonable to set this to 0 so that the shell will check on every prompt.

You can set the variable `MAIL` to a file where your mail is kept, but it's more powerful to use the variable `MAILPATH`, which you can give a list of places to check. This exists in both shells, and like the variable `PATH` it consists of pathnames concatenated with colons between the individual names. In zsh, MAILPATH has a companion variable mailpath. This is an array that contains the same information in a different form. (Many variables in zsh that contain colon-separated paths exist in pairs like this.) Arrays tend to be easier to deal with, so we recommend using mailpath.

You need to know where the system stores your mail. Typically, this is somewhere like /var/spool/mail/$USER or /var/mail/$USER. You may need $LOGNAME instead of $USER on some systems, or just insert your own username directly.

That may be the only place where mail arrives; you only need to check other files if they are specially configured. For example, if you run the command procmail to sort mail into a particular file when it arrives, you can add those files to the mail path. Let's suppose you have this or some other mail sorting program which filters mail from the zsh mailing list into the file ~/Mail/zsh-new. The following code will check for mail using either bash or zsh:

```
MAILPATH=/var/spool/mail/pws:\
~/Mail/zsh-new'?New zsh list mail'
```

The following code is supported only by zsh:

```
mailpath=(
  /var/spool/mail/pws
  ~/Mail/zsh-new'?New zsh list mail'
)
```

Note that as with all assignments in bash and zsh there is no space immediately before or after the = in either case. There are quotes in both versions for the question mark and the text after; this is needed because of the special character ? and the spaces inside the list item. As you probably guessed from the phrase, that text gives a message to be printed when the shell finds mail in the file named just before. We haven't bothered giving the main mail file a prompt, since there's a reasonable default. In zsh this is "You have new mail". (Note that the variable MAIL doesn't take a prompt; it must contain just a single filename.)

You can put the variable substitution $_ inside the prompt part and it will be turned into the filename. Make sure you use single quotes around this; as we explained for prompts, that prevents the variable from being expanded when you define MAILPATH or mailpath, which isn't what you want.

Scheduling Commands to Happen Before Prompts

It's possible to tell the shell to execute any command line at a particular time of day. You may know that Unix has facilities called at and cron, which can execute a set of commands at a certain time of day. The shell facility is useful when you need the output from commands to appear on the terminal; at and cron have no knowledge of your terminal. Hence the shell's built-in facility is often used for printing messages such as reminders to yourself. We're mentioning the facility here because is it always occurs just before the prompt for a new command line is printed, like the mail check. In fact, it occurs just after the mail check, assuming that both tasks are scheduled to occur. It's a very simple command:

```
sched 17:34 echo Time to go
```

This prints the message on your terminal the next time after 17:34 that the shell is about to print a prompt. The `sched` command on its own lists scheduled events with the event numbers (the first thing on the line), and `sched` *-num* with the number of the event removes the scheduled event.

If you're going to use `sched` with a command significantly more complicated than what we've shown, it's probably better to put the command in a shell function, described in Chapter 13. Otherwise, it can be quite complicated to decide what parts of the line are evaluated immediately when you type `sched` or have it run from an initialization file, and what parts are run only when the alarm goes off. Burying the second set inside a function makes this completely clear.

Watching for an Idle Terminal

Assigning a number to the shell variable TMOUT gives it a timeout value in seconds. If the terminal is idle for this long, the shell will exit.

```
zsh% TMOUT=30
```

Wait 30 seconds and your terminal will disappear. You may see the message "zsh: timeout" go floating by. That's quite useful for security on a dumb terminal, since it will usually log you out; it's less useful on a graphical display, where you will need to have the screen locked to prevent people doing unpleasant things while you are away. However, it's also useful if you have a terminal window where you are logged in as root. Then if you go away from the terminal the shell will exit, preventing anyone else from gaining root access. The timeout works by sending a signal, SIGALRM, to the shell. In `zsh`, you can define a function TRAPALRM to handle this signal as an alternative to the shell exiting. See the section "Trapping Signals" in Chapter 13 for an explanation of trapping signals. The following `zsh` code updates a clock in an `xterm` title bar every 30 seconds:

```
TRAPALRM() {
  print -nP "\e]2;%T\a"
  TMOUT=30
}
TMOUT=30
```

This uses several of the features we have met during the chapter. `print -nP` prints a string with no newline at the end using prompt escapes. The escape %T outputs the time. The string also contains the terminal escapes for inserting a string into the title bar, and resetting the output to normal afterwards. Finally, the function sets the timeout back to 30 seconds so that it will be re-executed then. After defining the function, we start the timeout for the first time. Nothing will happen until you leave the terminal alone for half a minute; then the time will appear. As long as you don't type anything, it will continue to be updated.

Summary

In this chapter we have seen the following:

- The various prompt variables that the shell uses to decide how to format information to display

- The system of prompt escapes that tell the shell to insert special information like the current directory or the time

- Similarities and differences between bash and zsh in outputting this information

- How to use the terminal's capabilities to enhance the output, whether by adding color or putting text in the window's title bar

- How the shell outputs information when telling you about the time a command has taken, or when asking you whether to correct spelling, or when telling you about logins and logouts

- How the shell can output other information between finishing a command and printing a new prompt, such as indicating the presence of new mail, or giving you a message at a certain time

In the next chapter we will have a closer look at how files and directories work in Unix. Whether the shell is running programs or manipulating input, it interacts with files a great deal. Knowing a little more will therefore help you work more efficiently.

## CHAPTER 8

Files and Directories

This chapter talks a bit more about files and directories and what the shell can do with them. Refer back to the section "The Filesystem: Directories, Pathnames" in Chapter 1 for an introduction to files if you're vague on the basics. Specifically, the topics covered in this chapter include

- Exploring the various types of files present in a Unix filesystem

- Learning how to make one type of file, links, work for you

- Finding files and commands

- Making changing directories easier

- Referring to directories in a shortened form in both shells, particularly zsh

- Using braces to expand a set of filenames (or other arguments) without repeatedly typing the same text

- Redirecting the input and output of commands

One key area related to file handling is so important that the entire next chapter is devoted to the topic. That's filename generation, also known as "globbing" or pattern matching.

Types of Files

In this section we'll introduce the various file types. You will already be familiar with the simple types; however, we're guessing that there are others that may be new to you.

Directories

We list directories first because the first thing you need to know about a file is what directory it's in. By now you are familiar with the current directory, and how to change it with cd. We'll reveal some more magic with cd below. You also know the difference between absolute filenames (those that begin with a / or ~) and relative filenames (those that don't).

Regular Files

Regular files are exactly that; the files that you typically call a "file," such as a text document or JPEG image. But to the computer everything is just a name in a directory, even another directory.

That's why when you execute ls you see directories mixed in with everything else. In the following listing we use the -l option to see the full file details. Regular files are the ones with a dash in the first character:

```
% ls -l
total 8
-rw-r--r--    1 pws       users          73 Aug  5 22:42 plain.txt
drwxr-xr-x    2 pws       users        4096 Aug  5 22:42 subdir
```

The first entry is a regular file, while the second is a directory.

Executable Files

The third type, executable files or external commands, is really just a subset of the second type. Unless you're using Cygwin, the only distinction between a command or executable script and any other type of file is that the *execute permission* is set. We introduced the notion of an executable script file in the section "Making a Script File" in Chapter 2; as far as the permissions are concerned, the same idea applies for all other executable files. Let's copy a command from another directory into the one shown in the previous listing (I simply copied it from /usr/bin, in fact):

```
% ls -l
total 8
-rwxr-xr-x    1 pws       users      557656 Aug  5 22:48 cvs
-rw-r--r--    1 pws       users          73 Aug  5 22:42 plain.txt
drwxr-xr-x    2 pws       users        4096 Aug  5 22:42 subdir
```

That new first file, with all the x's, is a command. Usually commands live in the directories given by the variable PATH rather than just lying around anywhere, but there's nothing special about the directories in PATH. You can add any directory you like to PATH, regardless of what the directory contains. (You will need an absolute path to make sure it always refers to the same directory.)

Cygwin inherits the Windows requirement that executable files are those ending in .exe. (Windows can execute files with other suffixes such as .bat and .com. A .bat file is a set of commands like a script, and a .com file is a type of executable that is less common than an .exe file.) There is no real executable bit in the permissions; Cygwin just makes it up for you based on the suffix. It does a little bit extra, however; if you try to run prog as a program but it doesn't exist, Cygwin will look for a file in the path called prog.exe and run that instead. This gives you a hybrid of Unix and Windows command handling. Actually, newer Windows filesystems do have the concept of an execute permission. What's more, not just executables but shared libraries—.dll files, which provide support for programs—need to have execute permission.

Links

The link is a type of file many expert shell users find a big help. A link is a pointer to another file. More precisely, it is an entry in the filesystem that indicates where another file is to be found. Actually, there are two types of link on Unix systems, referred to as hard and symbolic (or soft) links. It's quite important to know the differences between them.

Hard Links

A *hard link* is really just another name for the same file, either in the same directory or somewhere else. File renaming works by creating a hard link to the new filename:

```
% echo Hello >firstname
% mv firstname secondname
```

This example starts by creating a file firstname by writing the string Hello into it, then renames the file to secondname. Although the underlying process isn't obvious, it does it by creating secondname as a hard link and removing firstname. Note that despite the name of the command mv it will always try simply to rename a file if it can; it will only actually move it if it needs to store the contents somewhere else—for example, on a different disk. Moving to a different directory on the same disk is done simply by renaming.

You can make the system skip the delete stage by replacing the mv with ln for link. Now both names are valid, until you delete one of them. Here's the mv example with the steps spelled out:

```
% ln firstname secondname
```

The file now has two names, firstname and secondname. You can see this from the following command. The 2 in the second column for each file is the number of links to the file:

```
% ls -l
-rw-r--r--    2 pws     users        6 Jun 24 22:41 firstname
-rw-r--r--    2 pws     users        6 Jun 24 22:41 secondname
```

How can you tell they're really the same file? Unix assigns a unique number to each file on a filesystem, called the *inode*. The option -i to ls shows this number; you can combine -i with the -l as ls -li, if you like. The following code shows that the inodes of the two files are the same:

```
% ls -i
653340 firstname   653340 secondname
```

Now we delete the original name of the file, leaving the second as the only name:

```
% rm firstname
```

The details of renaming and moving files can be more complicated. In particular, if a file is moved to a different filesystem, it always needs to be copied. This means that making a hard link isn't sufficient. Therefore, moving a large file to a different filesystem takes a lot more work than moving it somewhere else on the same filesystem. Another detail is that modern Unix systems can perform renaming in a single step. This means that programs will always see either the old name or the new one for a file.

Symbolic Links

Hard links have their limitations. For one thing, you can't make hard links to a directory. For another, as we just pointed out, hard links to the same file have to be on the same filesystem.

The symbolic link was invented to get around these limitations. It's also called a soft link, to distinguish it from the hard link. You create a symbolic link with ln -s. Here's a simple example:

```
% echo You have my word on it. >original.txt
% ln -s original.txt link
% ls -l
total 4
lrwxrwxrwx    1 pws     users              12 Aug  6 23:10 link -> original.txt
-rw-r--r--    1 pws     users              23 Aug  6 23:10 original.txt
% cat link
You have my word on it.
```

The new file is simply a pointer to the original. When we reference link, we find ourselves looking at the original file. The long directory listing for a symbolic link starts with l. The permissions after that aren't useful and you should ignore them; the important permissions are the ones for the file the link is pointing to. The length of the link—the 12 just before the date and time—is simply the number of characters of the name being linked to.

It's quite useful to think of the link as simply a place to hold the name of the file pointed to, original.txt. So, for example, if you deleted original.txt the link would still be there, pointing at a file that no longer exists. If you tried to edit link, it would re-create the file original.txt when you saved any changes.

There are a few times when the system doesn't follow the link but uses it directly. You've seen one, ls -l. Another important case is when you delete the link. Then only the link is removed; whatever it points to isn't touched. It's the same if you use mv to rename a link; the link is modified, while what it points to stays put. However, if you copy a link with cp, then the contents are copied, so that the file you're writing to will contain a separate copy of those contents, not just another pointer back to the original.

As we've hinted, you can create symbolic links to directories. There's a special option -L to ls to make it follow the link. Take this example:

```
% ln -s ~ myhome
% ls -l myhome
lrwxrwxrwx    1 pws        users          27 Jan 11 18:45 myhome -> /home/pws
% ls -lL myhome
total 116
drwx------    3 pws        users        4096 Jan 10 20:39 Desktop
drwx------    3 pws        users        4096 Jan  5 20:51 Mail
drwxr-xr-x    3 pws        users        4096 Dec 19 19:30 bin
drwxr-xr-x   16 pws        users        4096 Dec 19 19:42 src
```

The file myhome provides a link to my home directory. You can use myhome just as part of a pathname, for example myhome/Mail. This always works, not just in the shell but anywhere you can give a path.

The way relative pathnames are handled by symbolic links takes a little getting used to. Suppose we want to create a link in subdirectory subdir to file in the directory we're in. You might think you'd do this:

```
# Wrong!
% ln -s file subdir/link
```

You can see why that's wrong if you remember two things:

- Symbolic links store a pointer to a filename as a string.

- When a link tries to find the referenced file, the system starts looking from the directory the link was in, not the current directory. Think about it—it has to, because otherwise symbolic links would refer to different files depending on where you accessed them from!

In this case, the string stored in subdir/link would be file. When you look at subdir/link, the system looks for file starting in subdir, and of course doesn't find it, because it's in the next directory up.

What you need to do is this:

```
% ln -s ../file subdir/link
```

It's a little bizarre, because from the directory you're in there is no ../file. If you want to keep your mind from reeling, you could do it like this instead:

```
% cd subdir
% ln -s ../file link
```

When you are sitting in the same directory in which you're creating the link, it becomes much more obvious what the link is referring to. Of course, you can always use an absolute path, but that will stop working if you rename an intervening directory, while the commands above just rely on the file being in the parent directory, whatever it's called.

Device Files

If you look in the directory /dev on a Unix system, you'll see a lot of files with cryptic names. (On many modern systems they're mostly in subdirectories rather than in /dev itself.) Running ls -l will show you lines beginning with b and c that correspond to special files, among other files. They refer to hardware *devices* that operate by blocks of characters (the lines with a b in the first column) and by individual characters (the lines with a c in the first column). A device is usually some peripheral attached to the computer. Unix is a little unusual in making devices look like files in this fashion.

For example, the terminal on most systems is known as a character device; if you write to the device, instead of the text ending up on the disk, it appears on the screen:

```
% echo Hello there >/dev/tty
Hello there
```

This is the same as if you hadn't redirected it. It's more useful in a command where most of the output goes somewhere else. For example, you could use the previous lines in a function or script that you use to create output for a file.

The special file named /dev/tty always refers to the terminal of the process writing to it, so it can be a different physical device for each process.

If you're using Cygwin, you won't find anything of interest in /dev, because Windows doesn't work that way. However, Unix programmers are so used to being able to use /dev/tty and other fixed paths that Cygwin pretends they exist and tries to do the right thing anyway. So don't be surprised to see references to /dev in scripts and functions that run on Cygwin.

On Unix, disks, mice, modems, and printer ports can also be accessed by special files. They are very rarely used directly from the shell, however. We'll now discuss a few devices that are useful in the shell.

The Null Device

The file /dev/null exists on all Unix, Linux, and similar systems. (The equivalent on Windows is NUL, with no directory name.) Any output sent to /dev/null is simply thrown away by the operating system. This is very useful for redirecting standard output when you aren't interested in the results. The following runs myprog with standard output thrown away. That might be useful if you know what the output will be and are not interested in it; the unwanted output might clutter up the output of a script, for example.

```
myprog >/dev/null
```

You can also redirect input from /dev/null. If the program reads its input, it will immediately see the end of the file. This can be used to stop a program reading from the terminal. /dev/null is often used with redirection; see the section "Redirection" in this chapter for more on that important topic.

The Zero Device

Although it's less useful for shell programming, there is a special file /dev/zero that provides an infinite stream of null bytes. That's an ASCII NUL, or character 0, not the character representing a printable zero in ASCII. We'll illustrate this by running the command od (standing for "octal dump") on the file. This shows the bytes in the file as a set of octal (base eight) numbers; here, as we've said, all the bytes are zero. The * indicates that the line above it is repeated. You will need to press Ctrl-c to stop the command endlessly reading zeros:

```
% od /dev/zero
0000000 000000 000000 000000 000000 000000 000000 000000 000000
*
```

This is very specialized; unless you are a system administrator, you are not likely to use /dev/zero.

FIFOs

A widely available, and quite useful, type is the *FIFO*, or first-in, first-out special file. It's basically just a pipe with a name—FIFOs are also called *named pipes*, in fact. They can be quite useful for some special uses. If you want to try one out, you'll need two terminal windows open in the same directory. In one window type the following:

```
% mknod fifo p
% ls -l fifo
prw-r--r--   1 pws    users          0 Aug  6 23:44 fifo
% echo Hello >fifo
```

(A more recent command that does the same as mknod but has a more obvious syntax is mkfifo. You use this as mkfifo *fifo*.) We put the ls -l in just to show you it really does look like a file, only with a different type. You'll notice the shell has apparently hung up at this point; that's because no one's attempting to read from the other end of the FIFO, so it can't finish writing. Now in the other window type the following:

```
% read var <fifo
% echo $var
Hello
```

When you read from `fifo`, the other terminal finishes writing, and the word `Hello` passes through the FIFO and into the shell variable var. Unlike a pipe created with |, a FIFO stays there until you delete it by hand; you can use it as often as you like.

One use for FIFOs is to send input to a running process. The process tries to read from a particular FIFO whose name you know. The FIFO doesn't have to have been created from the shell you're running, unlike a normal pipe. It doesn't even need to have been started by you at all. You simply need write permission on the FIFO, and this works just as it does for writing to a regular file. FIFOs can be a powerful way of communicating between different processes.

Here's an example. Some programs that deal with security need to accept random numbers from a file. The environment variable `RANDFILE` is often used to specify the name of the file. On some operating systems such as Linux, there is a special file (`/dev/random` on Linux) that provides random numbers. If there is no such file, you can consider writing a program to provide the random numbers. That's well outside the scope of this book, but let's suppose there is a program called `randomize` that produces random bytes on its standard output. (We'll talk about standard output in the section "File Descriptors" in this chapter.) We make the random numbers appear to be a file by creating a FIFO. Then we start `randomize` with its output to the FIFO. The command line ends with an ampersand to run it in the background:

```
% mknod /tmp/rng.fifo p
% randomize >/tmp/rng.fifo &
```

Now the file `/tmp/rng.fifo` can be used as a source of random numbers, for example by exporting `RANDFILE=/tmp/rng.fifo`. When you run a program that reads from that file, its input will actually come from the output of `randomize`. Note that when the reading program exits it's quite likely that `randomize` will exit, too, since it detects that there is nowhere to write its output to any more. (You might see a message such as "broken pipe" when `randomize` exits.) You can restart `randomize` to use it again, however.

Finding Commands and Files

You will often want to find something—either a command or another file—on your system. The procedures for finding commands and for finding files are a bit different, so we'll examine them separately.

Finding a Command

If you simply want to find a command in your path, you can use the built-in type, common to both `bash` and `zsh`, followed by the name of the command or commands, and the shell will print out its location. It's not restricted to external commands; if you give it the name of an alias, a shell function, or a shell built-in it will report what they are. Here is an example in `zsh`:

```
zsh% type cvs ll chpwd echo
cvs is /usr/local/bin/cvs
ll is an alias for ls -l
chpwd is a shell function
echo is a shell builtin
```

Note that the shell only gives you a location for a file for external commands, cvs in our example; otherwise it prints a message saying what type of command the shell has found. Here is a similar example using bash:

```
bash$ type cvs ll l echo
cvs is /usr/local/bin/cvs
ll is aliased to `ls -l`
l is a function
l ()
{
    less "$@"
}
echo is a shell builtin
```

We've shown a function, l, which acts as an abbreviation for calling the less command. As you can see, bash is a bit more verbose about functions. You can achieve a similar effect in zsh with one of the following commands or options:

- The functions command, which lists only functions but lists them in full.

- The which command. This is inherited from the C shell, but has slightly different behavior. This function also exists in recent versions of bash.

- The option type -f lists functions in full, but still lists other types of commands, too.

Actually, the basic command in zsh that provides all the other ways of finding commands is whence. It's used by which and type, although functions is different since you can also use it to set attributes for shell functions. All are simply whence with different options. That's useful to know if you're looking in the zsh manual pages. Otherwise, just stick with whichever version you like.

Like many zsh listing commands, whence takes the option -m for "match", which causes it to treat all its arguments like patterns. These are the same patterns used everywhere in zsh, and are the same patterns used for matching files that we discuss in the next chapter. They are not regular expressions as you use with grep. Make sure you quote the patterns to stop the shell from expanding them immediately as files in the current directory:

```
zsh% whence -m 'xg*'
/usr/local/bin/xgalaga
/usr/X11R6/bin/xgc
/usr/bin/xgettext
/usr/X11R6/bin/xgamma
```

A basic whence is less verbose than type, which is equivalent to whence -v. This, too, searches for all types of command, not just external ones:

```
zsh% whence -vm '*read'
_read is a shell function
_acroread is a shell function
zftpfn_read is a shell function
read is a shell builtin
timed-read is /usr/bin/timed-read
kspread is /usr/bin/kspread
ppmspread is /usr/bin/ppmspread
acroread is /usr/local/bin/acroread
```

We haven't talked about what happens when you add a new command somewhere in the command search path. Usually, this isn't a problem; the shell will search for the new command. However, if there is already a command of the same name later in the search path, the shell will use the old command instead of the new one. This is because the shell keeps a list of commands so that it can quickly find out the location from the name. The list of commands is called a *hash table* from the way it is stored. You can issue the command hash -r (or, in zsh only, rehash) to fix this. We talked a little about that in the section "Programs and the Path" in Chapter 2.

Finding Other Files

Suppose you know that a file lives somewhere under a particular directory, for example your home directory, but you can't pinpoint the exact location. The usual way of finding the file is to use the find command. Unfortunately, this command has a rather bizarre syntax. Here's how to find a file called addrs.txt under your home directory:

```
% find ~ -name addrs.txt -print
/home/pws/text/addrs.txt
/home/pws/text/writing/addrs.txt
```

The command accepts as input a whole series of options, some (like -name) with an argument, some (like -print) without. It starts at the directory you give first, in this case ~, and descends through all the directories below it, examining each file for a potential match, including subdirectories. The match criteria are determined by the supplied options, with each option representing a test. The option -name causes find to compare each filename with the argument that follows the option. If it matches, the test succeeds, and find goes on to -print. That doesn't look like a test, and in fact it always acts as if the test were true. It has the side effect of printing the filename including the directory portion of the name. The ~ is expanded to /home/pws in this output. (That was done by the shell before the command executed.)

The find command allows you to use patterns, but you must remember to put quotes around them so that the shell doesn't expand them to the name of files in the current directory. Here's an example of how you might find this confusing. Suppose you're looking for files ending in .c with the pattern *.c. You issue the following (incorrect) command:

```
% find . -name *.c -print
./testprog.c
```

Only one file was found, but you are sure there are more in subdirectories. What happened? The shell expanded the pattern *.c to testprog.c and then passed this argument to find. So the command only searched for files called testprog.c, and there was only one. Let's do it properly by quoting the pattern:

```
% find . -name '*.c' -print
./Src/main.c
./Src/options.c
./Src/utils.c
./testprog.c
```

Now find has been given the pattern as an argument, as you wanted. Once you've got the idea of find, you can read the manual for more of the long list of tests it can perform. We'll show you a few more examples.

First, let's consider how to test for the type of a file, in this case for a directory. Let's look for all directories called tmp. This time, we'll tell find to output more detailed information about the file. We can do this by using the option -ls, which produces output similar to the command ls -l, although with a few extra pieces of information. The output depends on the version of find; in the example we show, from GNU find, the first number on the left is the inode we mentioned earlier in our discussion of hard links:

```
% find ~ -name tmp -type d -ls
1114154   4 drwxrwxr-x  21 pws    users   4096 Sep 14 19:05 /home/pws/tmp
508128    4 drwxr-xr-x   2 pws    users   4096 Feb 25  2003 /home/pws/.gimp-1.2/tmp
```

The next example shows how you can make find choose one of a set of alternatives. This is most useful when the files you are searching for could have different names that aren't easily written in a single pattern. This example looks for some types of file that might have been generated by compiling on a Windows system:

```
% find . \( -name '*.exe' -or -name '*.obj' \) -print
./src/main.obj
./src/output.obj
./bin/program.exe
```

The code now includes parentheses with backslashes in front and -or in the middle. (The parentheses are quoted because they are special to the shell.) The effect is that the expression in parentheses is considered true if either of the two -name tests is true. You can have extra -or's, or extra levels of parentheses, if you need them.

Using find to Execute a Command

A more powerful feature of find is to execute a command for each file found. For simple actions, this can be done with another rather strange addition to the find command line. Here's a typical example that uses rm to remove the files it finds (anything ending in .o):

```
find . -name '*.o' -print -exec rm {} ';'
```

(That's about as cryptic as find gets.) The {} is replaced by the name of the file it found, with the path. The ";" indicates the end of the command line that followed -exec.

We've written it so that the command shows what it's deleting, but obviously you need to be careful here. You might want to start with just -print and then add -exec and its arguments. Alternatively, you might want to replace rm with rm -i, which asks you for confirmation on every file. Some versions of find allow you to use -ok instead of -exec; find will ask you for confirmation before executing the command for each file.

Running find in a Pipeline

When running find on its own isn't powerful enough, there are other ways of passing the names of files to other commands. One is to use find -print to get the list of names printed out, one per line. Then use the command xargs to run another command once for each line. Here's the previous example rewritten to use the combination:

```
find . -name '*.o' -print | xargs rm
```

The xargs command collects the output from find and runs rm with all the output from those lines as set of arguments. It's therefore often faster than find with -exec, which always runs one command for each file found.

Tip Filenames may contain space characters. This is very common on Windows, which uses a lot of spaces in the names of the directories it creates for you, such as My Documents. However, the problems caused by spaces in filenames occur regardless of the operating system. Spaces cause problems for xargs when it divides up the arguments passed to it. If you want to protect against this, you can tell both find and xargs that null characters (ASCII 0) are to be used to divide up the arguments instead. This is bound to work, since nulls aren't allowed in filenames. You need to modify both commands to tell them about the nulls:

```
find . -name '*.o' -print0 | xargs -0 rm
```

Not all versions of find and xargs understand this syntax.

Your last resort with a long list of files is to read them as a shell variable with the shell's read command and then process that variable. Running read in a loop to read output from find or a similar command is a common trick we'll meet in the section "Reading Input" in Chapter 13.

Tip With zsh you can often dispense with find altogether and use the shell's built-in ability to search through directories using **. Here's the rm example rewritten, including the list of files it's about to delete; it looks a lot more natural as a pair of commands. Note the option -l to print to make it output one argument per line:

```
zsh% print -l **/*.o
tmp/gas.o
zsh/sourceforge/4_0/zsh/Src/builtin.o
... lots of other hits...
zsh% rm **/*.o
```

We discuss ** in more detail in the section "Recursive Searching" in Chapter 9.

The locate Command

The locate command allows you to find commands much faster than find because it keeps a database of all the files on the system. It's quite a new addition to Unix and GNU-based systems and is not always installed. Some systems have `slocate`, a more secure version that is often installed under the name `locate`.

The output of the command is only accurate if the database is kept up to date. The database is updated either by `updatedb` or an option to `locate` itself. The update commands use a configuration file, usually `/etc/updatedb.conf`, to decide which directories to search and which not to. Then the update command must be run every now and then. If `locate` came in a package, all this may happen automatically. Otherwise, see the documentation that came with the program.

Once the database is present, `locate` is easy to use. If you give it part of a filename (any part), it will show the full path:

```
% locate grep
/usr/bin/bzgrep
/usr/bin/zipgrep
/usr/bin/pgrep
/usr/bin/zgrep
/usr/bin/pcregrep
/usr/bin/msggrep
/usr/bin/grep-changelog
/usr/bin/rgrep
/usr/bin/xine-bugreport
/bin/egrep
/bin/fgrep
/bin/grep
```

One of the problems with `locate` is often the sheer volume of output. If you know the exact name of the file you are searching for, try this:

```
% locate '*/grep'
/bin/grep
```

That works because when `locate` sees the wildcard * in the argument it doesn't add wildcards of its own. So this guarantees that grep is the last part of the path, with nothing following it. You can put wildcards anywhere in the argument.

Managing Directories with the Shell

You will certainly have used `cd` to change directories by now. Since changing directories is so common, several special features are associated with the command. Later we'll explain about a further enhancement, the directory stack, which allows you to juggle multiple directories. We'll start off with some features of `cd` that are common to both `bash` and `zsh`.

We've already met the `CDPATH` variable in the section "Quick Directory Changes with cdpath" in Chapter 3, so we won't mention it here.

Features of cd

Two common places you want to change to are your home directory, and the directory you were in before the current one. There are abbreviations for both of these.

- To change to your home directory, just type `cd` on its own. We explained this in the section "Relative Pathnames and Your Current Directory" in Chapter 1.

- To change to the directory you were in before, use `cd -`. This gives the following behavior:

```
% pwd
/home/pws/zsh/projects/zshbook
% cd
% pwd
/home/pws
% cd -
% pwd
/home/pws/zsh/projects/zshbook
```

- If you keep typing `cd -`, you will keep switching between the two directories. When you change directories the shell sets the variable `OLDPWD` to the directory you are leaving. We introduced it in the section "Taking Advantage of Shell Variables and System Commands" in Chapter 7.

Paths with Symbolic Links

If you have symbolic links pointing to directories, things can get quite complicated. The problem is that the directory you change to has a parent directory `..`, which is not the same as the directory where the link was. Suppose that a link `~/link` points to the directory `/tmp/there`, and you try to change to it:

```
% mkdir /tmp/there
% ln -s /tmp/there ~/link
% cd ~/link
```

The shell will detect that the link is to a directory, so the `cd` succeeds—but what is the directory where you end up called, `~/link` or `/tmp/there`? If you run the shell command `pwd`, displaying the current directory, it will output `~/link`; and so if you execute `cd ..`, as that would lead you to believe, you arrive in `~`.

However, if you run `/bin/pwd` while you are in `~/link` it will show you `/tmp/there`. (`/bin/pwd` works just like the shell's `pwd`, but isn't part of the shell.)

The reason for this is that the shell tries to be clever with symbolic links so that you can `cd` down into a link and then `cd ..` back out of it. However, as far as the operating system, and everything outside the shell, is concerned, there *is* no directory `~/link`; you are in the directory `/tmp/there`. (Remember, `~/link` is just a pointer as far as the operating system is concerned.)

You can prevent `pwd` from lying to you by including the option `-P` (for physical):

```
% cd ~/link
% pwd
/home/pws/link
% pwd -P
/tmp/there
```

Both bash and zsh have options so that the shell doesn't try to lie to you in the first place; you need to turn on the option chase_links in zsh, and physical (using set -o) in bash. This will result in the following behavior:

```
% cd ~/link
% pwd
/tmp/there
```

Symbolic links to directories are very useful. You need to decide whether you prefer the convenience of special handling, or whether you prefer the shell to be honest.

Other cd Options

Both bash and zsh have an option for lazy typists, cdable_vars; note in bash the spelling is strict and the option needs to be set with shopt -s cdable_vars. When this option is set, you can give cd the name of a shell variable without the $ in front and the shell will attempt to change directory to the expansion of the variable. (Yes, it just saves typing one character.)

bash has an option to check the spelling of directories: cdspell, set in the same way. If you have this set, the shell will correct small errors in the directories typed after cd.

Special zsh Directory Features

zsh's shortcut for cd, the option autocd, is extremely useful. If the option is set, you can type the name of a directory, and the shell will change to that directory:

```
zsh% setopt autocd
zsh% ~
zsh% pwd
/home/pws
```

It works just as if you'd typed cd before the directory name. In fact, the shell behavior is exactly the same as a cd command with a single argument. This means the shell will search the directory path given by the CDPATH variable in order to find the right directory. If the directory has the same name as a command, the command is executed instead. Because changing directories is a common task, this option is highly recommended.

The completion system understands this syntax, too, so the directories you type in place of the command can be completed. (In fact, directories can always be completed at this point, since they can contain commands. However, the completion system understands extra features of cd such as CDPATH, too.)

You can give the cd command two arguments. (You can't use autocd here.) These are a search and a replace string; the shell looks through the current working directory for the search string, replaces it with the second string, and attempts to change to that directory:

```
% pwd
/home/pws/zsh/4.0.7/Src
% cd 4.0.7 4.1.1
~/zsh/4.1.1/Src
```

(The shell tells you the new directory if it isn't obvious, hence the output at the end.) Note that the command is fairly stupid—it tries the first possible replacement of the search string in the directory name. If that doesn't work, it gives up even if replacing a later occurrence of the search string would give a directory that does exist.

Shorthand for Referring to Directories

We've seen the short way of referring to home directories, ~ for your own and ~bob for bob's home directory. There are many uses of ~ for referring to directories. We summarize all these uses in Table 8-1.

Table 8-1. *Uses of ~ for Referring to Directories*

Example	Meaning
~	The user's own home directory
~pws	The home directory of user pws
~var	The directory path given by the variable var (zsh only).
~+	The current directory, the same as $PWD
~-	The previous directory, the same as $OLDPWD
~+2	The second directory on the directory stack
~2	A shorter form for the second directory on the directory stack
~-0	The final directory on the directory stack

Both bash and zsh understand the syntax ~+ to refer to the current directory. It's a slightly shorter way of saying $PWD. Like all the family of substitutions beginning with ~, it only works if that character is at the start of the word and isn't quoted.

Also, ~- refers to the directory you were in just before the current one. (This is possibly more useful than ~+ since you don't usually need to refer to the current directory directly on the command line. The syntax should remind you of cd -, which would change to that same directory.)

In zsh (but not bash), you can actually give a name to *any* directory, not just users' home directories. To do this, set a variable to a full directory path. When you refer to that variable with a ~ in front, it substitutes the directory:

```
zsh% zb=~/zsh/projects/zshbook
zsh% print ~zb
/home/pws/zsh/projects/zshbook
```

In the section "A Few Simple Tricks" in Chapter 7, we mentioned that when a directory is given a name the prompt escape %~ will show the name of the directory with the ~ in front. This saves the space, which would be taken up by a long directory name. However, you need to refer to the directory name as in the previous example before the prompt will use the short form. There's a common trick for this: Use the command :, which does nothing but expand its arguments; see the explanation in the section "Parsed Comments" in Chapter 13. Here's an example:

```
zsh% zs=~/src/zsh/Src
zsh% cd ~/src/zsh/Src
zsh% PS1="%~%# "
~/src/zsh/Src% : ~zs
~zs%
```

(Remember the space between the colon and the ~zs.) Here, we set the variable zs to the path to a directory, then changed to that directory. We then set the prompt to include %~ in order to show named directories in the short form. To begin with, the prompt shows the short form for the home directory ~, but doesn't yet know about ~zs. We refer to ~zs with the colon command. Then the prompt abbreviates references to that directory. Usually, it is convenient to put the lines shown above (except for the line with the cd command) in your .zshrc file.

The Directory Stack

You sometimes find that you are switching between many different directories to do your work. To help you, bash and zsh have a *directory stack*. This is a list of directories you've visited, where the first in the list is the current directory. The shell then provides a simple way to switch to other directories in the list. The name "stack" is used because the first thing you put in is the first to come out: you can think of a pile of books where the nearest to hand is the one you last put on top.

The two basic commands are pushd and popd, which add a directory or remove the last directory added:

```
% pwd
/home/pws
% pushd zsh/projects/zshbook
~/zsh/projects/zshbook ~
% pushd ~/elisp
~/elisp ~/zsh/projects/zshbook ~
% popd
~/zsh/projects/zshbook ~
% popd
~
```

Each time you add something to or take something off the stack, the shell shows you the new stack; the current directory is always the one at the left of the list. If you forget what's on it, the command dirs will show the stack in exactly the same form. You can execute the command dirs -v to show an enumerated list, one entry per line. This is useful since the numbers can be used to refer to the directories with one of the shorthand forms using ~. Here's an example where we use the directory stack and then print the value of the item numbered 2:

```
zsh% dirs -v
0        ~/src/zsh
1        ~/tmp
2        ~/zsh/projects/zshbook
zsh% echo ~2
/home/pws/zsh/projects/zshbook
```

Many times you probably find you're switching between a small group of directories in an apparently random order. The pushd command can help with that, too. If you type pushd on its own, it will swap the two directories on the top of the stack. This is similar to what cd - does, except cd has no knowledge of the stack and only affects the current directory at the stack and nothing else. For example, if you use pushd to switch to a directory, then cd - to switch to the original directory, you end up with the same directory on the stack twice. This can be quite confusing, so we suggest you try not to mix pushd and cd - unless you have a good idea of the effect you are attempting to achieve. The following example shows the result of what we have just described. To avoid the problem, you should replace the cd - with pushd if you want to switch around the first two directories on the stack, or popd if you want to remove the first directory completely:

```
% dirs
~/tmp ~/src/zsh
% pushd  ~/zsh/projects/zshbook
~/zsh/projects/zshbook ~/tmp ~/src/zsh
% cd -
~/tmp
% dirs
~/tmp ~/tmp ~/src/zsh
```

You can also type pushd with a number beginning with a + or - (those are necessary, to stop the argument from looking like a real directory name). This brings the *number*th directory to the top of the stack, making it the current directory. With a plus, the numbers count from the left, where the current directory is +0 (yes, that works, though it's not extremely useful). With a minus, numbers count from the right, where the last directory is -0. This is not very sound mathematically, perhaps, but easy to remember because of the symmetry.

In zsh, when you use +*number* or -*number* the entire directory stack is cycled around to bring the directory you ask for to the top. For example:

```
% dirs
~/one ~/two ~/three ~/four
% pushd +2
~/three ~/four ~/one ~/two
```

In other words, if you think of the stack as having the first entry following the last entry in a loop, the order itself doesn't change but only which directory is first. This behavior can be quite confusing, and it is not the way bash and other shells work. They simply pull the directory to which you're referring to the top of the stack. That has the following effect:

```
% dirs
~/one ~/two ~/three ~/four
% pushd +2
~/three ~/one ~/two ~/four
```

The remainder of the stack apart from the entry ~/three stayed in the same order. There is a function pushd in the directory Functions/Example of the zsh source distribution that implements pushd in the same way as other shells.

The fact that pushd shows you the new stack makes it relatively stress free. If you want to get the adrenalin pumping, zsh has an option pushd_silent that stops the stack from being printed unless you ask explicitly with dirs.

A useful option is auto_pushd. If it's turned on, a cd or an auto_cd causes the new directory to be pushed onto the top of the stack. You can combine this with setting the variable DIRSTACKSIZE to a number that gives the maximum size of the stack, so that you don't overload the stack with too many entries. If the stack becomes too large, the ones at the far end from the current directory start to fall off when new directories are added.

Another useful option in connection with pushd is pushd_ignore_dups. When this is set, you never have the same directory name on the stack more than once. This feature is useful for the forgetful among us who are always putting directories onto the stack that are already there. It also works well with the auto_pushd option.

In zsh and recent versions of bash, you can refer to directories on the stack using a form of the ~ notation. In this case you use a tilde followed by the number you would need as an argument to pushd to make that directory the current one. This time, though, you can omit any plus sign between the tilde and the number:

```
% dirs
~/one ~/two ~/three
% echo ~2
~/two
```

The bash array DIRSTACK and the zsh array dirstack give you access to the stack from variables. These variables are useful for writing your own functions. For zsh you need the add-on module zsh/parameters; it may well already be loaded because it's used by the completion system. Otherwise, use zmodload -i zsh/parameters to load it. (The -i option stops the command from complaining if the module is already loaded, which is harmless.) The arrays' elements correspond to the directories on the directory stack in order, current directory first.

More Argument Handling: Braces

A list of comma-separated items in braces expands to those items. This works in all versions of zsh and recent versions of bash. The items don't have to be files, though generating filenames is one of the most common uses. We describe it here as a link between files and pattern matching, which we will talk about in the next chapter. The following is a simple example:

```
% echo {one,two,three}
one two three
```

So far, that's not very helpful—it's just like having different words on the command line. However, if you have something outside the braces, it appears with *each* of the items in the braces, not just the one at the end. It's important that no space appear before the opening brace or after the closing brace:

```
% ls myfile.{c,h}
myfile.c myfile.h
% echo BEFORE{one,two,three}AFTER
BEFOREoneAFTER BEFOREtwoAFTER BEFOREthreeAFTER
```

The first example is typical of the sort of thing you use this command for. The second shows the full glory of the syntax, and also makes the point that the arguments aren't restricted to files.

There are lots of places you can use braces that might not occur to you at first. For example, suppose you need to rename a file, and the new name is only slightly different. Let's suppose it's the same name with .bak on the end. You can complete the original filename by pressing Tab, or whatever key is configured to perform completion in your shell:

```
% mv bra<tab>
```

This gives you

```
% mv brace_expansion.xml
```

Now finish entering the line as follows and press Return:

```
% mv brace_expansion.xml{,.bak}
```

This is the same as

```
% mv brace_expansion.xml brace_expansion.xml.bak
```

(The first string in the braces was empty. However, the shell still output what was in front of the braces.) You made the shell do most of that work for you.

Here's a similar example. We use the tar command to create an archive containing the contents of a directory. The archive name is the directory name (project_cheapskate) with .tar added to the end. This is the usual convention for tar archives:

```
% tar cf project_cheapskate{.tar,}
```

■Tip Brace expansion is not a form of pattern matching. It always generates all the elements, whether existing files are there or not. In the next chapter we'll see various sorts of patterns that can pick out alternatives. For example, myfile.[ch] expands to whichever of the two files myfile.c and myfile.h actually exists.

If you find you'd rather have braces behave as normal characters, in bash you can turn off the braceexpand option; in zsh, you can turn on the ignore_braces option.

Generating Numbers with Braces

Newer shells offer a couple of other additions. Instead of commas, you can use a pair of numbers with two dots in between to signify the complete range between the two numbers. This syntax is borrowed from Perl. In zsh, it is also possible to pad the numbers with leading zeros:

```
% echo {1..10}
1 2 3 4 5 6 7 8 9 10
zsh% echo {01..10}
01 02 03 04 05 06 07 08 09 10
```

This is often used in conjunction with files. The following creates 10 files from data1.txt to data10.txt:

```
% touch data{1..10}.txt
```

Finally, there is a slightly more esoteric zsh option, braceccl, which is used with braces that don't contain either a comma or two dots. The name is a little hard to remember, but the ccl stands for "character class." With this option turned on, the shell generates the set of characters in the braces. The character - is special and turns into the range of characters, in the standard ASCII order, between the two:

```
zsh% setopt braceccl
zsh% echo BEFORE{a-e.}AFTER
BEFORE.AFTER BEFOREaAFTER BEFOREbAFTER BEFOREcAFTER BEFOREdAFTER BEFOREeAFTER
```

Note the characters are expanded in ASCII order regardless of the order they appear inside the braces.

Order of Braces and Tilde Expansion

Annoyingly, the order of ~ expansion and brace expansion is different in bash and zsh. In zsh, the braces are expanded first, and in bash the ~'s. This is not usually important, but it's a point to bear in mind if you're going to try clever things such as the following:

```
zsh% echo ~{nobody,root}
//root
```

Note that this doesn't work in bash. zsh has the option sh_file_expansion to swap the order, just to allow standardization, but you are not likely to need it.

Redirection

In the section "Writing Output to Files: Redirection" in Chapter 2, we showed you how to use > to redirect output to a file. Redirection is a power feature of the shell, and you can use it in various other ways, as you'll learn in this section. The syntax for all forms of redirection is quite similar to the form you've already seen for output.

Redirecting Input

The shell lets you redirect input as well as output. To redirect input, you use the symbol <. A typical use for that is for a program that usually takes input from the keyboard. A way of running a set of shell commands is to redirect them from a file:

```
% cat commands
echo "*** Today's Date and Time ***"
date
echo "****************************"
% bash <commands
*** Today's Date and Time ***
Tue Jan 20 22:51:44 GMT 2004
****************************
```

Here, the shell finds its input isn't a terminal, and instead of using the line editor to read the commands, it just reads them line by line from its input and executes them. The effect is the same as if you'd run the file as a script with bash ./commands. (We put the ./ in front because otherwise bash will try to search your PATH for the file.)

That behavior—either use files specified on the command line, or use the shell's input if there aren't any—is very common. Other programs we've met that do this include grep and cat. For this reason, it's less common to redirect input than output.

Preventing Files from Being Clobbered

When we say a file is "clobbered," we mean that new output has overwritten the existing contents of the file. Given the ease with which the shell can redirect output, this can be a real problem. Consider an output redirection:

```
% echo "**** Start of log file ****" >logfile.txt
% ./myprog >>logfile.txt
```

If the file `logfile.txt` existed, it would be overwritten by the first command. In the second command we deliberately avoid overwriting the file by using the double > to make the shell append output.

Both `bash` and `zsh` offer an option `noclobber` that you can set to stop this happening:

```
% echo "**** More log output ****" >logfile.txt
bash: logfile.txt: cannot overwrite existing file
```

The `noclobber` feature goes right back to the C shell, and it's been implemented in most of the new shells since then.

If you want to overwrite the file, you can delete or rename it, or you can use a special syntax that tells the shell you don't care whether the file already exists:

```
% echo "**** More log output ****" >|logfile.txt
```

That "pipe" symbol isn't a real pipe, it just combines with the > to override `noclobber`.

`zsh` tries to be clever if you set the option `hist_allow_clobber`. You'll see what happens if you repeat the example without the pipe symbol. `zsh` gives you the error, just as before. However, if you use the Up Arrow key to go back in the history, you'll find the shell inserted the pipe. So if you *really* meant to clobber the file, you now just press Return and the file will be overwritten:

```
zsh% echo "**** More log output ****" >logfile.txt
zsh: file exists: logfile.txt
zsh% <up>
```

The line now turns into the following:

```
zsh% echo "**** More log output ****" >|logfile.txt
```

File Descriptors

Like *standard input* and *standard output*, the shells have a *standard error* channel. By default, anything written to standard error goes to the same place as standard output, such as the terminal. The main use is to allow error messages to appear on your terminal when you have redirected standard output to a file. Together, standard input, output, and error can be referred to as standard channels.

The three standard channels are associated with numbers called *file descriptors*. This comes from a low-level feature of Unix—every input, output, and error channel associated with a process has a file descriptor. It's usually a small number, since the numbers are assigned starting from 0 up. The three standard channels all have fixed numbers:

0: Standard input

1: Standard output

2: Standard error

The numbers are valuable because you can use them with the shell's redirection feature to tell the shell where to send the output or to take the input. We haven't needed that because >file is shorthand for 1>file. Also, <file is shorthand for 0<file.

We showed you an example of this in the sidebar "Making Error and Progress Messages" in Chapter 2. Here's another example:

```
% cat example.sh
echo This is output from the program.
echo This is an error message.  Something is wrong. 1>&2
% bash example.sh >output.txt
This is an error message.  Something is wrong.
% cat output.txt
This is output from the program.
```

You can see that we've separated error messages and output. The error messages go to the terminal while the output goes to a file named output.txt. That 1>&2 isn't completely obvious at first: it means "take the standard output of the command, and instead send it to file descriptor 2," which is standard error. You can think of it as *copying* the file descriptor 1 onto 2—that's more or less how it actually works.

There's nothing to stop you redirecting file descriptor 2 as well, however:

```
% bash example.sh >output.txt 2>error.txt
% cat output.txt
This is output from the program.
% cat error.txt
This is an error message.  Something is wrong.
```

Without the &, what follows 2> is a filename instead of another file descriptor. It's just like > except that it redirects file descriptor 2, standard error. You can use the /dev/null special file instead of error.txt to discard the error messages completely.

You can use the shell's special exec command to reassign file descriptors to one another. The changes remain in effect for the rest of the shell, or until you reassign the file descriptors. You will usually only need this in scripts or functions. Here's an example that saves the standard output channel, redirects it temporarily to a file, then restores it:

```
# Save the normal standard output by using file descriptor 3.
exec 3>&1
# Redirect standard output to a file.
exec >output.txt
echo "This is output from the script, with no special redirection."
# Restore normal output by copying standard output back to 3.
exec 1>&3
echo "Normal output has been restored"
# To be tidy, we can use the special symbol - to close 3.
exec 3>&-
```

Save this in a file and run it as a script (bash `./`*filename*) and see what goes to the terminal, and what lands in the file `output.txt`. All the redirections we've shown are allowed after `exec`. This works in both `bash` and `zsh`.

File Descriptors as Files

On many recent versions of Unix and Linux, the file descriptors for input and output can be read as special files. Where this is available, the syntax is `/dev/fd/`*num* for file descriptor *num*, for example `/dev/fd/0` for standard input. (On recent versions of Linux, the directory `/dev/fd` may actually be a symbolic link, but that doesn't change the following description.) This probably seems a little strange—after all, file descriptor `0` is already the input, so why would you need to access it as a file?

One use is to send standard input to a command that only takes filenames and won't read from standard input. The same goes for a program that only writes to a named file. You can give such a program the filename `/dev/fd/0` as input or `/dev/fd/1` as output. Then it can, for example, read from or write to a pipe.

Here's a demonstration of the feature that creates a file using `cat` to join three files. The first and last are existing files with some text that acts as the head and foot of the output text. In the middle, `cat` will take what you type at the terminal (press Ctrl-d to finish). In a script, it would use the input to the script at that point.

```
% cat header.txt /dev/fd/0 footer.txt
Here is a message typed at the terminal.
^D
These are the contents of header.txt
Here is a message typed at the terminal.
These are the contents of footer.txt
```

Note that, even on systems that don't support the `/dev/fd` special devices, `bash` and `zsh` will emulate them when they are used in a redirection or in `[[ … ]]` style conditional expressions.

Here-Documents and Here-Strings

There is a standard shell feature called a *here-document* that allows you to supply input for a command directly within a script. For that reason, it has a syntax similar to input redirection. It's present in all the major shells, including `bash`, `zsh`, and `ksh`. It saves you the inconvenience of having to use a temporary file for the input to a command. Here's a simple but typical example:

```
mailx -s 'Errors running your job' $LOGNAME <<HERE
The job you submitted failed to run properly.
You should check the output file to see what happened.
HERE
```

(On your system the simple command for sending mail may be just mail or even Mail with an uppercase M rather than mailx. The history of Unix mail commands is rather tortuous.) This sends a mail message to the user running the job with the subject line given by the -s option and the text given by the here-document. The <<HERE tells the shell that the lines that follow the command contain data for the standard input of mailx, which is the body of the mail message. The input is terminated by a line containing just the string HERE. Be careful that it is *exactly* that, and nothing else—in particular, there must be no trailing white space. This is a common source of problems with here-documents. There's nothing special about the string HERE, however, as long as you use the same string after the << and on the line that terminates the here document. Any string without special characters in it will work, as long as the string doesn't appear as a line in the body of the here-document.

Command substitution and variable substitution work inside here-documents. This means, for example, you could put the name of the job that failed inside the mail message. (The variable substitution $0 is useful—if the command is running in a script, it expands to the name of the script.) If you put the string HERE inside quotes, substitution is turned off and the text sent to the command's standard input is exactly the text from the here-document.

If you put a hyphen in front of the string, then any tab characters at the start of lines in the here-document will be removed; the remainder of the line will be passed as input to the command. The main use of this feature is to make the script or function where the here-document appears a little neater by indenting the text. The following code gives an example; if you try it, make sure you used a tab character, not spaces, for the first line inside the here-document. To get that at the command line, you would need to press Ctrl-v before the tab to suppress any special interpretation. (That's assuming that Ctrl-v is the key sequence that makes the next character behave literally; this is the default.)

```
% cat <<-HERE
        Tabs were stripped
although they don't need to be present
HERE
Tabs were stripped
although they don't need to be present
```

In conjunction with the cat command, a here-document can be used to create or append to text files. For example, you might do the following to add some aliases to your .bashrc file:

```
$ cat <<END >> ~/.bashrc
alias scat='sed -n l'
alias spell='ispell -l'
alias ll='ls -lFb'
END
```

This demonstrates how you can mix a here-document with other redirections. It is even possible to use a here-document from the middle of a pipeline. The form this takes isn't obvious at first. All commands come first, with the content of the here-document following afterwards. Consider this example:

```
netcat -l -p 8080 <<END | head -2 >> requests.log
HTTP/1.0 200 OK
Connection: close

<html><body><h1>Hello!</h1></body></html>
END
```

This code uses a program called netcat to listen on a network port and serve up a simple web page. The here-document, which contains the simple web page, is used as input to netcat. The output from netcat is piped through head to extract just the first two lines of the web page request.

Here-Strings

zsh, ksh93, and recent versions of bash have an extension to the here-document syntax called a *here-string*. If you use three <'s in a row instead of two, the text following it becomes the command's standard input. That text is parsed like a normal shell command argument, so it can be a quoted string. Here's a terser variant of the here-document we showed earlier:

```
mailx -s 'Unlucky!' $LOGNAME <<<"Script $0 bombed."
```

The subject line of the mail will be Unlucky! and the body of the mail will be the string in double quotes. The occurrence of $0 will be expanded to the name of the script where the code occurs. This form of the syntax is a bit less clumsy than the standard here-document, so you are more likely to find it useful in an interactive shell.

Multiple Redirections

Sometimes you find you want the same output to go to multiple files. A particularly common example is to send data to the terminal as well as to a log file. The standard way of achieving this is by piping the output to tee, a command that is not part of the shell. The following example shows the output of a command being sent to the terminal as well as to the file file1.log. If you added other files as arguments to tee, the output would be sent to all the files as well as to the terminal:

```
% echo "*** Logging started at $(date) ***" | tee file1.log
*** Logging started at Mon Jul 26 22:38:28 BST 2004 ***
% cat file1.log
*** Logging started at Mon Jul 26 22:38:28 BST 2004 ***
```

zsh extends redirections so you can output to (or input from) more than one file without an external program. This feature is called *multios*, which is also the name of the option that controls it. It's on by default; execute `unsetopt multios` to turn it off.

Outputting to multiple files works like this:

```
zsh% echo "*** Logging started at $(date) ***" >file1.log >file2.log
```

Look in both files and you will see the same output. The shell copies the output to all files that have been opened on standard output. (The feature works on other file descriptors.) If you want to output to the terminal as well as another file, as in the example with `tee`, one of the redirections should be `>/dev/tty`.

Note that a pipe is treated as another use of standard output:

```
zsh% echo Script started. >logfile | sed 's/started/stopped/'
Script stopped.
zsh% cat logfile
Script started.
```

The output went to the file as well as to the pipe, where a substitution was performed on it. Unless you realize the shell treats pipes like other redirections, it's easy to assume that this is a bug.

You can also perform multiple input redirection using multios. Multiple redirections from input files make the shell concatenate the files in the order given:

```
zsh% cat filein1
These are results from the first run.
zsh% cat filein2
More results here, from the second run.
zsh% cat <filein1 <filein2
These are results from the first run.
More results here, from the second run.
```

We used `cat` to show the output, but in this case it was the shell that concatenated the files. All the program did was read its standard input; zsh fed it one file after the other.

There's a slight problem with output multios that you might notice if you use them in scripts or functions. (Those squeamish about how processes are handled should skip to the next section now.) Consider an example where you want to record the output for a command in a file, while also appending the output to a file with the output of every time you've run the program:

```
./mycommand >record.txt >>allrecords.txt
```

After mycommand has finished executing, the files may still not have had the output written to them. To see why, you need to know that the shell has to create an additional process for each redirection to copy the output to all the files in turn. The shell waits for mycommand to finish before executing the next command—but it doesn't wait for the processes, which are copying data to the two files to finish. They can take a little longer.

In versions of zsh from 4.2, the problem has been fixed for commands that run inside the shell. This apparently bizarre limitation is because the shell then has direct control over the processes forked to handle the multio output, and can wait for them to finish. You can then avoid the problem for external programs (those found by looking in your PATH) and for all commands in older versions of zsh like this:

```
{ ./mycommand } >record.txt >>allrecords.txt
```

The braces are an instruction to the shell to run a list of commands (or just one, in this case). The redirections apply to the braces as a whole, so the shell will wait for output to be written before it executes whatever command follows the line we've shown.

Null Redirections as Shortcuts

zsh lets you use redirections without commands (*null redirections*) as shortcuts for writing output or reading input. This example shows both at once; note that it won't work if the variable NULLCMD described below has been unset or changed:

```
zsh% >memo.txt
Reread the chapter on files before I go to bed.
<ctrl-d>
zsh% <memo.txt
Reread the chapter on files before I go to bed.
```

On the first line there is an output redirection with no command. zsh automatically adds the command given by the variable NULLCMD. By default, this is cat, so it executes cat >memo.txt. This copies input from the terminal to the file; you end the input with the special key Ctrl-d, for end of file (we mentioned this in the section "Basic Moving and Deleting" in Chapter 4). DOS aficionados might remember the equivalent feature, copy CON: memo.txt.

The next command is <memo.txt. This is an input redirection with no command. zsh adds the command given by the variable READNULLCMD to the line. The default for this is more, so zsh runs more <memo.txt, which displays memo.txt on the terminal. This is a useful shortcut, but it's nonstandard. Other shells, including bash, do nothing with <memo.txt and handle >memo.txt by creating an empty file. (These are both quite logical, in fact. They represent what you would get if you ran any command that doesn't use input or output with the corresponding redirections.) Luckily, they are not commonly used in shell scripts. We recommend that you use the null redirections only from the command line and in scripts and functions always type the command name in full.

You can turn this feature off by setting the option sh_null_cmd.

Summary

The following list shows the topics we have covered in this chapter:

- We discussed various different types of files: directories, regular files, links, and special files.

- We explained methods for finding commands and other files using the shell and related tools.

- We introduced various ways of managing directories, including the directory stack. Special care is needed when symbolic links refer to directories.

- We expanded our earlier explanation of the redirection operators <, > and | for managing input and output, and introduced some related concepts: *file descriptors, here-documents,* and *here-strings.*

- We demonstrated using the tee command to copy output to multiple files, and the multios facility in zsh to allow multiple input and output redirections.

In the next chapter we will fill in the big gap in our description of how the shell manages files, namely pattern matching. You'll see lots of examples of how the shell can be made to generate filenames from expressions with special characters. The features we'll describe are designed to work seamlessly with the subject matter of the present chapter, so it will be useful to have a good basic knowledge of files before proceeding.

■ ■ ■

## CHAPTER 9

Pattern Matching

Many beginning shell users shy away from learning how to take advantage of patterns in their everyday work, despite the fact that patterns are one of the most powerful features of the shell. Indeed, whatever your level of knowledge, we'd venture to say that you have used them already, perhaps most notably the * wildcard. In this chapter, we'll show you many more patterns along the same lines. Using patterns for file matching is often called *globbing* by shell programmers. It's a funny word (it's derived from "global," as in *global substitution*), but it does at least summarize this often-discussed procedure in a single term. We'll use the word to describe the process of generating filenames from patterns.

■**Note** The zsh manual refers to globbing as "Filename Generation" (type man zshexpn). In the bash manual (man bash) it's covered in the "Pattern Matching" section.

Matching filenames is not the only use of patterns, however. The shell uses the same form of pattern for other things, such as when comparing a string against a pattern. This is a useful thing to be able to do from scripts and functions. We'll show you some examples of this in Chapter 13. Most of what we discuss in this chapter will be applicable to testing strings, although some patterns are designed only for files.

We'll divide up this chapter into patterns understood by both bash and zsh, patterns understood by bash, and those understood by zsh. The last of those three will be by far the longest; globbing is one of zsh's real strong points. However, although the syntax is different, some of the advanced bash and zsh patterns can do similar things.

A note about language: unless you tell it otherwise, the shell will generate names of directories just the same as it will other files. So when we talk about "files" we will usually mean anything with a name in the filesystem, including directories. We'll usually say "regular files" when we mean the basic sort that have a - in the first column of their detailed ls -l listing.

Basic Globbing

A character or set of characters that have a special meaning in a filename is sometimes called an *operator* (though other names are used). We'll meet quite a few operators during the chapter; some of them are only available in one shell or another. Nearly all Unix-style shells support the simple operators. We summarize them in Table 9-1. Although they are generally available, you need to keep a lookout for subtleties. For example, later we'll see that there are occasions when * doesn't actually match all characters.

Table 9-1. *Common Globbing Operators*

Operator	Meaning
*	Zero or more characters
?	Any single character
[abc]	Any of the characters a, b, or c
[a-z]	Any character that lies between a and z
[^a-z] or [!a-z]	Any character other than one that lies between a and z

You need to remember it's the shell that expands patterns—not the program that runs with the file arguments. The shell passes down the expanded filenames, so the program itself never sees the patterns. (If your shell is running under Cygwin and you execute a native Windows command, the program may try to expand patterns in filenames after the shell has finished its own expansions.)

The most basic pattern character is *. We'll refer to it as a "star" in this chapter. It matches any number of characters, including none—in other words, file* matches anything beginning with those four characters, including just file:

```
% ls
File  Makefile  file  file.c  file.txt
% echo *
File Makefile file file.c file.txt
% echo file*
file file.c file.txt
```

Note that any letter given explicitly, like the f in file*, is matched exactly, as long as it's not part of an operator. Even the case of letters is important. bash has an option, nocaseglob, which if turned on makes the matching case insensitive. This is very useful for Cygwin, where the filesystem is case insensitive. For example, on Cygwin the names File and file refer to the same file (only one of the two could have appeared in the listings of the previous example). So the commands less file and less File have the same effect. It is therefore useful to have file* match the name File as well as file. zsh 4.2 and greater also has the option no_case_glob. If you are using an older version of zsh, you can make a particular pattern case insensitive by using one of the *globbing flags*. We'll meet these when we talk about extended globbing in the section "Extended Globbing," later in this chapter.

Even those simple rules have consequences you may not immediately realize, particularly if you grew up with patterns in DOS or in a Windows Command Prompt window. We've discussed some simple differences in the sidebar "Differences from the DOS Command Prompt."

DIFFERENCES FROM THE DOS COMMAND PROMPT

If you have experience using the DOS (or Windows) shell, you will find that under Unix even simple patterns like * behave a little differently. Here are a couple of things to notice.

1. DOS users often attempt to rename a group of files in one go using syntax like this:

```
mv *.c *.bak
```

Unix shells will not allow this, because the shell expands *both* of those stars straight away, or tries to. When it's done that, the mv command receives arguments that look like this:

```
mv prog.c utils.c oldprog.bak mydata.bak
```

As you can see, the arguments consist of all possible expansions. As a result, mv will complain and do nothing. That's because if mv has more than two arguments, the last must be a directory.

2. Unix shells recognize a single star as any character in a filename. In DOS, it doesn't match a dot; you need *.* to match both the filename and the extension. Under Unix, you can just use * to match both unless you're looking specifically for those files that contain a dot in the filename.

There is one important exception to the "star matches everything" rule: it doesn't match a dot at the start of a filename. There is a conspiracy between the shells and the ls command to keep files beginning with a dot out of your way; the shell won't match such files with wildcards, and ls won't show them.

Here is a simple example. We've used ls -a (for "all") to show the complete list of files, including those beginning with a dot:

```
% ls -a
.  ..  .mozilla  .zlogin  .zprofile  .zshrc  Mail  msg.txt
```

However, if we use * to match all the files, the ones beginning with a dot won't appear:

```
% echo *
Mail msg.txt
```

Whenever you specify the first character, the * can match anything else. This may be a letter:

```
% echo m*
msg.txt
```

However, you may also specify that a dot is the first character. Then the shell will match those files that were hidden before. The two examples below show any file beginning with .z, and any file beginning with a dot and containing an l:

```
% echo .z*
.zlogin .zprofile .zshrc
% echo .*l*
.mozilla .zlogin .zprofile
```

Under Unix, these are the *only* places where a leading dot is special—apart from programs such as graphical file browsers, which mimic the way `ls` lists files. The underlying filesystem doesn't care at all. It only cares about the two special files: `.` (a single dot), which refers to the current directory, and `..` (two dots), which refers to the parent directory. Any other files beginning with a dot behave like any other file. (If you're using the shell under Cygwin, things are more complicated, because there are more special characters.)

You can make the shells expand files beginning with a dot in patterns, however. In `bash`, you need `shopt -s dotglob` and in `zsh`, `setopt globdots`. We recommend you that you don't do that, except in functions where you only set it for a short time and make sure it is unset at the end; it can have very nasty effects when combined with `rm`. This can happen if you run `ls` to see what files are in a directory, then `rm *` to remove all those files. The `ls` command wouldn't show you files beginning with a dot. However, with the `dotglob` (bash) or `globdots` (zsh) option set, the shell does generate such filenames. Then the `rm` command deletes the files that you didn't even know were there. Since files beginning with a dot are often used for special purposes, such as the shell's own startup files, this is definitely a bad thing.

`zsh` never matches the special files `.` and `..` as patterns, though you can type them explicitly, of course. The shell assumes—and it's nearly always correct—that if you want to refer to the current or parent directory you will say so explicitly. `bash` is a little less consistent: if you use `.*` to match leading dots, it will show you both those files, but if you set the option `dotglob` and use `*`, it won't. The following example shows that happening. First we show all files, then we set the `dotglob` option and use `*` to generate filenames, then we use `.*` to show all files beginning with a dot. You can see that in the second case the two files `.` and `..` are missing, but they are present in the first and third cases:

```
bash$ ls -a
.  ..  Mail  .mozilla  msg.txt  .zlogin  .zprofile  .zshrc
bash$ echo *
Mail .mozilla msg.txt .zlogin .zprofile .zshrc
bash$ echo .*
.  ..  .mozilla  .zlogin  .zprofile  .zshrc
```

Tip In `zsh`, you can make a single pattern match dots at the start of the filename. This is usually more useful than making all patterns match dots. The following shows all files, including those beginning with a dot, which contain an `l`:

```
zsh% echo *l*(D)
.mozilla  .zlogin  .zprofile  Mail
```

That "`(D)`" is one of a set of *glob qualifiers* we'll meet in the section "Glob Qualifiers in zsh," later in this chapter.

Matching a Single Character

A ? matches a single character. As with *, this character can't be a leading dot unless you've asked specially for patterns to match them.

There are two common uses for the question mark pattern. The first is to match a given length of characters in the filename. In the following case, we look for files with a three-character extension:

```
% echo *.???
msg.txt
```

(If you're pedantic, you might note that one of those questions marks could match another dot. That's because none is at the start of the word, which is the only place dots are special.)

The second common use is to combine a question mark with a star to make sure at least one character is present:

```
% echo *
string. string.c string.h string.bak
% echo string.?*
string.c string.h string.bak
```

Here, we are looking for "true" suffixes, a dot followed by at least one more character. Aside from the number of characters matched, ? behaves a lot like *.

Matching a Restricted Range of Characters

Sometimes you want to match only a certain range of characters, for example only uppercase letters. To do this, you can put the characters you want to match in square brackets. This feature is usually referred to as a *character class*. In the simplest form, the square brackets contain every character allowed to match at that point in the pattern. However, it's very commonplace for the characters allowed to be within a range of consecutive characters, such as letters or digits, so there is a shortcut for this case. You can specify this by putting the first character in the range, then a - (hyphen), then the last character in the range, all inside the brackets. You can even mix individual characters with ranges. Let's consider a few examples. First, here are all the files that don't begin with a dot:

```
% echo *
1foo Mail MSG msg.txt
```

In the following example we echo files that start with an uppercase letter from the English alphabet:

```
% echo [A-Z]*
Mail MSG
```

In the following example, we specify that the first letter is either the digit 1 or an uppercase letter:

```
% echo [1A-Z]*
1foo Mail MSG
```

Note that the expression in brackets matches exactly one character. Therefore, in the previous example the [1A-Z] matched the M of MSG and the * matched the SG.

If you place a ^ (sometimes called a *caret*) immediately after the opening bracket, the sense is negated, so the shell matches any single character that is not one you specified. (Some shells such as ksh use a ! instead of a ^; you can do that in bash and zsh, too, but in zsh you will need to quote the ! at the command line to prevent it from being taken as a history reference.) Let's consider another example:

```
% echo [^a-z]*
1foo MSG
```

The first character was forced to be anything except a lowercase English letter. Once again, it can't be a dot, either, since it's a pattern at the start of a word. In addition, you can't match an opening dot even if you include it explicitly inside the brackets, so [.]* doesn't match any files. This is probably so that it is safe to use character classes in the more complicated forms of matching that we'll meet later.

If you are wondering whether you can put one of the special characters into a character class, you can. The rules are as follows:

1. A right bracket ("]") to be matched literally must come immediately after the opening left bracket, except for any caret (^) used for negation. The following example shows a directory with three files; first we match any files ending in a right bracket or an X, then any files that don't end in one of those characters:

```
% ls
file0  file[1]  fileX
% echo file*[]X]
file[1] fileX
% echo file*[^]X]
file0
```

2. A hyphen to be matched literally must come immediately after the left bracket, except for any caret used for negation, and any right bracket. (Some versions of bash apparently don't let you combine a hyphen and a right bracket in this way.) In the following example, we first list the files in the current directory. Then we show all files whose names end with a hyphen or a plus sign; then all files whose names end with a right bracket or a hyphen; then all files whose names don't end with a hyphen or a right bracket.

```
% ls
file-  file+  file[0]
% echo *[-+]
file- file+
% echo *[]-]
file- file[0]
% echo *[^]-]
file+
```

3. A caret to be matched literally must not come immediately after the left bracket. In the following example, we list all files, then show all those whose names start with a plus sign or caret:

```
% ls
_func  +note  ^readme
% echo [+^]*
+note ^readme
```

You can also include one of the characters], -, ^, or \ in a character class by escaping it with a backslash; for example, in bash [\]\-\^] will match any of the three characters that are special in classes. This is usually rather easier than the rules we just listed. Unfortunately, however, zsh won't let you escape a hyphen in that way—you must put the hyphen first, or after the caret for negation. A backslash also needs to be doubled to be treated literally in a character class.

Picking the Right Range of Characters

If you tried out some of these last examples you may have found that, on your system, [A-Z] is actually matching both upper- and lowercase letters. The traditional way of determining whether a particular character is in a range simply uses the relative positions of the characters in the character set. For Unix, in the past, that always meant the ASCII character set. In ASCII, all the 26 uppercase letters appear in unbroken order. The 26 lowercase letters follow on a little later, again in order. Most notably, this means that Z appears before a, and [A-Z] only matches the uppercase letters.

Unfortunately, as character sets have been extended to allow for further characters, problems have become apparent. For instance, [A-Z] would not match Ä. Also, even in the English language, conventional dictionary order would not put Z before a.

The modern way of handling a character class involves using the *collation order* for the current *locale*. We explain more about this in the section "Internationalization and Locales," later in this chapter. zsh still does things the old way, but even if you use zsh, you may find that character classes in regular expressions handled by commands like grep work differently from how they work in the shell. The collation order is even used by commands like ls to determine the order in which files are listed.

To allow things like uppercase letters to be matched, most modern Bourne-shell variants have an extension that lets you use names for character classes. You simply include an extra set of brackets, with a colon before and after the name, giving the complete result [[:*name*:]]. (This form isn't available in older shells; it was added by POSIX, a standard for Unix-like operating systems.) The possible names are shown in Table 9-2.

Table 9-2. *Named Ranges for Character Sets*

Name	Explanation
alnum	A letter or number.
alpha	A letter.
ascii	A character in the ASCII set.
blank	A space or tab. This is a GNU extension and might not always be available.
cntrl	A control character.
digit	A decimal digit (number).
graph	A printable character, but not a space.
lower	A lowercase character.
print	A printable character including space.
punct	A punctuation character, meaning any printable character that is neither alphanumeric nor one of the space characters.
space	A white-space character, usually space, (horizontal) tab, newline, carriage return plus the less usual vertical tab and form feed.
upper	An uppercase letter.
xdigit	A hexadecimal digit; an upper- or lowercase "a" to "f," or a digit.

This allows you to be more explicit in testing for files beginning with an uppercase character:

```
% echo [[:upper:]]*
Mail MSG
```

Note that the inner bracketed component works just like any other part of a character class. This means you can negate it, or combine it with other things:

```
% echo [^[:alpha:]]*
1foo
% echo [[:digit:]m]*
1foo msg.txt
```

Named ranges are often safer for scripts. However, they are still affected by internationalization. This means, for example, there may be differences in which characters are regarded as letters of the alphabet. This is usually an advantage. For example, as long as the shell has been told what character set you are using, you can pick up all uppercase characters, including accented ones.

Quoting Pattern Characters

You should know by now that if you want a special character to behave without its special behavior, you need to quote it either with quotation marks or a backslash. Luckily, you don't need to quote the whole word, so you can have special characters that retain their effect in the same word. In the following example we use quotation marks to suppress the special interpretation of square brackets that appear as part of filenames:

```
% ls
FILE.log     FILE[1].log  OUTPUT.log     OUTPUT[1].log
FILE[0].log  FILE[2].log  OUTPUT[0].log  OUTPUT[2].log
% echo 'FILE['*'].log'
FILE[0].log FILE[1].log FILE[2].log
```

Writing it like that made it quite clear that only the * was special to the shell. Although this works perfectly well, many people don't use characters that are special to the shell in the names of files they create, just to avoid having to quote them. Under Unix, the only characters that can't appear in filenames at all are the NULL character and a slash. That's because a NULL is used to mark the termination of the name, and a slash is used to separate directories. In Windows, it's more complicated; for example, you can't use colons because they represent drive letters.

Tip The patterns we've shown you using *, ?, and ranges are not the ones you use in programs that search text, such as grep, or scripting languages other than shells, such as awk and Perl. Those patterns are called *regular expressions*. See the sidebar "Globbing and Regular Expressions" for a more detailed explanation.

GLOBBING AND REGULAR EXPRESSIONS

A regular expression (or *regex* as it's commonly called) is designed for a different task than a globbing pattern. Globbing gives you a short way to match a complete word while regular expressions are useful when more powerful pattern matching is required. In fact, zsh patterns have been extended so far they can do all that most forms of regular expressions can. However, patterns in zsh are still based on the normal globbing form that's designed to match filenames easily. So the zsh extensions to pattern matching don't have the usual regular expression syntax. Here are the most obvious surprises:

1. In a regular expression, a dot doesn't just match a dot, it matches any single character; in other words, it does what a question mark does in globbing. To match a dot in a regular expression, you need to put a backslash before it: the backslash is the only form of quoting regular expressions understand.

2. The star in a regular expression doesn't match any number of characters; it matches any number of *repetitions* of the previous character, including zero repetitions. Thus a* in a regular expression matches any number of a's. The equivalent of a globbing star is therefore . *—any number of repetitions of any character, and it doesn't have to be the same character on every repetition.

Continued

3. A question mark in a regular expression designates zero or one of the preceding patterns. So a? means either nothing or a single a. There's no simple shell equivalent of this because it's not usually as useful.

4. Regular expressions are not automatically *anchored* to a beginning and an end of a string. That means they can match a string in the middle of some text, with other strings before and after. There are special characters for matching the start and end of lines or words. So to convert a regular expression to an equivalent globbing expression, you often have to add a * on either side of the pattern.

Since the basic shell never uses regular expressions as part of its filename-matching capabilities, it's a good idea to get into the habit of putting the whole of any regular expression inside quotes, to make sure it's passed down intact to the program that does use it. (There is actually an additional feature that uses regular expression syntax, but we won't discuss it here.) As you've seen, many of the same characters are special to both regular expressions and globbing. It's quite common for both to appear on the same line. Then the globbing expression should not be quoted, while the regular expression should. For example:

```
grep 'shell.*script' *.txt
```

The first argument is passed intact to grep. The second is expanded to filenames, and those names are passed down as a set of arguments. The whole searches files ending in .txt for lines containing shell and script in that order with any other characters in between.

Internationalization and Locales

In this chapter we see examples where the shell needs to decide how to order characters, or how to classify a character (as a letter, or a punctuation character, or whatever). The results are affected by variations in language, character sets, and other features between countries and even regions. Unix and related systems nowadays have support for local differences of this type. This goes under the heading "internationalization," sometimes rather obliquely abbreviated to "i18n" (count the letters). A set of information for a particular region is called a *locale*. The system can be quite complicated, so we'll just point out some of the more obvious features.

Programs that are sensitive to locales (not all are) look at environment variables to find out which locale to use. Often, the values of these variables are assigned by you or your administrator. The variables consist of a set of names beginning with LC_, and the variable LANG. The value of each variable is the name of the locale itself. Typical names look like en_US, which is the language and the country, but you may see variations such as en_GB.UTF-8 and de_DE@euro, where a particular character-encoding or other unique feature is noted in the name. To find out what locales are available on your system, try running locale -a or looking in /usr/lib/locale. zsh 4.2 can even complete them, as long as you have the completion system described in Chapter 10 loaded; try LANG=<tab>.

The default locale is called C, as in the programming language. It will always exist and so can be selected as a way of disabling the special behaviors associated with internationalization.

Two variables particularly affect the shell:

1. LC_COLLATE determines the sort order of characters.

2. LC_CTYPE determines the character handling and classification behavior.

You can override all of the LC_ variables by storing a value in LC_ALL. Furthermore, by storing a value in LANG, you can specify a fallback for any variable that is left unset.

One thing to be careful about is the character encoding used by the locale. This isn't necessarily trivial because your terminal emulator, shell, and files could have different ideas of the character encoding. Even the names of files may be encoded differently depending on your filesystem.

The old way of handling non-English characters was to have multiple character sets for different languages. This is gradually being replaced. The new system is based around a character set, called Unicode. (You may also see Unicode referred to as ISO 10646 or UCS, for Universal Character Set.) This is a code table for assigning numbers to characters; there are several alternatives for how to represent a sequence of characters as a sequence of bytes. The most useful such encoding under Unix is UTF-8, because it has the property that all characters that exist in the ASCII character set have exactly the same encoding as under ASCII. Multibyte sequences of bytes with the eighth bit set are used for other characters. To be clear: Unicode is a set of characters. UTF-8 is (maybe) the way those characters are represented on your system.

zsh does not currently handle multibyte character encodings such as UTF-8. There are other multibyte character sets, the most common being those in use for East Asian languages. For best results, you are better off avoiding such character sets in zsh. Recent versions of bash do handle UTF-8, at least for line editing.

If your terminal is set to use an 8-bit character encoding, and you are confused about locales, you can use a simple trick in zsh: set the option print_eight_bit. Then the shell will assume it can print 8-bit characters straight to the terminal in completion lists and so on. The shell will ignore the system's information about which characters are printable. Character encodings where this will work (assuming your terminal is configured properly) include the ISO-8859 family. These are common single-byte extensions of ASCII for adding accented characters found in many European languages.

Pattern matching is commonly used when the need arises to detect lower- and uppercase letters. Suppose my directory contains two filenames, one with only English letters, and one with European characters:

```
bash$ echo *
Orvieto Ötztal
```

The locale currently in use for deciding on the nature of characters (using the variable LC_CTYPE) is en_GB. This only knows about ASCII characters, which don't include any accented characters. So here's what happens when we look for words beginning with uppercase letters:

```
bash$ echo $LC_CTYPE
en_GB
bash$ echo [[:upper:]]*
Orvieto
```

However, there is another locale that is aware of characters in the UTF-8 Unicode encoding: en_GB.UTF-8. If we set LC_CTYPE to that value, the shell can now identify all uppercase letters in the character set:

```
% LC_CTYPE=en_GB.UTF-8
% echo [[:upper:]]*
Orvieto Ötztal
```

It may not be easy for you to reproduce this example, however, even if you have a sufficiently recent system. It depends on the locales that are installed on your computer and on the character set that is used by the terminal for output. Furthermore, bash and zsh don't make it easy to create filenames with characters that are not on your keyboard. These matters are well beyond the scope of this book.

Globbing in Bash

How does the shell deal with patterns that don't match any files? In bash the string is passed through to the command unchanged, with the pattern characters intact. (This is different from zsh. If a pattern fails to a match a file in zsh, the shell by default reports an error and doesn't execute the command.) So, for example:

```
$ ls
picture1.jpg  picture2.jpg
$ echo pic* slide*
picture1.jpg  picture2.jpg  slide*
```

Sometimes you need all the arguments to correspond to real files. There are various ways of dealing with this:

- You can use one of the tests we'll introduce in the section "Condition Tests" in Chapter 13 to test each argument to see if it's a file. It works, but it's clumsy.

- You can turn on the nullglob option with shopt -s. In that case any argument with a pattern in it that doesn't match a file will simply be removed from the command line. Arguments with no patterns or where the patterns are quoted are passed through unchanged as arguments to the command. So in the previous example, echo would show "picture1.jpg picture2.jpg".

- For bash versions 3.0 and greater, you can set the option failglob. In this case, if a pattern match fails, the shell prints an error message and doesn't execute the command line. This is similar to the default behavior of zsh.

Extended Globbing

If you find that you need some more sophisticated forms of pattern matching, you can turn on the extglob option. That makes available a set of patterns all with the same form: a special character, followed by an expression in parentheses. The expression in parentheses can consist of vertical bars (or pipe symbols), which in this context separate pattern alternatives. The presence of the surrounding pattern delimiters stops the shell from recognizing the bar as a real pipe, since it's meaningless in the middle of a pattern. This style of extended globbing comes originally from the Korn shell.

The simplest form is @(*expr*), which matches one of the alternative patterns found in the expression *expr*. Let's consider an example:

```
$ echo *.@(out|txt)
ham.txt msg.out msg.txt spam.txt
```

In this case the alternatives were simple strings, but they could be patterns, too. An advantage of the parentheses is that they make it easy to bury patterns recursively inside others. In the following example, we look for files starting with OUTPUT. We then look for two possible endings: first, files that end with .old where the previous part of the name is either .txt or .log; second, files that end with .bak. We've wrapped the long line in the output that resulted:

```
% ls
OUTPUT1.bak       OUTPUT1.txt       OUTPUT2.log       OUTPUT2.txt.old  prog.c
OUTPUT1.log       OUTPUT1.txt.old   OUTPUT2.log.old   OUTPUT.bak       prog.h
OUTPUT1.log.old   OUTPUT2.bak       OUTPUT2.txt       prog             prog.o
% echo OUTPUT*.@(@(txt|log).old|bak)
OUTPUT1.bak OUTPUT1.log.old OUTPUT1.txt.old OUTPUT2.bak
OUTPUT2.log.old OUTPUT2.txt.old OUTPUT.bak
```

If you're familiar with extended regular expressions, you might notice a resemblance to the patterns used by the command egrep, an enhanced version of grep. The difference is that bash has @ in front. The shell has other uses for parentheses, and the @ makes it clear which is meant. A list of syntactical variations of this form follows. In each case, *expr* can be a set of alternatives separated by a bar, but in all apart from the first it's also useful to have a single string or pattern with no bar:

- @(*expr*) matches exactly one of the alternatives in *expr*.

- ?(*expr*) matches either nothing or one of the alternatives in *expr*.

- *(*expr*) matches any number of repetitions, including zero, of the patterns in *expr*.

- +(*expr*) matches one or more repetitions of the patterns in *expr*.

- !(*expr*) matches anything except the patterns in *expr*.

You may notice that the code letters * and ? in the list above have similar effects to the same letters when used in regular expressions, as we described in the sidebar "Globbing and Regular Expressions." Here are some examples. We use fixed strings for clarity, but the expressions can contain patterns as complicated as you like:

```
$ ls
a   aone   aonetwo   aonetwoonetwo
$ echo a@(one|two)
aone
$ echo a*(one|two)
a aone aonetwo aonetwoonetwo
$ echo a+(one|two)
aone aonetwo aonetwoonetwo
$ echo a?(one|two)
a aone
```

> ■**Tip** You can't use slashes for directory separators inside parentheses. That's because pattern matching is only done on files within each directory. There's nothing to stop you from using patterns within more than one chunk of a filename, however, such as /@(usr|var)/@(spool|lib)/*.

Negative Pattern Matching

The form !(*expr*) matches anything except a pattern in *expr*. As before, *expr* can be a list of alternatives separated by vertical bars. The implications of not matching a pattern are more complicated than you might think at first:

```
$ echo !(a)*
a aone aonetwo aonetwoonetwo
```

What? We've told it not to match a at the start, and yet every single match it's come up with does. How come?

The matcher first finds the longest string that matches !(a), and then matches the star. Anything matches the star, so in each case we simply need any string that doesn't match a. In the case of a itself, that's an empty string, and in the case of the others, it's the entire string. The star then ensures everything else matches.

In other words, !(a) can match any string other than a. It could be b, but it could also be aa. The string matched is not required to be a single letter.

The most common uses of that syntax are when the entire file pattern is inside. For example, the pattern !(*.o) matches all files that don't end in .o. This is more intuitive than the previous example, because either the file matches the entire pattern or it doesn't.

> ■**Note** Compare this with the zsh extended globbing syntax ^*.o in the section "Negated Matches," later in this chapter. In fact, zsh supports all the operators that are provided by the bash extglob option. You make them work in zsh by turning on the option ksh_glob. (It has this name because ksh was the first shell to have this syntax.) Then you can try out all the examples in zsh, too. Most zsh users don't use the ksh_glob option, however, since zsh provides its own equally powerful patterns.

Ignoring Patterns

bash gives you a way of overriding the patterns matched by globbing. The variable GLOBIGNORE works like PATH in that it consists of different elements joined with colons. Each element represents a pattern that globbing should never match. Remember to quote the patterns when you first assign a value to GLOBIGNORE.

Note that GLOBIGNORE overrides the rule that files beginning with dots are not matched. In other words, if you want to continue to use that rule, you will need to add :.* to the end of the variable's value. Here are some examples.

```
bash$ ls -a
.  ..  .msg.list  ham  ham~  msg  msg.bak  msg~  newmsg
bash$ echo *
ham ham~ msg msg.bak msg~ newmsg
bash$ GLOBIGNORE='*~'
bash$ echo *
.msg.list ham msg msg.bak newmsg
bash$ GLOBIGNORE='*~:*.bak'
bash$ echo *
.msg.list ham msg newmsg
bash$ GLOBIGNORE='*~:*.bak:.*'
bash$ echo *
ham msg newmsg
```

In the previous examples we referred to two patterns that you typically don't want to see in results, because they represent two common strings used to specify backup files. However, you need to be sure you *really* never want them to be matched by patterns. You need a good reason to set GLOBIGNORE, and if you do it, it is likely to be only for a short chunk of code at a time.

Globbing in Zsh

zsh, like bash, has special options for dealing with failed pattern matches:

- In the default state, the shell outputs an error message when a pattern on the command line doesn't match a file. The command is not executed, and the shell waits for new input:

```
zsh% echo No*Such*File
zsh: no matches found: No*Such*File
```

Note that there was no output from echo because it was never executed. This can be quite useful since it enforces the habit of quoting pattern characters when you don't want them to act as patterns.

- If you set the option no_nomatch, you have the standard bash behavior: any patterns that don't match are passed to the command unchanged and no error is reported:

```
zsh% setopt no_nomatch
zsh% echo No*Such*File
No*Such*File
```

- If you set the option csh_null_glob, standard C shell behavior is followed. If there are several patterns on the command line, at least one must match a file or files; in that case, any that don't are removed from the argument list. If no pattern matches, an error is reported. This is a hybrid between zsh's default and full null_glob behavior. This behavior often matches the user's intentions. It's common to need at least one argument to a command, but not to care which of a set of patterns successfully generated a filename.

- If you set the option null_glob, patterns that don't match a file are unconditionally removed from the argument list. This is the same as the bash option nullglob. Note that the option csh_null_glob will be used if it is turned on as well as null_glob.

Suppose a directory contains some files that you'd like to match:

```
% ls
file1.h file1.c
% echo file1.* file2.*
???
% echo file2.*
???
```

The various ways the shell can handle this are summarized in Table 9-3. In the table, "Error" indicates that the shell prints a message saying the match failed and doesn't execute the command.

Table 9-3. *Options for Handling Failed Matches in zsh*

Option	echo file1.* file2.*	echo file2.*
Default	Error	Error
no_nomatch	file1.c file1.h file2.*	file2.*
csh_null_glob	file1.c file1.h	Error
null_glob	file1.c file1.h	Empty argument list

zsh also gives you a way of switching on the option null_glob for a single command. This means that if that pattern doesn't match a file, it will be removed, regardless of how other command-line arguments are handled. To get this effect, you put (N) after the pattern. This is a *glob qualifier*; see the section "Glob Qualifiers in zsh," later in this chapter.

If zsh can't understand a pattern—for example, the argument contains a [with no matching]—it will usually show a message and not execute the command. This is typically a good thing, particularly when you are learning about patterns. However, if you are lazy about quoting special characters, you can set the option no_bad_pattern. This causes the shell to pass any pattern it doesn't understand to the command without altering it. The following example shows what happens first with the option off, then with it on:

```
zsh% echo Options [a to d]
zsh: bad pattern: [a
zsh% setopt no_bad_pattern
zsh% echo Options [a to d]
Options [a to d]
```

Special Patterns in zsh

zsh's additional globbing operators are in two classes: those usually enabled, and those for which the option extended_glob must be enabled. The first set extends the operation of characters already special to the shell, and are enabled by default since they aren't likely to cause problems with compatibility. The second set uses characters that aren't special inside patterns unless the option is set. First, we'll talk about the ones available without a special option.

Grouping Alternatives

Like ksh and bash (with the extglob option set), zsh can interpret pattern alternatives that are surrounded by parentheses and separated by a vertical bar. The difference from ksh and bash is that the parentheses aren't preceded by a special character. Let's consider an example:

```
zsh% ls
dry.out  dry.txt  greasy.out  greasy.txt  normal.out  normal.txt
zsh% echo d*.(out|txt)
dry.out dry.txt
```

The drawback of this arguably more intuitive syntax is that there is a clash with other uses of parentheses. In particular, they can occur in two places:

- At the start of a command line to signal a set of commands to run in a subshell, as described in Chapter 13

- To show the start of a group in the tests starting with [[that we describe in the section "Condition Tests" in Chapter 13

Luckily, neither of these causes much of a problem: you almost never need a set of alternatives at the start of a command line, and zsh is good at guessing whether parentheses in tests are for grouping or for a pattern.

Unlike braces, parenthesized expressions refer to a single globbing pattern. This has particular implications when you are using one of the special options to handle failed matches. At this point, an expression such as d*.{out,txt} has already been expanded into the words d*.out d*.txt. If you try them both out with the options in Table 9-3 you will find the results are different.

■**Tip** Parenthesized groups in zsh are limited in the same way as bash; a single group can't contain a path that has a directory separator in it.

The uses we've shown for parentheses in zsh would cause other shells derived from the Bourne shell such as bash to report a syntax error. If you prefer to use only the syntax common to bash and zsh, you can set the option sh_glob to turn off this use of parentheses. However, it's still possible to turn on ksh_glob to use the patterns you'll learn about in the section "Extended Globbing," a bit later in this chapter. The combination of sh_glob and ksh_glob turned on and extended_glob turned off makes zsh work very like both bash and ksh. A problem you might notice when the ksh_glob option is in effect is that the form !(*pattern*) can be taken as a history reference. For better compatibility with other shells, you can turn off the option bang_hist.

Recursive Searching

Suppose you want to find a file that resides somewhere in the directory tree that starts with the current directory, but you don't know how deep in the tree it is. For example, it might be in scripts, or in scripts/zsh, or in functions/zsh/completion. In most shells you have to do something quite complicated to find the file:

1. You could use the tricks we discussed in the section "Using find to Execute a Command" in Chapter 8.

2. You could specify a list of possible directory levels, such as */* */*/*.

zsh has a simple replacement: the pattern **/ matches any number of directories (including none) to any depth. By "including none," we mean that **/*filepat* can match *filepat* in the current directory, too; if you don't want that, you can use */**/*filepat*.
Here is a simple example:

```
zsh% print -l **/*.txt
README.txt
src/config.txt
src/drivers/driver-list.txt
src/problems.txt
testing.txt
```

Note how at each level the directory entries are listed in alphabetic order; if any are themselves directories, all the files inside them to any depth appear at that point. This is one of the most commonly used zsh extensions. However, you should be aware of a few problems you may encounter:

- Operating systems limit the number of arguments that can be passed down to a program. This syntax can generate truly huge argument lists, which can result in an error message such as "argument list too long". If that happens, you need to split the arguments up—for example, using xargs as we did with find in the section "Running find in a Pipeline" in Chapter 8.

  You don't need to use xargs with commands that are part of the shell, because that error occurs only when you're starting a separate program. However, really large argument lists can take up huge amounts of memory. Using the xargs method avoids that.

- The shell isn't very fast at performing the search. If you experiment, you will probably discover that the find command can generate long lists more quickly. The fact that the find command can do additional tests on files it finds isn't much of an advantage, however. We'll see a bit later that zsh's "glob qualifiers" provide many of the same abilities.

- The form **/ does not follow symbolic links to directories. However, the variant ***/ does follow symbolic links, and this can cause problems. Keep in mind that ***/ will follow any link, even those that refer to a directory outside the parent of the directory containing the link. This can result in an infinite loop. Luckily, other operating system limits come into play first. If the length of the filename including all the directories is too long, you may see the message "file name too long". If the system has followed as many links as it will allow, you may see "too many levels of symbolic links". These limitations usually mean the effect of loops isn't too disastrous.

- A limitation of the pattern **/ is that you can't use it as part of a set of alternatives in parentheses since it matches across multiple directories. For example, the pattern (dir1/**/file1|dir1/**/file2).txt, which you might expect to find files called file1.txt below dir1 or files called file2.txt below dir2, actually fails to match.

- Be careful to make sure the ** occurs at the start of the pattern, or between slashes; if you put some other text next to it, or don't follow it with a slash, its behavior reverts to that of a single star. There is a way of recursive matching with a given pattern that you'll learn about in the section "Multiple Matches," later in this chapter.

Matching Numeric Ranges

zsh can also match ranges of numbers. The syntax in general looks like this:

```
zsh% ls
data1   data2   data3   data10   data20   data30
zsh% echo data<1-9>
data1 data2 data3
```

Either of the numbers can be omitted. In the simplest case, `<->`, the expression matches any set of digits. It even matches a number that's usually too large for shell arithmetic, because the shell doesn't need to do arithmetic; it just needs to match all the digits it encounters without turning them into an integer. If the first number in the range is omitted, it's taken as 0, and if the second in the range is omitted, it's effectively infinity. If both numbers are given, the first must be less than the second and the pattern matches any number in that inclusive range:

```
zsh% ls
data1   data2   data3   data10   data20   data30
zsh% echo data<1-9>
data1 data2 data3
zsh% echo data<10->
data10 data20 data30
```

The first example is different from the corresponding brace expansion, data{1..9}. That would generate all nine of the expressions, regardless of which files existed. Numbers with leading zeroes can be matched (for example, 0010 is treated by the shell in the same way as 10), but other forms of numbers, such as negative integers or numbers with a decimal point, aren't handled.

Usually files are sorted as strings, even if they contain numbers. However, it's possible to set the option numeric_glob_sort so that any ranges of digits within the pattern are sorted numerically:

```
zsh% echo file<->
file1 file10 file2 file20 file3 file30
zsh% setopt numericglobsort
zsh% echo file<->
file1 file2 file3 file10 file20 file30
```

You may think this looks much more sensible. Note that this occurs any time the files are matched by the same pattern; it doesn't matter whether you use the range syntax. This means file* would have worked just as well in that example.

Extended Globbing in zsh

When you set the option extended_glob, the characters ^, ~, and # become special wherever they appear unquoted. As you'll recall from the section "Shorthand for Referring to Directories" in Chapter 8, ~ is always special when it appears unquoted at the beginning of the word, where it is used to retrieve abbreviated directory names. The # character is also special when it appears at the beginning of a word: it makes the rest of the line a comment, which is ignored by the shell, as we explained in the section "Making a Script File" in Chapter 2. (In an interactive shell you need to turn on the option interactive_comments to achieve this effect.) Conveniently, the new uses apply only when they *don't* appear at the start of a word, so there is no clash.

Some users regularly use extended_glob—in many functions, for example. (We will discuss the use of options in functions in the section "Porting Scripts" in Chapter 13.) The only truly negative effect is that you have to get into the habit of quoting ^, ~, and # wherever you want to use them as normal characters.

Negated Matches

zsh offers two ways of asking for something that doesn't match a particular pattern. The simpler method is to put ^ in front of the pattern. For example, ^*.o matches every file in the directory except those ending in .o. (This feature comes from tcsh.)

The ^ often comes at the beginning but doesn't need to. The expression *pat1^pat2* means that the pattern *pat1* should be matched at the beginning, then anything that doesn't match the pattern *pat2* should be matched as the rest of the string. Let's consider an example:

```
zsh% ls
AAreadme  Areadme  HeHiHo  readme  abba
zsh% echo A^r*
AAreadme
```

Of the two files starting with A, one had an r next and so failed to match. The ksh and bash equivalent for this is A!(r*); note the * is inside the parentheses, which is why it is different from our first example of that syntax in the earlier section "Negative Pattern Matching."

You can use ^ for directories in the middle of a path; it just applies to that path segment:

```
zsh% ls /usr
X11R6  bin  etc  games  include  lib  local  lost+found  sbin  share  src  tmp
zsh% print -l /usr/^*bin/A*
/usr/lib/ADVX
/usr/local/Acrobat4
/usr/local/Acrobat5
/usr/share/ADVX
```

All the directories in /usr except the ones ending in bin were searched for files (including other directories) beginning with A. We could also have used the pattern /usr/^(bin|sbin)/A* or even /usr/^(s|)bin/A* to exclude those two directories and arrived at the same result.

Keep in mind that the ^ character is used to indicate control characters for the system's stty command and the shell's bindkey command. For example, in stty intr ^c, the last word was supposed to indicate Ctrl-c. Unfortunately, with the extended_glob option set, the text ^c expands to every file in the directory except one called c. Make sure you put quotes around words containing ^ if you use extended globbing.

Pattern Exceptions

Sometimes you find yourself thinking along the lines, "I need a file that begins with m, as long as it doesn't end in .txt". Exceptions allow you to turn that thought directly into a pattern. In zsh you can specify exceptions to patterns. This means that you can give a shell a pattern that it must match, and also a pattern that it must not match. The syntax is the pattern that must be matched, followed by a tilde character, ~, followed by the pattern that must not be matched.

In the first line of the following example, we show all files beginning with m. In the second line, we show files that begin with m but don't end with .txt:

```
zsh% echo m*
msg msg.out msg.txt
zsh% echo m*~*.txt
msg msg.out
```

The ~ operator works a little differently from the ^ operator we met earlier. You can see that by rewriting the last example using ^. In the following example, m matches the start of the word. Then we write ^*.txt to specify that the rest of the word should be anything except a string ending with .txt:

```
zsh% echo m^*.txt
msg msg.out
```

Compare this with the pattern m*~*.txt, where the parts before and after the tilde both referred to the whole word. We think that the example with ~ is a little clearer.

Note that everything to the right of the ~, including the slashes, is treated as one pattern. Therefore, a * in the portion after the ~ can match across multiple directories. So, for example:

```
zsh% echo **/*.c
config.c Src/Lib/Utils/prog.c
zsh% echo **/*.c~Src/*
config.c
```

The shell looked for all files ending in .c in all subdirectories. When it finished generating the list of files, it checked each filename against the pattern Src/*, and if it matched, it omitted those entries from the result.

You can eliminate any directory in the middle with a particular name using an exclusion pattern. In the following example, we're looking (searching recursively) for a file in a subdirectory, and the file's name must begin with an uppercase letter. We specify that no directory called CVS can occur in the middle of the path to that file:

```
grep **/[A-Z]*~*/CVS/*
```

This way of excluding directories doesn't work if the directory is at the start or end of the pattern, because of the slashes around the directory name (/CVS/). The slashes were necessary to stop other names that included the string CVS from matching. We'll meet a more powerful way of eliminating particular directories from a match in the section "Eliminating a Directory from a Recursive Pattern Match," later in this chapter.

Some text editors produce backup files ending in a ~. These don't cause any problem—a tilde right at the end of a word isn't considered special, because "excluding nothing" is useless. However, be careful when the backup files are numbered; Emacs, for example, generates names such as `prompt.c.~1.11.~` (a backup of version `1.11` of the file `prompt.c`). You would need to quote the tilde in the middle when referring to the file. If you use completion to get the file-name (typically by typing `prompt.c.<tab>`), this will be done for you; in fact, the completion system will quote the tilde at the end as well, which is unnecessary but harmless.

Multiple Matches

Sometimes it's useful to determine whether a character or group of characters is matched an indefinite number of times. For example, a name may have a repeated string in the middle and you want to match however many repetitions there are. The character # placed after a character or group allows that character or group to be matched any number of times, including zero. (It's similar to the character * in a regular expression, but that character was already taken in the shell.)

Note we said a *character* or *group*. If you put # after a single character, only that character is matched multiple times, whereas if you put it after something in parentheses or brackets, the whole expression is matched. Consider the following examples. First, we list the files in the directory. Next, we match a file whose name consists of zero or more uppercase A's followed by readme. Then we display all files consisting of any number of lowercase a's and b's. Finally, we show all files consisting of pairs of characters; in each pair the first character must be H, but the second can be anything:

```
zsh% ls
AAreadme  Areadme  HeHiHo  readme  abba
zsh% echo A#readme
AAreadme Areadme readme
zsh% echo [ab]#
abba
zsh% echo (H?)#
HeHiHo
```

You will probably find that you use this approach mostly with expressions in parentheses; in fact, you probably won't use it very much with files at all. It really comes into its own when matching against arbitrary patterns, which we discuss in the section "Condition Tests" in Chapter 13. This form is equivalent to the bash and ksh *(*pattern*).

Bear in mind that # only refers to the character or group immediately preceding it. In A#readme the # only refers to the A just before it. If the pattern had been BA#readme, it would have matched Breadme, BAreadme, BAAreadme, and so on. If you want it to match BABAreadme, BABABAreadme, and so on, you need to introduce parentheses and write the pattern as (BA)#readme.

A very close relative of # is ##. It indicates one or more occurrences of the preceding pattern. The two # characters act together; you should think of the two combined as a single special symbol. Let's consider another example:

```
zsh% echo A#readme
AAreadme Areadme readme
zsh% echo A##readme
AAreadme Areadme
```

That's just the same as writing AA#readme; again, the double hash is useful when something complicated appears in square brackets or parentheses before it. These two examples are equivalent to the bash and ksh patterns *(A)readme and +(A)readme, respectively.

Eliminating a Directory from a Recursive Pattern Match

You might expect a pattern like (files/*)# to match a hierarchy of directories in the form files/A/files/B, repeated indefinitely. However, this doesn't work. The shell doesn't apply the pattern inside the parentheses correctly when it spans multiple directories. There is one special case that does work: when there is only one slash in the parentheses, and it appears right before the closing parenthesis. Therefore, (file*/)#*.txt matches a directory tree where each path component except the final one starts with the string file—for example, filesA-Z/filesA-M/filesG-M/FISH.txt. Because the single # at the end indicates zero or more repetitions, the pattern will also match a file ending in .txt in the current directory. Doubling the # has its usual effect of ensuring that the expression in parentheses matches at least once. You can see that (*/)# has the same effect as **/. In fact, **/ is simply shorthand.

Repeating patterns for directories probably looks rather strange and not very useful. Actually, there are cases where it can help you. Here's one: CVS (Concurrent Versioning System) is a very common tool for keeping control of different versions of files laid out in a directory hierarchy. It's used by zsh as well as many other software projects. The tool maintains its own information about files in each directory in a special subdirectory called CVS. For example, the following output displays some of the directories in the current zsh tree, printed one per line for clarity:

```
zsh% print -l Src/**/
Src/
Src/Builtins/
Src/Builtins/CVS/
Src/CVS/
Src/Modules/
Src/Modules/CVS/
Src/Zle/
Src/Zle/CVS/
```

We've employed a trick that has yet to be introduced. You can place a / at the end of a file pattern, causing zsh to match solely directories. Note that the shell always outputs the slash at the end of each directory path. Those CVS directories just contain the special files; they're a bit of a nuisance if we only want the directories containing files specific to the zsh project. Here's how to prune the list:

```
zsh% print -l Src/(^CVS/)#
Src/
Src/Builtins/
Src/Modules/
Src/Zle/
```

In this example, we used ^ to make the directory pattern anything other than CVS.

As the previous output made clear, the directory names generated by the pattern include a / at the end for each directory matched, including the final directory. That means you don't need to add another slash when you want to find a file in the directory that's matched by the (^CVS/)#. For example, Src/(^CVS/)#zle_tricky.c matches the file Src/Zle/zle_tricky.c.

There is no equivalent in zsh for the ksh and bash pattern ?(*pat*), which matches zero or one occurrences of a pattern—unless you turn on the option ksh_glob and use ?(*pat*); we don't recommend ksh_glob unless you really prefer that syntax. However, you can do it in the same number of characters by using (*pat*|). That doesn't even require extended globbing. This expression consists of two alternatives: either it matches *pat*, or it matches nothing at all.

Glob Qualifiers in Zsh

A glob qualifier is a brief set of characters in parentheses at the end of a pattern that provides some restriction on the type of file to be matched. Along with the **/ pattern, glob qualifiers are probably the most used extension to filename generation in zsh. A pair of parentheses at the end of a file pattern can include a short description of the type of file you want to match. The "short description" can be as simple as a dot:

```
ls *(.)
```

This picks out all *regular* files—no directories, symbolic links, or other special file types. Note this works only when the closing parenthesis is the final character of the pattern. In this section we cover the most common forms. See the manual (man zshexpn) for more.

Single-Character Qualifiers

The simplest form is a single character denoting the type of the file you want to match. The dot is the most common. For example, the following command searches all the regular files in the current directory for the pattern mypat:

```
grep mypat *(.)
```

Any set of glob qualifiers such as the (.) in the previous example applies only to the file that results from applying all the glob expansions, not to any directories located earlier in the path. Consider the following example, where all regular files in the subdirectory Src are searched except those ending in .o:

```
grep mypat Src/^*.o(.)
```

The negation ^ doesn't apply to the qualifier, and the qualifier doesn't apply to the Src/ part. The list of files not matching *.o is generated, then all those files that *are* regular files are kept. (It's unlikely, but not impossible, that files ending in .o are directories or something more unusual.)

You can, however, negate the qualifiers themselves, separately from the pattern that precedes them: *(^.) matches all files that are not regular. Only ^ does this; you can't use the ~ feature in a glob qualifier.

File Types

The following is a list of the most useful qualifiers for file types:

- (.), which we've already introduced. This matches a regular file, that is, one which is not a directory, link, or one of the other types of special files we discussed in the previous chapter.

- (/), for a directory.

- (*), for an executable regular file. Remember directories can have executable permissions; they aren't selected by this qualifier.

- (@), for symbolic links.

As you saw in the earlier section "Eliminating a Directory from a Recursive Pattern Match," you can usually use a slash on its own at the end of a pattern to indicate a directory, but you can't combine it with other qualifiers. What's more, a slash on its own is appended to the argument. Therefore, */ might expand to subdir/ whereas *(/) would expand to subdir.

File Owners and Permissions

It's possible to refer to file owners and permissions using single-character qualifiers. The qualifiers r, w, and x indicate files that are readable, writable, or executable by the current user. Note that these modifiers apply to the person running the shell, not the person who owns the files. The same letters in upper case indicate files with those permissions for everyone. In other words, the qualifiers (R), (W), and (X) indicate files that are readable, writable, or executable by everyone on the system.

The following example shows three files. myfile is owned by the user pws, who is also the user running the commands. The username is represented by the command whoami. The file private is owned by root; only root can read the file, since the only r in the listing is in the second column, which applies to the owner of the file. The third file is rootfile, also owned by the user root. This is readable by other users; the three r's in the group of characters at the left show this. The *(r) picks out the file myfile, because the owner is the same as the user running the command and the user read permission is set, and rootfile, because all users are allowed to read it:

```
zsh% whoami
pws
zsh% ls -l
-rw-------    1 pws      users        239 Jan 18 20:36 myfile
-rw-------    1 root     staff        302 Jan 18 20:36 private
-rw-r--r--    1 root     staff       4096 Jan 18 20:36 rootfile
zsh% echo *(r)
myfile rootfile
```

The letter U refers to files owned by the user running the shell. For example, the following command lists all the files in the temporary directory owned by the current user (pws) and no files owned by other users:

```
zsh% ls -ld /tmp/*(U)
-rw-------    1 pws      users         239 Jan 18 20:36 /tmp/dcopoMNg4c
srw-------    1 pws      users           0 Jan 18 20:36 /tmp/esrv1000-pwslaptop
drwx------    2 pws      users        4096 Jan 18 20:36 /tmp/kde-pws
drwx------    2 pws      users        4096 Jan 18 20:36 /tmp/ksocket-pws
drwx------    2 pws      users        4096 Jan 18 20:36 /tmp/mcop-pws
drwx------    2 pws      users        4096 Jan 18 20:36 /tmp/ssh-XXt702x5
```

Combining Qualifiers

You can combine qualifiers inside the parentheses. The following example retrieves all executables that are both readable and writable by you:

echo *(*rw)

You can put a ^ at any point in the pattern, not just at the start, to flip the sense, so the following example matches executables that are readable but not writable by you:

echo *(*r^w)

The ^ is a toggle, so another one flips the sense back to positive matching. You can also designate a list of alternatives by using commas. The following example matches both directories and executable regular files:

echo *(/,*)

We haven't yet mentioned what happens with symbolic links. Usually, symbolic links are treated as a special sort of file that you can select with the qualifier @. However, if you put in a - (hyphen), qualifiers after it will follow symbolic links, so that *(-*) matches all executables, including those reached by following one or more symbolic links. Like ^, this works as a toggle and can go anywhere in the list of patterns.

Tip Sometimes symbolic links don't point to a real file. For example, if you execute ln -s /nonexistent ~/file, it creates a file in your home directory that points to a nonexistent file. Such links are referred to as "broken." A broken symbolic link often arises when the target file is deleted. You can find all broken links with the special pattern *(-@). The - qualifier tells the shell to examine the type of whatever file is referenced by symbolic links, whenever they are found by the * pattern. The @ qualifier tells the shell to find only symbolic links. The only files that match both requirements are broken symbolic links, which don't point to a real file. Thus, rm *(-@) removes all broken symbolic links from the current directory.

More Complicated Qualifiers: Numeric Arguments

Not all qualifiers are single letters; some take a numeric or a string argument. The numeric arguments are a little simpler, since they don't require special delimiters. We introduce several common numerical arguments in this section.

File Sizes

The letter L can be followed by a size in bytes to pick files of a particular size. You can think of it as standing for "length" (in bytes). It's usually more useful to precede the size with a + or -, to specify files with a size greater than (or less than) the size in bytes. You can also change the units to kilobytes or megabytes by putting a k or m immediately after the L (and before any plus or minus sign).

Here, for example, are all the files in the zsh source directory that are larger than 100 kilobytes, excluding .o files:

```
zsh% ls -l ^*.o(Lk+100)
-rw-r--r--   1 pws      user       182631 Sep  7  2002 TAGS
-rw-r--r--   1 pws      user       131308 Sep 26 20:50 builtin.c
-rwxr-xr-x   1 pws      user      1476478 Oct  6 23:38 zsh
```

File Timestamps

You can match files that were modified during a certain period using the qualifier m, a unit that defaults to days, and a number with an optional plus or minus sign in front of it for greater than or less than. Note that plus means "more days ago"—in other words, files older than the given number. This time, it's quite useful to omit the plus or minus, since "files modified six days ago" is meaningful, covering a full 24 hours. The difference is based on the current time, not the period from midnight to midnight; files modified one day ago are those modified between 48 and 24 hours before the present time.

The optional units to use instead of days are M (months), w (weeks), h (hours), m (minutes), and s seconds. This means (m-2) indicates files modified less than two days ago, while (mh+2) means files modified more than two hours ago. Note the position of the unit when it is present, immediately after the m. Here are all the files in my zshbook directory modified within the last hour:

```
zsh% ls -l *(mh-1)
-rw-r--r--   1 pws      user       52832 Oct 26 00:00 #p2c6_pattern_matching.ch#
-rw-r--r--   1 pws      user       51982 Oct 25 23:44 p2c6_pattern_matching.ch
```

The second one is the file containing this chapter. (The first is another file special to Emacs. If the file was edited but the changes weren't saved, every now and then Emacs saves the changes to a file with a # at the front and end so that they won't be lost if the system crashes. You need to quote those #'s if you refer to the file from the shell and you are using extended globbing.)

In the following example, we specify both ends of a range, picking up files modified between one and four days ago:

```
zsh% ls -l *(m-4m+1)
-rw-r--r--   1 pws      user       63849 Oct 23 16:44 p2c4_prompts.ch
-rw-r--r--   1 pws      user       67082 Oct 24 20:32 p2c5_files.ch
```

Files on Unix systems have three timestamps: the modification time, which we used earlier; the time of the last access of any kind; and a special one that refers to the changes to the file's current entry in the directory. You can use the qualifiers a and c for the access and change time, respectively. They both work in exactly the same way that m does. They're much less often used.

Counting Links

Another qualifier that accepts a numeric argument is l, representing the number of hard links. As with the previous qualifiers, including a plus or minus is allowed. As we showed in the section "Hard Links" in Chapter 8, the number of hard links to a file is the number shown by ls -l after the permissions; remember hard links are essentially alternative names for files. This command finds all regular files in the directory that have another name:

```
zsh% ls -l *(.l2)
-rw-r--r--   2 pws     user         12951 Nov 21 12:22 Makefile
-rw-r--r--   2 pws     user         12951 Nov 21 12:22 makefile
```

The link count for directories works a little differently because each reference to the directory from another directory takes up one link. The total number of links to a directory is usually two plus the number of subdirectories. The extra two links that are always present are related to the . and .. entries in directory listings. So the expression *(/l+2) refers to all subdirectories of the current directory that have at least one subdirectory of their own.

There's no simple way of counting the number of symbolic links to a file, because these links don't leave any sign on the file they point to.

More Complicated Qualifiers: String Arguments

A few qualifiers take a string as an argument. The argument is used to pass extra information to the qualifier, such as the username of a file's owner or a specification for a file's permissions. Because the syntax for qualifiers is rather terse, special care needs to be taken to mark where the argument starts and ends.

Specifying the File Owner

The qualifier u (for user) takes a string as an argument, namely the owner of the file. Here's a list of all files in the /var directory that are not owned by root:

```
zsh% ls -ld /var/*(^u:root:)
d-wx-wx-wt   2 apache   apache      4096 Mar  5  2003 /var/apache-mm
drwxr-xr-x   3 ftp      ftp         4096 Jun 28 21:19 /var/ftp
```

The colons are there to mark off the string root, so it won't be mistaken for additional qualifiers. Any pair of characters will do, except vertical bars—those are used to separate alternative matches and this can't be used in qualifiers. To make the appearance a bit more natural, if the delimiter is a character that looks like a form of opening bracket, then the matching delimiter is the corresponding closing bracket. (Angle brackets are allowed, too, just as in numeric globbing.) So we could have written the pattern as /var/*(^u{root}).

You can actually shorten that example. The qualifier u can also take a numeric argument; the number is the unique user id (UID) of the owner of the file. For root this is always 0, so we could have typed /var/*(^u0). For other users it's usually simpler to use the name.

File Permissions (Complicated)

One of the most complicated qualifiers is the letter f (for file), which checks for file permissions; it offers more options than the letters r, w, x, etc. The argument is a string similar to those accepted by the command chmod. (Type man chmod to learn more.) The letters u, g, and o mean user, group, and other (not owner!), and the letters r, w, and x mean read, write, and execute permissions. A plus or minus precedes the user specification, used to test whether the type of access is present or absent. You can separate sets like this with commas, assuming the comma isn't the delimiter you picked to separate the entire argument after the f qualifier. So:

```
# All files for which the owner has both read and execute permission.
echo *(f:u+rx:)
# The same, but also others don't have execute permission.
echo *(f:u+rx,o-x:)
```

Qualifiers for Ordering and Selecting

Normally the matches generated by globbing are sorted into the order of the names, with the effect of the option numeric_glob_sort taken into account. You can turn that option on for one pattern only with the qualifier n. However, sometimes you want to specify a different order—for example, sorting by the age of the files. You need to be careful if you list the files you've ordered using ls. In the sidebar "The ls Command and Globbing," we briefly explain the interaction between ls and globbing.

THE ls COMMAND AND GLOBBING

The ls command does its own ordering, so the files you pass as arguments may be output in a different order from the one in which they were listed on the command line. The default, as with the shell, is to sort the filenames according to the *collation sequence* specified by the locale; see the section "Internationalization and Locales," earlier in this chapter. This determines how every character in the character set is related to every other. You can specify reverse chronological order with ls -t. There are other relevant options as well; execute man ls to see them. To keep the output in the order generated by the shell (as modified by any locale settings), many of the examples in this chapter use echo and print to output the names in the order the shell generates them.

The spacing in the output from ls is modified, too: ls usually uses formatted columns. So sometimes we use echo just to make the output simpler.

More generally, beginners often use ls where the shell can do everything on its own. Consider the examples in the section "for and foreach Loops" in Chapter 2: we didn't need ls at all. Expressions like `ls` used to generate filenames are the wrong way to do it—use * instead.

The ls command comes into its own when you need specific information about files including directories. If you find you are using ls for some other reason, you might want to stop and think if using globbing would be simpler.

Ordering Files

You can change the order in which the files that match a pattern are passed as arguments to the command by using the qualifier o followed by a single letter that specifies a different sort order for the generated filenames.

Using (on) produces the default order: sorting the names according to the collation sequence similarly to ls. This ordering is a superset of alphabetical order. This isn't quite as useless as you might think, as we'll see. If you turn that into (On), the order is reversed. Here, we show both ls and echo output to emphasize the point in the sidebar "The ls Command and Globbing":

```
zsh% ls *(On)
1foo  MSG  ham.txt  msg  msg.out  msg.txt  newmsg  spam.txt
zsh% echo *(On)
spam.txt newmsg msg.txt msg.out msg ham.txt MSG 1foo
```

The arguments passed to the command were the same in each case, but in the first ls reordered them to name order sorted as we described for the qualifier (on) earlier. In the second case, we see reverse name order.

Several of the other forms of ordering are reminiscent of the qualifiers that take numbers after them. L sorts by file size, and m by the modification time. Those are the two most useful ones, but the other two timestamps a and c and the link count l also work. Note that the time order is most recent first with o ("increasing difference from now," if you like) and oldest first with O.

One special form of ordering uses the qualifier d for depth; it's most useful in combination with the ** and *** forms of recursive globbing and their more sophisticated counterparts such as our (^CVS/)# example. It means that the shell will search through all subdirectories of a directory before outputting the files within the directory itself. Note that if you use this on its own there is no other sorting—the files come out apparently randomly, however the records are stored on the disk. This means it's useful to combine this with another ordering, which is allowed: (odon) means the shell will sort by looking into subdirectories before examining the regular and other files in a directory (referred to as *depth first*), then by name. You can combine other forms of ordering in the same way.

Consider the following directories (associated with the KDE desktop) on my laptop, sorted alphabetically by name and then in depth-first order. The ordering qualifiers are combined with a slash so that only directories are matched by the pattern:

```
zsh% print -l .kde/share/apps/kon*/**/*(/)
.kde/share/apps/konqsidebartng/entries
.kde/share/apps/konqueror/dirtree
.kde/share/apps/konqueror/dirtree/remote
.kde/share/apps/konqueror/dirtree/remote/ftp
.kde/share/apps/konqueror/dirtree/remote/web
.kde/share/apps/konqueror/dirtree/services
.kde/share/apps/konqueror/profiles
zsh% print -l .kde/share/apps/kon*/**/*(/odon)
.kde/share/apps/konqsidebartng/entries
.kde/share/apps/konqueror/dirtree/remote/ftp
.kde/share/apps/konqueror/dirtree/remote/web
.kde/share/apps/konqueror/dirtree/remote
.kde/share/apps/konqueror/dirtree/services
.kde/share/apps/konqueror/dirtree
.kde/share/apps/konqueror/profiles
```

Note the way the entries ending in dirtree and remote appear later in the listing than their subdirectories. I think it looks neater with the subdirectories at the end, which means replacing od with Od in the qualifiers:

```
zsh% print -l .kde/share/apps/kon*/**/*(/Odon)
.kde/share/apps/konqsidebartng/entries
.kde/share/apps/konqueror/dirtree
.kde/share/apps/konqueror/profiles
.kde/share/apps/konqueror/dirtree/remote
.kde/share/apps/konqueror/dirtree/services
.kde/share/apps/konqueror/dirtree/remote/ftp
.kde/share/apps/konqueror/dirtree/remote/web
```

This way, complicated listings tend to put the longer entries later.

Changing What Is Displayed Using Qualifiers

In the section "Basic Globbing" earlier in this chapter we saw that the qualifier D turns on globbing for dots for the pattern. In the section "Globbing in zsh" you learned that the qualifier N turns on the null_glob option for that pattern only. So, for example, PROG*(N) expands to any files found beginning with PROG, but if no files are found, the argument is completely and silently removed. This is quite useful in scripts and functions to avoid causing unnecessary errors due to failed matches.

Other similar qualifiers include M to mark directories with a trailing slash. The qualifier T marks various types of file, not only directories but also executable files, which are given a *, and symbolic links, which are given an @. You need to be careful with T since the results are no longer files: the special characters become part of the string passed as an argument to the program. Therefore, you should only use T when the strings are to be displayed. Here we show the effect of both M and T on a directory dir and an executable file prog; M only marks the directory dir, while T marks both files:

```
zsh% echo *(M)
dir/ prog
zsh% echo *(T)
dir/ prog*
```

Colon Modifiers as Qualifiers

In the section "Modifiers" in Chapter 6, we talked about using expressions with a colon to modify values from the history. For example, :r removes a suffix, and :t strips all but the tail of the filename path. As we mentioned, you can use this feature with globbing, but the colon modifier must be surrounded by parentheses. Effectively, the expression with the colon is treated as a type of glob qualifier.

Colon modifiers must come after all other glob qualifiers. Also, note that you need to repeat the colon before each modifier. This is the same as for modifiers used as part of history references with the ! character. Consider the following examples:

```
zsh% echo ~/.z*(oL:t)
.ztcp_sessions .zshenv .zlogout .zcompdump .zshrc
zsh% echo ~/.z*(:t:s/z/ZED/)
.ZEDcompdump .ZEDlogout .ZEDshenv .ZEDshrc .ZEDtcp_sessions
```

The first example shows the base names of the files after sorting the files into size order, smallest first. The second changes the name of the files with a string substitution. This example makes clear a common effect of using modifiers: the resulting string no longer refers to a file, because some component of the name has been changed. This is like the M and T qualifiers, but unlike other glob qualifiers we have considered. They select files without altering the name.

Globbing Flags in Zsh

Qualifiers always come at the end of a file pattern. When the option extended_glob is turned on, zsh allows various *globbing flags* that can appear anywhere in the pattern and affect the way it is interpreted. They always have the form (#X), where X is a code character, possibly followed by a numeric argument. This works because a # following a parenthesis is usually meaningless; in normal extended globbing, it means any number of repetitions of the string preceding it, but there isn't anything just in front of the # character in this case. This allows us to use it for a different purpose. (The idea was stolen from Perl, which uses a question mark in the corresponding position of a regular expression for its own sort of flags.)

We won't cover the whole range of globbing flags in this section. *Approximate matching*, where the shell allows you to match strings that are a little different from the string in the pattern, is covered in the sidebar "Approximate Matching" in Chapter 14. It's used for the example in the section "An Example Widget: Correcting Spelling" in that chapter.

Case-Insensitive Matching

Flags are used when you'd like to perform case-insensitive matching. The form (#i) indicates that the pattern from that point on is to be considered ignoring case, so the uppercase and lowercase versions of a character are both matched by either the lower- or the uppercase character. Note that this applies only to literal characters in the pattern and not to any specified as part of a character class. If you want to stop case-insensitive matching, you can put (#I) at the point you want to turn it off:

```
zsh% ls
oREADME   READme   ReAdMe
zsh% print (#i)readme
README READme ReAdMe
zsh% print (#i)read(#I)me
READme
```

You can apply case-insensitive matching to a whole path with slashes by putting (#i) right at the beginning. Note, however, that doing so slows down the matching process. If the path starts (#i)/usr/, the shell must search the root directory for files with matching names such as USR or Usr. The only way of doing this is to read the entire directory and compare the names one by one. Thus it's usually better to put the (#i) at the point where you actually need case-insensitive matching to start—for example, ~/src/prog/(#i)README.

It shouldn't be necessary to read the entire directory for a pattern such as (#i)/usr/ in Cygwin, since filenames are all case insensitive, so that /usr and /USR refer to the same file. However, zsh only acquired the option no_case_glob in version 4.2; we discussed that option in the section "Basic Globbing" earlier. Without no_case_glob set, zsh reads the entire directory / to find /usr even in Cygwin.

A slightly more complicated variant is (#l), where only lowercase letters in the pattern match either upper- or lowercase; letters given in uppercase only match themselves. This, too, is turned off by (#I), not (#L) as you might think.

Summary

In this chapter we have discussed many aspects of pattern matching for generating filenames (known as globbing):

- The common forms of globbing: *, ? and character classes like [a-z].

- How international settings (locales) are important to the shell, for example, in the type and ordering of characters, and how this affects pattern matching.

- The special forms of globbing in bash; the forms @(pat1|pat2), !(pat), *(pat), +(pat).

- How to configure bash to ignore certain patterns.

- The many extensions to globbing in zsh: grouping alternative matches, searching recursively for files within the shell, matching numeric ranges.

- The additional power gained by the zsh option extended_glob: negated matches, excluding certain patterns from matching, matching an indefinite number of repetitions of a pattern.

- zsh glob qualifiers, which allow you to select files by their properties rather than by their name.

- The notion of a globbing flag in zsh that turns on a certain feature for a single pattern. Case-insensitive matching is a common use.

We haven't exhausted the possibilities of pattern matching. We'll have more to say when we talk about programming the shell in Chapter 13. For example, we introduce an extension to zsh's glob qualifiers where you can write your own qualifiers; see the section "Defining New Globbing Qualifiers" in Chapter 13.

In the next chapter, we return to the line editor and discuss how you can use it to complete the arguments of commands. Filenames are the most common type of argument to shell commands, and so completion has many features for selecting the file you want in a way complementary to the methods discussed in this chapter. However, we'll see that in bash and zsh the capabilities of completion go a long way beyond filenames.

CHAPTER 10

■ ■ ■

Completion

Shell completion started out in the C shell as a way to save the user effort when typing out long filenames. The user types the first few characters of a filename and presses a special key such as Tab or Esc. The shell then *completes* the remaining characters of the filename. Consider the following example:

```
% ls
index.html  intro.html  links.html
% cat l<tab>
```

expands to

```
% cat links.html
```

As you can see, I want to review `links.html`, and I only had to type the first letter and then press the Tab key, prompting the shell to complete the filename for me. It's quite a convenient feature indeed!

Modern shells have extended this basic idea well beyond its original scope. All manner of things can be completed: filenames, usernames, options, email addresses, words taken from the shell history, and anything else you can possibly imagine. When multiple completion candidates exist, the list of possibilities can be displayed, accompanied by descriptive explanations, and an interactive menu can be used to select among the possibilities. Also, it doesn't stop at merely completing extra characters: anything that involves intelligently interpreting your current command line to do something useful can be done—correcting typos and expanding patterns, for example.

Much of this control requires specific instructions to be written for each Unix command. `tcsh` was the first shell to offer such a capability, i.e., *programmable completion*, using a built-in with special syntax. `zsh` followed with a system based around a similar built-in, but this has since been superseded by a much more flexible system using shell functions. For `bash`, programmable completion is still a relatively new and immature feature. `bash` also utilizes shell functions. We will cover how to write such completion functions in Chapter 15. In this chapter, we will show you how to make use of the many functions that have already been written and how to configure them to work in the way that suits you best. Specifically, in this chapter we'll cover the following topics:

- Enabling the full power of the bash and zsh completion systems. We'll introduce many of the features this will make available to you.

- Configuring the display of completion matches. This includes coverage of how to enable the zsh feature of displaying descriptions alongside completion matches.

- Exploring the different ways in which completion can be configured to behave. This includes presenting interactive menus, expanding patterns, and correcting typos.

- Learning ways to control how the shell chooses the candidate completion matches.

- Seeing how the shell copes with some awkward situations. This includes removal of unwanted suffix characters and the case where one of the completion matches does not need any extra characters to be inserted.

Getting Started with Completion

To start, we'll enable the programmable completion functions that already exist for each shell. We can then see what completion can do and how to configure it.

bash_completion

The bash_completion project[1] aims to provide programmable completion functions for the most common Unix commands. Typically, it is installed as /etc/bash_completion (some Linux distributions install it there for you). To enable it, all you need to do is source this file. This is done by adding the following line in your .bashrc:

```
. /etc/bash_completion
```

That's all you need to do. Let's try it out and see that it works:

```
$ cd <tab>
```

bash should give you a list that only includes directories, leaving out any files (you can't cd to a file).

zsh's compinit

The zsh shell offers a collection of completion functions; a very much more extensive collection than bash, in fact. While the bash_completion project is maintained independently of bash, the zsh developers took a different approach and decided to distribute the completion functions with zsh itself. So you shouldn't need to do anything to obtain them.

The zsh completion system is enabled in a slightly different manner. You have to run compinit, which is an autoloaded shell function. So the necessary lines, typically run from .zshrc, follow:

```
autoload -U compinit
compinit
```

---

1. bash_completion is available from http://www.caliban.org/bash/index.shtml#completion.

The `autoload` command here tells `zsh` that `compinit` is a function that it should automatically read in when the function is first run. Autoloadable functions are discussed in more detail later on in the section "Autoloadable Functions" in Chapter 13, so refer to that section if running `compinit` produces some sort of error message. The `-U` option is there to prevent any aliases from being expanded (that feature being the key reason why `compinit` is an autoloadable function and not a sourced script).

The `compinit` function can also take a number of options. None of these are particularly important to understand. They either give you control over a dump file used to speed up the running of `compinit` (you may have noticed `compinit` taking a little while to finish the first time you ran it) or over a security check on the file permissions of the completion functions.

An alternative way to get started with the `zsh` completion system is to use the `compinstall` function. This is invoked in a similar way to `compinit`, first using `autoload`. As its principal function, `compinstall` guides you in an interactive manner through the many aspects of configuring completion under `zsh`. As its name is more suggestive of, though, it will also install the new completion system by adding the necessary lines to your startup file if they aren't already there.

If you're using a sufficiently recent version of `zsh`, you can also make use of completion definitions written for `bash`. There is a `bashcompinit` function that, when invoked *after* `compinit`, emulates the bash built-ins related to completion. Though it will allow you to use the entire bash_completion project, we would not recommend you do that because it would override many better native `zsh` completion definitions. It is better to pick out any functions that are of particular interest to you.

Completing Things Other Than Files

We showed you examples of completing filenames in the section "Building Pathnames by Completion" in Chapter 1 and at the beginning of this chapter. Filenames are not the only thing that can be completed, though. For example, if a word starts with a $, the shell will interpret it as a variable reference so it makes sense to complete variable names after a $. This both `bash` and `zsh` will duly do:

```
% echo $OS<tab>
```

expands to

```
% echo $OSTYPE
```

For another example, try completion after a tilde (~). As you might expect, this will complete usernames. `bash` will also complete hostnames taken from `/etc/hosts` if the current word contains an @ character. For this to work, you will have to make sure the `hostcomplete` option has not been turned off.

Sometimes, you might want to complete usernames, variables, or hostnames when the current word doesn't start with the requisite character. To do this `bash` provides a number of separate key bindings that you can use instead of Tab. These include Esc ~ for completing usernames, Esc $ to complete variable names, and Esc @ to complete hostnames. Additionally, there is Esc !, which will complete the names of commands, and Esc /, which will complete filenames. In the following example, we use Esc @ to complete the remaining characters of a hostname:

```
bash$ telnet loc<escape><@>
➤ telnet localhost
```

Before programmable completion was added, this was about the limit of what bash could do. Programmable completion allows the shell to see that the telnet command is being used and so complete hostnames, just with the Tab key. zsh does not have key combinations like these set up by default, but they can be enabled. Some of the completion functions define zle editor functions and become available after compinit has run. One such editor function is _bash_complete-word and to use it all you need to do is bind the keys. For example:

```
bindkey '\e!' _bash_complete-word
```

A Brief Tour of Programmable Completion

With bash_completion or compinit in place, you shouldn't need to remember special keystrokes for completing different types of things. Try completion after telnet and it should complete hostnames. Command options are often completed, a useful feature when working with long options. Consider the following example:

```
$ find -ex<tab>
➤ find -exec
```

For commands like cvs that take the name of a subcommand as their first arguments, these are also completed. Try cvs ann<tab>.

Many commands can only make use of certain types of files. For example, the command gunzip is only useful when used with compressed files. It therefore makes sense to only complete the names of compressed files after gunzip:

```
$ ls
docs.html  docs.tar.gz
$ gunzip <tab>
➤ gunzip docs.tar.gz
```

If zsh doesn't find any compressed files, it tries all files. This can be useful if you have an unusually named file. In bash, you can always use Esc / to complete all files.

Filename completion ordinarily uses the local filesystem to find out the names of files to be completed. Sometimes, however, the names of files need to come from some other source. For instance, when completing after tar xvf foo.tar, files are instead completed by looking inside the tar archive. Another case, which currently only works in zsh, is completion after scp *host*:. If you have password-less logins with ssh set up, zsh can complete files on the remote host.

When using the shell, if you're ever unsure what goes next or what syntax is necessary, try pressing Tab. It may not work but we expect you will be surprised at many of the unusual situations in which completion will do something useful. For an example of just such a situation, try this in zsh:

```
% echo $fpath[(<tab>
```

The shell lists subscript flags. These are special flags that allow array indexing to work in unusual ways. We will discuss them in more detail in the section "Reverse Indexing" in Chapter 12.

Completing Parts of Words

For the purposes of completion, the shell breaks the command line into suitable chunks. For the most part, this means that just the current word is completed. This isn't the whole story, though. As you have probably already seen, for file completion, the word is split at slashes so that you can complete files within a directory. bash also breaks words at colons. This lets bash do completion correctly in something like this:

```
$ PATH=/bin:/usr/bin:/usr/lo<tab>
```

Unfortunately, this can be inconvenient when colons are used in other contexts. For example, when completing URLs, you would not want the colon in http:// to be handled as a separator. There's not much you can do about the problem except quote any troublesome colons with a backslash. The backslash will have no effect on how the shell interprets the line when you finish it and press Return but it does stop completion from breaking up the word.

Command arguments sometimes take the form var=value. In this case, it can be useful to have files completed for the value part, ignoring anything up to and including the equals sign. bash will do this by default. In zsh, this is enabled as a side effect of setting the magic_equal_subst option. The main purpose of magic_equal_subst is to enable tilde expansion after an equals. In zsh, you will see many more places where only parts of words are completed.

In bash version 3, it is possible to configure the range of characters that delimit words for the purposes of completion. The characters are listed in the variable COMP_WORDBREAKS.

Configuring Completion

There are a number of different ways in which you can configure the completion system before you get embroiled in writing functions. Many features are controlled by simple shell options. bash also has readline variables that affect behavior (see the sidebar "readline Configuration" in Chapter 4). Next there are a number of different editor commands to which you can bind your Tab key. Each results in a fundamentally different type of behavior. Finally, in zsh there are what are known as styles, controlled by the zstyle built-in. Styles are essentially context-sensitive options that are not limited to "on" and "off" values. For more on styles, see the sidebar "Configuring Completion Using Styles." The remainder of this chapter is primarily focused on the many ways you can configure completion. bash users will find that most sections start with some material relevant to them but move on to concepts specific to zsh.

Listing and Formatting Possible Matches

If you have used completion in C shell or ksh, you will know that if it cannot insert any characters, it does nothing other than perhaps beeping at you. This isn't very useful. As we'll see in this section, newer shells handle the situation much more gracefully.

Listing Matches

You may have noticed that you hear a beep when the shell is unable to perform a requested completion. What do you do next? Typically you might decide to abort the line and run ls to see what files are there, offering a clue as to why it couldn't complete anything. That would only help when completing files, though. A far more useful feature is to list the possible completion *matches.* We saw how to do this back in the section "Building Pathnames by Completion" in Chapter 1: depending on your shell, you either need to press Esc = (ksh/bash) or Ctrl-d (csh/tcsh/zsh). So let's try it:

```
bash$ echo $HO<escape><=>
$HOME       $HOSTNAME  $HOSTTYPE
bash$
```

As you can see the three matches are listed and a new prompt is printed. Being able to see this is very useful. It's so useful, in fact, that it makes sense to do the listing anyway—in response to the Tab key. Both bash and zsh have this feature enabled by default (turning off the auto_list option in zsh would disable it). In bash, you'll find that the list is only displayed in response to a second press of the Tab key. zsh's bash_auto_list option emulates this behavior and setting the show-all-if-ambiguous readline variable to On in bash causes matches to be listed after just one press of the Tab key.

Requiring two strikes of the Tab key in bash makes sense because the listings of completion matches can easily add up to a lot of fairly similar lists scrolling up your terminal window. Information you want to refer back to can then have long scrolled off the top. zsh has a clever way of dealing with this: instead of reprinting a new prompt after the list of matches, it prints the list below the prompt. Subsequent new lists replace the previous one. Try typing cd /usr/<tab> and then add an s and press Tab again. Initially, it will list all the directories in /usr. Assuming that you have more than one directory there beginning with s, the second Tab press will replace the original list with a new one. If you don't like this, there is, as always, a way to disable it: unset the always_last_prompt option. If you consider disabling this option, be aware that menu selection, which is covered later, requires it to be enabled.

■**Tip** If at some stage, you find yourself actually wanting to keep zsh's completion list, there is an end-of-list editor command that you can bind to a key. When invoked, it will print you a new prompt below any current completion list.

Sometimes, the shell is able to insert some characters for you but the word is still not complete. This occurs where some initial characters are the same across all the matches. By default, zsh doesn't automatically list matches when this occurs. If you turn off the list_ambiguous option, then the matches will be listed. With show-all-if-ambiguous on, bash will list matches in this situation. In bash 3 you can instead enable the show-all-if-unmodified readline variable to make the behavior resemble the zsh default.

You may have noticed that the shell beeps when producing a list of completion matches. More precisely, it beeps whenever an ambiguous completion is attempted. This can cause quite a lot of beeping to occur, so to disable it you can turn the list_beep option off in zsh. In bash, you can set the bell-style readline variable to none, but note that this disables bash's use of the bell altogether.

Altering the Appearance of the List

In the previous section we showed how the completion system's ability to list completion matches can serve as a substitute for the `ls` command. One nice feature of `ls`, enabled by the `-F` option, is to show the type of each file. This is done by means of a trailing character:

- `/` for a directory

- `*` for an executable file

- `@` for a symbolic link

- `|` for a named pipe

- `=` for a Unix domain socket

- `%` and `#` for character and block devices, respectively

You can do this in completion listings too. In `bash`, you have to set the `visible-stats` readline variable to `On`, while in `zsh` it is enabled by default but can be disabled by turning the `list_types` option off.

Another feature of `ls`, enabled by the `-x` option, is to change the order of the listed files to be by rows first instead of columns. You can achieve the same effect in `zsh` by turning the `list_rows_first` option on and in `bash` by setting the `print-completions-horizontally` readline variable. This doesn't just apply to files, however: it will affect the order of all completion lists.

CONFIGURING COMPLETION USING STYLES

In the section "Shell Options" in Chapter 5, shell options were introduced as the primary mechanism by which shells allow their behavior to be configured. For completion, a much more powerful mechanism is needed. Styles serve this purpose in `zsh`. We'll provide a brief introduction so that you are comfortable with their use over the following sections.

Styles are defined with the `zstyle` command. `zstyle` takes a number of arguments. The first is a context string that allows a style to take on different values in different contexts. Don't worry too much about these for now; we start with simple context strings and will only slowly progress to the more complex ones. The second argument is the name of the style. All subsequent arguments give its value.

The context strings are made up of a colon-delimited list of tokens. Each token corresponds to some aspect of the current context when performing completion. When you set a style, you can use a pattern to match the range of contexts for which you want your style to apply. More specific contexts take precedence over vague ones. The least specific context pattern you might use would be `:completion:*`. This is useful for any settings that you want to make the default.

The actual make-up of contexts is as follows:

`:completion:function:completer:command:argument:tag`

This is useful to keep written down somewhere as a reference, but don't worry too much about it just yet. Each of the components will be introduced later as and when they are used in examples.

Formatting Messages

Along with the list of matches, zsh is able to display a number of useful informational messages. These are disabled by default but can be enabled using the format style. The format style is so named because the value of the style gives the format to print the message in.

The true command does not take any arguments, so if you try to complete after it, nothing will happen. Try it and see:

```
% true <tab>
```

Now if we set the format style, and try again, a message is displayed:

```
% zstyle ':completion:*' format %d
% true <tab>
no argument or option
```

The %d in the style's value is replaced by the actual text of the message. This allows a format such as Alert: %d to be used so that messages are preceded by the word Alert. Other special strings that will be familiar from prompt expansion in the section "Prompt Escapes in zsh" in Chapter 7 are also handled. So for instance, you can enclose the description in %S and %s to cause it to be displayed in standout mode.

■Caution If you did not run compinit as described in the section "zsh's compinit" earlier in this chapter, none of this will work. compinit does not just enable completion definitions for common Unix commands; it enables some more central functionality as well. Any configuration we describe that uses zstyle will be dependent on compinit having been run.

The context used for the style above extends the reach of the style across the whole completion system. Using a more specific context, we can make a style apply only in a more limited range of situations. In this situation, there are a number of types of messages and it can be useful to have a different format for each one. The different types of messages can be distinguished by the *tag* used when looking up the style. In the case of the simple example above for the true command, the messages tag is used. The tag is the last component of the zstyle context, so to restrict the format to those messages, the following style can be used:

```
zstyle ':completion:*:messages' format %d
```

Another possible message type is printed whenever completion is attempted but there are no possible matches. In this case, the warnings tag is used. So if we want zsh to print "No matches" in these cases, we can set the following style:

```
zstyle ':completion:*:warnings' format 'No matches'
```

If you now type cat qqq<tab>, the message "No matches" will be displayed unless a filename actually matches.

In the case of this message, it is possible to get a little more information. If you include %d somewhere in your message, it will be replaced with a list of the type of things zsh tried to complete. So let's try this style instead:

```
zstyle ':completion:*:warnings' format 'No matches: %d'
```

Now, trying the same example with the cat command, you should get the message "No matches: `file`". For many commands, completion is tried for a whole variety of different types of things together. So you may see messages along the lines of "No matches for: `process ID` or `job`".

You may have surmised from these messages that the completion system knows what type of object it is completing. Indeed, this is the case. The types are identified by a tag, and each tag can have a corresponding description. It can be useful to see these descriptions anyway, even when completion does find matches. This is another type of message, using the tag descriptions. This time let's format them in bold:

```
zstyle ':completion:*:descriptions' format %B%d%b
```

Now, if you try completion with this style, you will see a description of the types of matches above the list of matches:

```
% more <tab>
file
bin          downloads  mbox       photos     src
```

The descriptions and messages tags are actually an example of special case in that they are only used when looking up certain styles. Normally, the last component of the context when setting styles contains the tag identifying the type of thing being completed. For example, there is a files tag (though its description, as seen in the example above, is just "file").

Grouping Related Matches

In some contexts, more than one type of thing can be completed. For example, if you have set the format style for the descriptions tag as described in the last section, the completion list may look something like this:

```
% no<tab>
external command
builtin command
alias
reserved word
parameter
no_proxy      nocorrect    noglob       nohup
```

In this list, all the descriptions for the types of match come first, before any matches. It would be nice to group related types of match. This is possible by means of the group-name style. Each group of matches needs a name to distinguish it. By using restrictive contexts for zstyle, this gives you a significant amount of control over what things are grouped together.

However, with a value of the empty string, the tag name is just used for the group name. In nearly all cases, that will probably do what you want. So let's try the completion again with that:

```
% zstyle ':completion:*' group-name ''
% no<tab>
external command
nohup
builtin command
noglob
alias
nocorrect        noglob          nohup
reserved word
nocorrect
parameter
no_proxy
```

As you can see, this is a big improvement in terms of presentation. Sometimes, as in the example above, it can give a list that is a bit large and spread out. In these cases, you can group related matches. For example, to group the different types of command together, separately from parameters (zsh's terminology for variables), you could do this:

```
zstyle ':completion:*:-command-:*:(commands|builtins|reserved-words|aliases)' \
    group-name commands
```

The -command- here in the context restricts the style to completion in command position. There are a number of these special *contexts*. They all appear in the fourth component of zstyle's context string, which is usually used for the name of the command being completed. For the tag, we match any of four possibilities using a zsh glob pattern. Set this style and try the previous example again. Note how it now groups some of the matches.

Another style, named separate-sections, causes completion matches to be further subdivided. The following example demonstrates:

```
% man write<tab>
manual page
write        writev   writevt
% zstyle ':completion:*:manuals' separate-sections true
% man write<tab>
manual page, section 1
write
manual page, section 2
write    writev
manual page, section 3
writev
manual page, section 8
writevt
```

Currently, this style is only used in one other place: when completing words for the dict command it separates matches from different dictionary databases.

Per-match Descriptions

zsh can also print descriptions against each match. These are disabled by default. To enable them, you use the verbose style:

```
zstyle ':completion:*' verbose yes
```

Now try this:

```
% declare -<tab>
option
-A -- specify that arguments refer to associative arrays
-E -- floating point, use engineering notation on output
-F -- floating point, use fixed point decimal on output
-L -- left justify and remove leading blanks from value
-R -- right justify and fill with leading blanks
-T -- tie scalar to array
and so on...
```

As you can see, each option has a description of its purpose so that you don't have to refer to the manual for this information anymore. This is one of the ways that completion has gone beyond its original scope. It is quick to type two characters so you wouldn't want to actually *complete* them.

One simple aspect of this list that you might want to configure is the characters that separate matches from their description. The list-separator style allows you to do this. So if you perhaps want to use # because it reminds you of shell comments you would use

```
zstyle ':completion:*' list-separator '#'
```

When we are completing command options, there is another style that affects these descriptions: auto-description. If a particular option hasn't had a description defined for it but it takes an argument, the description for the argument can be used. As an example, consider fetchmail's --auth option. If we try completing options for fetchmail, the --auth option is listed but with no clue as to what it does. If we then try again after first setting the auto-description style, it will generate a description:

```
% zstyle ':completion:*' auto-description 'specify: %d'
% fetchmail --<tab>
--auth   -- specify: authentication types
and so on...
```

It can do this because it knows that the --auth option takes an argument for which it has the description "authentication types".

Handling Lots of Matches

If there are many matches, you may see a message like this:

```
$ ls /usr/lib/<tab>
Display all 1266 possibilities? (y or n)
```

This solution is a compromise: questions like this can be disruptive because you have to answer them before you can continue typing, but having to watch a huge list scroll past can be as bad if not worse. Fortunately, there is a better way. The matches can be displayed in an internal pager similar to more or pg, with scrolling under your control.

In bash, this feature is controlled by the page-completions readline variable and defaults to being on. In zsh, this particular feature is made available by a separate module named zsh/complist. To enable this feature, you need to load this module and set the list-prompt style to specify the format of a prompt, which will be displayed at the bottom of the screen. For example:

```
zmodload zsh/complist
zstyle ':completion:*:default' list-prompt '%S%M matches%s'
```

The value of list-prompt can include the usual prompt escapes along with a number of special sequences, such as the %M in this example. If you now try the last example again, it will display the first screenful of matches. While scrolling, a number of editor commands take on a different meaning. It is basically designed so that pressing Tab again will advance to the next screen of matches, pressing Return will advance just one line, pressing Ctrl-c will abort the listing and return you to the prompt, and any other key will stop the listing and work as normal. It is possible to configure what different keys do. You just need to use the listscroll keymap for key bindings to apply when scrolling. We showed how to do this in the section "Keymaps" in Chapter 4. For example, if you're used to pressing q to exit from your pager, you might be interested in this:

```
bindkey -M listscroll q send-break
```

Make sure you have loaded the zsh/complist module before trying to bind the keys—the keymap won't exist until the module is loaded.

Paging in bash is very similar to the more pager and is not configurable.

Types of Completion

Completion isn't limited to just adding extra missing characters. As we'll see here, it can be configured to behave in a number of ways. In this section, we'll introduce the following approaches:

- **Menu completion** allows you to cycle through the possible completion matches until you get to the one you want.

- **Menu selection** allows you to select a match from an interactive menu.

- **Expansion** takes such things as variable references and file-matching patterns and expands them in place on the command line. This allows you to see the arguments exactly as they will be passed on to the command when it is run.

- **Approximate completion** corrects any typos or mistakes in what you have already typed.

Menu Completion

Up until now, we've only seen how completion works by default. Menu completion does things differently. It doesn't bring up a menu of the possible matches as you might guess from the name (see the section "Menu Selection" a bit later for more on that). Instead, it lets you cycle through the available matches. Each time you press Tab, the current word is replaced by the next possibility.

To enable this in bash, you need to bind your Tab key to the menu-complete editor command. The command to do that is

```
bind 'tab: menu-complete'
```

In zsh, menu completion is enabled by setting the menu_complete option. There is also a menu-complete editor function if you want to use a different key to invoke menu completion. Furthermore, there is a reverse-menu-complete editor function so if you find that you have gone past the match you wanted to select, you can go back to it.

The zsh default is that the menu_complete option is not set but another option, auto_menu, is. auto_menu causes menu completion to be used after a second consecutive request for completion. So in effect, menu completion is started by pressing the Tab key twice.

Menu Selection

zsh has an extension of menu completion: menu selection. On one level, menu selection is the same as menu completion in that repeatedly pressing the Tab key cycles through the possibilities. Menu selection also takes over the list of matches below the prompt and operates it in a manner more befitting the term "menu." This means the currently selected match is highlighted and you can use the cursor keys to move around and select the appropriate match. Figure 10-1 shows menu selection being used to select an option to the bzip2 command. This is a compression command similar to gzip. At the moment the --stdout option is highlighted. If the Up Arrow key is pressed, the --quiet option will be highlighted.

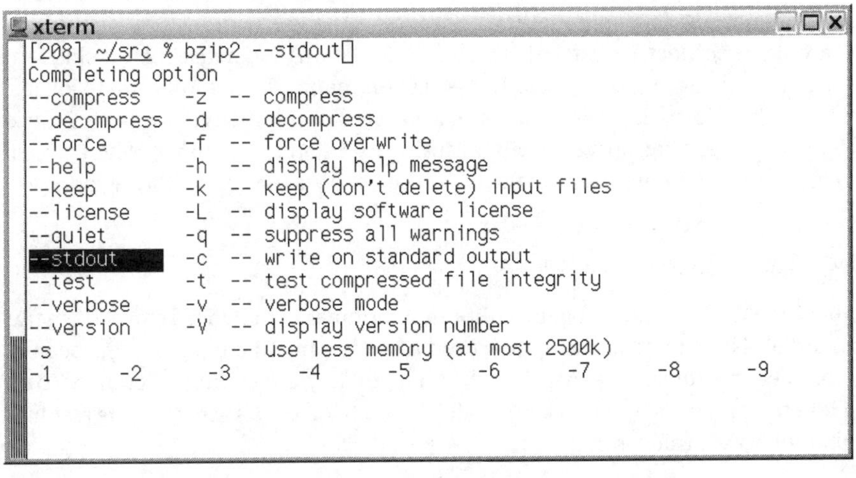

Figure 10-1. *Terminal window showing menu selection in action*

■**Note** A nice feature of zsh 4.2 is that matches are listed on the same line as any other matches that have the same description. The result of this is shown in Figure 10-1. There, options to the command bzip2 are listed as completion matches. As an example, you can see that both -c and --stdout appear on the same line. The two options have the same purpose, so they have same description.

Like completion list scrolling, menu selection is a feature of the zsh/complist module so you will need to load that with zmodload. To enable menu selection, you then need to set the menu style:

```
zstyle ':completion*:default' menu 'select=0'
```

The number (0 in this example) specifies how many matches there should be before menu selection is started. You can also use the word "long" in place of the number to start menu selection only if the list of matches is too long to fit on the screen. With these exceptions, menu selection is started whenever menu completion starts.

To allow the behavior of keys in menu selection to be configured, the zsh/complist module defines a menuselect keymap. You just need to ensure the module is loaded and then bind keys in that keymap. For example:

```
bindkey -M menuselect '\C-o' accept-and-menu-complete
```

Now, if you press Ctrl-o while in menu selection, it will *accept* the currently selected match, but remain in menu selection allowing you to select another match from the same list to form the next word on the line. This is often useful when you want to pass several files from the same directory as arguments to a command: you won't have to retype the name of the directory.

You may choose to use a different key combination, of course. We suggested Ctrl-o because the behavior is reminiscent of that of accept-line-and-down-history first discussed in the section "Executing Commands" in Chapter 4.

Menu selection is particularly suited to completing things that are not meaningful words so typing them is not natural. Examples of this are process IDs and X window IDs. Using the menu style with a suitable context, we can enable menu completion (and hence menu selection) for these cases. To demonstrate this we'll use the xkill command. xkill allows you to kill a window on your display. Normally, it asks you to select a window interactively with the mouse but using the -id option, you can specify a window using its unique ID number. When added as completion matches, X window IDs have the tag windows, so we use that in the tag part of the context:

```
zstyle ':completion:*:windows' menu on=0
```

The number in the style's value is again a minimum number of matches before the menu completion is started. The menu style can also be used to disable menu completion in specific contexts. Try completion after xkill -id with and without this style to see the difference. To do so, you might find the zstyle -d option useful. It allows you to delete a style. Usage is just the same except that the style's value is missing:

```
zstyle -d ':completion:*:windows' menu
```

You can also leave out the name of the style, but that will remove any other styles that use the same context:

```
zstyle -d ':completion:*:windows'
```

Expanding Variables and Patterns

If you look to see what editor command is bound to the Tab key, you will probably find that the command is called expand-or-complete. So what does the "expand" part of this do? Well, it expands just about anything on the command line that would otherwise later be expanded by the shell before the line is executed. This includes, among other things, variable substitution, history substitution, and command substitution. This lets you see the result of various substitutions before you commit to running a command line by pressing Return. Let's demonstrate this feature:

```
% echo $CFLAGS<tab>
  ➤ echo -O2
% echo `which less`<tab>
  ➤ echo /usr/bin/less
% echo =less<tab>
  ➤ echo /usr/bin/less
% echo !#<tab>
  ➤ echo echo
% echo /etc/z*<tab>
  ➤ echo /etc/zlogin /etc/zprofile /etc/zshenv /etc/zshrc
```

The third of these expansions (=less) uses a feature we haven't yet seen. It's explained in the section "Finding the Full Path to a Command in zsh" in Chapter 11.

■Tip The undo key is often useful in conjunction with expansion. If you are a vi or Emacs user, you will probably find it bound to a familiar key combination, and if not, you may want to bind it to whatever your text editor uses, Ctrl-z perhaps. As you use the more advanced aspects of completion, you will find it to be invaluable.

There is an alternative in the case of filename expansion (the last of these examples). Instead of expanding all the files, of which there could be many, menu completion can be used, allowing you to select just one of the possible files. To enable this, turn on the glob_complete option.

There is a better way of doing expansion based on shell functions. It is newer and has the advantage of being much more configurable. To enable it, the first thing you will want to do is disable the original, internal expansion. To do this, you need to bind the Tab key to the plain complete-word editor command. The Tab key actually produces a Ctrl-i in effect, so the command for this is

```
bindkey '\C-i' complete-word
```

Different types of completion are handled by functions that are called *completers*. For expansion, there is a completer named _expand. So next we need to tell the completion system that we want to use it before doing normal completion. The default list of completers is actually _complete (which does normal completion) followed by _ignored (covered in the section "Completing Ignored Matches," later in this chapter). So the style we want is

```
zstyle ':completion:::::' completer _expand _complete _ignored
```

We now have the completer enabled but we have a bit more work to do if we want it to behave in a useful manner. If you try expansion at this point then, assuming you've set up grouping of completion matches by their tag, you'll see behavior similar to the following:

```
% echo /etc/z*<tab>
expansions
/etc/zlogin    /etc/zlogout   /etc/zprofile /etc/zshenv    /etc/zshrc
all expansions
/etc/zlogin /etc/zlogout /etc/zprofile /etc/zshenv /etc/zshrc
original
/etc/z*
```

Note that under the "all expansions" heading is a single long match containing all the files and not five separate matches. So if you select the single long match all the filenames will be inserted on the command line.

You probably don't want it to offer all these matches, though. The original string is easily reached with undo anyway, and you probably only want one of the other two groups. Which of those you choose depends on whether you liked the glob_complete option or not. Fortunately, you can restrict which matches are added by their tag. First you need to know what tags the matches are added with. To help you with this, there is a _complete_help function. Let's try it out with an example. Ctrl-x followed by h is usually bound to _complete_help, so that appears as <ctrl-x><h> below:

```
% echo /etc/z*<ctrl-x><h>
tags in context :completion::expand:::
    all-expansions expansions original  (_expand)
```

This gives us the names of the tags used for the three groups we saw in the completion listing. If we just want to insert the one match with the all-expansions tag, we can then use this style:

```
zstyle ':completion:*:expand:*' tag-order all-expansions
```

The third component of the zstyle context is the name of the completer with the leading underscore omitted. In this case, we want our style to affect the _expand completer so we use expand. If you try expansion with this style, it should now just insert the list of files.

If you restricted it to just the expansions tag instead, you would achieve an effect similar to the glob_complete option. You can also combine more than one tag. For example, the following style is like glob_complete but the original string is included as a match:

```
zstyle ':completion:*:expand:*' tag-order 'expansions original'
```

Two styles allow you to limit the types of expansion:

- If you set glob to false, then filename generation (globbing) will not be done.

- If you set substitute to false, then most substitutions introduced by a $ are disabled.

So if you only want variables and not files to be expanded, you could use the style

```
zstyle ':completion:*:expand:*' glob false
```

This may be useful if you want to use another completer, _match, to handle glob patterns. You may notice that the expansion of variables and named directory references is not always done. If you press Tab immediately after a variable reference, it is expanded, but if you add a subsequent slash, completion carries on with no expansion having taken place. There are two styles, both on by default, that control this:

- keep-prefix preserves a tilde or variable expansion at the beginning of the word.

- suffix preserves a tilde or variable expansion if there are no further characters following the last one.

As an example, try completion after echo ~/.z*. The expanded list of files will include the initial ~. With keep-prefix disabled, the expansions would contain the full location of your home directory instead. The suffix style does not have as strong an effect. If you complete after ~/, it will prevent expansion of the tilde, allowing normal completion to proceed. The subtleties of these styles are really quite complicated, and our advice would be not to try to understand them fully but to experiment until things work in a way that you like.

The _match completer provides an alternative way to handle glob patterns in completion. Instead of performing filename expansion, the pattern is matched against the completion matches you would get from normal completion. So completion after declare m*path would add matching variables such as mailpath, manpath, and module_path as matches. _match is covered in more detail in the section "Stand-alone Completion Widgets" in Chapter 15.

Approximate Completion

Approximate completion provides a way of using the completion system to correct typos and spelling mistakes. It is controlled by the _approximate completer. Typically, you would put this after the normal _complete completer to give _complete precedence.

Approximate completion is done by first looking for matches that differ by one error from what was typed. An error could be an additional character, a missing character, an incorrect character, or two characters transposed. Additional characters at the cursor position don't count as an error, though: when doing completion you generally expect extra characters to be filled in where the cursor is positioned. Anyway, if matches differing from the original string by one error are found, they are added as matches. Otherwise, the completion system goes on to look for matches with two errors, then three errors, and so on.

Obviously, there needs to be a point at which _approximate gives up; otherwise, it would be able to transform your word into something that doesn't even vaguely resemble the original. You can, therefore, use a max-errors style, which allows you to specify a maximum number of errors that should be allowed. The following should give you an example of approximate completion in action:

```
% zstyle ':completion::::::' completer _complete _approximate
% zstyle ':completion:*:approximate:*' max-errors 2
% zstyle ':completion:*:corrections' format '%B%d (errors: %e)%b'
% nowhere<tab>
corrections (errors: 2)
where              whereis           whereis-archive
original
nowhere
% gerp<tab>
    ➤ grep
```

The `format` style with the `corrections` tag allows it to print the number of errors in the heading above the matches.

If you set the maximum number of errors to a fixed number such as 2, you might find that this setting makes the approximate completion mechanism overly aggressive with short words and insufficient for longer words. Making the style depend on the number of characters of the word typed so far requires more information than is contained in the `zstyle` context. Fortunately, there is a way. By using the `-e` option with `zstyle`, you can use the final arguments as a string to be evaluated each time the style is looked up. This evaluated string returns a value in the `reply` array. So for example:

```
zstyle -e ':completion:*:approximate:*' max-errors \
    'reply=( $(( ($#PREFIX+$#SUFFIX)/3 )) )'
```

The word currently being completed is stored in the `PREFIX` and `SUFFIX` variables—they contain the parts before and after the cursor, respectively. So taking their combined length in characters divided by 3, as here, allows one mistake for every three characters typed.

There is also a very similar completer named `_correct`. It is identical to `_approximate` except that it doesn't allow extra characters at the cursor position. If you use both in your list of completers, `_correct` should therefore either come before `_approximate` or have a larger `max-errors` value.

Controlling Matching

The term *matching* is used to refer to the process in which possibilities are compared against the word typed so far on the command line to see if the possibility should be thrown out or used. At the simplest level, this just involves looking at what appears before the cursor and selecting possibilities that start with that string.

Case-Insensitive Matching

One way in which you can affect the matching process is to make it case-insensitive. In bash, if you set the `completion-ignore-case` readline variable to `On`, completion will thereafter be done case-insensitively:

```
$ ls
README
$ less Read<tab>
    ➤ less README
```

This is a global setting and so applies for completion in all contexts. zsh's system is quite complex and provides a special *matching control* syntax. Fortunately, you don't need to understand the details of this syntax to do most things. A few basic constructs are sufficient for the common situations. Matching control is specified by using a matcher-list style. To specify that case-insensitive matching should be done by default, you can set

```
zstyle ':completion:*' matcher-list 'm:{a-zA-Z}={A-Za-z}'
```

This type of match specification involves two character correspondence classes. Characters on the left side appearing on the command line are considered to match the corresponding character on the right in a completion possibility. This means that you can achieve one-way case-insensitivity with this style:

```
zstyle ':completion:*' matcher-list 'm:{a-z}={A-Z}'
```

This can be quite useful because typing capital letters generally requires explicit extra keypresses and thus is more likely to be done deliberately. So such a deliberate action is preserved while lowercase characters can be freely converted to uppercase.

If you use the _approximate completer, you may find that this causes it to change what you've typed just a bit too much. However, because the completer appears in one of the components of the zstyle context, it is easy to exclude one by using a negated pattern as we saw in the section "Negated Matches" in Chapter 9. In this case, the relevant style is

```
zstyle ':completion:*:(^approximate):*' matcher-list 'm:{a-z}={A-Z}'
```

In some cases, matching control is applied automatically by the completion system. For example, try this:

```
setopt cO_mpLE_te_in<tab>
```

If it seems strange that this does complete, remember that shell options are case-insensitive and that any underscores are ignored.

Prefix Completion

If the cursor is positioned in the middle of a word when completion is invoked, there are a number of different ways in which that can be treated from the perspective of deciding which possibilities match. In bash, the suffix is considered when matching but is strangely also preserved after completion. Here is an example of the bash behavior:

```
bash$ ls -d /usr/l*
/usr/lib  /usr/local  /usr/lost+found
bash$ cd /usr/l<tab>oc
```
➤ cd /usr/local/oc *with the cursor positioned over the second o*

The default in zsh is to handle matching as if the cursor is at the end of the word. So in the previous example, it would complete the word to /usr/local/. With the complete_in_word option turned on, however, matching is done by expecting the characters after the cursor to be at the end of any matches. The option is off by default because it can take a little while to get used to but once you are accustomed to using it, you'll find it can be very powerful. To give an example, if you complete h.html with the cursor positioned over the dot, it will complete to any files starting with h and with an .html extension. I often find it is useful with the look or dict commands: try completing fless with the cursor over the l and it will match words starting with f and ending in less.

An alternative approach is provided by the _prefix completer. It performs completion with any suffix completely ignored. You can use it instead of the normal _complete completer, but it is quite common to use it after _complete so that it will only be used if that failed. To use it, you need to have the complete_in_word option turned on. _prefix doesn't actually do completion itself. Instead, it looks up the completer style and calls other completers to do completion; it just hides any suffix first. To set it up you can use the following:

```
setopt complete_in_word
zstyle ':completion::::::' completer _complete _prefix
zstyle ':completion::prefix:::' completer _complete
```

If you want to keep the number of styles down and don't want a different set of completers to be used with _prefix, you could replace the two styles with this one:

```
zstyle ':completion::*:::' completer _complete _prefix
```

Adding the star (asterisk) to the completer component of the context here allows this style to match when looked up by the _prefix completer. _prefix knows to miss out the _prefix completer itself so you don't need to worry about it calling itself again.

The following is an example of a case where _prefix can be useful. We want to add the command sudo to the front of a command line, to force the operation in the rest of the command line to be run as root:

```
% chmod 644 file<ctrl-a>
% sud<tab>chmod 644 file
    ➤ sudochmod 644 file
```

The Ctrl-a took the cursor back to the beginning of the line (at least in emacs mode). Without _prefix, if you wanted completion to work here, you would otherwise have to insert a space and then move back a character. In this example, you would want to insert a space after sudo. This will not always be the case, but if you want a space to be inserted automatically for you, the following style will do that:

```
zstyle ':completion:*:prefix:*' add-space true
```

There is also an expand-or-complete-prefix editor command. This is like _prefix but is only useful nowadays if you don't run compinit.

Partial Completion

Along with case-insensitive completion, partial completion was one of the effects that first appeared in tcsh as "enhanced" completion. In zsh, partial completions can be defined using the matching control syntax that we have already seen for case-insensitive completion. Partial completion allows completion to match other words wherever particular *anchor* characters appear. By way of illustration, type cd /u/lo/b<tab> and notice how it expands to /usr/local/bin/. In this case, the / is taken as an anchor. The effect is similar to if you had placed the cursor over each / in turn and pressed Tab.

This effect can be useful in many places. For instance, a dot (.) makes a useful anchor when completing hostnames and newsgroups. You can use the `matcher-list` style to specify partial completions. If you want ., -, and _ always to be anchors, you can use the following style:

```
zstyle ':completion:*' matcher-list 'r:|[._-]=* r:|=*'
```

It isn't necessary to fully understand the syntax of these match specifications. Only a few common forms are used. The pattern to the right of the | and to the left of the equals sign matches the anchors. You can use the same basic recipe with any anchors of your choosing.

Matching control specifications can be combined. This last style actually uses two specifications. If you want to use case-insensitive completion in combination with partial matching, you can use this style:

```
zstyle ':completion:*' matcher-list 'r:|[._-]=* r:|=* m:{a-zA-Z}={A-Za-z}'
```

You can also specify the matching specifications separately so they are not tried together but are tried in turn until matching is successful. For example:

```
zstyle ':completion:*' matcher-list 'r:|[._-]=* r:|=*' 'm:{a-zA-Z}={A-Za-z}'
```

Reducing the Number of Matches

Sometimes the completion system will generate unwanted matches. For example, an application might create backup copies of any files you are currently working on. It is very rare that you would actually want to do anything directly with these backup files, so it can be annoying when completion matches them. Completion becomes more useful when it generates fewer matches, because an unambiguous match is more likely. For this reason, excluding such files is a useful thing to be able to do. In this section, we'll describe the following strategies for reducing the number of matches:

- Restricting filename completion to only certain types of files

- Excluding matches that are the same as any preceding words on the command line

- Not completing matches unless initial prefix characters have already been typed

PASTING COMMAND LINES

To take reducing the number of matches to its ultimate extreme, you can disable completion entirely for certain contexts. The question is, why might you want to do this? Every now and then, you will want to use the windowing system's cut-and-paste to copy text from another window, perhaps where you are editing your start-up file, into your shell window. It isn't uncommon for the text being pasted to include tab characters, especially as part of initial indentation. This looks just the same to the shell as if you had pressed the Tab key directly so completion is invoked. The result is somewhat unpredictable and as a result it is one situation where disabling completion is beneficial.

Continued

bash has a no_empty_cmd_completion option that, if turned on, disables command completion unless at least one character has been typed. This solves the problem for any tabs in initial indentation because command completion is always used at the beginning of a line.

The zsh equivalent of enabling no_empty_cmd_completion is to set the insert-tab style to true:

```
zstyle ':completion:*' insert-tab true
```

You may find this behavior is already in operation—the default has changed between zsh versions. A slightly better option is to set the style to pending. What this does is to check whether more characters are queued up for reading. This is commonly the case when you paste text and is unusual when you are typing the characters. Unfortunately, it isn't guaranteed to work on all systems.

To disable completion more generally for a particular context, you can use the tag-order style. This isn't fully covered until the section "Tag Ordering" in Chapter 15, but for disabling completion you won't need to understand the full details. As an example, to disable all completion in command position, you can do this:

```
zstyle ':completion:*:*:-command-:*' tag-order '-'
```

If you use this style it will likely be with some other zstyle context. However, the context shown in the example needs a little explanation. -command- is used to indicate completion in command position. This actually applies in slightly more cases than just the beginning of the command line, such as after pre-command modifiers like nice or time.

Another issue you may have noticed when pasting text is that the output and error messages can be a bit of mess, becoming mixed up both with the input you've pasted and with any prompts that the shell has added. There's a trick to get around this. It involves using a feature we won't cover until the section "Grouping and Subshells" in Chapter 13, but it's so simple it's worth mentioning here. Before you paste the text, type

```
zsh% {
```

(This works in bash, too.) Next, paste the text. Then type a closing brace at the final prompt:

```
cursh> }
```

When you hit Return on that line, the whole chunk is executed at once. That's basically all the braces do—they delimit chunks of commands to be executed by the shell in one go. That's why the continuation prompt shows cursh—to show it's waiting for the end of a list of commands to be run in the *current shell*.

Excluding Certain File Types

To reduce the number of matches for file completion, bash has a FIGNORE special variable similar to GLOBIGNORE, which we saw in the section "Ignoring Patterns" in Chapter 9. A colon-separated list of suffixes is assigned to it, and files with those suffixes are then excluded from completion. To demonstrate:

```
bash$ cc <tab><tab>
main.c   main.o   main.c\~
bash$ FIGNORE='.o:~'
bash$ cc <tab>
➤ cc main.c
```

This feature is actually inherited from the C shell, where the variable is instead named fignore and is an array instead of a colon-separated list. You can use the fignore array in zsh too, but it is a deprecated feature because it can only have one context-independent value and is limited to selecting files by suffix to be ignored. Instead, there is an ignored-patterns style. As you might guess from the style's name, its value is any pattern and not just a suffix. So the equivalent to the bash FIGNORE value above would be

```
zstyle ':completion:*:*files' ignored-patterns '*?.o' '*?~'
```

The ? is not essential; it just ensures that at least one character is matched (* can match zero characters).

Another common use of ignored-patterns is to avoid the directories that your source code control system uses to keep track of its things but in which you are for the most part uninterested. This style excludes CVS and SCCS directories but only for the cd command:

```
zstyle ':completion:*:*:cd:*' ignored-patterns '(*/|)(CVS|SCCS)'
```

Ignoring Matches Based on Other Criteria

There are two more styles that allow certain matches to be ignored. The ignore-line style causes matches that are the same as a word already on the command line to be ignored. This can be useful with commands that cannot take the same argument twice. For example, you don't want to remove the same file twice, so it can be useful when completing arguments following the rm command. You might use it as follows:

```
zstyle ':completion::*:(cvs-add|less|rm|vi):*' ignore-line true
```

The context shown here matches when completing the commands listed. cvs-add refers to completion after cvs add. Modifying the command part of the context in this way is common for commands like cvs that support subcommands. With this last style set, the following will now happen:

```
% ls
one two three
% rm two t<tab>
   ➤ rm two three
```

ignore-parents is used to ignore directories that it makes no sense to complete. For example, if completing after ../, you won't find it very useful to complete the current directory because if you wanted the current directory you would not have bothered to type ../ in the first place. The style can take a number of values to specify exactly what is excluded, but the most useful is probably to set it as follows:

```
zstyle ':completion:*' ignore-parents parent pwd
```

Completing Ignored Matches

The zsh fignore array has a useful additional feature. If no matches remain after removing those with the specified suffixes, it falls back to completing all matches anyway. This can now be achieved by using the _ignored completer.[2] Completers in general were described in the section "Types of Completion" in this chapter. The _ignored completer is like _prefix in that it calls other completers to do completion but it allows otherwise ignored matches to be completed. Again like _prefix, it defaults to using the completers that preceded it but does check the completer style. For example, suppose we use the ignored-patterns style we showed you earlier for ignoring files with a .o or ~ suffix and we do this:

```
% ls
config.o
% echo co<tab>
```

Our ignored-patterns style would prevent the filename from being completed. If we used the _ignored completer, it would still be completed. If there were also a file named config.c, however, that would be completed first by _complete instead.

In bash version 3, it is possible to enable this feature for files skipped by the FIGNORE variable by disabling, with shopt, the force_fignore option.

Requiring Prefixes

Having the ignored matches completed as a fallback by _ignored leads to another use of ignored-patterns. Consider for a moment how completion handles files beginning with a dot by default. If you go to a directory such as your home directory containing lots of dot-files and try completion, the dot-files are not listed. However, if you type the initial dot and try completion again, the dot-files will be listed. To demonstrate:

```
% ls -a
.  ..  .zlogin  .zshrc  Mail  bin
% ls <ctrl-d>
Mail/  bin/
% ls .<ctrl-d>
.zlogin  .zshrc
```

Using _ignored and ignored-patterns, you can replicate this behavior for the completion of other things. As an example, you might want to do this for functions whose names begin with _. Provided that you have _ignored somewhere in your list of completers, you can use this:

```
zstyle ':completion:*:functions' ignored-patterns '_*'
```

By convention, all the functions for the completion system have names beginning with _, and since there are many of them, this can be a wise thing to do.

In cases where all matches share a common prefix such as the % for jobs or the - before command options, the completion system defaults to requiring the prefix. This is done by simply checking for the prefix before adding matches and so does not rely on the _ignored

---

2. Tag labels and the tag-order style, mentioned in the section "Tag Ordering" in Chapter 15, also provide a means of doing this but in a more complex albeit more flexible way.

completer. It can be configured, however, using the `prefix-needed` style. To see how this works, create a couple of background jobs (see the section "Starting and Stopping Processes: Signals, Job Control" in Chapter 3) and then experiment with completion after `kill`. It will complete process IDs, but you have to type the prefix before jobs, options, or signals will be completed. Now try setting this style and see the effect it has:

```
zstyle ':completion:*' prefix-needed false
```

If you want this effect to apply only to jobs, you can instead do this:

```
zstyle ':completion:*:jobs' prefix-needed false
```

Most people prefer to leave `prefix-needed` in its default state, but it can be useful to set it to `false` for the `_approximate` and `_correct` completers, if you use them. To see why, consider the possibility that you make a mistake in typing the prefix itself. In the following example, an underscore has been typed instead of a dash. We enable approximate completion first but completion is unable to correct the mistake:

```
% zstyle ':completion::::::' completer _complete _approximate
% bzip2 _-dec<tab>
No matches for: `files', `file to compress', or `corrections'
```

Because the prefix itself was mistyped, options were not completed and approximate completion could not do its job. By setting the `prefix-needed` style to `false` for `_approximate` only, we allow this to work without affecting other completers:

```
% zstyle ':completion::approximate*:*' prefix-needed false
% bzip2 _-dec<tab>
  ➤ bzip2 --decompress
```

The extra `*` in the completer component of the context after `approximate` is there because `_approximate` includes the number of errors being tried there. So the context string being looked up here will actually be

```
:completion::approximate-1:bzip2::options
```

You may have noticed a similar problem with our use of the `ignored-patterns` style in our example for completing functions beginning with an underscore. The `_ignored` completer has to invoke `_approximate` if you want to be able to make corrections to ignored matches. A more efficient alternative is to exclude the `_alternative` completer in the context when you define the `ignored-patterns` style. In fact, it makes sense to limit the style to the `_complete` function. We do that by filling in the completer component of the style, which is highlighted in bold in the following example:

```
zstyle ':completion::complete:*:functions' ignored-patterns '_*'
```

Another style that applies when completing things that have a common prefix is `prefix-hidden`. When set, the prefix is not displayed with all the matches in completion lists. This can make the lists more compact but less clear.

Defining Different Words to Complete

Sometimes, the completion system does not seem to complete those words you want, and it is helpful to make it complete a totally different list of things. A common example of this is when completing hostnames. By default, a list will be built up of hosts from sources such as the /etc/hosts file. The list is therefore not always going to be what you want.

To deal with this, you could write your own _hosts function to override the default, but it is a sufficiently common case to have warranted a simpler mechanism in zsh. If the hosts style is set to a list of hostnames, those are completed instead. For example:

```
zstyle '*' hosts Indigo athlon ultra1
```

> **Tip** If you include ${REMOTEHOST:-${SSH_CLIENT%% *}} in the list of hosts with this style, then when you log on from a remote machine, it will try to complete the name of that remote machine. This is especially useful when you are logging on to remote servers from a dial-up Internet connection where you have no real hostname and your IP address is dynamic. The REMOTEHOST environment variable is set on some systems and the ssh daemon sets the SSH_CLIENT environment variable. If neither of these works on your system, you can try parsing the output of the command who am i.

In a similar vein to the hosts style, there is also a users style. It can be useful on a machine where there are a few thousand users, especially if this causes completion of users to be quite slow. By setting the style to just a list of those people you know or have to deal with, it will only complete them. For example:

```
zstyle '*' users fred joe harry
```

> **Note** We haven't included the usual :completion: prefix in the context for these styles because it is quite likely that something else unrelated to completion will make use of the same styles in the future.

When accessing accounts on various remote machines with commands like rlogin and ssh, you typically have to specify both a username and a hostname. Because there is a correspondence between these, the users and hosts styles are not ideal since you can't specify which usernames correspond to which hostname. There is a users-hosts style for this situation. The value for it is simply a list of all your accounts. For example:

```
zstyle ':completion:*:rlogin:*:my-accounts' users-hosts \
    opk@shell1 okiddle@ultra1 builder@server2
```

The my-accounts tag here is used for commands that are typically used for your own accounts. For commands like talk and finger, the tag other-accounts is typically used instead. Also, for commands where a port number can also be specified there are users-hosts-ports and hosts-ports styles.

Similar to the styles mentioned so far in this chapter, there are also groups, domains, and urls styles, all for specifying replacement words to complete. Sometimes however, you want to be able to specify additional words to complete along with those produced by the completion system. Two styles, fake-parameters and fake-files, exist that let you do just this.[3] The fake-parameters style allows you to specify the names of shell variables to complete. This is especially handy for completion of variable names when writing an assignment because the variable may not exist yet and so cannot be completed. If you specify the names of any long, and often used, variable names with the fake-parameters style, they can then be completed:

```
zstyle ':completion::*:(-command-|export):*' fake-parameters LD_LIBRARY_PATH
```

The context here picks out completion in command position (that includes variable assignments) and completion after export. fake-parameters also allows you to specify the type of the fake parameters, so for example where only array variables are completed, it can decide whether or not to include the fake variable. So in the previous example, you might want to use the value LD_LIBRARY_PATH:scalar.

fake-files is useful where your system recognizes file or directory names that don't really exist. For example, under Cygwin, the special directory /cygdrive allows access to filesystems by their drive letters. Normally, zsh can't complete /cygdrive because it doesn't exist in the root directory listing, but with the following style, it works:

```
zstyle ':completion:*' fake-files '/:cygdrive'
```

Note that the value specifies the *fake* file separately from the directory it is in using a colon to separate them.

Automatically Added Suffixes

Normally when the shell completes a word, it will also add a space following it. Sometimes, however, a space is not pertinent. A common example is when a directory name is completed. In this case, a slash is more useful because you can then go on to type (and complete) the name of a file in the directory:

```
% cd pub<tab>
  ➤ cd public_html/
```

Now by pressing Tab again, we can complete directories within public_html.

There are many other cases where suffixes are added. Often the suffix forms the separator character between two things such as an at sign (@) between a username and hostname. Though

3. In the 4.2 version of zsh, a fake style exists to allow this for the more general case. If you use it, make sure to specify a sufficiently restrictive zstyle context.

it makes a special case of slashes after directories, bash doesn't have zsh's concept of suffixes (or prefixes). To get around this, any suffix has to be included as part of the match itself. To see the result, try listing the possible completion matches after typing chown:

```
bash$ chown <escape><=>
daemon:    games:    list:      mail:      news:      root:      sync:      uucp:
etc...
```

See how all the users listed have a trailing colon. In zsh, you wouldn't see it.

Adding a suffix isn't always what you want, however. Some commands don't like it if you pass them the names of directories with a trailing slash (including some versions of rmdir). If public_html here was actually a symbolic link to another directory, the slash could actually be harmful because it could affect whether the target directory or the symbolic link itself is used. For this reason, recent versions of bash don't add a / suffix when completing a symbolic link that points to a directory. You can configure this by setting the mark-symlinked-directories readline variable. In bash 3 there is also a mark-directories readline variable that allows you to prevent the slash from being added to any directory name.

To deal with this problem, zsh has a clever feature. If the next thing you type doesn't "make sense"—in other words, it's not something that would typically follow a slash—zsh removes the slash:

```
% rmdir pub<tab>
   ➤ rmdir public_html/
% rmdir public_html/<return>
   ➤ "rmdir public_html" is run
```

This can be quite a surprising feature when you first see it: it seems unnatural for something to actually be removed from the command line. Once you are accustomed to this feature, you will find that it behaves predictably and is useful. If you really don't like it, the option auto_remove_slash can be turned off to disable it. This is just a regular option and not a style and so it can't, unfortunately, be adjusted for particular contexts.

zsh has two other options related to these "auto-removable suffixes." If you remember from the section "Expanding Variables and Patterns" earlier in this chapter, completion after a variable expansion can expand the variable for you. If you reconfigured how expansion works in your set-up, it may not do this and you will have to refer back to that section to learn how to reenable it. See what happens if you do this:

```
% print $HOME<tab>
```

I get:

```
% print /home/opk/
```

Notice anything? The HOME variable's value doesn't normally include a trailing slash. After doing the expansion, zsh looks at the resulting value, sees that it is the name of an existing directory, and so adds a slash. Unsetting the auto_param_slash option will disable this particular feature.

The second option also relates to suffixes added to variable references:

```
% print ${HOM<tab>
   ➤ ${HOME}/
```

Supposing you now decide that you want to use a modifier. Modifiers, which were discussed in the section "Other Uses of History Modifiers" in Chapter 6, are introduced with a colon. So try pressing : now. Note how both the slash and the closing brace are removed. The auto_param_keys option controls this, so if you don't like it, the unsetopt command is again your friend.

Exact Ambiguous Matches

If you invoke completion on a word and the word is already complete and the matching unambiguous, the completion system accepts the word. There won't be any characters to actually *complete* but there may be a suffix to add:

```
% cd /usr/bin<tab>
  ➤ cd /usr/bin/
```

Sometimes, though, one match may be exact but the completion is still ambiguous. Consider this example:

```
% ls -F
zsh-4.2.1/   zsh-4.2.1-doc.tar.bz2   zsh-4.2.1.tar.bz2
% bzcat zsh-4.2.1<tab>
zsh-4.2.1/   zsh-4.2.1-doc.tar.bz2   zsh-4.2.1.tar.bz2
```

In this example, the directory matches exactly but both files also match. This behavior is not quite ideal when you want completion to accept the exact match because you can only do that using menu completion. In practice, all that selecting the match would do in this case is add a slash as a suffix. Adding a slash manually is not a big inconvenience, so most people prefer this behavior. If you do want completion to accept exact matches, you can turn the rec_exact option on. (The name is short for "recognize exact".) That would result in only the directory matching in this example.

When accepting a match does more than adding a suffix, the issue becomes more serious. This occurs when using expansion:

```
% foo=/usr/local
% foobar=/usr
% echo $foo<tab>
```

So what should it do here? It could either expand the exact match, resulting in /usr/local, or it could offer the two variables as matches. The default behavior is to complete the variable names. With old-style completion using the expand-or-complete editor command, the situation is treated just like the previous example. This means that both matches are considered unless the rec_exact option is set.

When using _expand from the new completion system, the behavior is instead controlled by the accept-exact style. This has the advantage over rec_exact that it only applies to the _expand completer:

```
zstyle ':completion:*:expand:*' accept-exact true
```

With this style, completion will now expand $foo. In zsh 4.2, it is also possible to use the value continue for the style. This will force completion to continue after _expand has finished, allowing all three possibilities to match:

```
% echo $foo<tab>
all expansions
/usr/local
parameter
foo     foobar
```

Summary

In this chapter, we have shown you how to do the following:

- How to make use of the bash_completion project or enabling zsh's completion system by running compinit.

- How to configure zsh's completion system using the style mechanism. We looked at how zsh displays matches and examined certain aspects of the completion behavior.

- How to make the completion system expand substitutions on the command line.

- How to configure zsh's completion system to correct typos and spelling mistakes or to ignore the case of words when completing.

- How to make completion more useful by avoiding unwanted matches.

The shell completion system can make it a lot easier and quicker to accomplish basic tasks from the command line. The aim of this chapter was to make it possible for you to take full advantage of the completion system's power. We will return to the topic of completion in Chapter 15 when we show you how to write your own completion definitions. In the next chapter, however, we explain the details of how you can control separate processes using the shell's job control features.

CHAPTER 11

■ ■ ■

Jobs and Processes

One of the areas in which the shell is particularly powerful is that of job control. Job control allows you to have more than one process using a single terminal. On modern computers where it is easy to have several terminal windows open on your display, job control is perhaps not as valuable as it once was, but it is still extremely useful. Many of the basics were introduced in Chapter 3, but in this chapter we complete the picture. We also cover a number of other advanced topics related to processes. In particular, we examine the following topics:

- Details of the ways in which you can manipulate jobs from the shell

- How to control what happens to jobs when the shell exits

- How to control the way the shell interprets the output from command substitutions

- Process substitution—and advanced forms of command substitution

- Resource limits that allow processes' use of resources such as memory to be restricted

- How to change the name of a process and what such changes mean

Mastering Job Control

Job control was first introduced in the section "Starting and Stopping Processes: Signals, Job Control" in Chapter 3. We showed you how to both stop jobs and run them in the background. Then you could have several commands running at once, just as long as they didn't need to use the terminal. We also showed you how to kill jobs that weren't running in the foreground using kill. However, there are a few things we need to add:

- Bringing a background or stopped job into the foreground (*resuming* a stopped job).

- Resuming a job quickly, without any special commands

- Telling the shell not to kill a job when the shell exits

- Telling the shell to ignore a background job completely

- Suspending the shell itself

In this section, we'll introduce these concepts.

Resuming Stopped and Background Jobs

We explained that when you press Ctrl-z it stops the currently running job, returning you to the shell prompt. Then when you type bg %*num*, where *num* is the number reported by the jobs command, the job resumes in the background.

In either of the two states—stopped or running in the background—you can use fg to bring the command into the foreground again. At that point, the command behaves just as if you'd never stopped it or put it in the background. When a job is running in the foreground, it has control of the terminal. Key combinations such as Ctrl-z or Ctrl-c always affect the foreground job.

This behavior is commonly used in conjunction with text editors. Many Unix users have a text editor running in the background all the time. When they want to use it, they run fg to bring it back to the foreground. When they want to execute some other command, they press Ctrl-z to go back to the shell prompt. This isn't helpful if your text editor has a separate window on your display, however—there's no point in stopping it when you switch to the shell window.

It's a little more complicated if the command is actually running inside the shell. For example, job control with shell functions can be a problem (see Chapter 13). zsh tries to handle this by treating the function as if it were a separate command, so you can stop a function and put it into the background. However, there's no way of bringing it back inside the shell that started it. You can use fg to bring it into the foreground, but it continues to run as a separate process. It's essentially a *subshell*, which we describe in the section "Grouping and Subshells" in Chapter 13. bash doesn't have that feature at the moment.

For people who frequently stop and restart foreground jobs, the shells provide a couple of shortcuts for doing this.

- You can use fg on its own to bring to the foreground the command that was most recently stopped or put in the background. The jobs command shows the job in question with a + after the job number.

- Instead of fg %*num*, you can simply type %*num* on its own. The shell takes special account of any command beginning with %, and looks to see if it corresponds to a job to bring into the foreground.

- If your jobs all start with different command names, you can use the name of the command after the % to resume the job. For example, use %vi if the job is running the editor vi. (You don't need any of the arguments to the command.) That means you don't need to find out the job number.

- bash and zsh both support an option, auto_resume, that allows you to bring a job to the foreground by typing its name without % in front. In bash, it's actually a shell variable that can be set to exact or substring. In zsh, it's an ordinary shell option. Setting auto_resume=substring in bash means you don't even need to type the full name of the job, just part of it. (That can lead to some odd effects if you're not careful, though. Short command names can easily match a job by accident.) Let's consider an example:

```
zsh% stty susp '^Z'
zsh% setopt auto_resume
zsh% vi
<ctrl-z>
zsh: 1535 suspended  vi
zsh% vi
[1]  + continued  vi
```

You may not see all those lines if vi clears the terminal when it starts and doesn't restore it when you suspend it. The stty command ensures that Ctrl-z is the suspend key; refer to the section "Other Tips on Terminals" in Chapter 4 for an explanation of that. In bash, you can only auto-resume a job if it's stopped, not if it's running in the background. (The jobs command will tell you if you're not sure which is the case.) In zsh, you can auto-resume jobs that are running in the background, too.

Most job control commands don't work in scripts or in any noninteractive shell. In particular, the %num syntax isn't available. That's because job control is based around a *controlling terminal*. The foreground job is the one that is attached to the terminal. That doesn't apply in a script. You can still start background jobs by putting & at the end, though. You just can't ever bring them to the foreground after starting them.

Use of the Terminal by Background Jobs

One problem you may notice when putting jobs in the background is that they can still write their output to the terminal. If they do, the output will be mixed up with any output from the job you are running in the foreground. One way to deal with this is to redirect the program's output when you first run it.

The same problem doesn't exist for background jobs trying to read from the terminal. If a background job tries to read from the terminal, the terminal driver automatically suspends it:

```
% { read; } &
[1] 1914

[1]+  Stopped                 { read; }
```

(You may have to hit Return again before the shell tells you the job is stopped.)

Using the stty tostop command, it is possible to extend this feature. Then background jobs are stopped when they attempt to write to the terminal, as well as when they read from it. You can bring such jobs back to the foreground at your convenience. To disable the feature, execute the command stty -tostop.

Letting Sleeping (or Background) Jobs Lie

So what happens to a job once you exit the shell? In most cases, there is little point in keeping jobs around so it is common for the shell to kill any remaining jobs upon exiting.

By default, zsh kills any running jobs when you exit the shell. It does this by sending each job the SIGHUP signal. We met this signal briefly in the section "Starting and Stopping Processes: Signals, Job Control" in Chapter 3 as part of the command kill -HUP. That's an explicit request to send the same signal to a process. In contrast to this, bash leaves running jobs alone by default.

Stopped jobs are treated differently: the operating system itself kills them. Actually, bash will kill any stopped jobs first (using the SIGTERM signal), but the key point is that they are always killed.

The shell usually warns you about any stopped or background jobs when you try to exit. After the warning, it returns you to the prompt, so you can do something about the jobs. If you type exit again immediately, the shell will exit without another warning. It also does this if you type jobs, then another exit—the shell assumes you have seen the list of jobs and are satisfied.

There are various ways in zsh of preventing the shell from killing jobs on exit:

- Set the option nohup. Then the shell won't kill running jobs when it exits. (Stopped jobs will be killed by the operating system anyway, though the shell won't do this deliberately.) The shell will still warn you about stopped and background jobs, however. You can disable the warning, too, by unsetting the option check_jobs. This is the easiest choice if you're not concerned about old jobs hanging around.

- If you want some but not all commands to be left running when the shell exits, you can put nohup in front of any command line. This tells the command to ignore any SIGHUP sent to it, so that the command will be left running when the shell exits. For example, you might use nohup for a program that downloads a large file. Any output from the command is put in a file named nohup.out. Note that nohup doesn't automatically run the command in the background so you still need to end the command line with &.

- You can use the shell's disown command to tell the shell to ignore the job completely. The shell won't send SIGHUP to the job. This method has the side effect that no job control commands will work. Even jobs won't show the command any more. If this isn't a problem, you can start the job in the background with &! at the end of the line instead of &. This immediately disowns the job.

Tip You can use disown any time you don't want a job to appear in the list, not just to ignore SIGHUP. The same is true for the &! syntax to start a job in the background and disown it. The latter is quite useful with commands that bring up a new window, since normally you interact with these directly rather than from the terminal. For example, you can start a new terminal emulator with xterm &! and it won't appear in the shell's job list.

All the commands fg, bg, and disown use the job marked with a + in the jobs list whenever you don't give them a job number.

bash works a bit differently. We mention it second because by default it doesn't kill running jobs when it exits, so you're less likely to become aware of the issue. However, if you set (with shopt -s) the huponexit option, bash will also send the SIGHUP signal to running jobs. Note, however, that the option only has an effect from an interactive login shell. See the section "Login Shells" in Chapter 5 for what we mean by that.

With huponexit set, nohup, which is a standard external command, is also useful in bash. Since nohup is not part of the shell, you can't use it with commands that are built into the shell or with shell functions. It will work with scripts, however.

The disown command is also available in bash and works like it does in zsh, removing the job completely from the shell's list of jobs. However, in bash you can also execute disown -h %*num* to tell the shell that you don't want the job to be sent SIGHUP when the shell exits. In this case you can still do job control. The &! syntax doesn't exist, unfortunately.

Reducing the Priority of Background Jobs

Since you don't usually want background jobs to slow down your use of the terminal or other windows, zsh runs background jobs at a lower priority. (This only happens if you start the job in the background—in other words, with an ampersand at the end of the command line.) In Unix jargon, this is referred to as a larger *nice value*, because the less the program hogs the computer, the more nice to you it's being. If you want a background job to run at the normal priority—for example, because it's running in another window and you need it to respond quickly—you can turn off the option bg_nice.

bash doesn't alter the priority of jobs started in the background. You need to use the external command nice to reduce the priority of a command—just put it at the start of the command line. You can do this with foreground commands, too, and because it's an external command it works with zsh as well. There's also a command renice to increase the niceness of a command that is already running. (Only the root user can decrease the niceness of a running command.)

The following is an example of the nice command being used to lower the priority of a job run in the background. The command make is often used to compile software. For large software packages, this can be a long task and consume many system resources. Therefore, this is a good example of when reducing the priority is beneficial. As the command executes in the background, we also redirect both the standard output and standard error channels to a file:

```
% nice make >make.log 2>&1 &
```

Suspending the Shell Itself

One thing you may have wondered about is why pressing Ctrl-z when you are at the shell prompt doesn't suspend the shell itself. The shell disables this because if the shell stops, the terminal is unlikely to be picked up by another process. This would be annoying because it is then not very convenient to arrange for the shell to be sent a SIGCONT signal so that it can start again. We showed how you can start one shell from another back in the section "Starting Shells" in Chapter 5. If you do this, perhaps because you are comparing features of bash and zsh, it would be nice to be able to suspend a second shell and return to the first.

We told you that Ctrl-z causes a signal to be sent to the foreground process. Since Ctrl-z doesn't work, let's try sending the signal directly. As we saw in the section "Expansion and Substitution" in Chapter 1, we can retrieve the shell's process identifier from $$. So we can try this:

```
bash$ zsh
zsh% kill -STOP $$

[1]+  Stopped                 zsh
bash$
```

As an alternative, both shells have a suspend built-in that does the same. However, it is a tad cleverer. Try running it and it is likely you will see this:

```
% suspend
suspend: can't suspend login shell
```

This makes sense because a login shell is typically not run from another shell. However, there are times when you use a command like rlogin or telnet to log in to a remote machine and it would be nice to suspend the connection and return to the shell on the local machine. Suspending the shell running on the remote machine is not going to help. What you need to do is suspend the actual rsh or telnet client. These are what your local shell is running. Fortunately, both can be suspended:

- When you run telnet, you may notice that it prints a line like the following:

  ```
  Escape character is '^]'.
  ```

  What that means is that you can press Ctrl-] to escape. Try pressing it and telnet will drop out of whatever you're doing on the remote machine and print its own prompt. If you type help at this prompt you will see that telnet actually has a range of its own commands. However, what we're more interested in is that you can now press Ctrl-z to suspend telnet.

- rlogin has a number of special escape sequences. In their case, you need to type a tilde (~) followed by Ctrl-z. This has to be at the beginning of a line so you may need to press Return first. This sequence will get you straight out and back to the original shell. There are a number of other escape sequences. You might be able to use ~? to list them. These escape sequences also work with ssh and with the remote shell command that is variously either rsh or remsh.

To return to the suspended shell, use fg or any of the special forms, just like with any other command.

High-Power Command Substitutions

We met command substitution in the section "Command Substitution" in Chapter 2. An expression with backquotes, `...`, is treated as a mini-command line of its own. It is run when the shell parses the command arguments—before the main command is started—and the output from it is put back into the main command line. It's a very commonly used shell feature, and there's more to it than what we said. In this section you'll learn

- How to control the way the substitution is divided into words

- How to make command substitution arguments behave a bit more like file arguments (we'll explain, if that sounds cryptic)

- zsh's shortcut for getting the full name of a command, including the directory

Command Substitution and Command Arguments

An expression in backquotes, `` `...` ``, is equivalent to the same expression inside $(...). The second form wasn't understood by older shells, so the first is still more commonly used. However, the second form is better if your shell supports it. (Backquotes are also called "backticks," since they look a little bit more like ticks than quotes in many typefaces.)

With simple substitutions it's not obvious why the newer form is better. Here's why: command substitution can include *any* set of shell commands. They might even include more command substitutions. If you use $(...) you don't need to worry—the parentheses are always paired, so it will work without any changes to the commands inside. If you use backquotes, however, you will need to quote any backquotes inside.

Here's an example complicated enough for the difference between the form with backquotes and the form with parentheses to be significant. It uses the command strip, which removes debugging information from executable files. It's quite common for advanced Unix users to strip files in order to save disk space, provided they are sure they will not want to debug the programs:

```
strip $(file $(cat filenames) | grep 'not stripped' | cut -d: -f1)
```

This expands the contents of the file filenames, which contains a list of filenames. The shell runs the command file on this list. We pipe this output to grep, which looks for any files that have been marked "not stripped". This message from file indicates an executable command that contains debugging symbols. We further pipe the output to cut to extract just the names of the files. The command substitution then passes the filenames to the strip command.

If we'd used backquotes, the inner substitution would have had to be `` \`cat filenames\` `` to prevent the shell from thinking that `` `file ` `` was the command substitution. We'd have

```
strip `file \`cat filenames\` | grep 'not stripped' | cut -d: -f1`
```

That works, but if you use the form we recommend, it doesn't need any backslashes for quoting.

Quoted Command Substitution

Both backquotes and the $(...) form work differently when they appear inside double quotes. (As with variable substitution, they don't work at all inside single quotes.) As we've seen, the output from an unquoted substitution gets turned into a whole set of command arguments. However, if the substitution is quoted, there is only one word. This is important if the substitution is to output a single argument that may have spaces in it. Let's consider an example:

```
% mkdir 'Program Files'
% touch 'Program Files/myprog'
% echo 'Program Files' >mydirs
% ls $(cat mydirs)
ls: Program: No such file or directory
ls: Files: No such file or directory
% ls "$(cat mydirs)"
myprog
```

In the first attempt at ls the space caused the directory name to be split into two, which ls saw as different filenames. In the second attempt, the quotes stopped that. (Filenames of this kind are extremely common in Windows.)

(By the way, you might think you could put the quoted form 'Program Files' into the file mydirs. Try it if you like; you'll see it doesn't work. That's because when the command substitution takes place, the shell has already parsed quotes. It doesn't do this again after the command substitution. So any quotes that come out of the file are treated as if they were normal characters.)

In the section "Variable Expansion Flags" in Chapter 12 we'll show how you can embed a command substitution inside a variable expansion to give you more control over the splitting.

We've already mentioned in passing that the output from command substitution doesn't get re-evaluated. For example, if the output contains $ characters, they won't be used to introduce substitutions, because the shell has already dealt with those. They'll simply be inserted onto the command line as literal $ characters.

It's not quite that simple, in fact. The real rule is that the shell continues with substitutions in the same order it always does them. In bash, that means that pattern characters that come from command substitution are active, because globbing occurs after command substitution:

```
bash$ ls $(echo '*')
...files in the current directory...
```

If you try that in zsh, you'll just see *. However, zsh does the substitutions in the same order as bash. The difference is that characters that come from substitutions are never special in zsh; they are treated as if they were quoted. You can switch to the bash behavior by setting the option glob_subst. (The same effect applies to variable substitutions, too.)

Sometimes you *do* want a command line to be reevaluated completely. For that you can use the shell's eval command, which we come to in the section "Variable Indirection" in Chapter 12.

Process Substitution

Process substitution is a specialized form of command substitution. Like ordinary command substitution, special syntax is used to indicate a command to be executed. Unlike ordinary command substitution, what is substituted is not the output of the command. Instead, it's a filename. There are three forms:

- <(*commands*): The *commands* are executed. The expression is replaced with the name of a file that can be read for the output of the commands.

- >(*commands*): The *commands* are executed and the expression is replaced by a filename, as before. However, this time the file is for writing: anything sent to it is used as input for the commands. The output of *commands* is not captured in any way.

- =(*commands*): This works just the same as the <(...) form. The only difference is that the filename is guaranteed to be a regular file. The other two forms use special files.

bash, zsh, and ksh93 all support the first two forms. The third form is a zsh extension that is not available in the other shells. We'll show examples of all three in order.

The <(…) Substitution

You can use the <(...) form when you need to combine output from multiple commands. Here's a way of extracting certain fields from a password file (/etc/passwd on standard Unix and Linux systems). The password file includes lines of information with each line containing fields separated by colons:

```
root:x:0:0:Root Account:/root:/bin/zsh
pws:x:1000:1000:Peter Stephenson:/home/pws:/usr/local/bin/zsh
```

(Real password files are much longer. We've just picked a couple of entries as an illustration.) The first field is the username, as you would use with ~*user*, and the fifth is the real name of the user.

Suppose we want to extract just those two fields and print them out. We will use the cut command to extract the fields. We need to tell it the number of the field using the -f option and the field delimiter (the colon) using the -d option:

```
zsh% cut -d: -f1 /etc/passwd
root
pws
```

Now we're going to use the paste command to piece the output from two cut commands back together. paste reads lines from two files, and joins each line together with a tab, though you can use the -d option to specify another delimiter. Here's what we get:

```
zsh% paste <(cut -d: -f1 /etc/passwd) <(cut -d: -f5 /etc/passwd)
root    root
pws     Peter Stephenson
```

What paste sees is two filenames. These contain the output from the cut commands.

The >(…) Substitution

The >(...) substitution works a bit like a pipe. In fact, it's implemented with a named pipe on some systems. As with <(...), if you want to redirect into the filename, you need to put a > in front.

Redirecting error messages away from the terminal is a good use. Shells don't make it easy for you to redirect standard error to a pipe while leaving standard output alone. To illustrate, suppose you are running make to compile a program. This produces some informational messages on standard output to indicate what it is doing. In addition, warning and error messages are sent to standard error. You decide you want to filter out any error messages from the standard error, saving them to a log file. You want to throw away any warning messages while keeping the normal informational output. Assuming that the error messages are tagged with a suitable word like "Error" we can achieve this as follows:

```
make 2> >(grep Error >logfile.txt)
```

The 2> redirects standard error. The substitution after that removes lines that don't contain Error, and saves the result to logfile.txt. Note that this appears as standard output from grep, not as standard error. The standard output of the original command is untouched; you can pipe it or redirect it as you like.

Tip As you can see from the example in this section, the >(. . .) form of substitution can be used in place of a filename after normal redirections. The same applies to <(. . .) and =(. . .) substitutions. This makes sense if you remember that the shell is substituting a filename. Note that in bash, there must be a space between the two > (or <) characters as in > >(. . .). In zsh the space is not required.

There is one important difference between ordinary pipes and the >(...) form. In the second case the shell won't wait for the command to finish. That usually doesn't matter. It wouldn't matter in the example we just showed unless you immediately tried to look at logfile.txt. You will notice a problem if you let the command in the substitution write to standard output or standard error. Then it's possible that the output comes after the command has finished, and appears mixed in with the next command line. The problem is very like the one we mentioned at the end of the section "Multiple Redirections in zsh" in Chapter 8, and the fix is similar, too:

```
{ make } 2> >(grep Error >logfile.txt)
```

The =(...) Substitution

The <(*commands*) form has its limitations. It is implemented to be as efficient as possible, with various consequences:

- The shell doesn't wait for the *commands* to finish before running the main command line. The command reading from the file needs to wait until data is ready. This usually works fine: in Unix jargon the read operation *blocks* until the data is ready or the program generating it exits.

- The file whose name is substituted on the command line is a special file: either a named pipe, or a file of the form /dev/fd/*num*, which we introduced in the section "File Descriptors as Files" in Chapter 8.

We can see the special file being substituted by using echo as in the following example:

```
% echo <( true )
/dev/fd/12
```

The shell opens a new file descriptor for the output of the commands in the parentheses. In this case, it has used 12. Sometimes, however, you need a regular file, not a special file. That's because the special files are streams of data, which when read are forgotten. Some commands need to be able to go backwards and read earlier parts of the file. (This is called a *seek* operation.)

To get around this problem, zsh provides the substitution =(*commands*). You use this in the same way as <(*commands*); however, the shell creates a regular file to hold the output of *commands*. Usually this is in the temporary directory /tmp, but with the permissions set so that no one else can read it. It is removed automatically by the shell as soon as the main command finishes.

A common use for this substitution is to view the output of a command using a text editor. This can allow you to make some changes to a command's output from your favorite text editor before you cut and paste it to another program that has limited editing capabilities. Other common features of text editors such as color syntax highlighting can also be a reason for using them instead of a pager. For example, to view the output of the indent command (which formats source code), you might do the following:

```
emacs =(indent -st < file)
```

Finding the Full Path to a Command in zsh

One very common use of command substitution is to expand the full path to a program. For example:

```
% echo $(which ls)
/bin/ls
```

zsh has a simple shorthand form for this: =*command* (no parentheses this time). The *command* must live somewhere in your PATH. The expansion doesn't work for shell functions, aliases, or commands built into the shell. (Old versions of zsh expanded aliases with the same syntax, but this was removed because it was confusing.)

```
zsh% echo =ls
/bin/ls
zsh% ls -l =zsh
-rwxr-xr-x    2 root     root      1941200 Jan 30 12:16 /usr/local/bin/zsh
```

There are numerous uses for this:

- You need the full path to a command when you run a debugger such as gdb or dbx to follow program execution.

- If the command is a script, you can run a pager to examine the contents, for example less =*script*.

- The command strings searches a file (typically a program) for occurrences of strings. You can run strings =*prog* to look for strings embedded in the program *prog*. This can sometimes gives hints if you are mystified about what *prog* is doing.

You can quote the = just like any other special character to remove its special effect. If you find this feature annoying and don't need the special behavior, set the option no_equals to turn it off. A common point of conflict is that some mail programs use an initial equals sign for specifying mail folders. Fortunately, they generally accept a plus sign instead.

Like tilde, the equals sign is only special at the start of the word.

■**Caution** Don't confuse =*command* with =(*command*). They have completely different effects.

Resource Limits

Unix-style systems allow *limits* on the resources used by a process or user. They are enforced by the operating system since every process, not just the shell, has limits. However, there are shell commands to alter the values of the limits. Like the current directory, these values are inherited by any processes started from the shell.

Both shells have the command `ulimit` for manipulating limits. `zsh` also has the command `limit`, which it inherited from the C shell. This uses names instead of option letters for manipulating particular limits but is otherwise much the same. However, we'll mostly discuss `ulimit`.

To review a summary of the limits that exist, execute `ulimit -a`. You will get something like this:

```
core file size        (blocks, -c) unlimited
data seg size         (kbytes, -d) unlimited
file size             (blocks, -f) unlimited
max locked memory     (kbytes, -l) unlimited
max memory size       (kbytes, -m) unlimited
open files                   (-n) 1024
pipe size         (512 bytes, -p) 8
stack size            (kbytes, -s) 8192
cpu time            (seconds, -t) unlimited
max user processes           (-u) 256
virtual memory        (kbytes, -v) unlimited
```

This is from a recent version of `bash`, which helpfully tells you the option to `ulimit` to use for altering each limit. However, the limits differ slightly between versions of Unix and Linux, so you may see another list.

For each limit, you can use `ulimit -X value` to set the limit. The *X* is one of the letters given in the output above. The *value* is a number in the units indicated in that list. You can also use the value `unlimited` to remove a limit.

We'll look briefly at the limits you're most likely to alter.

The Core File Size Limit (-c)

When a program exits in response to certain signals, it produces a *core dump*. This is a file, usually called `core`, in the program's current directory. A debugger such as `gdb` or `dbx` can read the `core` file and tell you more about what the program was doing when it died. This is very handy for programmers. If, following a programming error, a program tries to do something bad such as access memory not allocated to it, the operating system makes it dump core. It is also possible to make a process dump core by sending it the `QUIT` signal. However, unless you actually want to debug the program, the `core` file is useless. These files also tend to be quite large so many people turn off core dumps. This can be done by limiting their size to 0:

```
ulimit -c 0
```

The only other sensible value is `unlimited`, which allows a full core dump. You can use this if you need to debug a program you are using, or if the maintainer of a program tells you they would like to see debugging information.

The Memory Size Limits (-m, -s, and -v)

You can limit the amount of memory a process is allowed to use. If it reaches the limit, requests to allocate more memory will be refused. The values of these limits are specified in kilobytes so, for example, 8192 means 8 megabytes.

Usually you don't need to limit the memory allowance for a program. However, occasionally you may find a program starts to take so much memory that it causes problems for other programs; then you may decide to limit the memory. It's very likely that a program won't work properly when it reaches this limit. It's quite possible that it will exit abnormally, maybe dumping a core file as we just described. So you should use these limits carefully.

Memory management is a complicated issue, but there are three particularly useful types of limit.

- The main memory, also known as the *resident set size* in Unix jargon. You set a limit for this with ulimit -m. You might want to set a limit for this if you find a program is hogging all the RAM. One sign of this is constant disk activity and a very slow response to commands entered. (This is sometimes called *thrashing*.)

- The stack memory. As well as storing data, the stack is used to remember where a program should return to after the end of a call to another routine. This limit, set with ulimit -s, is the one that is most often applied. Sometimes a program can get into an infinite loop in which a routine endlessly calls itself. Limiting the stack causes such a program to run out of space and terminate.

- The *virtual* memory, also known as the *address space*. Unix systems are able to store parts of programs temporarily on disk in an area called the *swap*. The virtual memory includes this plus any other memory the program can in principle access. For example, there may be areas the program has asked to access but don't yet contain any data. A system may not reserve space for this until it is needed. Because of these features, not all virtual memory is necessarily in RAM at any one time. You can set a limit for virtual memory with ulimit -v if you are short on swap space.

The ps command will tell you the details of memory usage, although there are other more sophisticated ways of looking for memory hogs such as the top or prstat command. Graphical interfaces you can use include gtop, which is the GNOME system monitor (and sometimes called gnome-system-monitor).

The Process Limit (-u)

You can limit the number of processes a user can have with the command ulimit -u. Some programs have a habit of creating lots of new processes. Every now and then, one of these gets out of hand and refuses to stop creating processes. This is known as a *fork bomb* after the system's way of starting a new process, which is to create a copy of the existing process (*forking* it). If you have such problems, you might want to set a process limit. A few hundred ought to be enough for an ordinary user, depending on your system.

Hard Limits and Soft Limits

By default, ulimit deals in *soft* limits. Any limit changes will be subject to the constraints of the *hard* limit. You can see the hard limits instead of the soft ones by using ulimit -Ha.

Hard limits can be reduced by any user for their own processes but can only be increased by the root user. You set a hard limit with the -H option, for example:

```
ulimit -Hu 256
```

The difference between hard and soft limits is only relevant when setting them. Since the soft limits are never larger than the hard ones, the soft limits will always be the ones that are applied.

Lying About the Program Name

It's an odd fact about Unix that the name of a program is not necessarily the same as the command you execute. The name is reported when you run the ps command, and is available inside the program as the first argument passed to it. (In the shell the substitution $0 tells you this.)

zsh has a trick to allow you to set the program's name to anything you like. Set the environment variable ARGV0 to the name you want just for that program. (The name is historical. It's borrowed from the arguments to a program written in the C programming language.) Try this:

```
ARGV0=sh zsh
```

You'll almost certainly find that zsh looks and behaves different from normal. That's because it sees that it's called sh and uses a completely different set of options, to make it more like a standard Bourne shell. We'll say more about this in the section "Porting Scripts" in Chapter 13.

If you use ARGV0=rzsh (or anything beginning with an "r"), zsh becomes a *restricted shell*. We explain what that means in the sidebar "Restricted Shells."

RESTRICTED SHELLS

Both bash and zsh as well as ksh support the idea of a restricted shell. Such a shell runs as normal, but certain features are turned off to make it harder for the user to do damage, whether deliberate or accidental, to the system.

For example, if the user of a restricted shell tries to change directory, the message cd: restricted appears. Likewise, any attempt to run a command with a / will be rejected because external commands must be found by looking through the $PATH list.

The shell will enter restricted mode if its name starts with an r. A standard way to arrange this is to make a symbolic link, for example:

```
ln -s /usr/local/bin/zsh /usr/local/bin/rzsh
```

This example assumes that /usr/local/bin/zsh already exists. If your bash came in a package or preinstalled, it's possible there is already a link, rbash, to do this for you.

Setting up a restricted shell is difficult. You need to rewrite the start-up files to provide a limited $PATH, which includes only the commands you want the user to be able to run. However, shells are intrinsically so powerful you will also need to think about all the possible ways a user can get round the restrictions. This is not for the faint hearted; the proper use of restricted shells is beyond the scope of this book.

You can disguise the name of any command like this, but as you can see it may have side effects.

bash doesn't have a direct equivalent of ARGV0, but it does have something similar. In the section "File Descriptors" in Chapter 8 we saw the exec command and how to use it for manipulating file descriptors. exec actually has another distinct use. It lets you run another command without creating a separate process for it. The result is that the new program replaces the shell. bash adds an option to exec that changes the program's name. One use of exec is if you have a system where you can't change your shell. By putting the following in the .bashrc file, it will replace itself with zsh with a program name of sh:

```
exec -a sh zsh
```

zsh has another feature used for lying about its name. With the -Z option to jobs, it is possible to change the name and arguments of zsh after it has started running. The change affects what is seen in the output of the ps. Its main use is to convey status information from scripts running in the background.

Summary

In this chapter, we have shown you how to do the following:

- Switch between different jobs in a single terminal.

- Control which jobs are killed when the shell exits.

- Control how output from command substitutions is split into words by the shell.

- Use process substitution to extend the benefits of pipes and filters to commands that expect to perform their input or output on a file.

- Restrict a program's use of system resources.

- Change the behavior of a program by changing its name.

That's the end of the second part of the book, our explanation of bash and zsh features. In the third part, we will largely be leaving interactive features of the shell behind and moving on to programming with the shell. As in other programming languages, learning how to use variables for storing information effectively is key to writing programs. So, we begin in the next chapter by covering the numerous types of variables. In the next chapter, we also cover the shell's built-in support for mathematical operations.

PART 3

■ ■ ■

Extending the Shell

In this third part of the book, we show you how to bring together many of the shell features described in the previous two parts to build simple programs. We then demonstrate creative ways in which you can apply this knowledge to extend components of the shell. We pay particular attention to the ways in which you can enhance the abilities of the shell's line editor and completion system.

CHAPTER 12

■ ■ ■

Variables

A *variable* is a named placeholder for a value. Whenever you want the shell to remember something, you can store it in a variable. As an analogy, imagine that a variable is a box; the variable's name would be the label on the box.

We have already made quite extensive use of variables in this book. In this chapter we'll expand upon your knowledge of the topic, introducing a number of concepts that will help you make effective use of variables in your daily scripting tasks. In particular, we will cover the following topics:

- Making the shell remember a list of values using arrays

- Seeing what happens when variables are expanded on the command line

- Storing numbers and using the shell's math facilities

- Substituting a default value when a variable is unset

- Returning just a part of a variable's value

- Using zsh's associative arrays to map strings to values

- Searching for data stored in variables

- Making variables that point to other variables

Given that we've already used variables in this book, we'll start by briefly reviewing what we've already covered. In Chapter 3, we explained that the shell handles two types of variables: *environment variables* and *shell variables*. Bourne-derived shells such as bash and zsh make less of a distinction between the two types than the C shell does. In this chapter, we will be discussing the more general shell variables.

Shell variables can be scalar or nonscalar. (Environment variables are always scalar.) The majority of the variables we have seen so far in this book have been scalar. A *scalar* is a single unit of information, typically either a number or a string of one or more characters. The syntax for setting a scalar variable should by now be quite familiar:

```
% name=value
```

If you're used to programming in other languages, note that spaces on either side of the equals sign are not allowed.

Similarly, using a $ symbol before a variable's name will be familiar as the way to retrieve a variable's value. So for example, if we have assigned the number 4 to a variable named x, we can then use $x in place of the literal value 4:

```
% x=4
% echo $x
4
```

The variable name can also be enclosed in braces. This is necessary if you want to have letters immediately following a variable expansion. For example, if the variable x denotes a length in millimeters, we might write the following:

```
% echo ${x}mm
4mm
```

If we had written $xmm, the shell would try to find a variable named xmm to expand.

In the first section, we'll discuss arrays, a type of nonscalar variable. We'll return to the topic of scalar variables in the section "Variable Attributes" later in this chapter.

Arrays

We have seen how scalar variables can be used to hold a single item, be it a filename, a number, a word, a character, or a line of input. It is frequently the case, however, that you need to manage a whole collection of values together. This might be several words, a list of directories, 100 numbers, or a few filenames. For these situations, the shell supports *arrays*. An array can hold as many different items as you like. An individual item in an array is called an *array element* and can be used much like an ordinary scalar variable. The elements of an array are maintained in sequence. To refer to an individual element, you use its position, or *index*, in the sequence.

Note We've already seen scalar variables that contain a list of values. The PATH environment variable, for example, contains a list of directory names separated by colons (:). Environment variables are always scalar. This is because of the limited way in which Unix stores the environment variables of processes. Using separator characters makes it possible to store a list of values in an environment variable. However, proper arrays are more convenient to manipulate.

If you are curious as to exactly how environment variables are stored for each process, Linux makes a process's environment visible in the /proc special filesystem. If you are using Linux, you can run the following command to see the environment of your shell. We use $$ to expand the process ID of the shell, but you could look at the environment of a different process.

```
cat -v /proc/$$/environ
```

What you will see looks like a series of scalar assignments. They are separated by the null character. That would be invisible if we hadn't used the -v option to cat. With the -v option, null characters appear as ^@.

Constructing an Array

There are two ways to assign values to an array. The 1988 version of ksh only supports the old way. bash allows only the new way. zsh and ksh93 support both.

Let's review an example involving storing three strings—*one*, *two*, and *three*—in an array named arr. If your shell supports both methods, you can use the old way:

```
set -A arr one two three
```

or the new way:

```
arr=( one two three )
```

It is worth remembering the old syntax because it can be useful if you ever use ksh88. The old syntax will be mentioned again in the section "Variable Indirection" later in this chapter, but apart from that we will stick to the new syntax. The new-style assignments have the advantage of being much more similar to assignments to scalar variables.

Inside an array assignment, you can use any shell substitution or expansion. This allows you to save the result of an expansion, so that you can reuse it or in case you want to inspect the result of the expansion before passing it to a destructive command like rm. For example, you can save the result of a zsh recursive file search as follows:

```
zsh% src_files=( **/*.[ch] )
```

In bash you can't match files recursively using globbing, but you can use the find command in a command substitution. We said that you can use any shell substitution in an assignment, and that includes command substitutions. So a similar example that will work in bash is as follows:

```
bash$ src_files=( $(find . -name '*.[ch]' -print) )
```

If you have filenames containing spaces, such as A source file.c, you will find that the bash example won't correctly create just one array element for each filename. We'll explain why this happens in the section "Word Splitting" later in this chapter. In order to work at all, this example depends on the fact that the shell allows values in an array assignment to be separated by newlines—find outputs the name of each file it finds on a separate line. That the shell allows newlines to separate array elements means that an array assignment can be split over multiple lines without putting backslashes on the end of the line. So, for example, the following creates an array with three elements:

```
arr=(
  'first element'
  'second element'
  'third element'
)
```

If you want array elements containing spaces or newlines, then you need to use quoting as we've done for the spaces in the example above. You can confirm that this command creates an array with only three elements by including the # flag in a variable expansion. For an array, it makes the expansion return the number of elements in the array. So to see how many elements are in the arr array, we can do the following:

```
% echo ${#arr}
3
```

Accessing Array Elements

Array variable expansions are written just like regular variable expansions except that they are followed by an index in brackets. The brackets are called the *subscript operator* and the index inside them is commonly referred to as the *subscript*. Let's try it out using a simple subscript that consists of just 1:

```
bash$ arr=( one two three )
bash$ echo ${arr[1]}
two
```

If you try running the same commands in zsh, you will notice that you get a different result. This is because the first element of a zsh array is numbered 1 while bash starts from 0. This isn't the only way in which zsh arrays are different. If you want zsh to act like bash or ksh, you can turn the ksh_arrays option on.

Note that we place braces around the expansion to force the index to be considered a part of it. zsh actually doesn't require braces around array indexes so you can write

```
zsh% echo $arr[1]
```

Note that in array expansions, you can use further variable expansions for the index inside the brackets. This could be another array element. Mathematical expressions, which we'll come to a little later, are even allowed inside the brackets. To demonstrate these two features, the following uses, as an array index, the result of adding 1 to the value of a variable named offset:

```
zsh% offset=1
zsh% echo $arr[1+$offset]
two
```

In ksh, regular string variables are actually treated as arrays containing just one element. For this reason, if you leave the subscript out in an array expansion, just the first element of the array will be expanded:

```
$ echo $arr
one
```

bash behaves likewise. zsh will expand all the elements of the array instead:

```
zsh% echo $arr
one two three
```

If you want the same in bash you need to use one of two special forms: either ${arr[@]} or ${arr[*]}. We'll come to the differences between these in the section "Array Expansions" later in this chapter.

It is also possible to use array indexes in assignments. This allows you to change just one element of an array at a time. So, we could store the string "zwei" as element 1 of array arr with this command:

```
arr[1]=zwei
```

If the array arr doesn't exist, it will be created. In zsh, you can even replace a range of values in an array"

```
arr[2,3]=( zwei drei )
```

What this actually does is first remove elements 2 and 3 and then insert the new elements in the array. You don't even need to insert as many elements as you remove. As a result of this, an element (or elements) can be deleted from an array in zsh by assigning () to them. So the following command will remove the second element of the arr array:

```
arr[2]=()
```

zsh's array ranges tend to be most useful when accessing an array. You can use the value -1 to indicate the last element in the array, so the following retrieves all elements from the second to the last in an array:

```
zsh% arr=( one two three )
zsh% echo $arr[2,-1]
two three
```

If you want to retrieve the last element of an array in bash, you can't use an index of -1. Instead, you can make use of the # flag, which, as we saw earlier, allows you to retrieve the length of an array. So to retrieve the last element of an array you need the following:

```
bash$ echo ${arr[${#arr}-1]}
three
```

With ordinary variables, the # flag causes the expansion to return the length of the variable in characters. As the following demonstrates, this even works for an array element:

```
$ echo ${arr[1]}
two
$ echo ${#arr[1]}
3
```

Array Attributes

There is one built-in command that we are going to be referring to frequently in this chapter: declare, also referred to as typeset. In bash and zsh, it doesn't matter which of the two names you use—they are both the same command. In ksh, you don't have the luxury of being able to choose—only typeset is available. We use declare throughout, mainly because we think it is a better name.

The declare command allows you to specify the type of a variable or to specify one or more attributes for a variable. To specify that a variable is an array, you use the -a option. Thus, the following command will create an empty array:

```
declare -a arr
```

If arr already existed as another type of variable, declare -a converts it to an array. To demonstrate this, we need to be able to determine the type of a variable. bash's declare command includes a -p option that allows us to do this. It outputs a variable in the form of an

284

assignment statement that could be used to re-create the variable. Here, we use it to see the effect of applying declare -a to a scalar variable:

```
bash$ var=string
bash$ declare -a var
bash$ declare -p var
declare -a var='([0]="string")'
```

This shows that the variable has become an array containing just one element. The syntax used in the array assignment that was output may be unfamiliar. When you're assigning to an array in bash, any of these will work:

```
arr=( [0]=one [1]=two [2]=three )
declare -a arr=( [0]=one [1]=two [2]=three )
declare -a arr=( one two three )
```

In addition to a variable's type, declare allows a number of attributes to be set. zsh has one such attribute, specified with the -U option, which can be very useful with arrays. It removes duplicate values in an array. For example, in your startup file, you may want to add a directory to your path but it is better if it doesn't then appear in your path multiple times:

```
declare -U path
path=( ~/bin $path )
```

Try this, repeating the second command multiple times. It should have no further effect on the path. There is no easy way to do this in bash. As with all the attributes specified with declare, you can remove them by using a plus in front of the option—declare +U path in this case.

This brings us to another feature of zsh—*tied arrays*. The path array is the companion of the PATH variable—if you modify one, changes are reflected in the other. Other variables like mailpath/MAILPATH (which we saw in Chapter 7) work similarly. Using an option to declare, you can tie together any other two variables in a similar manner. For instance:

```
declare -T LD_LIBRARY_PATH ld_library_path
```

The scalar variable will contain each of the elements in the array separated by colons. zsh 4.2 allows you to choose a different separator character.

Word Splitting

In the section "Constructing an Array" earlier in this chapter, we showed how substitutions such as command substitutions can be used inside an array assignment. An important aspect of the shell you should be aware of when doing this is how the shell decides where to divide the result of the substitution into separate array elements. This is an issue that is not just relevant to array assignments. When the shell executes a command, any parameters are passed to the command in the form of a list. The shell, therefore, needs to split each command line you type into the separate elements of this list. This process is called *word splitting* and the elements are called *words*. These "words" are distinct from English words: they are maintained separately like array elements and can contain characters such as spaces.

When using variables, you need to be careful because word splitting may happen on the result of a variable expansion. So if your variable contains spaces, it will be broken up into several words. Before the shell had arrays, this could be useful, but more often than not it is a nuisance. For this reason, zsh doesn't do word splitting on variable expansions.

To demonstrate how a particular command line is broken down into words, we'll use the printf command. printf allows some text to be output in a specific format. It has the useful feature of reusing the format string if more arguments remain. So if you use a format string such as '%s\n' it will print each word on a new line. We're going to use it frequently so let's create an alias for it:

```
alias showargs="printf '>>%s<<\n'"
```

Now we can see just how a command line is broken into words:

```
% showargs one 'two three'
>>one<<
>>two three<<
```

■**Caution** zsh only gained printf as a built-in command in version 4.2 so this may depend on an external printf command. On some Unix systems the external printf command doesn't reuse the format string until all arguments have been printed so this alias won't work. If you find that this is the case on your system, you can try using zsh's print command instead. print has a useful -l option, which makes it print each argument on a new line (the l stands for line).

Returning to word splitting in variable expansions, the examples that follow illustrate how bash and zsh differ. In the first example, bash expands a variable:

```
bash$ var='one two'
bash$ showargs $var
>>one<<
>>two<<
```

Let's repeat that task in zsh:

```
zsh% var='one two'
zsh% showargs $var
>>one two<<
```

As we saw in the section "Control Shell Interpretation with Quoting" in Chapter 3, quoting can be used to make the shell ignore the special meaning of spaces. So we can prevent the word splitting for bash by putting the variable reference in double quotes:

```
bash$ showargs "$var"
>>one two<<
```

In zsh, you can emulate the Bourne shell behavior by turning the sh_word_split option on. In the sidebar "The Dangers of Word Splitting," we explain why zsh behaves differently by default. We would only recommend using sh_word_split for compatibility when you're running scripts not originally written for zsh.

There is one situation where the bash behavior can be useful. If you put a command with parameters in an environment variable, then when the variable is expanded the shell will separate the parameters from the command name. To demonstrate this, consider the PAGER environment variable. Programs such as man look at the variable to decide what program to use so that their output can be viewed a page at a time. It is common to set it to less or more, but you can actually include options in the variable. So it is perfectly acceptable to set PAGER to less -s. The -s causes consecutive blank lines to be squeezed into one. If, in zsh, you now try to use the PAGER environment variable (which is not uncommon in a script) you will see the problem:

```
zsh% nroff -man zshall.1 | $PAGER
zsh: command not found: less -s
```

It is looking for a command named less -s and not finding one. If you try the same command from bash, it should successfully run less with the -s option. zsh provides a workaround to let you do this, which we will come to shortly. Using a value such as less -s doesn't cause problems from programs like man because the value is passed to a shell. This shell then treats it in much the same way as if you had typed it at the command line.

THE DANGERS OF WORD SPLITTING

In this section, we explain how the shells behave with respect to word splitting. What may not be clear is why they behave as they do. In particular, why does zsh behave differently?

The first point to note is that word splitting on variable expansions is rarely useful. Without some modern shell features, it would have more uses. It allows, for example, a list of filenames to be separated when passed to a command, but arrays now serve this purpose. Word splitting also allows a command to be separated from its parameters when they are stored together in a variable. This is what we did in the example with PAGER, but if we didn't want to export PAGER to child processes in the environment, it would be better to use an alias or a function.

In addition to not being particularly useful, word splitting can be a nuisance in many situations. For example, it is very common to assign the name of a file to a variable. A common pitfall is to forget to quote this variable when using it. For example you might write a script that looks roughly like this:

```
for file in *.old; do
  # do some other things
  rm $file
done
```

When you test this little script, it may appear to work fine. However, try running the script in a directory containing a file with a name that contains a space. In this case, the rm command receives two arguments for this file instead of one. It won't delete the file as expected and may even delete different files. Even if you're not using destructive commands like rm, this behavior can cause scripts to fail or do unexpected things.

To summarize, word splitting was originally useful because it allowed for a sort of poor man's array. Given that it is no longer needed for that purpose in modern shells, zsh avoids its disadvantages by disabling word splitting by default. If you use bash, you will find that you need to put double quotes around variables to avoid the splitting. If you ever want your variable to be split, you almost certainly ought to be using an array.

Sometimes, you may find that you want to have a variable split. This most commonly occurs when a list of values is stored in an environment variable. For example, the cvs command looks for a list of filenames in the CVSIGNORE environment variable. One solution is to use a tied array as shown in the previous section. The other way is to specify that you want your variable to be split. You do that with an equals sign like this:

```
zsh% var='one two'
zsh% showargs $=var
>>one<<
>>two<<
```

So, returning to our earlier example, if you want to make use of PAGER from a zsh script, you can make it work when PAGER includes options by using the expansion $=PAGER. There are a few other characters that are used in a similar way to equals. Remembering them can be difficult. In this case, it might help if you consider that an equals sign consists of two separate lines that are split from each other.

Array Expansions

So how is a variable expansion split into words when you have an array? You may recall that we stated there are two methods for retrieving all the elements of an array: ${arr[@]} and ${arr[*]}. The first form results in each element of the array being a separate word while the second form amounts to joining all the array elements together with a space[1] between each element and treating the resulting string like a scalar variable expansion. One of the reasons why the difference isn't always obvious is that, if you use ${arr[*]} outside double quotes in bash, it is promptly split up again at all the spaces that were used to join the array elements.

```
bash$ arr=( one 'two three' four )
bash$ showargs ${arr[*]}
>>one<<
>>two<<
>>three<<
>>four<<
bash$ showargs "${arr[*]}"
>>one two three four<<
bash$ showargs "${arr[@]}"
>>one<<
>>two three<<
>>four<<
```

In the first case, it wouldn't matter if we used @ instead. Without the quotes even the array element containing a space is broken up. In zsh you would need an equals sign for the words to be split ($=arr[*]). In the second case, the words are joined together with a space and the quotes prevent word splitting. The last case is the most useful: each array element forms one word. This is the default in zsh:

---

1. Actually the first character of $IFS (internal field separator) is used as the separator. This happens to be a space by default.

```
zsh% showargs $arr
>>one<<
>>two three<<
>>four<<
```

If you don't use array expansions on their own but have adjacent text, the text is made to adjoin the first or last element of the array:

```
% showargs "BEFORE${arr[@]}AFTER"
>>BEFOREone<<
>>two three<<
>>fourAFTER<<
```

This isn't particularly useful, especially if you compare it to how brace expansions work (see the section "More Argument Handling: Braces" in Chapter 8).

```
% showargs BEFORE{one,two\ three,four}AFTER
>>BEFOREoneAFTER<<
>>BEFOREtwo threeAFTER<<
>>BEFOREfourAFTER<<
```

With the rc_expand_param option on, arrays in zsh work like this. The "rc" in this option name refers to the rc shell, since this is a feature borrowed from rc. The option is off by default but we recommend turning it on.

Note rc is the default shell for the Plan 9 operating system. A Unix port is also available; see Appendix B for the web address. rc has a similar level of functionality to the traditional Bourne shell but has the advantage of a much cleaner syntax. zsh has a few rc-inspired features. In addition to the rc_expand_param option, there is an rc_quotes option. This allows literal single quote characters to be included in quoted text by doubling them. In the following example, we use this to output a single quote character.

```
zsh% setopt rc_quotes
zsh% echo 'one of rc''s features'
one of rc's features
```

You can also use a caret character to turn on rc_expand_param for a single expansion, so you should see the same result from BEFORE${^arr}AFTER as we saw with braces.

Braces and array expansions can be mixed. With rc_expand_param, that produces all the possible combinations, which can result in quite a lot of words. With the option unset, the brace expansion is applied against just the first (or last) element of the array:

```
% showargs {A,B}$^^arr{C,D}
>>Aone<<
>>Bone<<
>>two three<<
>>fourC<<
>>fourD<<
```

Using two carets as in this example turns off rc_expand_param for the single expansion.

Variable Attributes

There are a number of attributes you can set for variables to achieve useful effects. You set these attributes using options to the declare command. Some alter the output format; for example, -u and -l convert the result to upper or lower case, respectively. Setting these attributes doesn't just apply to the variable's current value—any new value assigned to the variable is similarly affected. There are also options for justifying the output value: -R for right justification and -L for left justification. To demonstrate this, the following example applies both the -u and -R options to a variable holding the string hello. When the variable is expanded, the string is converted to uppercase and padded with spaces to be 10 characters wide.

```
% declare -u -R 10 greeting='hello'
% echo $greeting
     HELLO
```

To turn the effects off, we use a plus in place of the minus in the options:

```
% declare +u +R greeting
% echo $greeting
hello
```

A further attribute, similar to the one set with -R, is set with the -Z option. It uses zeros instead of spaces to pad out any space on the left. This can be useful with numbers.

Further attributes are available that affect other properties of a variable. The export command, which was first introduced in Chapter 3, is the same as using declare with the -x option. There are quite a few commands such as export that are specialized forms of declare, each corresponding to a particular option. Another is readonly, which is equivalent to declare -r. That allows you to protect a variable from having its value changed.

If you want to be sure of removing all attributes from a variable, the best way is to unset it. There is an unset built-in that lets you do exactly this. So to get rid of the greeting variable we created, we would do the following:

```
% unset greeting
```

That is generally useful as a better alternative to assigning an empty value to a variable. It won't work for a read-only variable, however: that is the one attribute you have to remove manually.

Numeric Variables and Arithmetic

In the past, to perform mathematical calculations from the command line, separate calculator programs such as bc were necessary. From shell scripts, the external expr command was typically used (and still is where portability is an issue). ksh88 added the let built-in command to do calculations directly in the shell. For instance, the following example performs the calculation 3×4 and assigns the result to the variable named product:

```
let product='3*4'
```

Although you can use let, the following syntax is preferred because it avoids the need for quoting:

```
(( product=3*4 ))
```

If the variable product didn't exist before, it will be created with an integer type. While integer variables act in every way like a string variable, they are more efficient because no conversion back and forth between ASCII and binary representations takes place.

You can also declare integer variables with the declare built-in or (in zsh) with integer:

```
declare -i product
```

or

```
integer product
```

It is a good idea to use this for any variables you want to use in calculations. Calculations like ((product=3*4)) will not change the type of product. This is worth remembering because its effect can be surprising when unforeseen. A declaration such as local product, which we introduce in the section "Functions and Variable Scope" in Chapter 13, will create product as a string variable. It would then remain a string when used in calculations.

If you don't want to assign the result of a calculation to a variable but want it to appear in place like a variable expansion, you can do that by adding $ before the opening parenthesis:

```
echo $(( 3 * 4 ))
```

Arithmetic evaluation like this occurs in one or two other places. Array subscripts for example can be any mathematical expression. The syntax rules for mathematical expressions are a lot like those for the C programming language. For instance, variables are referred to by name without an initial $. So for example, let's multiply the variable i by 3 when specifying an array index:

```
zsh% a=( one two three four )
zsh% integer i=1
zsh% echo ${a[ 3 * i ]}
three
```

The range of available mathematical operators supported by bash and zsh are shown in Table 12-1. They are the same as those available in C with the exception of **, the exponentiation operator, which C lacks.

Table 12-1. *Mathematical Operators Ordered from Highest to Lowest Precedence*

+ - ! ~ ++ --	Unary plus and minus, logical NOT, bitwise NOT, increment, decrement
<< >>	Bitwise shift left, right
&	Bitwise AND
^	Bitwise XOR
|	Bitwise OR
**	Exponentiation
* / %	Multiplication, division, remainder
+ -	Addition, subtraction
< > <= >=	Comparison: less, greater, less or equal, greater or equal
== !=	Comparison: equal, unequal
&&	Logical AND
|| ^^	Logical OR, XOR
x?y:z	If *x* then *y* else *z*
= += -= *= /= %= >>= <<= &= ^= |=	Assignment
, (comma)	Sequence separator

Number Bases

Sometimes it can be useful to operate in bases other than decimal (base 10). Inputting numbers in other bases works in both bash and zsh. You can specify hexadecimal (base 16) and octal (base 8) using the standard C convention: writing 0x ("zero x") before a hex number and 0 ("zero") before an octal number. In the following example, we input the number 255 using each of those bases in turn (in other words, we show that both FF hex and 377 octal are equivalent to 255 decimal):

```
$ echo $(( 0xff ))
255
$ echo $(( 0377 ))
255
```

Alternatively, you can specify an arbitrary base. The following example specifies 255 using base 12:

```
$ echo $(( 12#193 ))
```

The standard C convention for octal is disabled by default in zsh, though. This is because it is inconvenient when parsing strings with initial zeros as is common for time strings. You can enable this feature by turning on the octal_zeroes option.

zsh goes a step further and allows you to output numbers in a different base. There are two ways to do this. In an arithmetic expression, you can specify the output base in brackets. For example, the following outputs a number in hexadecimal:

```
% echo $(( [#16] 255 ))
16#FF
```

Alternatively, when you declare an integer variable, you can specify its output base with an argument to the -i option. The following example uses this method to output a number in hexadecimal:

```
% declare -i 16 i=255
% echo $i
16#FF
```

It is also possible to have the output using the standard C conventions. For this, you need to turn on zsh's c_bases option. Observe the following:

```
% setopt c_bases
% echo $(( [#16] 255 ))
0xFF
% setopt octal_zeroes
% echo $(( [#8] 255 ))
0307
```

Floating-Point Numbers

Another zsh (or ksh93) extension is support for floating point numbers—numbers with a decimal portion. When specifying a number, you may need to include the decimal point if you want to have decimal values in your result—much the same as in a C program. Contrast these two commands to see the difference:

```
% echo $(( 1 / 3 ))
0
% echo $(( 1. / 3 ))
0.33333333333333331
```

Floating point variables are defined with an option to declare or with a variant of it named float. There are actually two such options to declare: -F and -E. The difference between them relates to the output format: with -E, engineering notation is used. The following example displays the same number in each of the two forms:

```
% declare -F f='1.0/3'
% declare -E e='1.0/3'
% echo $f
0.3333333333
% echo $e
3.333333333e-01
```

You can also specify how many significant digits you want in the output values. In the following example, we specify three significant digits:

```
% declare -F 3 f='1.0/3'
% declare -E 3 e='1.0/3'
% echo $f
0.333
% echo $e
3.33e-01
```

If you are concerned about the output format, it is probably better to use printf, though, because it has support for a wider range of output formats. It handles specifics of your locale so if you are in a country where a comma is used for a decimal point then it will handle that. zsh 4.2 has printf as a built-in so no precision is lost if you pass the name of a variable directly instead of using an expansion. The following example demonstrates this:

```
% declare -F 3 f='1.0/3'
% printf '%f\n' $f
0.333000
% printf '%f\n' f
0.333333
```

zsh also has a number of more complex mathematical functions such as the common trigonometry functions. They are in a separate loadable module, which you need to first load. Modules are loaded with the zmodload command:

```
zmodload zsh/mathfunc
```

This provides most of the mathematical functions available in C, so you can do things like the following:

```
(( pi = 4 * atan(1) ))
```

Refer to the zsh documentation for the complete list of available math functions.

Complex Variable Expansions

As we have already seen, zsh allows special flags to be specified in variable expansions to do certain things like control how word splitting works. There are quite a few more things you can do from within variable expansions, including quite a few tricks that will work from older shells. We'll start with these and move on to the more advanced features for which you'll need zsh.

Alternative and Default Values

Sometimes, if a variable is unset or empty, it can be useful to have a default value as a substitute. You might handle this using an if statement, as we'll see in the next chapter, but that can be quite a long way of expressing it. So to specify a default value in an expansion, you can use ${*variable:-default*}. For example, you might have a script that uses the PAGER environment variable to choose a suitable program to pipe output into, but it is wise to specify a default in case the user has left it unset:

```
ls -l | ${PAGER:-more}
```

A similar substitution performs the inverse: the word on the right is substituted only when the variable is set. This takes the form ${*variable*:+*alternative*}.

For example, from a script you might use the following to print a file using lp. If the dest variable is set, it will be substituted with the -d option preceding it:

```
lp ${dest:+-d$dest} file
```

That is, if the dest variable has been set, the shell will execute lp -d*DDDD* file, where *DDDD* is the value of dest; otherwise the shell will simply execute lp file. lp's -d option allows the destination (print queue) to be specified. So this would allow the default destination to be overridden in a script by setting the dest variable.

Patterns

We saw in Chapter 9 that the shell offers a fairly powerful mechanism for matching filenames using patterns. Generating lists of files is not the only place that the shell allows you to use these patterns. As we'll see, a number of variable substitution forms make use of these patterns. These are very similar in effect to using sed's s command on a variable's value except that sed uses real regular expressions. We'll refer to these substitution forms as *pattern operators* because they all use a special operator character after the variable name and are followed by a pattern.

Let's look first at the operators ${*variable*#*pattern*}, ${*variable*##*pattern*}, ${*variable*%*pattern*}, and ${*variable*%%*pattern*}. These operators expand *variable*, removing text that matches *pattern*. The operators # and ## remove text from the left side (beginning) of the value; % and %% remove text from the right side (end). (Here's a tip to help you remember which operator removes from which side. The number sign # may be used at the left side of a number while writing, for example, "task #1" to mean "task number 1." Also, the percent sign % is used at the right side of a number as a percentage—for example, "95%" meaning "95 percent.") The single-character operators # and % remove the least text possible; the double-character operators ## and %% remove the most text possible. Some examples should make all of this clear.

The following example examines the HOME variable and removes from the beginning of its value the part matching the pattern:

```
% echo ${HOME##*/}
opk
```

In this case my home directory is /usr/people/opk so the /usr/people/ part has been removed.

You may spot here a minor difference in how the pattern is interpreted from how it would be for globbing. The difference is that the star (*) is able to match slashes (/) separating directory names: slashes are only considered special when doing globbing. So zsh's **/ and ***/ forms, along with features like zsh's glob qualifiers, can't be used here (though globbing flags such as (#i) can be).

When we are using patterns to match filenames, the question of exactly how much of a filename the pattern matches doesn't matter: we are only interested in whether the pattern matches the whole filename or not. When removing the matching portion of a variable, however, the question does matter. The pattern */ matches all of /, /usr/, and /usr/people/, so how does it decide which to remove?

With the ${*variable*##*pattern*} form we used here, the longest possible match is removed. There is a second form that takes the shortest match:

```
% echo ${HOME#*/}
usr/people/opk
```

The reason we showed the other form first is that that is how regular expressions normally work. Or, to use the standard terminology for this behavior, regular expressions are *greedy*.

As we said, the related pattern operators with % and %% allow you to remove from the end of a value the part that matches a pattern. For example, ${HOME%/*} will remove the last component of the path to your home directory. In zsh, you can use ${HOME%%[^/]#} to leave a trailing slash.

Caution When using pattern operators to remove directory names from a path, be careful if the path might contain a single slash (/), which is the root directory. The result might be the empty string being substituted. Though they are less flexible and will only work from zsh, it can often be safer to use C shell style modifiers. For example, ${HOME:h} can be used instead of ${HOME%/*}.

The pattern operators we have shown so far anchor the pattern to either the beginning or the end of the word. Modern shells also have a third form that is not anchored. This form is more similar to sed's s command. It looks like ${*variable/pattern/string*}.

One common use of this is to access a directory that has a similar path to the current directory. In the following example we expand the PWD variable, replacing src with bin to run the program /home/opk/dev_ws/bin/test-subsystem/test:

```
% pwd
/home/opk/dev_ws/src/test-subsystem
% ${PWD/src/bin}/test
```

In that way you can quickly access a program in a directory parallel to the current one. Note that this is similar to using two arguments to zsh's cd command as discussed in the section "Special zsh Directory Features" in Chapter 8 except that cd doesn't use patterns.

There is another similar form that looks like ${*variable//pattern/string*}. This doesn't enable greedy matching as you might expect; greedy matching is actually the default for both ${*variable/pattern/string*} and ${*variable//pattern/string*} substitutions.[2] Instead, this form causes all occurrences of the pattern to be replaced. So in bash you might use ${PATH//:/ } to return the directories of your path split into separate words. (Remember that in zsh you need to add an equals to enable word splitting (${=PATH//:/ })—or you can just use $path.)

Substrings

We've seen how you can use pattern operators to extract a substring from a string. Often, it is more convenient to specify a substring using numeric offsets into the string instead of using patterns that are matched against the string contents. Unfortunately, bash and zsh differ here. zsh allows array-like indexing to be used with scalar variables. In this example we extract the

---

2. As we mentioned before, greedy matching is the norm for regular expressions. To disable greedy matching, zsh has an (S) variable expansion flag.

substring starting with the third character in the original string and finishing with the fifth character:

```
zsh% a='123456789'
zsh% echo $a[3,5]
345
```

bash uses another new form: ${*variable*:*offset*:*length*}. The length part can be left out, leaving just ${*variable*:*offset*}.

Indexing is from zero so the same example for bash is

```
bash$ a='123456789'
bash$ echo ${a:2:3}
345
```

Note that in both bash and zsh the indexes can be mathematical expressions.

■**Note** zsh doesn't support the bash syntax at all—colons are used to introduce C shell style modifiers. Using modifiers with variables was mentioned in the section "Other Uses of History Modifiers" in Chapter 6. One of the most useful things about modifiers is that you can use them with bang history, globbing, and variable substitutions. Since we've shown you modifiers before in both Chapter 6 and Chapter 9, we won't do so again.

Nested Expansion

In the same manner that pipes allow several commands to be combined together to achieve a result, it can be useful to combine the effects of some of the forms of variable expansion that we have seen. zsh allows variable expansions to be nested to achieve this. For instance, the following example accepts a filename and removes an initial path and any file extension:

```
${${file##*/}%.*}
```

Constructs like this are commonly used inside for loops, which we'll cover in the next chapter. They enable you to intelligently adjust a filename to refer to a related file. For example, the following removes files in the current directory that have the same name (not counting the extension) as a .zip file in another directory:

```
for file in /project/documentation/*.zip; do
  rm ${${file##*/}%.*}.*
done
```

Unfortunately, with nested expansions, it becomes tempting to use many levels of nesting and to produce some horribly unreadable pieces of code. For this reason we won't say much more about this particular feature. There is a little more information in the sidebar "Nested Expansions" in Chapter 15 if you're curious to know more.

Expansion Flags

zsh offers various flags that can be specified inside variable expansions to enable optional behavior with respect to the expansion. We have already seen = and ^ for the sh_word_split and rc_expand_param options, respectively, as well as # for returning the length of a variable. Having run out of suitable characters to use like them, further flags that were added appear inside parentheses.

Many flags are available that provide a wide range of effects. Some of these flags are mentioned at other points in this book. This section offers just a sampling of some of the things they can do. Additionally, Table 12-2 lists some of the more useful flags. For the full list, you should refer to the manual.

Table 12-2. *Some Useful zsh Variable Expansion Flags*

Case Conversion

L	Lowercase
U	Uppercase
C	Capitalize initial letters of words

Sorting

a	Array index order (useful with O)
i	Case-independent ordering
o	Ascending order
O	Descending order

Splitting

f	Split at lines
s	Split at a specified character
z	Split into words, taking account of any shell quoting

Joining Words

F	Join words using newlines
j	Join words using a specified character

Length Counting (for use with the # flag)

c	Count characters
w	Count words
W	Count words, including empty ones

Quoting

Q	Remove one level of quoting

Table 12-2. *Some Useful zsh Variable Expansion Flags (Continued)*

q	Quote the resulting words
V	Make special characters visible
Padding	
l	Pad words on the left
r	Pad words on the right
Variable Information	
t	Return the type of a variable
k	Return associative array keys
v	Return associative array values
Expansions	
%	Perform prompt expansion on the value
e	Perform shell expansions on the value
P	Reinterpret value as a further variable name

Converting Strings to Upper or Lower Case

One simple flag converts all letters in the result to lower case. The flag is introduced with the letter L in parentheses. So for example, if you have a directory where all the filenames are in block capitals, you can change them to lowercase letters like this:

```
for f in *; do
  mv $f ${(L)f}
done
```

Note how we need to use braces, otherwise there would be a conflict with command substitution. There is a similar U flag that converts letters in the result to upper case. It is also worth noting that you could use a modifier here instead of the flag. There is an l modifier for converting to lowercase letters so the expansion would be ${f:l}.

Sorting Values

When writing scripts, it is often useful to be able to do sorting. Using the o flag, it is possible to sort an array. It doesn't have to be an array, though. zsh allows a command substitution to be nested inside a variable substitution. If you don't quote the command substitution, word splitting will apply. The result of word splitting can be treated in much the same way as an array. So for example, the following will produce a sorted list of users from the password file:

```
echo ${(o)$(cut -d: -f1 /etc/passwd)}
```

(The cut command returns the first field from each line of /etc/passwd.) Compare this to the following, where we have quoted the command substitution. This means that the result is not split into separate words that can be sorted. The output of cut is not altered, so the result is one username per line:

```
echo ${(o)"$(cut -d: -f1 /etc/passwd)"}
```

Splitting Strings

There is also a flag for splitting a string directly. This allows us to use a separator character of our choosing. Taking the fifth field of the password file instead of the first demonstrates how this might be useful. This is because the fifth field often contains spaces that we want to preserve.

In the following example, the s flag defines the separator character. It takes an argument in much the same way as we saw for some glob qualifiers in the section "More Complicated Qualifiers: String Arguments" in Chapter 9. Also similar to glob qualifiers is the way we can clump several flags together in the same parentheses so the o, p, and s flags appear together as ops. The p flag here allows us to use the \n escape sequence to indicate a newline:

```
echo ${(ops:\n:)"$(cut -d: -f5 /etc/passwd)"}
```

Splitting the result of expansions into lines like this is quite a common thing to do so there is another flag, f, which provides a shortcut for it. So, the following is the same as the previous example:

```
echo ${(of)"$(cut -d: -f5 /etc/passwd)"}
```

We'll see the f flag again in the section "States" in Chapter 15. It is often useful when generating completion matches.

Matching Patterns Against Arrays

In the same way that some common Unix commands such as cut, sed, and awk allow you to repeat an operation on every line of their input, pattern operators, when used with an array, will act separately on each element of the array. Being able to repeat an operation across all elements of an array is one thing that makes arrays very powerful. For example:

```
$ files=( /lib/lib* )
$ echo ${files[@]##*/}
```

Here we have used filename generation to create a list of files in a directory other than the current one. As you'll see if you look at the files array here, filename generation includes the full path of the files matched. In zsh we can remove these by using a modifier (/usr/lib*(:t)), but not all arrays are created this way. In the second line, we use the a ${...##...} style substitution. By using the [@] subscript, we signal to bash that it shouldn't just take the first element of the array. The result is that the path component is removed from every element in the array in the expansion.

zsh includes an additional substitution operation, one that is mostly used with arrays. It takes the form ${*variable*:#*pattern*}. Each array element is matched against the pattern and those that match are discarded. So for example, ${pipestatus:#0} discards all elements that consist of the single character 0 (zero). This leaves only the values in the pipestatus array that are not zero. Whenever you run several commands in a pipeline, the exit status for each of the commands is put in pipestatus. So with this expansion, only the exit status for commands that failed are expanded. bash offers a similar variable named PIPESTATUS.

What actually tends to be more useful is the opposite—returning just those elements that do match the pattern—much like the grep command returns just those lines that match a regular expression. The M variable expansion flag reverses the sense of the pattern operators, causing them to return what they would otherwise remove. The :# operator allows us to pick just those elements that match a pattern. For example, here we find that the only element of path matching *X11* (in other words, containing the string X11) is /usr/X11R6/bin:

```
% echo ${(M)path:#*X11*}
/usr/X11R6/bin
```

Associative Arrays

Associative arrays are a feature specific to zsh and ksh93. Like ordinary arrays, they can contain more than one value. How they differ is that instead of being indexed by number and being in a well-defined order, they are indexed by a text string that is known as the *key*. Values in an associative array are not in any particular order. Note that elsewhere you may see associative arrays referred to as *hashes*. In this section we cover just zsh's handling of associative arrays. There are a few differences in the syntax for ksh93, but the basic principles are the same.

To create an associative array, you need to invoke declare with the -A option. Assignments then look like regular array assignments. The values in the assignment are expected to alternate between keys and values, so there must be an even number of them. For example, the following will create an associative array with the keys "pres", "vicepres", and "secr" having the values "Pamela", "Victor", and "Sam", respectively:

```
declare -A people
people=(pres Pamela vicepres Victor secr Sam)
```

The keys can be used to index into the array in much the same way as for ordinary arrays. This means that assignments to individual elements are also possible. Here we add a fourth element to the associative array with the key "treas" and value "Tammy":

```
people[treas]=Tammy
```

This indexing is more useful when accessing the array, however. Here, we show the value corresponding to the key "vicepres" being retrieved:

```
% echo $people[vicepres]
Victor
```

If you take the value of the whole associative array, all the values will be returned. To demonstrate this, observe the following:

```
% echo $people
Sam Tammy Victor Pamela
```

Again, this is entirely consistent with ordinary arrays. As we see here, elements of an associative array come in no particular order. You may even see the four values in a different order. Sometimes, it can be useful to extract the keys of an associative array. For this, the k variable expansion flag is used:

```
% echo ${(k)people}
secr treas vicepres pres
```

There is also a similar v flag that extracts the values of an associative array. With this being the default, it may not seem very useful, but it can be combined with k to return both the keys and values together:

```
% echo ${(kv)people}
secr Sam treas Tammy vicepres Victor pres Pamela
```

You may notice that this paired list of keys and values is similar to how we assigned to the associative array in the first place. This can be useful if you need to add elements to an associative array. The following line uses this feature to add a further three elements to our associative array:

```
people=( ${(kv)people} driver Don clerk Clara cleaner Charles )
```

If you are using zsh 4.2, there is actually an easier way to do this using a += assignment. So we could instead write the previous example as follows:

```
people+=( driver Don clerk Clara cleaner Charles )
```

One final point: to delete an element of an associative array, you need to use the unset built-in command. Here we delete the element with the key "pres":

```
unset 'people[pres]'
```

We'll now consider an example use of an associative array. Back in Chapter 7 we mentioned a colors autoloadable function that is used by the prompt themes. This function defines associative arrays that map meaningful color names to their associated terminal escape sequences. For example, $fg[red] produces the output necessary to turn the text (in other words, the foreground) red. The variable is both more readable and easier to remember than the direct escape sequences. In Chapter 7 we showed an example that output a word in red text on a yellow background using the escape sequences directly. We can rewrite that example as follows:

```
% autoload colors
% colors
% echo "${fg[red]}${bg[yellow]}WHAM$reset_color"
WHAM
```

In addition to allowing more readable code, the associative array is more flexible. For example, we can use the k subscript flag to retrieve a list of available colors:

```
% echo ${(k)bg}
cyan white yellow magenta black blue red default green grey
```

You may see the colors listed in a different order. Remember that unlike ordinary arrays, associative arrays are not ordered. If you want, you can always sort the result using the o flag that we mentioned earlier:

```
% echo ${(ok)bg}
black blue cyan default green grey magenta red white yellow
```

Another way in which the associative array is more flexible than using escape sequences directly is that you can put the name of the color in another variable. This makes it easier to make the colors used by a script configurable. For example, you might assign the name of a color to the variable col and then use $fg[$col] when outputting the escape sequence.

Bringing this all together, the following example displays all combinations of foreground and background colors. (Actually there are a few more combinations if you use the bold attribute too.) It first iterates through each background color in alphabetical order. It then uses each key to retrieve the escape code from the associative array. The inner loop is just doing exactly the same for foreground colors. This would be difficult to do without using associative arrays.

```
for bgc in ${(ko)bg}; do
  print -n "$bg[$bgc]"
  for fgc in ${(ko)fg}; do
    printf '%s%-8s' $fg[$fgc] $fgc
  done
  print $reset_color
done
```

Reverse Indexing

zsh provides a number of mechanisms for searching arrays or doing reverse lookups. Alongside this we need to introduce yet another type of flag—the *subscript flag*. These look much like variable expansion flags except that they appear at the beginning of the subscript—the expression enclosed in brackets used for indexing into the array. You may find that you need to take care about quoting inside subscripts. The manual goes into a lot of detail on how subscripts are parsed, but as a general rule remember that they are interpreted in much the same way as if they were in double quotes.

With associative arrays, subscript flags allow elements to be found by specifying a pattern to match keys or values against. Normally associative arrays are looked up by their key, so we'll try the reverse and look them up by value. Naturally enough, the flag for reverse lookups uses the letter r.

Now we just need a suitable associative array to search. zsh's completion system uses the _comps associative array to map commands to the functions that handle completion for them. It is useful to be able to search in it, so we'll use that. If you haven't enabled the completion system, you'll need to refer back to Chapter 10 for details on how to do so.

So to perform a reverse lookup for the _mail function, we can do the following:

```
% echo ${(k)_comps[(r)_mail]}
mailx
```

This tells us that _mail handles completion for mailx. Note how we have used the k variable expansion flag so that it returns the key and not the value. The subscript flags actually imply whether keys or values are returned by default, but it is worth remembering that you can always choose which you want by adding (k) or (v) as appropriate.

The r subscript flag causes it to stop searching after it finds the first match—mailx is not the only command handled by _mail. To see all matches, we need to use R instead:

```
% echo ${(k)_comps[(R)_mail]}
mailx mail Mail nail zmail mush
```

As was mentioned, these flags allow patterns to be used in searching. In the previous example we used a literal word—"_mail"—but we could have just as easily used a pattern. Without using any subscript flag, you have the effect of matching the key against a literal word. If, however, we want to match the key against a pattern we need the i subscript flag. It allows a pattern to be used but doesn't do the lookup in reverse. For instance:

```
% echo ${(v)_comps[(i)ps*]}
_ps
```

This gives us the name of a completion function that handles a command whose name starts with ps. The result is perhaps not surprising since there is a _ps function that completes PostScript files. If we used the I flag instead, it would search for all possible matches. Change the flag and try it again. You should see that some functions are listed more than once. If you're using zsh 4.2, there is a u variable expansion flag that is useful in this situation. It removes duplicates from the result (it stands for *unique*). Let's add that in and observe the result:

```
% echo ${(vu)_comps[(I)ps*]}
_ps _psutils _pspdf _pids _pscp
```

Subscript flags can also be used for reverse lookups on ordinary arrays. This can be quite useful interactively for referring to a particular array element—its index is generally going to be a meaningless number but you are likely to have some idea of the value. For instance, suppose we want to remove the Java directory from the path. We could look at the path and count the index, but it is common to have a rough idea of the name of directory. In the case of Java, we might know that the name of the directory contains "j2sdk". In the following example, we use a subscript flag to search for this and remove the directory from the path:

```
% echo $path
/home/opk/bin /usr/local/bin /bin /usr/bin /usr/local/j2sdk1.3.1/bin /usr/games
% path[(r)*j2sdk*]=()
% echo $path
/home/opk/bin /usr/local/bin /bin /usr/bin /usr/games
```

The second command there may be more typing than path[5]=() but you would need to look it up in order to know that it was, for example, the fifth element of the array.

There are more subscript flags, providing a number of further facilities, but this should have given you a good idea of the most useful features and some of the ways in which you can use them.

Variable Indirection

Variable indirection is a very powerful technique. One of the possibilities it opens to us is the ability to mimic associative arrays in bash. Variable indirection refers to the practice of using a variable to store the name of another variable. We then need to take an indirect route, via the extra variable, to access the actual variable's value. So for an associative array, we need to arrange for something like assoc_$key to be evaluated and then treated as a variable name itself.

First let's define our bash "associative array." The following defines one similar to the fg associative array used in the zsh example. We use a string variable for each element of the array. Note how you can assign to more than one variable on a single command line:

```
fg_black=$'\e[30m'   fg_red=$'\e[31m'   fg_green=$'\e[32m'
fg_yellow=$'\e[33m'  fg_blue=$'\e[34m'  fg_magenta=$'\e[35m'
fg_cyan=$'\e[36m'    fg_white=$'\e[37m'
```

You can already use these variables to display text in a fixed color. To achieve the flexibility of associative arrays, however, we need to be able to store a key in another variable. In this example, the keys are the names of the colors. It is not possible to use a variable substitution such as ${fg_$color} or to use variable substitutions on the left-hand side of an assignment. Instead, we need to make use of the shell's eval command.

Note In the section "Constructing an Array" earlier in this chapter we mentioned that there are two ways to assign values to an array. bash only supports the new way, and that is what we use in this book. However, the old method has an advantage when using variable indirection.

Let's see an example. Suppose we want to set the array named arr. That name arr is stored in the variable var. The following example won't work because the variable expansion ($var) isn't allowed on the left-hand side of an equals sign:

```
var=arr
$var=( one two three )
```

But the old method will work:

```
set -A $var one two three
```

The eval command takes a complete command line after it. This command line is parsed by the shell twice:

1. The first time the shell reads the line, it is parsed normally.

2. The shell then executes the eval command. All the arguments are turned into a single string. This string is processed exactly like an ordinary command line.

Given this double evaluation, eval lends itself very nicely to doing variable indirection. Let's see an example. Here, we first store the string "blue" in the variable named color. We then use this variable in both an assignment and an expansion to manipulate the variable fg_blue:

```
color=blue
reset_color=$'\e[0m'
eval "fg_$color=$'\e[34m'"
eval "echo \${fg_$color}Hello\${reset_color}"
```

Note how it was necessary to put a backslash before the first $ on the last line. This ensures that the $ is preserved until the second time the string is evaluated (after $color has been expanded). The last $ is also quoted with a backslash to delay the expansion of reset_color until the second evaluation. This is not essential, but the shell will otherwise see the [character and spend time trying to evaluate the string as a glob pattern. In zsh, this causes an error unless the bad_pattern option is turned off.

USES OF EVAL

Variable indirection isn't the only use of eval. Evaluating a chunk of code contained inside a variable is another use. The variable might contain a command-line input by the user, for example. (You need to be careful since eval allows *any* shell command line to be executed, including potentially dangerous operations.)

```
bash$ var='ls -l ~/.zshrc'
bash$ $var
ls: ~/.zshrc: No such file or directory
bash$ eval $var
-rw-r--r--    1 pws      users        11780 Jun 20 14:34 /home/pws/.zshrc
```

Without using eval, the tilde is not expanded so ls looks for .zshrc in a directory that is actually named ~. When we used eval, $var was expanded first. Then this string was run as a command line. It had the same effect as if the value in the variable had been typed at the command line.

bash provides a second, more convenient, way of accessing variables with a level of indirection. This involves using an expansion of the form ${!*var*}. So we could avoid the second eval in the previous example as follows:

```
var=fg_$color
echo "${!var}Hello${reset_color}"
```

Unfortunately, this required us to first construct the full variable name in an additional variable. This technique is powerful enough that we can do most of the things we covered for zsh associative arrays in the previous section. bash has one further feature that is worth a mention, though. An expansion of the form ${!*prefix**} will expand to all the variables with names starting with the given prefix. This is similar to using the (k) flag in zsh to extract all the keys of an associative array. To demonstrate this feature, let's list all the variables starting with fg_:

```
bash$ echo ${!fg_*}
fg_black fg_blue fg_cyan fg_green fg_magenta fg_red fg_white fg_yellow
```

Another common use for variable indirection is when specifying the name of a variable as a parameter to a function. Functions and parameters to them are covered in the next chapter, so you may want to skip over the rest of this section and come back to it later.

Consider this function:

```
double() {
  local i=${!1}

  (( i = i * 2 ))
  eval "$1=$i"
}
```

This function takes the name of a variable as its parameter. It uses the variable indirection methods we've seen to first obtain the value of that variable and then assign a changed value to it. This means we can do the following:

```
bash$ num=3
bash$ double num
bash$ echo $num
6
```

Being able to have function calls of the form `double num` can allow scripts to become much more readable. The alternative would involve calls of the form `num=$(double $num)`.

This particular trick is also useful in `zsh`, but the syntax is slightly different. Instead of using `${!var}`, there is a `P` variable expansion flag (the P stands for "parameter"). So in `zsh`, the first line of the `double` function would need to be

```
local i=${(P)1}
```

`ksh93` has another, nicer, way of doing variable indirection. This uses something called *named references*. A named reference is a special type of variable that points to another variable. You can use the reference in exactly the same way as any other variable (no need for `eval`), and it will be the same as if you had used the variable it points to. Using this, our `double` function would look like this.

```
function double {
  nameref i=$1
  (( i = i * 2 ))
}
```

In this function, the variable `i` just becomes another name for the variable passed as a parameter. We've used the different function syntax so that `ksh93` will make the reference variable local.

Summary

In this chapter we discussed the use of shell variables for storing different types of data. A scalar variable can hold a single value such as a string or a number, or you can use an array variable or associative array to store multiple values. The shell includes mechanisms for performing transformations on, searching for, and analyzing data stored in variables. In the following chapters, we will show how to combine many of these mechanisms to solve complex real problems. The next chapter explains how to write programs using the shell. These programs frequently make use of variables to store data.

This chapter has also given you an insight into the way the shell interprets what is on the command line. In particular we discussed how the contents of a command line are broken into separate words before being passed to a command. This is one of the more idiosyncratic aspects of the shell, but it has wide implications. A good understanding of this aspect of the shell will help you to avoid common mistakes.

CHAPTER 13

■ ■ ■

Scripting and Functions

A shell script may contain no more than a few commands, although the shell offers a complete programming language. Using features like loops and condition tests can allow you to do very powerful things just from the command line. Often, however, it can be useful to save a set of commands in a file for later reuse. This aspect of scripting was largely covered in Chapter 2. In this chapter we focus on more advanced uses of scripting where the script needs to make decisions based on its inputs or to the result of previous operations. A particular aim of this chapter is to introduce ways in which shell programming can be used to extend the base functionality of the shell. That theme continues into the following two chapters, where we show how to write line editor widgets and completion functions to customize the shell's interactive environment.

The structure of this chapter is as follows:

- We start with an overview of the basic programming syntax offered by the shell. This includes how to control the flow of execution by evaluating conditions, how to repeat sections of code in a loop, and how to separate sections of code that you want to run more than once into subroutines, or *functions*.

- Next, we cover input and output. This includes how to read and write files from a script and how to handle command-line arguments.

- zsh's automatic function-loading mechanism is explained next. This is used to manage the many functions that are a part of the completion system, so this is relevant to Chapter 15.

- Next we move on to ways to extend the shell using shell code. This includes intercepting certain events to run code and how to write functions that act as additional glob qualifiers in zsh.

- Finally, we discuss a number of techniques for debugging shell scripts.

WHY WRITE SHELL SCRIPTS?

You may wonder why anyone would choose to use the shell when writing a program to perform anything more than the simplest task. After all, there are other scripting languages such as Perl, Python, and Ruby that are in many ways more capable. They certainly have their place and in many situations we would advocate their use over the shell. Nevertheless, you will find situations when a shell script is a good choice:

- When most of what you want to do involves calling other Unix commands. This is a natural application of the shell.

- When you have already constructed most of the program interactively from the command line.

- When you want to make changes to the current shell's environment or current directory. This is only possible from a shell function or sourced script.

- When portability is an issue: you can rely on the Bourne shell existing anywhere. Scripting languages like Perl and even the newer shells like bash and zsh are potentially unavailable. Note, however, that issues related to writing portable shell scripts are beyond the scope of this book.

However, if you need complicated data structures, a lot of text parsing, or access to low-level routines, or if speed of execution is a consideration, then the shell is probably not your best option.

Because the shell is the foremost way of interacting with a Unix system, familiarity with it is perhaps the main reason for using it for scripting. Nevertheless, it is very useful to be aware of what it can do. You'll need to be comfortable with writing shell code to make the most of the following chapters on programming the shell line editor and completion systems.

Programming with the Shell

In this section we will cover the various programming facilities made available by the shell. This will enable you to write shell code. We use the term *shell code* here when talking about programming instructions written for the shell. A shell *script* is, strictly, when you put together some shell code in a file to be run by a separate shell instance. In Chapter 2 we showed how to put together a script. Here we'll show you how to make shell code follow different paths in different situations, how to define how a path is chosen, and how to repeat commands using loops.

Control Flow

The shell provides us with a number of control flow statements. The most basic is the if statement, which is used to make decisions. Its full form, including the optional else and elif parts, is as follows:

```
if condition; then
  commands
elif condition; then
  commands
else
  commands
fi
```

More than one `elif` part can be used. As we saw in the section "Building Our Script" in Chapter 2, the *condition* is really just a command with its exit status being used to indicate true or false. In fact, the condition can contain more than one command and the status of the last one is used. The Unix convention is for an exit status of zero to indicate success. So if you want to do something only if the previous command succeeded, you might write something like this:

```
if grep -q word file; then
  echo file contained word
fi
```

In this example, we use the exit status from the grep command. grep attempts to match a regular expression against its input. A status of zero indicates that the regular expression matched, one indicates that it didn't, and a higher value would mean an error occurred. Only a status of zero is regarded as *true* for the purposes of conditions. The -q (quiet) option to grep here tells it not to output the matching lines. If your version of grep doesn't support the -q option, you can always use redirection to send the output to /dev/null instead (see the section "Redirection" in Chapter 8).

Note You may often see if statements where the then appears at the beginning of the following line. The shell expects the next command after the condition to be "then". A newline is the most common way of separating two commands, so using newline as the separator is quite natural. Instead of using a newline, we use a semicolon. A semicolon is an alternative way of separating two commands in the shell. Functionally it is exactly the same as a newline. It can also be useful interactively if you want to type a couple of commands and have them run without a break in between. For example:

```
sleep 10 ; kill %1
```

Here the shell will run the kill command as soon as the sleep command has finished.

Condition Tests

There is one command that is used more often than any other in conditions: that is the test command and its synonym [.The test command has a variety of options that allow you to do common things like check for a file's existence, check the type of a file, and compare two values. So for example, we can write the following to test whether a filename stored in the variable file has a .txt extension:

```
if test ${file##*.} = txt; then
  echo file has .txt extension
fi
```

Note that because `test` is like any other command, it can't tell the difference between an expanded variable and a literal string. So if your variable happens to be empty or its value looks like an option, you may run into problems. This is often an issue when comparing two strings. Try this to see why:

```
$ value=''
$ [ $value = val ]
bash: [: =: unary operator expected
```

More useful in this case would have been an exit status of 1 (false). Unfortunately, what the `[` command sees is exactly the same as if you had typed just

```
$ [ = val ]
```

Using double quotes around variable expansions solves this dilemma. Quoting doesn't help where you have a value that might look like an option to `test`. For this reason you may see a condition where an extra character has been added on both sides of the comparison operator, as in the following example:

```
if [ X$1 = X-z ]; then
```

Due to issues such as this, there is a newer way of doing conditions. These are instead delimited by double brackets (`[[ ... ]]`). They are given special handling by the shell so that they work better. Unless you need to support older shells, we would recommend using them instead.

These newer conditions are in many ways similar to the old form; they understand a similar set of condition codes. The available condition codes are listed in Table 13-1. && and || can be used within the condition as AND and OR operators, respectively (the `test` command uses -a and -o instead).

Table 13-1. *Conditional Expression Operators*

Operator	Purpose
-b *file*	Tests if *file* is a block special file.
-c *file*	Tests if *file* is a character special file.
-d *file*	Tests if *file* exists and is a directory.
-e *file*	Tests if *file* exists.
-f *file*	Tests if *file* exists and is an ordinary file.
-g *file*	Tests if *file* exists and has its setgid bit set.
-k *file*	Tests if *file* exists and has its sticky bit set.

Table 13-1. *Conditional Expression Operators (Continued)*

Operator	Purpose
-n *string*	Tests if *string* is nonempty.
-o *option*	Tests if *option* is turned on.
-p *file*	Tests if *file* exists and is a named pipe (fifo).
-r *file*	Tests if *file* exists and is readable.
-s *file*	Tests if *file* exists and has a size greater than zero.
-t *file descriptor*	Tests if *file descriptor* is open and associated with a terminal device.
-u *file*	Tests if *file* exists and has its setuid bit set.
-w *file*	Tests if *file* exists and is writable.
-x *file*	Tests if *file* exists and is executable.
-z *string*	Tests if *string* is empty (length zero).
-G *file*	Tests if *file* exists and is owned by the current group.
-L *file*	Tests if *file* exists and is a symbolic link.
-O *file*	Tests if *file* exists and is owned by the current user.
-S *file*	Tests if *file* exists and is a socket.
file1 -ef *file2*	Tests if the two filenames refer to the same file.
file1 -nt *file2*	Tests if *file1* is newer than *file2*.
file1 -ot *file2*	Tests if *file1* is older than *file2*.
string == *pattern*	Tests if the string matches the pattern.
string != *pattern*	Tests if the string doesn't match the pattern.
string1 > *string2*	Compares strings based on their ASCII values.
string1 < *string2*	Compares strings based on their ASCII values.
string =~ *regex*	Tests if the string matches the regular expression (bash 3 only).

So for example, you might place the following in your zsh startup file to test whether the shell is interactive and has a terminal before running the mesg command:

```
if [[ -o interactive && -t 0 ]]; then
  mesg y
fi
```

The mesg command allows you to control whether other people have write permissions for your terminal. Write permission is necessary for others to be able to use the write or talk commands to talk to you.

The == operator (which can also be written as just =) is worth a special mention because it is one of the most useful. It allows you to compare a string against a pattern. The patterns used are the same as those we saw in Chapter 9 for matching filenames, with the exceptions we described for variable expansions in the section "Patterns" in Chapter 12. In particular, slashes don't have any special meaning.

For example, the following will test if the current directory is below the current user's home directory:

```
[[ $PWD = $HOME/* ]]
```

Note that it isn't necessary to quote the pattern to protect it from filename generation. [[...]] style conditions are handled specially by the shell, so in this example, it knows not to expand $HOME/* to the list of files in your home directory. Often, you will only want to compare against a literal string instead of a pattern. To do this, just quote any characters that have special meanings in patterns.

Sometimes it is useful to do comparisons of numbers as opposed to strings. For this, there are additional operators, not listed in Table 13-1, such as -eq (equal) and -lt (less than). If you want to deal with numbers instead of strings, it is both more efficient and more readable to make use of the shells arithmetic mode. So, for example, instead of using the condition [[$val -ge 3]], you can write ((val >= 3)).

Note that the notions of true and false for math evaluation are similar to those used by the C programming language. This is the reverse of how the exit status of a Unix command is interpreted. This means that if the number resulting from the math evaluation is nonzero, the return status will be zero. There are a number of useful tricks making use of this. For example, you might test whether an array is empty as follows:

```
if (( ! ${#array} )); then
```

Arithmetic mode is another thing that is specific to the more modern shells. If you want to write a script that will work in the Bourne shell, there is an expr command that evaluates number-based expressions.

Control Operators

There are a couple of short forms that you can use instead of an if statement. These use the AND (&&) and OR (||) control operators. If you connect two commands with && or ||, they are run in order in the same way as if they had been connected using a semicolon. The difference is that the exit status of the first command decides if the second command is to be run. So you could instead write

```
grep -q word file && echo file contained word
```

The || operator has the opposite effect. The second command becomes like the else part of an if condition. So:

```
grep -q word file || echo "file didn't contain word"
```

To do this with an if statement, you would use the ! operator,[1] which negates the exit status of the following command:

```
if ! grep -q word file ; then    ·
    echo "file didn't contain word"
fi
```

You can even combine the two forms if you want to consider the exit status of more than one command:

```
if grep -q word file && grep -q word otherfile; then
    echo files both contain word
fi
```

Furthermore, several commands can be chained together with the && and || operators:

```
grep -q word file && grep -q word otherfile && echo files both contain word
```

If you try mixing the two operators in a series, you may find that they don't work in the way you expected. The two operators are actually left associative. To understand what we mean, try running this:

```
true || false && echo hello
```

You may have expected it to get no further than the true command because it is followed by || but that is not the case: it goes on to execute the echo command. When handling the &&, it takes the result of the entire preceding sequence, which is true. The effect of the || is merely to prevent the false command from running. Try the following to confirm that this is indeed the case:

```
echo true || echo 'not executed' && echo hello
```

It is more common to use the two control operators combined in the opposite order with the && appearing first. That provides a short way to write simple if-then-else statements. Consider the following example:

```
grep -q word file && echo file contained word || echo "file didn't contain word"
```

If grep finds the word in the file, it returns success and the first echo command will be executed. If grep returns false, the entire expression before the || operator will evaluate to false and the second echo command will execute. In theory, it is possible that both echo commands would be executed: If for some reason the first echo command was to fail, the overall result of the expression before the || operator would be false and the second echo command would be executed. So for the command in the middle, you need to stick to something that can be safely relied upon to return true.

---

1. Be aware that the ! operator isn't available in some older sh-compatible shells.

Let's see another example of this. Some systems have a getent command that allows information such as the list of known hosts to be retrieved. Traditionally, this information was available in files, /etc/hosts in the case of hostnames. The following defines a function, findhost, which searches for a particular hostname. It uses the result of the which command to decide whether to use getent or to look in /etc/hosts.

```
which getent >/dev/null && findhost() { getent hosts $1 } ||
    findhost() { grep $1 /etc/hosts }
```

Case Statement

Sometimes, it can be useful to evaluate a value against a series of possibilities. You can do this with the case statement. For example, it is common in startup files to do different things depending on the terminal type. A case statement is useful in this situation because $TERM can be compared against a series of possible values. One characteristic that differs among different terminals is the escape sequences generated by function keys. In this example, we bind the appropriate sequence for the Insert key.

```
case $TERM in
  (aixterm|iris-ansi*)
    bindkey '\e[139q' overwrite-mode
  ;;
  (xterm|dtterm)
    bindkey '\e[2~'   overwrite-mode
  ;;
esac
```

■**Tip** You will often see case statements where the patterns don't have the opening parenthesis, for example xterm|dtterm). This is an older version of the syntax. Text editors, and sometimes even the shell itself, prefer to find matching parentheses, so we suggest you use the form presented in this section.

The parentheses enclosing each of the patterns are a necessary part of the syntax. Also of particular note, especially to bash users, is that alternatives always work in case patterns. You don't need the special @(pat1|pat2) syntax.

Each pattern is tried in turn until one matches. If you want a catch-all condition at the end, use the pattern *. The double semicolon is used to terminate the commands for each branch of the case statement. If you want a particular case to fall through and also run the commands for the next case, ksh and zsh allow you to use ;& instead. For example, let's suppose we want to extend our previous example to handle the rxvt terminal program. rxvt generates the same escape sequence for the Insert key as xterm but differs in other areas. For instance, rxvt generates \eOD for Ctrl-Left Arrow. We can add a branch to the case statement to bind this key for rxvt but also, by using ;& to terminate the branch, have execution continue into the xterm branch. The resulting case statement is as follows:

```
case $TERM in
  (aixterm|iris-ansi*)
    bindkey '\e[139q' overwrite-mode
  ;;
  (rxvt)
    bindkey '^[OD'    backward-word
  ;&
  (xterm|dtterm)
    bindkey '\e[2~'   overwrite-mode
  ;;
esac
```

You don't need to place the pattern, commands, and terminating semicolons on separate lines. Where there is only one command, it is common to put them together on a single line. Let's revise one of the branches of the previous example:

```
  (xterm|dtterm) bindkey '\e[2~'    overwrite-mode;;
```

More Looping

In Chapter 2, the for loop was briefly introduced. The for loop is not the only type of loop you can use; it just happens to be the one that is most useful when using the shell interactively.

Like most programming languages, the shell offers a while loop. Its use is very similar to the if statement and looks like this:

```
while condition; do
  commands
done
```

The condition is similar in structure to that used by the if statement. It is evaluated first and before each subsequent iteration of the loop. Looping only continues when the condition evaluates to true. There is a variant of this: the until loop, which is identical except that looping continues for as long as the condition is false.

Modern shells offer another type of for loop. It is modeled on the C language's for loop and uses mathematical evaluation to determine whether the loop should continue execution. Consider the following example:

```
for ((i=1;i<5;i++)); do
  a[$i]=$i
done
```

This is another way of doing a=({1..4}). See the section "Generating Numbers with Braces" in Chapter 8 for an explanation of this form of expansion.

zsh offers another loop construct, inherited from C shell. It is known as the repeat loop and is very simple: you just supply a number and the loop runs that number of times. So for example, the following will remove the first five directory components from the beginning of a pathname:

```
repeat 5; p=${p#*/}
```

Note that we have omitted the do and done keywords in this loop. If you have the short_loops option turned on, zsh allows you to do this with for and repeat loops if they contain only one command.

We mentioned that the condition for an if statement can contain more than one command and the status of the last command determines the result of the overall condition. The same applies to the condition for while and until loops. This feature is the reason why the short_loops option only works for repeat and for loops: a short-form while loop would be indistinguishable from the beginning of a while loop containing more than one command as its condition. Using more than one command in the condition effectively allows you to have a loop with an exit condition in the middle because both the condition and loop body are run for each iteration of the loop. It is rarely used for that purpose, however, because, as we'll see in the next section, the shell provides another way to exit from the middle of a loop.

The break and continue Statements

Sometimes, you want more control over when you exit from a loop. For this, there are the break and continue statements. break is used to exit immediately from a loop. It is often useful if an error occurs. For instance, in the example from the section "Building Our Script" in Chapter 2, we might want to bail out of the loop if the cd command fails. The change to that example is highlighted in bold.

```
for dir in `echo "$PATH" | tr ':' ' '`; do
  cd "$dir" || break

  for file in *; do
    [[ -x $file && ! -d $file ]] && echo "$file"
  done

done | sort > proglist
```

You may be wondering what would happen if we put the break inside the inner loop: which loop would it break out of? The answer is that it would just break out of the inner loop. If you wanted to break out of an outer loop, you can pass a number to break specifying how many levels you want to break out of. So in this case, you could use break 2.

On the other hand, the continue statement causes control to advance to the next iteration of the loop skipping any following commands. Like break, continue can be passed a numeric argument to allow execution to skip to the next iteration of an outer loop. If, in the example above, we wanted to do a lot more for each file it finds, we might use

```
for file in *; do
  [[ -x $file && ! -d $file ]] || continue
  echo "$file"
  # lots more commands…
done
```

■**Tip** Occasionally, you may want to write a loop where there is no exit condition at the beginning of each iteration: the only way out of the loop is a `break` command in the middle. For these situations, there is a `true` command that always returns success and so can be used as the loop condition as follows:

```
while true; do
```

Parsed Comments

There is another command functionally equivalent to the `true` command mentioned in the last section, it consists of just a single colon. Like `true`, the command itself doesn't perform any useful action but the shell parses and evaluates its arguments. This is in contrast to a comment, introduced with #, which the shell simply ignores. As we will demonstrate, forcing the shell to evaluate a set of arguments does have some uses.

One use of the colon command is to comment out a command that spans multiple lines. This might be a command with a large here-document or a command where lines end in a backslash or where quotes span several lines. When we place a colon before the command name all the lines are, in effect, commented out. Be careful if you have any command substitutions, though: command substitutions are still evaluated and may have unwanted side effects. Note that you can't use a colon to comment out multiline structures that consist of several commands such as a `while` loop or pipeline: it applies to one command only. You can use a colon to comment out a single command in a series, however. Earlier in this chapter, we showed the following example:

```
grep -q word file && grep -q word otherfile && echo files both contain word
```

If this appears in a script and you want to temporarily skip the command in the middle, you can comment out just that command alone as follows:

```
grep -q word file && : grep -q word otherfile && echo files both contain word
```

Another way you can use the colon command is to fill in an area of a script that you have yet to write while you test those parts of the script that have been written. In most cases you can leave areas blank or use conventional comments, but in some places the shell expects to find a command. To see one such place, try the following in bash:

```
if true; then
  # comment
fi
```

The following error is returned:

```
bash: syntax error near unexpected token `fi'
```

It doesn't like the lack of commands inside the `if` statement. By substituting # with :, it will still be a comment but this time the script will run.

Perhaps the most common way in which the colon command is used is to give it arguments where the process of evaluating those arguments has side effects. There are two variable expansion forms that have a side effect. Suppose that you are writing a script that expects an environment variable, which I'll name VAR, to be set. When you use an expansion of the form ${*variable*:?*error message*}, it will print an error message and exit if the variable is not set. Your script can, therefore, use a line like this at the beginning.

```
: ${VAR:?error: VAR not set}
```

Another similar situation is that we may want to assign a default value for the variable. In Table 13-1 we included the -z condition code, which allows us to test whether a string, and hence a variable expansion, is empty. Making use of that, we could write the following:

```
[[ -z $VAR ]] && VAR='default value'
```

You may remember from the previous chapter that default values can be achieved in a substitution by using the ${*variable*:-*default*} form. There is a variant of this, using an equals sign, that actually assigns the default value to the variable if the variable is unset or empty. Using this and the colon command, the equivalent of the previous example would be

```
: ${VAR:=default value}
```

Grouping and Subshells

Sometimes, it can be useful to group several commands together. Perhaps you want to redirect the output from several commands to a file. For an example, let's write a backup script that backs up several disks and writes output to a log file. The ufsdump command allows a single file-system to be backed up. It needs to be passed some options and the name of the tape and disk devices. So we might use something like this:

```
ufsdump 0f /dev/rmt/0n /dev/dsk/c0t1d0s0 > logfile
ufsdump 0f /dev/rmt/0n /dev/dsk/c0t1d0s1 >> logfile
```

Because there are two separate redirections, this script will close the log file and reopen it between the two commands. A more efficient method involves the grouping of commands between curly brackets, also known as *braces*, like this:

```
{
  ufsdump 0f /dev/rmt/0n /dev/dsk/c0t1d0s0
  ufsdump 0f /dev/rmt/0n /dev/dsk/c0t1d0s1
} > logfile
```

Another use for this grouping is with job control. When we place & after the closing brace, a single background job is created that will run both commands. So for example, to cause a build to be run in the background in an hour's time, you might use

```
{ sleep 3600; make; } &
```

You may also have seen something similar to this that uses parentheses instead of braces. This introduces a subshell: the shell *forks* creating a copy of itself as a separate process. A subshell inherits just about everything from its parent but inside it, changes to things like the current directory, traps, or any variables are lost. This can be quite useful. The following common trick uses tar to copy a directory structure to another place:

```
tar cvf - . | ( cd /somewhere/else; tar xvf - )
```

Because the cd command is run in a subshell, the current directory is changed only for that subshell.

What is perhaps more important to know about subshells is that they can be introduced indirectly in other ways with unexpected results. One way is with pipes: a pipe expects two communicating processes, but what if both commands are shell built-ins? Try executing the following in bash:

```
bash$ var=before
bash$ echo after | read var
bash$ echo $var
before
```

The read command is a built-in that reads its input into a variable. We introduce it in more detail in the section "Reading Input" later in this chapter. In this case, we would expect read to set the variable named var to after. So why doesn't read change the variable? As you've probably now guessed, read is being run in a subshell. So why does it work in zsh? Because zsh runs echo in a subshell instead. To be more explicit, zsh runs all but the last command of a pipeline in a subshell, while conversely bash runs all but the first. This means you can see the same effect in zsh with the following:

```
zsh% echo after | read var | :
```

The zsh behavior is less likely to be a nuisance, but there is one case that occasionally surprises people: when you use the jobs command (see the section "Starting and Stopping Processes: Signals, Job Control" in Chapter 3) to determine which background jobs are running. You probably expect to be able to read the output like this:

```
zsh% sleep 60 &
zsh% jobs | read line
zsh% echo $line

zsh%
```

In bash, this works. In versions of zsh up to and including 4.0, you get no output, even if jobs on its own gives you a list of jobs.

The reason is that in zsh the jobs built-in is run in a subshell. This subshell, unlike the main shell, has no jobs. Therefore, there is no output. In zsh version 4.2 this has been fixed, but only by having zsh remember the list of jobs as they were when the subshell was started. It's possible that the list has changed by the time it is recalled in the subshell, since the subshell doesn't get to see what's happening in the main shell. However, if you only use it to process output right away with read or some other command, that won't be a problem. If you are using zsh 4.0, you can implement a similar solution yourself by using a temporary file to remember the output, and process that:

```
zsh% jobs >/tmp/jobs.$$
zsh% read line </tmp/jobs.$$
zsh% rm /tmp/jobs.$$
zsh% echo $line
[1]  + suspended  vi foo
```

Tip The special variable $$ (see the section "Expansion and Substitution" in Chapter 1) is a common way of creating the name of a temporary file name that's unlikely to clash with an existing one. $$ expands to the shell's process ID and there can only be one process with a given ID at any one time. We'll use the same trick in the section "Trapping Signals" in this chapter.

The other notable places where you will have a subshell is inside command substitution and process substitution. See the section "Command Substitution" in Chapter 2 and the section "Process Substitution" in Chapter 11.

Functions and Variable Scope

Though they are sometimes known as *procedures* or *subroutines*, *functions* are a feature of nearly all programming languages. Functions allow programs to be divided into separate blocks and for the details of one part of the program to be hidden from another. In the shell, functions are often used for creating interactive shortcuts. We have seen this use of functions already, but shell functions can also be used within scripts or even within other functions; instead of control returning to the command line when the function finishes, execution continues with the next line after the function call. Functions are a feature common to all modern sh-compatible shells, but C shell and early versions of the Bourne shell don't support them.

Defining a function is very simple. Reiterating the example from Chapter 2:

```
findpgm() {
  grep "$1" $HOME/proglist | column
}
```

There are actually two different syntaxes used for functions. We could instead write

```
function findpgm {
  grep "$1" $HOME/proglist | column
}
```

The reason for this is historical: the name() {} syntax was added to the Bourne shell by Steve Bourne at around the same time as David Korn added the function name {} syntax to the Korn shell. Only the former syntax is defined in the POSIX specification, but either will work in modern shells.

One thing to be aware of if you write ksh scripts[2] is that in ksh the two syntaxes have different semantics. With the latter syntax, variables and traps (we'll discuss traps later) are local to the function, making the functions more script-like. This reflects the difference in how they were implemented in the two shells.

In both bash and zsh, all functions follow the simpler semantics. You have to state explicitly if you want local variables or traps. Note that the positional parameters (such as $1) are always local, though. Local variables are declared using the local built-in, which is yet another variant of declare.

Local variables in both bash and zsh have what is called *dynamic scope*. This means that if you call another function, it will be able to see all of the calling function's local variables. To see what I mean, try this:

```
function inner {
  echo $var
}

function outer {
  local var=local

  inner
}

var=global
outer
```

If you run this in bash or zsh, it will print local: the inner function sees the outer function's local variable. In ksh93, the situation is different. First, the local command needs to be replaced with typeset. More significant is that ksh93 uses *static scoping*, which means it will print global. The behavior of typeset in ksh93 is similar to that of the my keyword in Perl. ksh88 used *dynamic scoping* like bash and zsh.

Note that there is no such thing as a local function. If you declare a function inside another function, it will be available globally.

Porting Scripts

As you may have noticed, zsh offers a number of options that make it behave in ways more similar to other shells. This can be very useful if you have, for example, a ksh script that you want to run with zsh. bash doesn't have any equivalent options, but like many GNU programs, it does look at the POSIXLY_CORRECT environment variable. If it is set, it will alter a few minor things to achieve better compliance with the POSIX specification. You can also use set -o posix or invoke bash with the --posix option to achieve the same effect.

---

2. ksh is generally a good choice for scripts: it is more widely available on commercial Unix systems and scripting is perhaps where it is strongest.

■**Note** The POSIX standard specifies the behavior of common components of Unix-like operating systems. This includes requirements for the shell's features and behavior. If you want to ensure that your script runs in all the mainstream shell variants, the easiest way is to restrict yourself to using the features standardized in the POSIX specification.

In zsh, you're saved the hassle of determining the ideal set of options in order to emulate a particular shell. If you install zsh under the name of a different shell, such as "ksh" or "sh" (or use a link), it will set the options to best emulate that shell. You can also use the emulate command to specify another shell to emulate after zsh has already started. Don't expect the emulation to be perfect, however, especially the C shell emulation—zsh is really too unlike the C shell to do a half decent job of emulating it. By default, only those options likely to affect portability of scripts and functions are altered.

■**Tip** Passing the -R option to emulate will additionally change options affecting the interactive environment.

When writing shell functions, it is often convenient to use features that are dependent upon specific options. Once features that you have enabled in your own startup file become familiar, it is only natural to want to use them from shell functions too. If you then give a copy of your function to someone else they may find it doesn't work from their setup. By using emulate with the -L option, it is possible to make functions more resilient. With the -L option, all options and traps (covered in the section "Traps and Special Functions" later in this chapter) will be restored after the function exits. It is, therefore, not uncommon to use the following line at the top of a function:

```
emulate -L zsh
```

In order to effect local changes to options, what this actually does is turn the local_options option on. If you only want to change a few particular options in your function, you can set local_options directly. For example, if you want to use extended globbing in your function, you might start your function with the following:

```
setopt local_options extended_glob
```

Input and Output

In the traditional view of a computer program, the program has some input coming into it, performs some processing on the input, and produces some output. For a program to be at all useful it needs to produce some form of output. Most of this chapter concentrates on the processing aspect of scripts, but in this section we will consider input and, to a lesser extent, output.

Let's begin this section by considering output. The output from a script can take many different forms: you can invoke an audio player to play sound files or output some text to a printer, or the "output" might take a more subtle form, such as rearranging some files on the filesystem. In this section, we look at just two of the more basic forms that output can take: printing text and returning an exit status from a script.

The input to a program can also take different forms. One of the more obvious ways that a script or function receives input is with arguments passed to on the command line. We describe not only how to access these arguments but also how to solve common problems that occur when trying to interpret the arguments.

Another common way in which a script or function receives input is by reading lines of text. The text can come from a variety of sources. We look at how you can read text from a file and from the output of another command, and how to read text that is typed by the user. Once information has been read in, a script typically has to make sense of it. We demonstrate some powerful techniques for parsing the text and extracting meaningful parts of it.

Writing Output

Output typically is performed by the echo command. We've seen it many times before. When run, it simply writes out everything you give to it as an argument:

```
% echo these are the arguments
these are the arguments
```

That looks really nice and simple, doesn't it? Unfortunately, things aren't usually quite that simple. The trouble is that the echo command *might* interpret some escape sequences in its arguments. These are the same escape sequences we talk about in the sidebar "POSIX Quotes." You can often enable or disable this behavior with the -e or -E options, respectively, but again, implementations vary. The reasons for these variations are largely historical and have to do with the old BSD and System V Unix split. The upshot is that you need to be careful when using echo in scripts, particularly if you are using variable expansions as the arguments to echo.

As one solution to the problem, zsh and ksh also include a very similar command named print. Unless you need your script to run in bash or an older shell, we recommend using it instead. print also has the advantage of having a number of interesting options that allow you to do things like print the arguments arrayed in columns and sorted.

The most portable way to output text is to use the printf command. It works very much like the C printf() function, so you need to provide it with a format string. For example, you can write this:

```
% printf '%s\n' 'hello there'
hello there
```

Note that not all shells have printf as a built-in (including zsh 4.0). It should exist as an external command, so this just means your script will be a bit slower.

POSIX QUOTES

In the section "Control Shell Interpretation with Quoting" in Chapter 3, we noted that there are three kinds of quoting. This was not entirely true. Newer shells offer an additional set of quote marks. We will refer to this third kind as *POSIX quotes* because they are defined by POSIX. They consist of a dollar symbol followed by single quotes.

POSIX quotes also behave like normal single quotes. There is one key exception, however. In POSIX quotes, you can additionally use a number of escape sequences. For example, you can use $'\t' to get a tab character. You can also use $'\n' as a nicer alternative to breaking lines. For example, you can use

```
% PS1=$'%~\n%#'
```

instead of

```
% PS1='%~
%#'
```

The available escape sequences are roughly the same as those available in strings in the C programming language.

Exit Statuses

The *exit status* of a command is the one form of output that is sent directly back to the code from which the command was called. We've talked a lot about the exit status of commands before. When any Unix command finishes, it returns a number to indicate its status when it finished. We've seen how to determine and use the exit status of commands, but how do we indicate our exit status from a shell script?

Tip When a command is killed by a signal, the exit status is 128 plus the signal number. In both bash and zsh, you can translate the exit status into the signal's name by using the -l option to kill. For example, to see that an exit status of 130 corresponds to the INT signal we can execute the following:

```
% kill -l 130
INT
```

Normally when a function or shell script finishes, it passes on the exit status of the last command executed. It is important to be aware of this because it can often cause your shell script to return 1 even when it finishes successfully. To avoid this, you need to explicitly specify your exit status. From a shell script you do this with the exit command. For example, to exit with a status of 0, you would use the following:

```
exit 0
```

This will exit the script immediately even if there are more commands following in the script.

The `exit` command terminates the currently running shell process. Functions don't run in a separate process so if you try this from a function, it will cause your shell to exit. Functions, therefore, have a separate command: `return`. For this reason, the status after leaving a function is often referred to as the *return status*. The `return` command is used in the same way as `exit`; thus, to return from a function with a status of 1, you would write

```
return 1
```

That finishes our coverage of output, and for the rest of this section, we'll consider input to programs. We'll start with the positional parameters. These refer to the arguments passed to a command when it is called. In some respects, they can be thought of as the opposite of the exit status: information is passed between the command and the point at which it is called but in the opposite direction.

Positional Parameters

One of the more noteworthy forms of input to a shell script or function consists of the parameters passed on the command line. From within a script or function, these parameters are on hand in a set of variables that are referred to as the *positional parameters*.

We have seen one of these already: $1, which contains the first argument passed to our function or script. There is a whole collection of these: $2, $3, and so on up to $9, each containing the next parameter. After 9 you need to use braces: ${10}, though zsh allows $10, $11, and so on. A $# variable contains the number of parameters that have been supplied. You can also view all the positional parameters together with the $* string or $@ array.

The difference between $* and $@ is exactly the same as for ${arr[@]} and ${arr[*]} array expansions as was described in the section "Array Expansions" in Chapter 12. Functionally, you will only see the difference when you use them in double quotes:

```
% set -- one two three
% printf '%s\n' "$*"
one two three
% printf '%s\n' "$@"
one
two
three
```

Using the `set` command as in this example allows you to set the positional parameters. zsh also allows conventional assignments to be used for them. For example, `5=five` will assign "five" to $5.

THE MANY USES OF SET

You may have noticed that the set command has more than one use. This can be confusing because most commands only do one thing. To clarify the situation for set, here is a summary of its uses:

- **Setting options:** by using options, and -o in particular, set allows you to turn options on and off. This is similar to zsh's setopt and bash's shopt. See the section "Setting Options with set" in Chapter 5.

- **Assigning to the positional parameters,** which we cover in this section. This is normally seen beginning with set --. The "--" is only actually necessary if the following arguments could cause this form to be confused for one of the other two.

- **Assigning to arrays:** set -A is the old way of assigning to array variables, which we mentioned in the section "Arrays" in Chapter 12.

The first two uses go back to the Bourne shell. In particular, there was no other way of setting options apart from set -o, so this use is still common. (Remember that in bash the options set using set -o are distinct from those set using shopt -s.)

There is one positional parameter we haven't mentioned yet: $0. It contains the name of the script itself as it was typed on the command line. This has a number of uses. As we saw in the section "Login Shells" in Chapter 5, the shell itself looks at its 0th argument for an initial dash to decide if it is to be a login shell or not. In scripts, it is not uncommon to use a hard link to allow one script to have two different names and alter its behavior slightly depending on the script name. This isn't unique to scripts: gzip and gunzip are typically a hard link to the same file. Another common use for $0 is when printing the command name in an error message. For example, you might begin your script with

```
if [[ -z $1 ]]; then
  echo "${0##*/}: parameter expected" >&2
  exit 1
fi
```

If you try this out in a function as opposed to a script, you will be in for two nasty surprises. The exit statement here exits the shell and says that we want to use an exit status of 1. It won't just return from the function. In a function, we need to use a return statement instead. So if you tried this in a function, your shell would exit and the window associated with it would disappear and you wouldn't see the first nasty surprise. The first surprise would be that instead of printing the name of your function the error would look like this:

```
-bash: parameter expected
```

In zsh, it would work as expected (unless you turn the function_arg_zero option off). In bash, you have to use the FUNCNAME special variable instead to get the name of the function. Note that as of version 3, FUNCNAME is an array containing the names of all functions in the current call stack. This means that the first element contains the name of the currently executing function, the second element is the name of the function that called that, and so on. zsh has a similar array named funcstack provided by the zsh/parameter module.

One more feature provided by zsh is that the positional parameters can also be accessed via argv and ARGC special variables. These come from C shell, but zsh is really too unlike C shell for them to ever be useful in running C shell scripts. argv is an array corresponding to $@ while ARGC is a scalar and corresponds to $#. One use for argv is if you want to assign to a particular positional parameter where the index of the positional parameter is held in another variable. For example, the following assigns the value five to $5:

```
index=5
argv[index]=five
```

It is not possible to write @[index]=five. argv is also sometimes used with subscript flags. So for example, we might use $argv[(I)-X] to search for the -X option in the positional parameters. In this case, we could have used $@[(I)-X] but argv is somewhat more readable.

Option Parsing

Most Unix commands accept a number of options along with normal arguments. For example, here the arguments to grep include the -v option and two further nonoption arguments:

```
grep -v '^#' .zshrc
```

It is common when writing a script or function to want to accept options. Unfortunately, having options complicates the job of picking arguments out of the parameters: instead of the first main argument being reliably in $1, options might move it up to $2 or beyond.

A common way to handle parameters is to loop through them. One way to loop through the parameters is with a for loop. If the in keyword and following list of words is left out of a for loop, it will loop through the positional parameters instead. So we might have something like this:

```
for par; do
  case $par in
    (-a) aopt=1;;
    (-b) bopt=1;;
    (*)  arg=$par;;
  esac
done
```

A shortcoming of this method would be exposed if we add another option into the mix where that option expects to be followed by an argument of its own. Handling the parameters one at a time in this way doesn't allow us to look ahead and consume two arguments in one iteration. We could maintain some state information ready for the next loop iteration, but there is an easier way.

The shift statement moves all the parameters up a place. So $2 becomes $1, $3 becomes $2, and so on. Used inside a while loop, this makes for another way of looping through the parameters.

```
while [[ $1 = -* ]]; do
  case $1 in
    (-a) aopt=1;;
    (-b) bopt=1;;
    (-c)
      carg=$2
      shift
    ;;
  esac
  shift
done
```

When processing the -c option, the code shown picks up the following argument from $2. At the end, any arguments that haven't been processed remain in the positional parameters, starting from $1. This code is sufficiently flexible to handle most option parsing situations.

One thing that the above code doesn't allow is for options to be clumped together, for example as -ab instead of -a -b. If you program in C, you may be familiar with the getopt() function, which allows this for C programs. Unix has a similarly named external command for use in scripts. In addition to this, there is a shell built-in named getopts. The built-in is a little bit more convenient to use, so let's look at it here.

To use getopts, you need to give it a specification describing the expected options. This is just a list of option letters. Any option that expects an argument should be followed by a colon. getopts is therefore of little use if you want to have long option names, though the previous two methods will work fine for you. Here is our example using getopts:

```
while getopts "abc:" par; do
  case $par in
    (a) aopt=1;;
    (b) bopt=1;;
    (c) carg=$OPTARG;;
    (?) exit 1;;
  esac
done
shift $(( OPTIND - 1 ))
```

Positioned as the condition of the while loop, getopts controls the loop, causing it to stop when it reaches a nonoption argument or the argument --. It uses three variables to provide the status. The first contains the current option with the leading dash removed. This is the one named with an argument to getopts—in this case par. The other two variables have fixed names: OPTARG provides any argument to an option such as for the -c option here and OPTIND is an index into the positional parameters and serves as the loop iterator. As shown in this example, OPTIND can be useful at the end of the loop with shift to remove all the option arguments. If passed a numeric parameter, shift will shift the parameters by that many places. zsh also allows shift to be used with arrays if given the array name as a parameter.

zsh has one further built-in—named zparseopts—for parsing options. It was developed with the peculiarities of completion functions in mind but can be useful elsewhere. What is unusual about completion functions is that they don't generally want to dissect all the options passed to them: instead they want to just pick out the few that are of interest and have the remainder ready for passing on unchanged, either to further completion functions or the compadd built-in. If you want to accept your own options from a completion function, you need to carefully avoid option letters that clash with compadd options and, because they may be passed mixed in with the compadd options, use zparseopts to extract them.

To use zparseopts, first divide up the list of possible options into those you want to throw away, those you want to look at, and those you want to keep ready for passing on. Like getopts, it needs specifications to describe the possible options. Unlike getopts, though, each option is in its own word, which means long option names can be handled. Specifications are just the option name followed by a colon if an argument is expected. Here is an example:

```
zparseopts -D -E -a garbage C=usecc O:=subopts J: V: 1 2 X:
```

By using the -D option here, all the specified options are removed from the positional parameters. Any others are left in "$@" ready to be passed on to another completion function. The specified options are put into the garbage array (defined with the -a option) where they can subsequently be ignored. The exception to this is the -C and -O options for which we have explicitly defined an alternate variable. So in this example -C or -O options are put, along with their arguments, into the usecc and subopts variables, respectively.

Without the -E option, it would stop at the first option for which there is no specification. Often you just want to extract one option from the parameters, and this is very useful for doing that. It is also common to just give specifications for options you want to remove.

That brings us to the end of our coverage of the positional parameters. Next we'll consider another form that input to a script can take: text read from a file or a command's output.

Reading Input

Earlier we saw how to use commands like echo to output information but haven't yet focused on reading text as input. The two most common sources from which text can be read are the output of another command or the contents of a file. From within a script, the aim is typically to read this input into a shell variable and then use some form of processing to make sense of it. In this section, we show you first how to read text in and then describe various techniques for parsing the input so that your script can make use of it.

In the section "Command Substitution" in Chapter 2, we saw one way of getting at the output of another command. For convenience, we often want the input in a shell variable. This is simple with command substitution—we simply use the expansion in an assignment. For example:

```
input="$(ps)"
```

This is fine when the input is another command's output, but what if you want to read in a file? The answer is to use the cat command. For example:

```
input="$(cat config.ini)"
```

This is so common that there is a special form of command substitution that does this without running the external cat program:

```
input="$(<config.ini)"
```

The trouble with this is that the entire input has been read into the variable. More often than not, it is more convenient to be able to deal with the input in smaller chunks such as a line at a time. While you could chop it up, it is easier and more efficient to just read the input in one line at a time. The shell provides a read built-in for this purpose. read takes one line of text from standard input and assigns it to a variable, REPLY by default. If there are no more lines of text available, read returns false. This is useful with a while loop as follows:

```
while read; do
  echo $REPLY
done < config.ini
```

Note how we place the redirection after the done keyword to redirect standard input for the whole while loop. This is similar to using redirections with commands grouped in braces as we described in the section "Grouping and Subshells" earlier in this chapter. It is also possible to pipe the output of a command into a while loop as we show here:

```
ps | while read; do
 echo $REPLY
done
```

Depending on the format of the input being read, it is likely that the line will need to be further broken down. Splitting a string into separate words is easy in general because you can use the shell's usual word splitting as described in the section "Word Splitting" in Chapter 12. In this case, you can ask read to do the splitting for you. If passed the -a option in bash or -A in zsh or ksh93, read will split the input into words and store the results in an array. Alternatively, you can specify a list of variables, one for each word. That even works in ksh88. For example, this will read the output from the ps command and output just the process ID and command:

```
ps | while read pid tty time cmd; do
  echo $cmd $pid
done
```

The shell's word splitting isn't confined to splitting up words at space and tab characters. It actually uses the characters listed in the IFS (internal field separator) variable as separators when splitting things into words. For example, we can use this to separate the fields in a password file:

```
while IFS=: read user pw uid gid name home shell; do
  echo $user $name
done </etc/passwd
```

Note also how the IFS variable is only changed for the read command.

Another way of breaking a line of input down is to use patterns. The variable expansion forms we showed in the section "Patterns" in Chapter 12 are powerful enough for most purposes. For example, let's say we are reading a configuration file where each line is of the form *option=value*. We want to split this into the name of the option and the value. To do this, we might use

```
option="${line%%=*}"
value="${line#*=}"
```

Backreferences

zsh has another, very powerful, way of doing this: *backreferences*. They are enabled in a pattern with the (#b) globbing flag. When enabled, parentheses in the pattern are active and can be referred back to by using shell variables. Each parenthesis matched where backreferences are turned on causes the shell to set an entry in the array match to the substring matched, and entries in the arrays mbegin and mend to the position of the substring inside the full string. Up to a maximum of nine parentheses are matched.

Here's how we might read in our configuration file using backreferences to break down the lines:

```zsh
#!/bin/zsh

# All globbing flags, including (#b), need this option turned on.
setopt extended_glob

# We'll store the result in an associative array.
declare -A results

while read line; do
  case $line in
    # ignore any blank lines or comments
    (|\#*) ;;

    # match configuration lines using backreferences
    ((#b)([^=]##)=(*))
      # store the result
      results[$match[1]]="$match[2]"
    ;;

    *)
      echo "Syntax error" >&2
      exit 1 # use 'return' from a function
    ;;
  esac
done < config.ini
```

Using a case statement allows us to compare the line against a pattern. We could have used [[$line = *pattern*]] instead.

If you use backreferences in a function, remember the feature sets three arrays. It's usually sensible to make all three invisible to anything outside the function by including the statement at the top of the function:

```
local match mbegin mend
```

bash 3 adds support for a form of backreferences but using regular expressions instead of shell patterns. An additional =~ operator is available in condition tests allowing a value to be matched against a regular expression. After matching, the BASH_REMATCH array contains any matching portions of the value: its first element contains the part of the value that matched the whole regular expression and subsequent elements contain parts of the value matching sections of the regular expression enclosed in parentheses. Using this to match lines in our configuration file example, we might use the following condition:

```
[[ $line =~ '^([^=]+)=(.*)$' ]]
```

This should place the option and value from our line in the second (index 1) and third elements of BASH_REMATCH, respectively. Note that the regular expression needed to be quoted. Unlike shell patterns, regular expressions are not automatically anchored at the beginning and end. This means that the regular expression only needs to match somewhere in the middle of $line. That's why the initial element of BASH_REMATCH is useful. To ensure that the regular expression matched the whole of $line we included the ^ and $ operators at the start and end of our regular expression, respectively. The $ is not actually needed in this example because .* will match as many characters as possible: as with shell patterns, matching is greedy.

Asking the User for Input

In this section, we will cover the special case where your script reads input typed by the user.

If you have tried using the read command without redirecting standard input from a file or pipe of some sort, you will see that it will use the regular standard input to the shell. You might want this if you intend your script to be used in a pipeline. In other circumstances, standard input will be the terminal device. In other words, reading from it will return a line of text typed by the user.

For example, if you need to prompt the user for an e-mail address in a script, you might write

```
echo -n "Enter e-mail address: " >&2
read -r address
```

The -r option to read stands for raw. It prevents backslash escapes being interpreted in the input. Because displaying a prompt is very common, you can specify it directly from read. In ksh or zsh, this would be

```
read -r 'address?Enter e-mail address: '
```

For bash, the prompt is specified with a -p option:

```
read -r -p 'Enter e-mail address: ' address
```

If you use the -e option, bash will use readline. This means that you will get many of the features associated with entering information on the command line. For example, you will get filename completion and be able to recall lines from the history.

In zsh, the read command doesn't have an equivalent option; -e does something entirely different. Instead, you can use the vared built-in, which does use the zsh line editor, for reading user input. For example:

```
vared -c -p 'Enter e-mail address: ' address
```

The -c option creates the variable if it doesn't already exist.

The vared built-in is also useful from an interactive shell as a way of editing the value of a variable. To see how it works, try this:

```
% vared PATH
```

When you're editing arrays with vared, the first character in $IFS is used to separate elements. This will normally be a space but it can be nice to use a newline instead. The following alias is useful for this:

```
alias lvared="IFS=\$'\n' vared"
```

To edit the path, you can then do lvared path. Each directory in the path will then be placed on a separate line.

Propagating Functions

Once you have built up a good collection of functions, you will come across the issue of where to store them in a tidy fashion and how you make them available. Initially, the obvious place to put them is your startup file or files sourced from your startup files. For small functions this is fine, but if you have a great many functions, it can take surprisingly long to read them all in. In this section, we will show you some ways of managing them better.

Exporting Functions

bash allows functions to be exported. This means that function definitions are kept in memory so when a new shell starts, they can be loaded quickly. The declare command applies to functions if passed the -f option so that can be combined with -x for exporting. Consider the following example:

```
bash$ foo() {
> echo in foo
> }
bash$ declare -fx foo
bash$ bash
bash$ foo
in foo
bash$ zsh
zsh% foo
zsh: command not found: foo
zsh% echo $foo
() {  echo in foo
}
```

As we can see, what bash is actually doing when running a command is treating the function as if it was a normal environment variable that begins with (). When the second instance of bash executes, it sees this environment variable and handles it specially, creating a function. However, when we run any other program such as zsh, we see nothing other than a strangely named environment variable. If you initialize your functions in your .bash_profile file, they will then propagate to subshells without each subshell rereading them.

Autoloadable Functions

We mentioned that the process of loading many shell functions into memory each time the shell starts can be time consuming. Exporting functions in the environment as bash allows wastes memory if you have a lot of functions, and it still doesn't solve the problem of having the definitions of many functions cluttered together in one startup file.

Consider what happens when you run an ordinary command from the shell. The command is found by searching the directories in $PATH and only then loaded into memory by the operating system. This is a system that works well. So, what if we could use the same system for shell functions? The operating system can't run shell functions but it can run scripts, so one solution is to convert our functions to shell scripts and store them somewhere in $PATH. This solution has a limitation, however: shell scripts are run in a separate shell instance. Often when we write a shell function, we want that function to be run in the current shell instance. A function running in the current shell instance has access to information denied to scripts such as to shell variables, and it has the ability to make changes that affect the current shell, for example to the current directory. Functions controlling the line editor and completion system, which we show you how to write in the following chapters, also need to run in the current shell instance.

The function autoloading mechanism of ksh and zsh takes the idea of loading commands when they are executed and applies it to functions. The functions are found by searching directories listed in $FPATH for a file that has the same name as the function.

In a similar fashion to the path array dual of PATH, zsh has a fpath array that is somewhat easier to manipulate than the FPATH string. It is common to create a directory for these functions within your home and add it to fpath from your startup file:

```
fpath=( ~/.zfunc $fpath )
```

You need to add the directory because unless you have a very old version of zsh the fpath will already contain a number of directories for such things as the completion system.

If you have used ksh's autoloadable functions, you will find that there are a few differences. One is that in ksh, files containing autoloadable functions include the surrounding function *name* {...} syntax to introduce and name the function. The other difference is that zsh doesn't automatically pick up functions by searching fpath: you need to use autoload on every function. In ksh, FPATH is searched after PATH so autoload is only used for a function with the same name as an external command.

Let's try this with a simple function. Create a file named newfunc in the directory you added to fpath and put the command echo hello in it. The file doesn't need to have any special permissions such as execute—you only need to be able to read it. If you try to run it now, it won't work because autoload has not been executed. We've already seen autoload used for functions like compinit in the section "zsh's compinit" in Chapter 10 and promptinit in the section "Prompt Themes" in Chapter 7. We just need to pass autoload the name of our function:

```
zsh% autoload newfunc
```

Now, you should be able to run the function:

```
zsh% newfunc
hello
```

Having to use autoload before using every function would obviously be rather tedious, so this is one thing you will want to do from your startup file:

```
autoload -- ~/.zfunc/[^_]*(:t)
```

That omits any files beginning with an underscore because `compinit` will autoload them. The (`:t`) modifier removes any directory portion from the expansion—we only want the name of the function.

Traps and Special Functions

Being able to run shell code in response to events other than the user executing a command from the command line allows you to extend the way the shell works in new, powerful, and interesting ways. Traps and special functions allow this to be done. Traps let you specify code to be run whenever a signal is sent to the current process. This means, for example, you can add some cleanup code to be run if someone kills your script. Special functions are invoked directly by the shell when certain events occur, such as a new prompt being printed or the current directory changing. In this section we demonstrate some of the uses for which traps and special functions can be applied.

Trapping Signals

In the section "Starting and Stopping Processes: Signals, Job Control" in Chapter 3, we learned how to send signals to a process using either the `kill` command or with special key combinations such as Ctrl-z. Using traps, these signals can be picked up within the shell allowing you to run shell code in response. This concept is perhaps best illustrated with an example. A typical use of traps is to clear up any temporary files if the script is interrupted by the user with Ctrl-c:

```
trap 'rm /tmp/temp-$$; exit' INT TERM
```

Note how we include an `exit` command to ensure the script still exits after clearing up the temporary file. This will also respond to the `TERM` signal, which is what the `kill` command sends by default. In addition to `INT` and `TERM`, there are quite a few signals that, by default, cause programs to terminate. Of these, it is common to trap the `HUP` signal often so as to do nothing more than ignore the signal. If you want to ignore a signal, disabling any default behavior, you can specify the empty string as the command argument to `trap`. Here we specify that the `HUP` signal should be ignored:

```
trap '' HUP
```

If you subsequently want to restore the default handling of a signal, you need to remove the trap. This is done by passing a dash (`-`) as the command argument to `trap`. So to make `HUP` signals terminate our process again we would use the following:

```
trap - HUP
```

If a signal isn't used to tell a process to exit, then it amounts to a rudimentary way of having one process communicate with another. Two signals, `USR1` and `USR2`, are made available for user-defined purposes. If you want to use a signal for some custom purpose, you can use one of these. It isn't possible to pass any information with a signal, though, so they are only useful for synchronization, perhaps to tell another process when a file is ready for it to read. There is an example using the `USR1` signal in the section "Keeping Other Input Away from the Command Line" in Chapter 14.

Most signals are sent in response to some event occurring. In zsh, the TMOUT variable we saw in Chapter 7 is used in conjunction with the ALRM signal: when the time elapses an ALRM signal is sent. By trapping ALRM, you can do something more useful than exiting the shell:

```
zsh% TMOUT=30
zsh% trap 'echo Do something.' ALRM
```

If you haven't typed anything for 30 seconds, you will see the message, and again 30 seconds later, until you unset TMOUT. The command run when this alarm goes off doesn't need to be before a prompt; that's because it's done using the operating system's own signal facility. This also means that the prompt is not redisplayed after the "Do something" appears, making the display look a bit messy. Some magic with the line editor that we'll meet in the section "Outputting Messages" in Chapter 14 can help there.

The shell also makes available a set of fake signals. These are signals that aren't known to the operating system and can't be sent with the kill command but that the shell allows you to trap. They allow you to intercept certain operations of the shell.

The EXIT fake signal is triggered any time the shell exits, whether it does so normally or in response to some signal. For tasks like clearing up temporary files, this can be a lot more convenient than trapping a whole host of signals.

Similar to the EXIT trap, bash version 3 has a RETURN fake trap that is triggered whenever a function or sourced script returns. In zsh, if you define the EXIT trap within a function, it will be triggered when the function exits. zsh will also restore any previous EXIT trap when the function exits. In general, traps are not restored when a function returns. zsh allows all traps to be made local to a function by turning the local_traps option on. This is similar to the local_options option we saw in the section "Porting Scripts" in this chapter.

The other two common fake signals are intended to aid debugging: DEBUG and ERR, which are triggered after every command and commands returning a nonzero exit status, respectively. In zsh, the ERR trap is instead named ZERR because some operating systems already have a signal named ERR.

Special Functions

zsh supports a number of special functions that allow you to run code in response to certain events. In concept, they are very similar to fake signals, but they happen to be implemented as functions.

The most basic of these functions is precmd, which is executed just before the prompt is printed. You can try it out like this:

```
zsh% precmd() { print About to show the prompt...; }
About to show the prompt...
zsh%
About to show the prompt...
zsh%
```

Thoroughly boring, but you get the picture. You can do pretty much anything with a function, so this is very powerful. In particular, we recommend using this wherever possible instead of putting a command substitution inside the prompt itself. precmd is a useful place to set the variable psvar for use in %v substitutions:

```
precmd() { psvar=( "$(read_thermometer)" ); }
PS1='%1v deg C%# '
```

This shows a hypothetical system with a command read_thermometer that outputs the temperature in degrees Celsius to standard output. We use psvar to put the result in the prompt. This keeps commands cleanly inside the function where they belong, so they don't clutter up the prompt.

A close relative of precmd is preexec. This is a function that is run just after you've hit Return to execute a command line and before it's executed. It gets the command line as an argument. You might, for example, want to parse it in some way to put it into the title bar while the command is executing.

The function periodic is run about the same time as precmd (just after, as it happens), but only if $PERIOD seconds have elapsed since the last time it was run. It allows you to implement your own custom things much along the lines of the built-in mail checking and watching of logins and logouts that we described in Chapter 7. Note that setting $PERIOD to 0 is pointless since you would get the same effect as precmd.

Finally, the function chpwd is run whenever the directory changes in the shell.

A common use of the chpwd function is to put the current directory in the window's title bar. Each time the current directory changes, the title bar can be updated to reflect the new current directory. Let's see how we could go about making this happen.

Putting messages in the title bar is something we might want to do from more than one place. Dealing with the terminal escape codes each time is not very nice, and it's quite useful to have a separate function that does that. So let's create one:

```
header() {
  case $TERM in
    (sun-cmd)
      print -nP "\e]$*\e\\"
    ;;
    (*)
      print -nP "\e]2;$*\a"
    ;;
  esac
}
```

It isn't possible to know if the terminal understands the particular escape sequence, but by using a case statement we can choose one based on the value of $TERM. There are two types of terminal: the old OpenWindows sun-cmd, and everything else that works like xterm —nearly all do, even the Cygwin terminal, and more pop up with each new type of desktop, so it's hard to keep up. But it does mean it's unsafe to use this command if you don't have a windowing system running; anything could happen, probably including a beep.

Note we've used print -nP; -n just suppresses the final newline, and the -P allows the prompt escapes. This means we can treat the argument to header as a prompt. So, for example, header "%n@%m: %~" will put your username, hostname, and current directory in the title bar.

Putting this together, the following should update the title bar every time the current directory changes:

```
chpwd() {
  header "%n@%m: %~"
}
```

Replacing Built-in Commands

We are not limited to traps and special functions if we want to intercept an operation within in the shell. By replacing a built-in command with a function, we can extend the built-in by adding extra functionality to it. Our function can go away and do whatever it wants before calling the real built-in.

If you want to create a function that replaces a built-in, the main thing you need to be aware of is the order in which the shell resolves a command. In bash and zsh, functions come before built-ins, so we just need to create a function with the same name. This opens a way to make up for the lack of a chpwd function in bash: we just need to have a wrapper function named cd. You would also need to do the same for pushd and popd, if you use them.

Note that ksh resolves built-ins before functions. Aliases are resolved before built-ins, though, so you can use an alias to call your function:

```
newcd() { … }
alias cd=newcd
```

Instead of showing you yet again how to modify the title bar, we'll do something different. In the section "Special zsh Directory Features" in Chapter 8 we showed how zsh's cd command does a form of search and replace on the current directory if it's passed two arguments. So what we'll do here is extend bash's cd command to do the same.

```
cd() {
  if (( $# > 1 )); then
    if [[ $PWD = *$1* ]]; then
      builtin cd ${PWD/$1/$2}
    else
      echo "$FUNCNAME: string not in pwd: $1"
    fi
  else
    builtin cd "$1"
  fi
}
```

The first thing this does is to check if it was given more than one argument. If not, the real cd is called. You need to precede this command with builtin; otherwise the function will call itself. In the first branch of the if statement we handle two arguments. The PWD variable contains the current directory so we can apply a substitution on that. It also prints an error message if the first argument doesn't appear in the current directory.

You can improve this function in a few ways. It doesn't take much effort to get its return status right for one thing. It also doesn't handle options to cd properly. To deal with them, you may want to refer back to the section "Option Parsing" earlier in this chapter. Alternatively, if you have a copy of the bash source, have a look in the examples directory and you will find a decent version of this function.

Defining New Globbing Qualifiers

In the section "Glob Qualifiers in zsh" in Chapter 9, we showed how there are various qualifiers that can be used with filename generation to restrict the list of filenames generated by criteria other than their filename. Though there are many of these qualifiers, thus allowing files to be selected by many different criteria, at some stage you may find that you want to select files according to some property for which there isn't a predefined glob qualifier. For this situation, zsh allows you to extend the shell's filename generation to handle this additional property by writing your own glob qualifier. In this section, we will show you how to write these glob qualifiers: as you most likely have already guessed, they are written using shell code.

Restricting the List of Files Generated

The majority of glob qualifiers restrict the list of files generated to only certain types of files. For example, / causes only directories to be generated. We'll start by showing you how to apply your own restriction on the filenames generated.

The syntax for including shell code in a list of glob qualifiers involves first specifying the letter e (for evaluate). The e is followed by a delimited string to specify the shell code to be evaluated. The rules for this were showed for other qualifiers in the section "More Complicated Qualifiers: String Arguments" in Chapter 9. The shell code is run for each filename with the REPLY variable set each time to the filename in question. The return status of the shell code then determines whether the filename is to be generated.

Let's see an example. Suppose that you want to know which files in the current directory also exist (or don't exist) in another directory. The conventional way to do this is to write a for loop:

```
for f in *; do
  [[ -e /other/directory/$f ]] && print $f
done
```

With the (e) glob qualifier, the equivalent would be

```
print -l *(e:'[[ -e /other/directory/$REPLY ]]':)
```

In addition to being shorter, this has the advantage that you can use it as an argument to any command. To pass all the files together to a command, you would otherwise need to make the script more complicated or use xargs as we described in the section "Running find in a Pipeline" in Chapter 8.

Quoting can become a little awkward. In the example above, it was necessary to add quotes to preserve the "$" symbol. For this reason, it is a good idea to define short functions for any such pieces of shell code that you use frequently:

```
in() { [[ -e $1/$REPLY ]] }
```

Now, we need only write

```
print -l *(e:in /other/directory:)
```

With these functions, it is common to want to negate their effect. In this case, we might want files that are *not* in the other directory. You actually have two options in this case. You can either use an exclamation mark before the command to negate its return status: *(e:! in /other/directory:) or you can use the "^" glob qualifier, which negates the meaning of any following qualifiers: *(^e:in /other/directory:).

You might need to be a little careful about this, though. If, for example, your function only works for directories and you include a test for whether $REPLY is a directory in the function, then the negation also applies to this test, which won't be useful. A good demonstration of this is the following function, which checks for empty directories:

```
empty() { [ -z $REPLY/*(DN[1]) ] }
```

■**Tip** The `empty` function presented in this section demonstrates an unrelated but useful trick. By using the old single bracket ([...]) condition test instead of the new double bracket one ([[...]]), we allow filename generation to apply. The "D" qualifier here forces any dot files to be included, "N" allows it to return nothing instead of a "no matches found", error and "[1]" causes it to only expand one filename. This allows us to test whether a particular glob pattern generates any files.

Create a new empty directory or two and try this out:

```
% mkdir empty
% print *(e:empty:)
% print *(^e:empty:)
```

In the first of the two lists, all the files in the current directory will be listed. Unfortunately, from within the function, there is no way to prevent ordinary files from getting into one or other of the lists. You just have to remember to use the slash glob qualifier with the function:

```
% print *(/e:empty:)
```

In zsh 4.2.1, an F glob qualifier has been added for finding nonempty (full) directories. This issue also applies with it: it needs to be combined with the / qualifier if negated unless you want the names of regular files to be generated.

Modifying the Results

When you use the history modifiers in a glob qualifier list as described in the section "Colon Modifiers as Qualifiers" in Chapter 9, you can alter the expanded filenames and the results do not have to be an existing file. There are, however, limits to what you can do with the history modifiers. For instance, they don't allow substitutions involving patterns. In this section, we will show how you can make changes to the generated filenames using the e glob qualifier.

By modifying the REPLY variable in the shell code for the (e) glob qualifier, you can replace what appears in the list for the filename. It is perhaps now clearer why the variable is named REPLY. With this, we can now do a substitution using a pattern:

```
print **/*(e:'REPLY=${REPLY/(src|include)/new}':)
```

So if a file named src/code.c was found, new/code.c would be substituted for it.

You can also use the reply array instead. This allows more than one word to be added to the list for each file. You might want to take the filenames and also the same names with a different extension as in this example.

```
print -l *.c(e@'reply=( $REPLY ${REPLY:r}.h )'@)
```

Note how we've had to resort to the character @ to delimit the shell code because more common choices are used in the shell code.

Accessing Extended Filesystem Attributes

We'll now present an extensive example to further demonstrate what can be done with the e glob qualifier.

Many filesystems allow for extended attributes to be associated with files beyond the basics that are common across Unix systems. The standard Linux ext2 filesystem, for instance, has a few attributes that can be changed or listed using the chattr and lsattr attributes. If you need to access these attributes, perhaps to operate on those files with the append only flag set, there will be no built-in zsh glob qualifier. This is a situation where a function using the (e) glob qualifier comes to your aid.

Such a function becomes especially useful when you consider modern filesystems such as SGI's XFS that allow user-defined attributes to be specified for files. If you are using version 2.6 of the Linux kernel, extended attributes are supported by some other filesystems. They may need to be enabled (tune2fs -o user_xattr *device* for ext2 and ext3). Alternatively, see the link in Appendix B for kernel patches and more information. If your filesystem or operating system don't support extended attributes, don't worry. The examples presented in this section may give you ideas for other things you can do from glob qualifiers along with some insight into how you can go about making those ideas work.

The getfattr and setfattr commands allow extended attributes to be manipulated. If you are using the IRIX operating system, you may need to use the attr command instead but it should be straightforward to adapt our examples.

One situation where user-defined attributes are useful is with a collection of photographs from a digital camera or scanner stored on your computer. You could use a separate database to store information about things like where and when a picture was taken, or which people or animals are featured in it, or if you're more serious about photography, you might want to record your camera settings. When you store this information in extended attributes, directly associated with the image files, it becomes much more convenient. This is especially so when you can use a zsh glob qualifier to perform a query of this "database," sending the results straight to your image viewer. To associate information you just use the setfattr (or similar) command:

```
setfattr -n user.year -v 1990 oldpicture.jpg
```

The "user" prefix is a name space. It is there for user-defined attributes. Other name spaces, such as "root", may exist but you probably won't have the necessary permission to use them.

■Caution Many backup programs like tar are not yet aware of extended file attributes so you may want to include a dump of the attributes (from getfattr -d) with your backups or use a program like xfsdump that does handle them.

To begin with, we'll write a function that just checks for the existence of a particular attribute. The return status of getfattr isn't particularly helpful so we'll just check if it produces any output. We'll pass the name of an attribute as a parameter:

```
fattr() {
  [[ -n $(getfattr -n user.$1 $REPLY 2>/dev/null) ]]
}
```

Now, we can use *(e:fattr year:) to pick out any files with the year attribute set. Taking this further, we want to be able to query the value of the attribute. To do this, we need to save the value of the attribute in a local variable and then perform a comparison:

```
fattr() {
  local val=$(getfattr -n user.$1 --only-values $REPLY 2>/dev/null)
  [[ -n $val && ( -z $2 || $val = $~2 ) ]]
}
```

The first line of this function gets the value of the attribute. The --only-values option allows us to get just the value that is more convenient for comparing. The second line then determines the return status. If no value was found, we want to return failure. If then no value was supplied for comparison to be against, it returns success. The final component of the test does the comparison of the value against $2. The tilde (~) there turns on the glob_subst option, which we saw in the section "Quoted Command Substitution" in Chapter 11, for this single expansion. This allows us to do more powerful searches by treating the result of expanding $2 as a shell pattern.

Tip The tilde flag can be used wherever you want the result of a variable expansion to be treated as a pattern. You may have a very complex pattern that includes a particular chunk multiple times. It can even be used with globbing; try this:

```
% glob='~/*(/)'
% echo $~glob
```

Note that this is actually how shells other than zsh always behave.

With this function we can now perform simple queries in our directory of photographs and have the results directed to the command line of our image viewer. For example, if I want to view all my pictures taken in Salzburg, I use the following:

```
xv *(e:fattr place Salzburg:)
```

We can even chain together more than one test. The following views all photographs taken in Salzburg during 2002 or 2003:

```
xv *(e:fattr place Salzburg:e:'fattr year 200\[23\]':)
```

Note how the pattern needs to be quoted.

As you can see, writing your own functions for use in glob qualifiers is very powerful and can allow you to use filename generation in ways unimagined before.

Debugging Scripts

We have now shown you how you can use the shell to write powerful programs to automate repetitive tasks. It should be evident that it is a flexible language able to handle demanding jobs. An important part of programming is debugging. In this section, we look at the shell features and tools available to make debugging scripts easier.

Trace Information

When debugging a program, what you need is the ability to see the steps taken by the program that led it to producing an erroneous result. With the xtrace option on, the shell shows each command line as it is executed. This may seem a somewhat basic mechanism, but it is actually very useful when debugging. If you are accustomed to compiled languages you may be more used to using a debugger to step through code. The problem with stepping through code is that you have to go forwards toward a problem instead of being able to work back from it. With trace information, it is often possible to isolate a problem more quickly because all the information is in front of you.

We can see how this works from an interactive shell. If you turn on the xtrace option:

```
set -x
```

then every time the shell executes a command, it prints $PS4, followed by the line to be executed after expanding variables, file patterns, and so on. The following demonstrates this directly from the zsh command line:

```
zsh% set -x
zsh% echo $ZSH_NAME
+zsh:2> echo zsh
zsh
```

Before executing the echo, zsh printed a line with: a +, which indicates a trace; the name of what was executing—here just the shell, but it could be the name of a script or function; and the line number, which is 2 here but will be larger if your shell has been running for a while. Then it prints what it's about to execute; note that the variable has already been expanded. bash behaves a little differently in detail, but the idea is very similar.

Now, if you take a script or function you can turn on the xtrace option at the start of it and run it again to get more information. You can also alter PS4 if you find you need to know other things about the state of the shell and how it is changing during the trace.

One thing you may just be wondering about is our use of set -x to turn the option on here. You can use setopt xtrace or set -o xtrace if you prefer. Options that have come from the Bourne shell heritage are often known by their single letter forms. For a script, you can even specify the option as an argument to the shell:

```
#!/bin/sh -x
```

In zsh, you can also enable tracing for a function by setting the *trace* attribute for it:

```
functions -t func
```

This has the advantage that you don't need to modify the function to turn tracing on. There are two other similar options that can be useful in debugging:

noexec (or -n)—This prevents commands from being run and just checks the syntax.

verbose (or -v)—This causes each command line to be printed exactly as it appears in the script before any expansion.

■**Tip** The nounset (or -u) option can save a lot of heartache with bug hunting for misspelled variable names. Normally, expanding an unset variable results in the empty string. With the nounset option set, an error will be returned instead.

The bash Debugger

For some problems, the trace information just doesn't given you enough information about the state of the program at a particular point during its execution. In such a situation, you may want to revert to using a traditional debugger.

There are a few such debuggers available. A ksh debugger has been around for some time. bash users will find themselves in a better position—in the examples directory within the bash source, you will find the bashdb script. There are also enhancements to this script, including changes to bash itself, available from a separate bashdb project. See Appendix B for more information on obtaining this. Many of the changes from the bashdb project have been merged into bash version 3 but we would still recommend downloading bashdb directly.

The interface for the bash debugger is modeled on the dbx and gdb debuggers, which you may know of from debugging compiled programs. So you may find the interface to be quite familiar.

To use the debugger, you simply run bashdb with the name of the script as a parameter. It will then prompt you with the current line in the script and its line number. Using commands you can step through the script, print the values of variables, set breakpoints, and do other things you would expect to be able to do in a normal debugger. Table 13-2 shows some of the most common commands. This is taken from a recent version of the bash debugger, which may differ from what you have. In any case, you can always run help to get a list of available commands.

Table 13-2. *Common bash Debugger Commands*

Command	Purpose
break	List breakpoints or set one at the specified line
continue	Continue running until the next breakpoint or the end of the script
delete	Delete a breakpoint
list	List sections of the script
next	Single step, stepping over function calls or sourced files
print	Print the values of variables
step	Single step, stepping into function calls or sourced files
help	Find out about the available commands

Note that many commands can be shortened to their first letter. So you can use "n" instead of "next" or "s" instead of "step".

Summary

While much of this book has focused on using the shell interactively, in this chapter we have explained many aspects of a shell's noninteractive mode. In this mode, the shell accepts commands from a script or function instead of the user typing commands manually.

At the beginning of this chapter, we showed you how to make your scripts more intelligent than is possible with a simple list of commands by making decisions within the script to control the flow of execution through a script. We showed the syntax for other constructs allowed in shell code such as loops and functions, enabling you to write full programs using the shell. The next major section of the chapter explained how to pass information in and out of a shell program. In particular, we showed how to take information that is input in the form of shell arguments or lines of text and make sense of it by breaking it into its component parts.

One of the aims of this chapter was to demonstrate how you can use shell code to extend the base functionality of the shell. We showed how to intercept signals, built-in commands, and some other special events to insert shell code to modify the shell's behavior. We also demonstrated how to extend the shell's filename generation facility by adding your own glob qualifiers. In the following chapter we will continue the theme of extending the shell's basic facilities by showing you how to write shell code to extend the zsh line editor. We'll return to bash at the beginning of the final chapter when we discuss completion functions. Completion functions rely heavily on the use of shell code and many of the shell features discussed in this chapter.

CHAPTER 14

■ ■ ■

Writing Editor Commands

Sometimes you may find that zsh's line editor doesn't quite provide the features you'd like, or that you'd like a quick way of performing frequent tasks. For example, there are commands to move the cursor by characters, words, and lines; maybe you frequently want to move a certain number of characters, or to a particular character, instead. Maybe a command you use frequently to search in the shell's history doesn't leave the cursor in the position you want. Maybe you'd like an editor command to delete a complete command-line argument, even if the argument consists of a complicated quoted expression. Perhaps a command behaves slightly differently from the way it does in another shell; you've seen that bash often differs slightly from zsh, and you might want to imitate the bash behavior.

zsh allows you to write new editor commands as shell functions. This is the subject of this chapter. These shell functions can call one or more existing editing commands, so you can easily put together a set of commands. What's more, we'll see how special shell variables exist that allow you to change the editor buffer directly by the use of substitutions and assignments.

The structure of this chapter is as follows. First we'll introduce the notion of a *widget*, an editor command. Then we'll provide a step-by-step set of instructions for creating shell functions to extend the line editor. Next, we'll show you how shell variables can add a great deal to your ability to edit the command line. The presentation of features ends with a discussion of a couple of matters we glossed over earlier: numeric arguments, which you can pass to an editor command to modify its behavior, and error handling.

Once we've introduced those features, we'll show you some case studies illustrating various ways that zsh users have found to make their editing tasks easier. Then we will put a lot of what we've learned into a usable example. We'll finish the chapter with some more advanced features that help when you're writing widgets that need to read their own input or output messages, and briefly describe some additions that appear in version 4.2 of zsh. (The rest of the chapter assumes you're using version 4.0 of zsh.)

Note that we're describing zsh alone. It's possible to extend bash's command-line editor, the readline library, but you need to write your own functions in the C programming language. Doing so is well outside the scope of this book. Users of bash should skip to Chapter 15.

Widgets and Functions

You'll find the zsh documentation refers to line editing commands—including the ones we've already introduced with names like up-line-or-history and universal-argument—as *widgets*. This name is quite useful, since it allows us to be clear about whether we are talking about something the editor does when you hit a key. Words like "command" or "function" are more ambiguous since they can imply normal shell commands. So from now on, we'll refer to all commands inside the line editor as *widgets*. If you're not familiar with the word, it means much the same as "gadget," and it was used by the X Window System for a completely different purpose (apparently a contraction of "window gadget"). The use in zsh is separate from any other.

The editor widgets introduced in Chapter 4, such as the two we mentioned in the previous paragraph, are built into the shell rather than written as shell functions. That makes them faster and more powerful, but unfortunately you can't use them as examples for shell functions you write yourself. However, zsh ships with various widgets that are described in the manual in the section on user contributions toward the end (type man zshcontrib). Most likely they are installed somewhere along your function path, so you can look at them for ideas of shell functions you might want to write to extend the editor. We'll sometimes talk about *widget functions*, when we mean shell code written to extend the editor. Let's be clear about the distinction:

- A *widget* is any editing command, whether implemented within the shell or added by you. All the editing commands that we've met before this chapter are implemented within the shell, with the exception of those related to the completion system.

- A *widget function* is a piece of shell code that extends the line editor by adding a new widget. It is always a shell function.

Simple Recipe for a Widget

All widgets are created in basically the same fashion. We'll illustrate this by creating a widget that moves the cursor backward 10 characters along the command line. It's not possible to do that with a single built-in widget in zsh, so this gives you a quick way of moving the cursor a long distance. We give it the logical name backward-ten-characters. For this, we'll just need one feature of widget functions: the shell variable CURSOR, which controls the cursor position. It's just an index into the line with the standard zsh convention that the first character is 1. When the widget is entered, the value $CURSOR is the current cursor position. You can also alter the variable CURSOR to change the position. So all we need to do for our new widget is subtract 10 from the value.

Step 1: Write the Function

You'll often want to put the function into a file in your function path, then mark it for autoloading from your .zshrc. Here's the function, for which we'll use the same name as the widget, backward-ten-characters:

```
(( CURSOR -= 10 ))
```

It's just a simple arithmetic evaluation to subtract 10 from the variable's value. Of course, the cursor may be fewer than 10 characters from the start of the line. However, the shell will silently handle this problem and place the cursor at the start. You only need to worry about it if you want the shell to do something else—for example, beep.

That code should be placed in a file called backward-ten-characters in a directory mentioned in the fpath array. If you want the function always to be available, you need to add the following to your .zshrc to tell the shell to load the function when necessary, as we described in the section "Autoloadable Functions" in Chapter 13:

```
autoload backward-ten-characters
```

If you just want to try it out once, you can run that command immediately instead.

Step 2: Create the Widget

The syntax to tell the shell that the function is to be treated as a new widget is as follows:

```
zle -N backward-ten-characters
```

Again, you need to add this to .zshrc if you always want the widget to be available. There's no easy shortcut to make the shell recognize widgets automatically, so you need a line like this for every widget you add.

In the example we just offered, the widget had the same name as the function. That's usually the best way of doing things, but actually it's not required. If you give two arguments to zle -N, the first is the widget (the name you use in bindkey commands) and the second is the function (which the shell finds in your fpath). Due to the potential for confusion, the only time you will want to do that is if the same function can be used for different purposes. We'll explain what this means later in the chapter in the section "Case Study 1: Multiple Tasks in Widgets."

Actually, that's all there is to it—you can now use the widget backward-ten-characters just like any other editor widget. However, to make it more useful, there is usually a third step.

Step 3: Bind the Widget to a Key

Now you just use bindkey as you would with a built-in widget, as we explained in the section "Configuration and Key Binding: readline and zle" in Chapter 4. If you don't, you will have to execute the widget by pressing Esc x and then typing the full name of the widget. That's fine for occasional use, but tedious if you're intending to use the new command a lot. Again, you can add the appropriate command to .zshrc:

```
bindkey '^xb' backward-ten-characters
```

If you've followed everything through, the next time you start the shell you can press Ctrl-x and then press b to move the cursor 10 characters back along the line.

The facilities normally available inside shell functions don't allow you to control the line editor. For that, an additional mechanism is required. zsh actually provides two ways of controlling line editing: one by means of commands, and one by means of shell variables. We'll introduce both in this section.

Calling Widgets from a Function

Several uses of the zle command have already been introduced, notably the ability to tell the shell that a widget has been newly created by using zle -N. The zle command can also be used inside widget functions to call another widget, just as if you'd typed the keystroke bound to the widget. This is very useful, because it immediately provides all the facilities of the widgets you already know about to help you extend the editor. In this case the zle command doesn't require an option letter, just the name of the widget you are calling. We'll illustrate that by creating a widget that simply calls an existing widget. First, let's remind ourselves what the widget is that takes the cursor to the end of the line when the user presses Ctrl-e. (We're assuming throughout that you use the emacs keymap; remember you can type bindkey -e to ensure this.) The bindkey command can be used to output the name of the widget:

```
zsh% bindkey '\C-e'
"^E" end-of-line
```

The widget we want to call is named end-of-line. Here's how we write a widget function that calls this built-in widget. The function is called example-widget:

```
example-widget() {
  zle end-of-line
}
```

This is different from the form of the backward-ten-word function because here we're assuming you'll type it in directly to the shell, rather than autoload it from a file. (However, this time we haven't shown the shell's prompts, in order to make the text of the function clear.) Finally, we'll tell the shell about the new widget:

```
zsh% zle -N example-widget
```

Because this is just an example, instead of binding it to a key we'll execute it by name. Type a line of text and move back to the beginning of it. Then press Esc x, after the prompt type example-widget, and press Return. The new widget is executed and the cursor jumps to the end of the line.

Executing a single command isn't much use. The following modifies the example to go to the end of the line, then backward one word. Already it's starting to look more like a useful shortcut:

```
example-widget() {
  zle end-of-line
  zle backward-word
}
```

Note that you don't need to execute the zle -N command again; the new function replaces the old one.

Special Variables in zle

In the function backward-ten-word we showed how altering the value of the variable CURSOR moved the cursor on the command line. This is one of a set of variables that have a special meaning to the line editor. Since variable substitution in zsh is very powerful, editing the command line with variables allows you to do quite lot without too much work.

In the following list we summarize the most common variables that have a special meaning in editor widgets. It's not a complete set; consult the manual (man zshzle) for more. You can alter the values of the variables except where we note that a variable is read-only.

These variables are only special inside zle widgets. You are entirely free to use variables of the same names in your own functions or on the command line, where they will behave normally. The only limitation is that you won't be able to see global variables of the same name as a zle variable inside a zle widget.

CURSOR—The character position of the cursor on the command line.

BUFFER—The contents of the current editing buffer. Possibly multiple lines.

PREBUFFER—The contents of any lines already read, if you are editing at a continuation prompt.

LBUFFER—The part of BUFFER to the left of and above the cursor.

RBUFFER—The part of BUFFER to the right of and below the cursor.

NUMERIC—The numeric prefix passed by Esc *digit* or by the universal-argument widget. If there is none, the value is not set. Numeric prefixes are introduced later.

WIDGET—The name of the editor widget currently being executed.

LASTWIDGET—The name of the immediately previous editor widget that the user called using a key binding, or of a widget function called with zle *widgetname*. Don't worry if this sounds complicated; there's a special section "Case Study 4: Chaining Widgets Together," to illustrate the use of LASTWIDGET.

KEYS—The set of keys used to execute the current widget. A raw string of characters, which may well not be printable.

There are two pairs of variables that you will use frequently in widget functions. Alongside CURSOR, there is the variable BUFFER, which is a scalar containing the entire contents of the editing buffer after the most recent prompt. (If you are at a continuation prompt, the lines before are in PREBUFFER, which you can read but not alter.) Hence CURSOR is essentially an index into the string BUFFER. That means you can use zsh's standard notation for subscripts in parameters, which we described in the section "Substrings" in Chapter 12. Here's a quick reminder: variables in zsh such as BUFFER that represent a string can be followed by a number in square brackets (the subscript). A single number gives an index into the string, picking out the *index*th character in the variable's value. A subscript consisting of two indexes with a comma in between picks out the range of characters between the two positions, including the positions of the subscripts themselves. The indexes are treated by the shell as numeric expressions, so they can contain variables like CURSOR that represent a number. A negative index counts from the end of the string, with -1 representing the last character. Here are a few common ways of using this feature with zle variables:

- The character at the cursor position is ${BUFFER[CURSOR]}.

- The string to the left of the cursor can be extracted by ${BUFFER[1,CURSOR-1]}.

- The string from the cursor to the end is ${BUFFER[CURSOR,-1]}.

It's so common to need the string before the cursor, and the string from the cursor to the end, that there are variables that let you do this: LBUFFER and RBUFFER. These are simply another way of presenting the information in CURSOR and BUFFER. All four variables can be altered; which you use is determined simply by convenience.

LBUFFER and RBUFFER provide a simple way of manipulating text at the variable position without needing to use subscripting. The following example, when executed inside a widget function, inserts the string prefix just to the left of the cursor, and the string suffix starting at the cursor position:

```
LBUFFER="${LBUFFER}prefix"
RBUFFER="suffix${RBUFFER}"
```

After those assignments, the variables CURSOR and BUFFER would also reflect the changes. In other words, the value of CURSOR would be increased by 6 (the length of the string prefix) and the value of BUFFER would include the string prefixsuffix in the middle.

Note that the shell doesn't know how to alter the cursor position when you change BUFFER. It makes its best guess about what to do—keep it the same. However, the shell will never leave CURSOR pointing off the end of BUFFER. It's up to you if you want to set CURSOR as well as BUFFER.

Now you immediately have all the power of variable substitutions available. Here are a few simple things you can do; return to Chapter 12 for a quick refresher if you need to.

```
# Replace all the single quotes on the line with double quotes.
BUFFER=${BUFFER//\'/\"}
# Move the cursor back to the last preceding uppercase letter.
# (Note the first test, to avoid an infinite loop.)
while [[ CURSOR -gt 1 && ${RBUFFER[1]} != [[:upper:]] ]]; do
  (( CURSOR-- ))
done
```

Remember that zsh is capable of editing multiline expressions. All the text, including the newlines, appears in BUFFER and the other variables. Usually, you won't need to worry about this, since the shell will handle adding and removing of newline characters just like any other. If you need to add a newline, the easiest way is to use the special form of quoting that interprets backslashes in the same manner as the built-in command print: $'\n' is a single newline character. Strings can include real newlines, too; in other words, just press Return in the middle of a string. The following code, when executed inside a widget function, adds an extra line echo Hello at the end of the editing buffer. If you press Return, the shell will execute the echo command after the command already on the command line (assuming that is a complete command):

```
BUFFER=${BUFFER}$'\necho Hello'
```

Making Widgets Behave Naturally

You already have quite a range of tools for building new widgets. In this section, we'll show some ways of making your new widgets behave like built-in widgets so that they integrate seamlessly together. First, we'll introduce a feature that applies to many built-in widgets, too: you can pass numbers to them. That's often useful for making a widget repeat its behavior without you having to type it repeatedly. We'll show you how to make your own widgets handle numbers. Next, we'll look at error handling, so that you can handle problems such as an expected piece of the buffer that you want to modify not being found. Proper error handling alerts the user that something has gone wrong.

Passing Numeric Arguments to Widgets

Many widgets that move the cursor or insert something into the command line can be repeated by passing them a number referred to as a *numeric argument*. There are two ways of passing that number to the widget. The simplest is to press Esc and then the number, then the key that executes the widget. If the number has more than one digit, you must press Esc before each digit. So, for example, to pass the number 10 to a widget you need to press Esc 1 Esc 0.

To see numeric arguments in action, type a command line of more than three words, then press the keys Esc 3 Esc b. If you are using the emacs keymap where Esc b is bound to backward-word, the cursor will move backward three words along the command line. Try this with some other movement commands and you'll see that using a numeric argument to repeat the widget's action is a common feature.

Numeric arguments have an effect with insert commands, too. For example, when you type a printable character the shell usually adds the character to the command line. If you type a numeric argument before it, the shell will insert it that many times instead of just once, so Esc 5 X inserts the letter X into the command line five times.

The use of the Esc key is quite clumsy with long numbers. The shell provides another way of entering numbers with a special widget, universal-argument. The advantage is that any string of digits after this number is treated as a complete decimal number. When the shell finds any key that isn't a digit, it stops looking for a number. The numeric argument is applied to whatever follows the number. You should bind the widget to a key for it to be useful; for our example we'll use the following command:

```
bindkey '\C-xu' universal-argument
```

Now press Ctrl-x and type u40X. The shell will insert 40 X characters into the command line. If you don't type a number, universal-argument behaves as if you typed 4; and if you type the key for universal-argument several times, it multiplies the argument by 4 each time. So Ctrl-x u Ctrl-x u * inserts a line of 16 stars.

It's possible for the user to pass a numeric argument to a widget function in just the same way as to any other widget. Inside a widget function the numeric prefix appears in the variable NUMERIC. This isn't set unless the user gives a numeric prefix. Since that's the usual case for just about every widget, you should always handle the case of NUMERIC being unset. Here's a replacement for forward-char. The expression ${NUMERIC:-1} tests the value of NUMERIC; if that is not empty, it substitutes the value, else it substitutes the string after the :-, namely 1:

```
(( CURSOR += ${NUMERIC:-1} ))
```

It uses the fact that if there is no numeric prefix, NUMERIC is actually empty (and not zero, as you might have guessed); refer to the section "Alternative and Default Values" in Chapter 12 for an explanation.

Here's a more flexible version of backward-ten-characters: if you give it a numeric argument *num* it will move *num* times 10 characters backward; otherwise it will move 10 characters backwards as before:

```
(( CURSOR -= 10 * ${NUMERIC:-1} ))
```

If you call another widget with the zle command within your widget, the shell will usually pass down the existing value of NUMERIC. For example, a widget function containing zle forward-char will automatically handle numeric prefixes without your interference. Suppose you want to create a widget that skips a number of characters, then inserts a string (in the following example, a single quote) at that position. Here's an example widget that does that:

```
example-widget() {
  zle forward-char
  LBUFFER=$LBUFFER"'"
}
```

If you call that widget with a numeric argument, you will see that the cursor moves forward the number of characters given by the argument, then inserts a single quote. The zle forward-char is affected by the numeric argument, but variable assignment is not. However, that's not always what you want—you may want your widget to handle the numeric prefix by examining $NUMERIC and the widget you call to see some other value entirely. The shell allows you to pass an explicit numeric value. In the following example we pass the numeric argument 10 to the widget backward-char:

```
zle backward-char -n 10
```

This is yet another version of backward-ten-characters. To make a widget see no numeric argument at all, use the option -N:

```
zle backward-char -N
```

This ensures that backward-char behaves in its default fashion—in other words, go backward a single character, regardless of the presence of a numeric argument in the widget that calls to zle. Note that the -N comes *after* the widget name—it won't work anywhere else.

Handling Errors

When the line editor encounters an error, it usually beeps. Each widget decides for itself what it considers to be an error condition. It's therefore up to you to decide how to handle errors in your own widgets. In this section we'll demonstrate the features you can use.

It's possible to cause a beep by calling zle beep inside a widget. This appears to the user just as if an error had occurred. The beeps are suppressed by setting the option no_beep. However, zle beep has no effect other than making the shell beep. If you want to indicate that an error occurred in a function widget, the widget should call the return built-in with the argument 1, just like any other function. The shell detects this nonzero status. If the widget was called directly during editing of the command line, rather than from another widget, the shell will beep as if you'd called zle beep. In the following we rewrite our example widget backward-ten-characters to indicate a return value 1 if there were not enough characters for it to be able to move the full 10:

```
if (( CURSOR > 10 )); then
  (( CURSOR -= 10 ))
else
  return 1
fi
```

The advantage of using a return value is apparent when you call the widget from inside another widget. Then the return status can be used within the calling widget just like that of any other command. Here's an example. Suppose we want to call `backward-ten-characters` but handle the error gracefully:

```
if ! zle backward-ten-characters; then
  zle beginning-of-line
fi
```

The definition of `backward-ten-characters` that we showed most recently will return a nonzero status if there are fewer than 10 characters before the cursor. The calling widget detects this status in the `if` and simply goes to the start of the line. Instead of going to the beginning of the line, you could have handled the failure of `backward-ten-characters` by outputting a message, for example; we'll see how to do that later. The calling widget also has the option of passing a nonzero status value back to its own caller to indicate an error has occurred; then the shell will beep after the calling widget returns. Alternatively, the calling widget may simply ignore the return status from `backward-ten-characters` by executing `return 0`. So return statuses are very flexible. You can see why we recommend using a return status to indicate a failure by considering the following alternative definition of `backward-ten-characters`:

```
if (( CURSOR > 10 )); then
  (( CURSOR -= 10 ))
else
  zle beep
fi
```

In that case, the shell beeps as soon as it finds that the cursor can't be moved 10 characters. The calling widget has no effect on this. Furthermore, no return status is passed back, so the calling widget can't tell that `backward-ten-characters` failed.

Return statuses are even useful when the calling widget doesn't handle them explicitly. Suppose the last line of the calling widget was the following:

```
zle backward-ten-characters
```

Because there is no `return` command, the status value returned by this function is the status value from the `zle` command. So the return status is propagated back to the shell; it will beep if `backward-ten-characters` failed.

Occasionally you may want to make sure the line editor stops what it's doing right away. That might be appropriate, for example, if the widget were in a state from which you were unable to recover. To abort right away, use the command `zle send-break`. This is the widget executed by default when you press Ctrl-g in the `emacs` keymap. When you call `zle send-break`, the shell doesn't finish executing the rest of the function where the command occurs, nor any calling functions. It clears the command line, redraws it, and waits for you to type a new key.

Case Study I: Multiple Tasks in Widgets

Many widgets occur in pairs, for example `backward-char` and `forward-char`, bound by default to the Left and Right Arrow keys. Often your own widgets will be in pairs, too. You now know how to write two separate functions to implement such widgets. However, it's often neater in such cases to write a single function to implement both widgets. That's particularly true if they have code in common. However, even if there is very little in common between the two widgets, it's much easier to keep the implementation of the two widgets consistent when the code is in a single function.

To demonstrate this feature, we'll create functions like `delete-word` and `backward-delete-word`, but where a "word" is everything up to the next or previous whitespace character. We'll interpret this simply, so the whitespace will have this effect even if it's quoted.

Let's name the function `delete-space-word`, which will be autoloaded, as usual, and the two widgets `delete-space-word` (for deleting the word following the cursor) and `backward-delete-space-word`. Again, we'll assume it's in a file in your function path. To tell the shell about it, we need to execute the following:

```
autoload delete-space-word
zle -N delete-space-word
zle -N backward-delete-space-word delete-space-word
```

Now here's the body of the function `delete-space-word`:

```
# Set up the options for the function
emulate -L zsh
setopt extended_glob

# Test whether we are the forward or backward widget.
if [[ $WIDGET = backward-* ]]; then
  # Backward: remove any whitespace from end of left buffer
  LBUFFER=${LBUFFER%%[[:space:]]#}
  # Now remove non-whitespace before that
  LBUFFER=${LBUFFER%%[^[:space:]]#}
else
  # Forward: remove any whitespace from start of right buffer
  RBUFFER=${RBUFFER##[[:space:]]#}
  # Now remove non-whitespace after that
  RBUFFER=${RBUFFER##[^[:space:]]#}
fi
```

There are three parts to the function. First, we set up some options. We are going to need extended_glob for the patterns; to avoid making assumptions about what options are normally set, we set the zsh default options locally using `emulate`.

Next, we need to test which widget we are implementing. The special variable `WIDGET` contains this information. We simply test if the name starts with `backward-`. The widget could have a different name, as long as the first word is `backward` for a widget going backward. This is the standard zsh naming scheme.

Finally comes the actual code for changing the buffer in the two cases. Because they're so similar, we've decided to bundle them together in a single function. While there's no need for them to be together, putting them there means that if you ever change the behavior you'll see right away what needs to be done for both.

We use the standard variable substitutions to remove the first part of the right buffer, if we're moving forward, or the last part of the left buffer, if we're moving backward. We explained those in the section "Patterns" in Chapter 12. The doubled ## and %% ensure that we remove the longest possible match, from the head of the string or the tail of the string, respectively. The character classes with a # afterward match any number of occurrences of space characters or, with the ^, any character other than a space character.

The reason there are two statements in each branch of the if is to mimic another piece of standard shell behavior when handling words. First, it deletes any whitespace between the cursor and the next (or previous) word. Only then does it look for the word and delete that.

As an exercise, you can add code that uses NUMERIC to delete multiple words at once. If you want to be really sophisticated, you can use a negative value for NUMERIC to switch the forward and backward behaviors. This is what the built-in widgets do, though you may never have noticed.

Case Study 2: Overriding Widgets

In some cases it's useful to replace an existing widget with one of your own. This can be quite convenient because any key bindings automatically refer to the replacement widget. Suppose you don't like forward-word's behavior because of what it considers to be a word. You can create a new widget called forward-word that works the way you want.

Replacing an existing widget is trivial if the replacement function does everything you want on its own. Use zle -N to create the widget in the normal way, giving it the name of the editor widget you want to override. The shell will use the widget you've created in preference to the built-in widget.

For example, you could have used the name delete-word for the widget we called delete-space-word. Then the shell would call our function instead of the built-in widget whenever the user asked for the widget, whether by name or key binding. The following example uses the same function, delete-space-word, but creates widgets with the names delete-word and backward-delete-word, overriding the built-in widgets with the same names:

```
autoload delete-space-word
zle -N delete-word delete-space-word
zle -N backward-delete-word delete-space-word
```

Note the test for the pattern backward-* in the function delete-space-word in the previous section. This causes the replacement widget backward-delete-word to delete backwards. That's a good reason for testing the name using a pattern, in this case backward-*, when you select the widget's behavior. If the test had been [[$WIDGET = backward-delete-space-word]], the widget with this name would have deleted forwards. Then you couldn't have used the same function to override backward-delete-word.

If you make a mistake overriding a widget such as delete-word, it's not a big problem; you can still continue editing. However, it's possible to override even the most basic widgets. If you make a mistake here, it can stop the shell working entirely. Nonetheless, it can still be useful to override such widgets, since you can add extra functionality to the existing widgets.

We'll illustrate this by redefining the widget accept-line. This is executed when you press Return to execute a line. If you redefine accept-line, it's necessary to call the original widget during the execution of your adapted version; otherwise the shell will never see the edited command line. For this purpose the shell has another name for every built-in widget. The alternative name is identical except that it has a "." in front. Therefore in this case the name would be .accept-line. So to override accept-line you should define a widget accept-line of your own that calls your special code and then runs zle .accept-line.

Here's a function to be used as the `accept-line` widget that puts the first word on the command line into an `xterm` title bar:

```
print -n "\e]2;${BUFFER%%[[:space:]]*}\a"
zle .accept-line
```

In this example, we stripped off everything starting from the first occurrence of a space character to the end of the buffer. Then we added xterm escapes to put this into the title bar. Finally, and crucially, we've called `.accept-line` to pass the command line to the main shell for execution. Don't forget that, or you'll never be able to execute any command line at all! In emacs mode you can press Esc x and type `.accept-line` to execute the line. If you want to be careful about such problems redefining widgets, you can create a widget that contains the following code:

```
bindkey -A main .safe
```

When executed, this causes the line editor to use the `.safe` keymap, which is guaranteed to allow you to type and execute command lines. You should then repair the damage to the keymap you were using, and switch back to it with another `bindkey -A` command.

To undo the behavior of the redefined widget, you must tell the shell that the `accept-line` widget is now to be the same as the `.accept-line` widget. You do that with an alias:

```
zle -A .accept-line accept-line
```

There are more sophisticated possibilities where instead of simply redefining `accept-line` you provide commands for switching on the special behavior, and switching it off again. This gives the user an easy way of selecting either the new or the original behavior. The best way of doing this is to give the special version of `accept-line` its own name, say `my-accept-line`, and use aliases to switch the special behavior on and off. Let's suppose the function to switch the special behavior on is called `special-on`, and the function to switch it off again is called `special-off`. You can write the two as follows, regardless of what your function `my-accept-line` does:

```
special-on() {
  zle -A my-accept-line accept-line
}
special-off() {
  zle -A .accept-line accept-line
}
```

For once, we've shown the functions in full, instead of as they'd appear for autoloading. You can use these as widgets, but if you're on the ball you may have noticed that they're perfectly ordinary shell functions. Unlike the use of `zle` to call other widgets, which only works inside a widget function, other uses are always available. It would be hard to define a widget if you had to do it from within another widget! So you can simply run `special-on` and `special-off` as commands, if you prefer.

Case Study 3: Locating Command-Line Arguments

When you press Return to execute a command line, the shell divides the line up into arguments to pass to the command. Sometimes it's useful to be able to analyze the arguments in the line editor before the command is edited. This allows your widgets to manipulate complete command arguments in one go, even if they are quoted expressions.

Extracting the full argument is tricky to do using just ordinary pattern matching, but luckily the shell can help you: the variable expansion flag (z) splits a scalar into an array using the shell word-splitting rules described in the section "Expansion Flags" in Chapter 12. If this flag is applied to the contents of BUFFER, the array looks much like the command and its arguments the shell will see later. Note, however, that (z) does not strip quotes from words, so for example the string 'one word' will appear in the array exactly as that, quotes and all. That's fine for many purposes, but note that this is not the argument the command receives. The equivalent command argument would be one word, a single argument with an embedded space but no quotes. If, for example, the word was a filename, you would need the expression without the quotes in order to examine the file.

This isn't the end of the story, however. Two problems remain:

- How do you know where the cursor resides?

- The user is still editing the command line, so the word may not yet be complete. How do you find the word so far?

If you feel your heart growing faint at this point, it may be time to consider whether you can use a completion widget instead. Completion handles all the fiddly little details of word splitting for you. However, in a moment we present a chunk of a function for those who feel sufficiently bold to try it out. It determines the word under the cursor and the number of characters between the start of the word and the cursor. You can use these values with the CURSOR and BUFFER variables to extract the full word from the command line. Later we'll see an example where this code fragment fits.

The code simply creates a couple of variables for you to use later. (They're not special variables.) We've put them in upper case so that they stick out. The other variables are only needed internally. We have assumed all the default zsh options are set, but you can safely set extended_glob and numerous other options without affecting the way the code works. After it has run, the current shell argument under the cursor is stored in WORD, and the index of the cursor into that word is stored in WORDPOS.

```
# Local variables.
# (If you put this into its own separate function, WORD and WORDPOS
# shouldn't be made local to that, but to the function calling it.)
declare bufwords wordnum leftchars sofar WORD WORDPOS
```

```
# Split the line up to and including the cursor.
sofar="$LBUFFER$RBUFFER[1]"
bufwords=(${(z)sofar})
# This is the index of the word the cursor is on.
wordnum=${#bufwords}
# This is that word up to the cursor position.
sofar=${bufwords[$wordnum]}
# This is the distance we are into that word.
WORDPOS=${#sofar}

# Split the full line into words.
bufwords=( ${(z)BUFFER} )

# Extract the word the cursor is on from the full array.
WORD=${bufwords[$wordnum]}

# Possibly the cursor was just after the word; then
# the last character of the word isn't the character at the
# cursor position...
if [[ $RBUFFER[1] != $WORD[$WORDPOS] ]]; then
  (( WORDPOS++ ))
fi
```

You can use WORDPOS together with CURSOR to find parts of the word. You can use the length of the word, given by ${#WORD}, to find where it ends.

Case Study 4: Chaining Widgets Together

Sometimes it's useful to know the name of the most recently executed widget. As we'll see, when you chain a series of widgets together you can sometimes help the user if a later widget takes account of what the previous one was doing. The widget in question is stored in the variable LASTWIDGET. When you enter a widget called by the keyboard or Esc x, the last widget was the previous widget called in that fashion. In other words, it's the name of the editor action the user thinks they executed before the current one. Remember that typing a key that inserts a character is also a widget, namely self-insert.

Here's an example that uses LASTWIDGET to maintain your position on the command line when you move up the history list to the line you've just entered. In the following example, the position of the cursor is saved in the variable __savepos. We do this by changing accept-line as we did earlier in the chapter. The function up-history, which is designed to override the real widget of that name, checks whether we've just called accept-line and have set __savepos. If we have, we go back up a line and restore the cursor position. Otherwise, we just go back up a line.

```
accept-line() {
  # Execute the line as normal, but first save the position.
  __savepos=$CURSOR
  zle .accept-line
}
up-history() {
  # Only use the special behavior if we just executed a line,
  # and only if that left us a saved position.
  if [[ $LASTWIDGET = accept-line ]] && (( $+__savepos )); then
    # Go up a line and save the position.
    zle .up-history
    CURSOR=__savepos
  else
    # Just go up a line normally
    zle .up-history
  fi
}
```

Approximate Matching

zsh allows you to use patterns that match a given string approximately—in other words, strings that don't exactly match the pattern you have given but are close. It's not so common to need this feature in a pattern to find files typed on the command line, so we've kept the description of approximate matching until we needed it.

To turn on approximation, use (#a*num*), where *num* gives the number of mistakes you are prepared to allow. The extended_glob option must be set. Each mistake is any one of the following:

- A character omitted that should be present

- A character present that shouldn't be there

- A character replaced by an incorrect character

- Any two characters transposed (in the wrong order)

Here are some simple examples:

```
zsh% ls
AAREADME  AREADME  READ.ME.txt  README  READ_ME  READme  REARME  ReAdMe
zsh% echo (#a1)README
AREADME README READ_ME REARME
zsh% echo (#i)(#a1)README
AREADME README READ_ME READme REARME ReAdMe
zsh% echo (#a2)README
AAREADME AREADME README READ_ME READme REARME
```

Note how turning on case-insensitive completion with (#i) allowed us more matches without the need to approximate. (We could have written (#ia1) instead of (#i)(#a1).) With (#i), READme matches README with no errors; without it, it gives two. Approximation is behind the use of approximate completion we saw in the section "Approximate Completion" in Chapter 10.

Approximation is implemented fairly simply and applies only to strings, not to other patterns. For example, [a-z] will always only match a single lowercase ASCII letter, regardless of approximation. You can mix approximation with the case-insensitive matching introduced in the section "Case-Insensitive Matching" in Chapter 9. With both together, a matches a or A without approximating, but any other letter would require an approximation.

An Example Widget: Correcting Spelling

Correcting the spelling of the name of a file is one of the tasks that straddles the boundary between needing an editor widget and a completion widget. In the following example, we'll depend on the former widget type to implement this feature. The key part of the method we use for correcting spelling is the extended globbing flag (#a*num*) that we just discussed.

Using completion could improve the example in a couple of ways.

- In completion, the shell itself decides what the current word is.

- The shell takes over the task of deciding how to handle the possibility that there are multiple matches.

In this example, we've used a simple method to determine where the cursor is positioned.

The function uses the parameter expansion syntax as well as extended globbing. Note in the after assignment that the first ## and the second have completely different meanings. The first is part of parameter expansion (remove the longest match at the head of the string), as we described in the section "Patterns" in Chapter 12. The second is part of extended globbing (match the previous expression at least once) as we described in the section "Multiple Matches" in Chapter 9. The whole remainder of the expression before the closing brace is passed to the shell's pattern matcher.

You can achieve better handling of embedded spaces by using the previous example for matching the current word. We've written this function in such a way that inserting that entire function where we've indicated will work correctly.

```
emulate -L zsh
# We need extended globbing for pattern matching
setopt extended_glob
# We use this to avoid errors when approximation fails.
setopt null_glob

# The maximum number of approximations we will allow.
integer max_approx=3

# *** You can replace this chunk with the more sophisticated ***
# word-finding code shown above.  That's why we've used the same
# names for WORD and WORDPOS.  The variables are not special to the shell.
local WORD before after
integer WORDPOS endpos
```

```
# What's before the current word:
# everything except consecutive non-spaces at the end of the left buffer.
before=${LBUFFER%%[^[:space:]]##}
# Position of the start of the current word.
# Add one to the length of the `before' string because we are on the
# character after.
(( WORDPOS = ${#before} + 1 ))

# What's after the current word: everything except consecutive
# non-spaces at the start of the right buffer.
after=${RBUFFER##[^[:space:]]##}
# Position of the end of the current word.
(( endpos = ${#BUFFER} - ${#after} ))

# Remove quotes in the filename.
WORD=${(Q)BUFFER[$WORDPOS,$endpos]}
# *** End of word-finding chunk. ***

# Now try to find a file to match.
integer n_approx
local -a files

# Start at zero in case there really is a file of the given name
# (i.e. no approximations are required to match).
for (( n_approx = 0; n_approx <= max_approx; n_approx++ )); do
  # There may be many matches, so use an array.
  # Scalar assignment doesn't do globbing anyway, so wouldn't work.
  files=( (#a$n_approx)$WORD )
  if (( ${#files} )); then
    # Found.  We don't make a choice, just insert the first file with
    # ordinary shell quoting (the (q) flag).
    # For multiple matches, completion would be more appropriate.
    BUFFER="${BUFFER[1,$WORDPOS-1]}${(q)files[1]}\
${BUFFER[$WORDPOS+${#WORD},-1]}"
    return 0
  fi
done

return 1
```

We'll demonstrate how the widget works. Suppose the code above is in a file named example-widget in one of the directories contained in the fpath array. Let's load it and bind it to a key sequence to make it easier to use:

```
zsh% autoload example-widget
zsh% zle -N example-widget
zsh% bindkey '\C-xE' example-widget
```

In the same directory as the file `example-widget`, we type the following:

```
zsh% ls eximple-wudget<ctrl-x><E>
```

The filename changes to the corrected version:

```
zsh% ls example-widget
```

The widget will also add missing characters at the end of the filename. If you type `example-wid`, press Ctrl-x, and then press e, it will append `get`. Since we've limited the maximum number of characters that the function will correct to 3, `example-wi` wouldn't be corrected. Increasing `max_approx` inside the function will make it add more characters. However, spelling correction isn't a very good method for completing filenames. For that you can simply add * to the existing name rather than looking for corrections. Indeed, you can alter the function so that it performs both correcting and completing. If you'd like an exercise, see if you can work out how to make the function find a complete filename of any length where the part typed by the user contains spelling mistakes. For example, you should be able to make the function turn `exim` into `example-widget` without increasing the value of `max_approx`. Hint: there's a trivial change to the function that will make this work.

If you have experimented by using the widget to correct `example-wid`, you will have seen that the cursor stays on the g that the widget added. That's because there's no code in the function to move the cursor after the filename has been corrected. As another exercise, you could try to make the widget work more naturally when the cursor is at the end of the word that's being corrected. You'll find the information present in the variables is already sufficient for you to tell whether the cursor is at the end of the word when the widget starts. If it is, you should move the cursor to the end of the new word after the widget has altered the line buffer. Again, all the information is present for you to do this.

■Tip The example just above offers an interesting trick. The word on the command line may have quotes that are stripped off when it is passed to a command. Sometimes you will need the word as it will be passed as a command-line argument after you press Return. The most common example is if you want to treat the word as a filename, which may have special characters quoted. You can get that with `${(Q)WORD}`. Then, for example, the word `Program\ Files`, with a quoted space, turns into `Program Files` by the usual rules of quotation. You can use this unquoted form as a filename.

Input and Output Within Widgets

Many widget functions need to read input from the user, or output a message. Of course, this is just what the line editor is doing for the shell as a whole, but sometimes a widget function has own its reasons for reading or writing characters. Often both are combined in the same function. For example, it's common for a function to print a message like `Type y to proceed, or n to abort`, then read a key that the user types. In this section we'll discuss the mechanisms that let you do that.

Examining User Input

It can be useful for a widget to determine which keys caused the current widget to be executed. The most obvious example of this is for the widget self-insert. This is bound to every character that inserts itself into the command line when typed. Using the key to determine which character to insert clearly saves writing a huge number of very similar commands. This feature means you can write your own widgets and have them behave differently depending on the keys to which they're bound. You can use the KEYS variable to peek at that key or those keys. This is a literal string of characters, not a string as formatted for bindkey. So, for example, the keystroke Ctrl-e appears as a single character, numbered 5 in ASCII. A simple example is the following function that does the same as self-insert:

```
LBUFFER="${LBUFFER}$KEYS"
```

Here's a more complicated example that inserts the name of a digit, which it takes from the last key typed:

```
# Make a lookup table of digit names.
local names
names=(zero one two three four five six seven eight nine)

# Extract the digit from the last character of $KEYS.
local digit=${KEYS[-1]}
# Make sure it is a digit.
if [[ $digit = <0-9> ]]; then
  # It is, so look up the word to add from the table.
  # Remember zsh arrays start from 1, not 0, so add 1
  LBUFFER=${LBUFFER}${names[digit+1]}
fi
```

Create a function widget named insert-digit containing this code as we've already described. Now bind a key sequence ending in a digit, for example bindkey '\C-x1' insert-digit. Then when you press Ctrl-x and then 1, the string one appears on the command line.

Sometimes you may even need to read in a new key, such as when you want the user to select a particular course of action from a list of choices. This is accomplished with the command read -k *variable*. The read built-in usually reads an entire command line into a variable (or a set of variables) at once. We demonstrated this behavior in the section "Reading Input" in Chapter 13. Using the option -k will cause just a single keystroke to be read. This is handled specially in zle. The shell takes a single character from the keyboard without disturbing the line you are editing. The value read is raw character stored in the variable in the same way normal line editor input is stored in KEYS.

When you read a key, it's stored as the raw character read from the keyboard, not as one of the symbols the shell usually uses for characters. This is exactly the same format we described for the value of the variable KEYS. Those numbers are hard to remember and it's much clearer if you can use the symbols instead. The shell's arithmetic handling provides a little extra syntax for this purpose. Consider the following example. When you execute it as a widget, it reads in a new key and tries to insert that in upper case. However, it treats a couple of keys in a special fashion if it reads them:

```
local key

# Loop until we read a special key.
while true; do
  # Read in a new key.
  read -k key
  if (( #key == ##\r )); then
    # Special action for carriage return (<return>).
    zle accept-line
    return
  elif (( #key == ##\C-g )); then
    # Special action for <ctrl-g> (abort).
    return 1
  else
    # Assume it's a real character and insert the
    # uppercase version.
    LBUFFER="${LBUFFER}${(U)key}"
    # Redisplay the line.    zle -R
  fi
done
```

We'll discuss the effect of the zle -R command in the next section. If you turn this into a widget and run it, the shell will read characters from the keyboard and insert the uppercase version of the key until you press either Return to end the line or Ctrl-g to abort what you are doing. It's a simple caps lock. For example, type echo, then execute the widget, then some lowercase text, then press Return. The text after the widget appears in upper case, and is then echoed to the terminal. You can probably think of ways to improve it.

The #key in the arithmetic evaluation takes the first character of $key and turns it into the number that represents that character. For example, the a character's ASCII encoding is 65. Don't worry about remembering this; just keep in mind that each character has a unique ASCII representation. The ##*keynum* treats *keynum* in the same way as a keystroke used in key bindings and turns that into a number, too. Hence, you can compare characters read in with those in the normal notation.

There are more complicated examples of this sort among the functions distributed with zsh. In particular the widget function incremental-complete-word reads in keys one at a time using read -k and tries to find completions to the word so far as you type. You'll find it could do with some improvement; there's a chance for you to use your new knowledge. The commands predict-on and predict-off put you into or out of a mode where the characters you type are inserted by examining KEYS, but the function also searches the history to try to guess the word you are typing. (Both functions are defined inside the file named predict-on.) If you can follow these functions, you will have a very good understanding of editor widgets.

Outputting Messages

You may need to make zle output a message. For example, you may want to print a prompt to tell the user to type a character that can be subsequently read using read -k. You can do this with zle -R followed by a message as a single quoted string. If you give further strings, they are formatted in columns like the output for possible completions of a word.

This example prompts for a character, reads it, and inserts it:

```
local key
zle -R 'Type a key:'
read -k key
LBUFFER="${LBUFFER}$key"
```

Note that the output from zle -R only lasts until the next time zle redraws the display. That means the shell has to pause afterwards for the user to be able to read the message. Here, read -k waiting for input will have that effect. If you use zle -M instead, it outputs a message below the command line that the line editor itself won't delete. It will eventually be overwritten when new output is added.

Keeping Other Input Away from the Command Line

If you use the shell's notify option to tell you immediately when a background job exits, you may notice it has a neat feature that prevents the message that appears from making a mess of the line you are editing. The editor exits temporarily, then the message is printed, and then the whole command line is redrawn just as it was. If you've never seen that, try the following example:

```
zsh% setopt notify
zsh% sleep 5 &
```

Then simply wait for the message. Type something while you're waiting, and see how that gets redisplayed.

There is an option to the zle command, zle -I, that provides the same behavior for you to use. If you have an ordinary shell function that often runs in the background (as in the section "Grouping and Subshells" in Chapter 13), you can use zle -I to make sure the output is kept tidy. One reason for that is to run a function when a timer expires or a signal is received. Here's a function that sends you a message after 10 seconds using the signal USR1. Most people don't use that signal for anything in the shell—if you already are, you will probably know, and shouldn't try this example.

```
# Function to send the shell a signal in ten seconds.
signal_me() {
  sleep 10
  kill -USR1 $$
}
# Function executed by the shell when it receives the signal.
TRAPUSR1() {
  zle -I
  print "Time's up."
}
# Start the first function in the background.
signal_me &
```

If you run this function in the background and wait, you should see Time's up printed neatly before the line is redrawn. If you still have the notify option turned on, you will also see the message saying the background job finished. That's the shell using the same display mechanism for its own purposes.

The two functions TRAPUSR1 and signal_me are needed because the special zle handling must take place in the main shell, where the line editor is running. We use the trap for that, since traps always run in the main shell when it gets a signal. The other function runs in the background, and can't communicate directly to the line editor in the main shell.

New Features in Version 4.2 of zsh

The line editor is one of the places where there are significant extensions in 4.2, the latest version of the shell. Here, we'll briefly describe a few of them. See the shell's documentation for more information.

There are new variables that give you direct access to the cut buffer, where killed text is put first of all, and the kill ring, where it goes when you kill some more text. (See the sidebar "The Kill Ring" in Chapter 4 for a short introduction to the kill ring.) In 4.0, you could do this only indirectly using the built-in widgets. The scalar CUTBUFFER is the space where the last killed text lives, and which will be inserted by yanking. The array killring contains the sequence of pieces of text that were killed. Normally, only the yank-pop widget uses the kill ring. The array killring provides the chunks of text in the same order as yank-pop. Both CUTBUFFER and killring can be set as well as read. This allows you to make the kill ring larger or smaller.

The two variables PREDISPLAY and POSTDISPLAY allow you to set parts of the visible command line that can't be edited. The widget function read-from-minibuffer, which is supplied with the shell, uses these in a widget that prompts for and reads input below the main editing area. This gives a much more natural and powerful way of reading extra input than was available in 4.0. It's much more like the way you enter text to use in searches, for example.

There are extra contributed functions, too. One set gives a powerful way of telling the shell what it should consider as a word for editor commands that move across or kill or delete words, replacing the WORDCHARS variable. This uses the shell's *styles* mechanism, which we met in the sidebar "Configuring Completion Using Styles" in Chapter 10. For more information look for the entry on select-word-style in the section of the manual on contributed functions.

Summary

In this chapter we've considered one particular topic, adding your own commands to zsh's line editor, in some detail. Here are some of the features of the line editor that we've examined.

- We introduced the concept of a *widget function*, a piece of shell code for a specific editing task. We showed how to create such a function to extend the editor.

- We showed two main ways of editing text from a widget function: calling other widgets with the zle command, and changing the state of the editor with variables such as BUFFER and CURSOR.

- To make widget functions behave more like zsh's built-in widgets, we discussed numeric arguments and error handling.

- We showed you some case studies in writing widgets for common tasks: making the editing behavior depend on the widget's name; overriding widgets; and examining command-line arguments. We also discussed the usefulness of testing the name of the previous widget to make widgets run smoothly one after the other.

- We introduced zsh's mechanism for approximate matching of patterns, often useful in widgets.

- We presented an example widget, for spelling correction, to put a lot of this information together.

- We demonstrated how the line editor can read characters inside your widgets, and how it can output status information separate from the line it is editing.

- At various points we mentioned that example widgets are supplied with zsh. These make a good starting point if you wish to learn how to write widgets effectively.

In the next chapter, we will consider a more specific task performed by the line editors of both bash and zsh: completion. We will you show you how to write functions in both shells to extend completion. As an introduction, the sidebar "Editor or Completion Widget?" discusses how functions that extend zsh's completion behavior, also called widgets, differ from the editor widgets we have introduced in this chapter.

EDITOR OR COMPLETION WIDGET?

We've seen in this chapter that editor widgets give you nearly complete control over what's on the command line. However, in the next chapter we're going to discuss a different sort of widget used for completion. Why, and what's the difference?

Completion widgets don't use the low-level ways of changing the command line that we're talking about here. The special variables introduced in this chapter are available, but they're read-only. To change the command line, you need to go through a completely different procedure.

Although you can't change everything in completion widgets, instead you can change the word the cursor is on in quite complicated ways without doing too much work. You tell the completion system the possible ways the final word can look; it does all the tasks necessary to allow the user to pick the one they want. In particular, the completion system is very good at deciding the current context where editor widgets don't give you much help. By "context", we mean whether the text is part of a word, if it's a command, if it's a piece of special syntax, and so on.

Which to use? The best answer is to consider whether the task you have in mind can be implemented as a set of choices to supply to the user. If it can, use a completion widget as described in the next chapter. If it can't, you probably want an editor widget, and should look at the information in this chapter.

That's not a complete answer, though: some tasks could be implemented either way. In that case, you need to decide between the simplicity of the interface of an editor widget or the power available in a completion widget.

CHAPTER 15

■ ■ ■

Writing Completion Functions

In Chapter 10 we showed how you can take advantage of the completion systems of bash and zsh. This included fairly advanced techniques for configuring their behavior. In this chapter, we build on this, with some more advanced ways to configure completion. The bulk of this chapter however, pertains to writing your own completion functions. In particular, we cover the following topics:

- Specifying simple definitions to enable the shell to complete the arguments of a particular command

- Writing a function, either for bash or zsh, to handle completion for a particular command

- Making use of the many zsh functions that allow you to do powerful things easily in your completion functions

- Associating descriptions with completion matches and grouping matches of a similar type together

- Enabling your completion functions to be configurable using styles

- Configuring the way zsh's completion works using an advanced mechanism: tags and tag labels

- Creating separate completion widgets in zsh, allowing completion to have different behavior depending on which key it was invoked with

Completions

The term *completions* is used when referring to the definitions that describe what the shell should complete depending on the existing words on the command line. To avoid confusion we use the term *matches* when referring to the list of possibilities generated by the completion system in a given situation, although you may see them referred to as *completions* elsewhere. For many commands, you will find that there is as yet no completion definition and the shell resorts to completing filenames. This will be especially true for any programs or shell scripts you have written yourself. By writing a completion for such commands, you can make the shell complete words that are valid arguments to the command. This chapter shows you how to write your own completions.

When programmable completion first appeared in tcsh, a complete built-in allowed completions to be specified using a special syntax roughly resembling sed expressions. zsh initially adopted a similar built-in—named compctl—but using more traditional command options. Unfortunately, these completions were hard to read and the many options meant that while writing them you had to keep the manual close at hand. Though improvements could have been made by using long options, completion definitions require more expressive power than was possible using sequences of options. Rather than define a whole new syntax, it made sense to make use of the existing zsh scripting language. So completions in zsh are now defined using shell functions. The old compctl-based system is not covered in this book, but it still works if you want to use it.

bash followed zsh's lead with a shell function–based system that was clearly inspired by zsh's. In some respects, it resembles a hybrid between zsh's new and old systems. As you will see, its flexibility is lacking in some areas.

There is quite a lot you can achieve without resorting to writing whole shell functions, however. For example, in bash to complete hostnames after the telnet command (which makes a network connection to another host) you can use

```
complete -A hostname telnet
```

The -A option specifies an action. In this example, the action is hostname, indicating that hostnames should be completed. bash provides a number of similar actions for completing words from particular groupings. For many of these actions, there is a short form using a single option so, for example, we can use -j instead of -A hostname. In general, it's probably better to stick with the -A option because it's more readable.

In zsh the _hosts function performs hostname completion. So in zsh, you would use

```
compdef _hosts telnet
```

■**Note** If you see a "command not found" error for compdef, you will need to make sure you first enable the new completion system. See the section "zsh's compinit" in Chapter 10 for details on how to do this. Also, make sure that the directories containing zsh's completion functions are listed in the fpath variable.

In fact, zsh also has a function named _telnet that does a better job of completing for telnet than merely completing hostnames.

It is common to want to restrict completion for a command to certain types of files. In Chapter 10 we demonstrated how completion after gunzip is restricted to only those files it can uncompress. Completions of this kind are easy to define and are powerful enough to make a difference. For instance, you might want to restrict completion to .jpg image files for the gimp image editor. In bash you can specify that like this:

```
complete -A file -X '!*.jpg' gimp
```

In this example we specify that we want to complete filenames using the file action and we also specify a pattern with the -X option to indicate that some matches should be excluded. The pattern starts with an exclamation mark (!) because we want to exclude those matches that don't match the pattern rather than those that do. If you have more than one command that uses the same completion definition, you can list all of their names as arguments to complete (the same applies to zsh's compdef). Typically you also want to specify a range of file types so the pattern needs to be more complicated. So you might use the following to additionally complete arguments to the gimp-remote command and to match .jpeg and .png files:

```
complete -f -X '!*.@(jp?(e)g|png)' gimp gimp-remote
```

Note that you will need to have the extglob option turned on in your setup for this to work. It is an invaluable option when writing completions because there is a lot of pattern matching. In this example, we use the -f option to specify that we want to complete filenames. This is the short form of -A file. One noteworthy aspect of the exclusion pattern is that it also applies to directories. It is, however, quite common to want to use gimp to edit an image file that is in a subdirectory. Starting with version 3 of bash, if you pass the option -o plusdirs to complete, it will additionally complete directory names. Let's now create a similar completion definition for zsh. To achieve this, you already run into the need to write a shell function. File completion is handled by a _files function. This supports a -g option that allows you to specify a glob pattern to restrict completion to certain types of files. In zsh 4.0, you can't specify these arguments with compdef.[1] It is still very simple, however:

```
_gimp() {
  _files -g '*.jpg(-.)'
}
compdef _gimp gimp
```

The (-.) at the end of the pattern is a glob qualifier (see the section "Glob Qualifiers in zsh" in Chapter 9). This restricts the files matched to regular files or symbolic links to regular files. We do this because gimp expects its argument to be an image file and not something like a directory. _files can still complete directories, however. In the section "Ordering with File Completion" later in this chapter we show how the behavior of _files in this regard can be configured.

The functions that make up zsh's completion system are all autoloadable. This has the advantage that functions are only loaded into memory when they are first called. As you may recall from the section "Autoloadable Functions" in Chapter 13, autoloadable functions are each stored in a separate file and the shell searches the directories listed in $fpath to find these files. You don't need to use the autoload command to mark your completion functions for autoloading; when compinit runs, it looks for functions with an initial underscore (_) in their name and also at the first line of the file. If the first line contains a special tag, it autoloads it. So for this function, you might create a file with the following contents:

```
#compdef gimp

_files -g '*.jpg(-.)'
```

If this is placed in a directory in your $fpath when compinit executes, it will be picked up, marked for autoloading and defined for the gimp command. Note that the function body doesn't need to be surrounded by _gimp() { ... }.

---

1. In zsh 4.2, you can use compdef '_files -g "*.jpg(-.)"' gimp.

So far in this section, you have learned how to replace, for a particular command, the default filename completion. In our example for the gimp command, this meant that the names of image files could be completed for each command argument. However, many commands expect each argument to be something quite different. A shell function allows programming logic to be used to make decisions. From a function, you can therefore find out which command argument is being completed and act accordingly. To demonstrate this ability, we'll write a function to handle completion for the chown command. The syntax for the chown command is

```
chown owner file...
```

or

```
chown owner.group file...
```

where we have omitted some options to make the example simpler. Our aim is to make the shell complete usernames for the first argument to chown and filenames for any subsequent arguments. Additionally, when completing after a dot (.) in the first argument, we want to complete the names of groups. Modern systems use a colon (:) instead of a dot to separate the user and group. Unfortunately, as was mentioned in the section "Completing Parts of Words" in Chapter 10, a colon is treated specially by bash and it splits the word up at the colon. This makes things a little complicated so, for bash, we will stick with the dot.

We'll write our completion function first for bash and then for zsh. Users of each shell will find it useful to still read through both sections because the shells have a fair amount in common.

bash Example

The first argument to chown needs to specify the new owner and group while the remaining arguments are all filenames. When calling a completion function, bash sets a number of special variables that tell the function information, such as what is currently on the command line and where the cursor is. These variables are shown in Table 15-1. The COMP_CWORD variable is particularly relevant to our example. We can use it to determine if we are on the first word (and want to complete users and groups) or if we are on a subsequent word (and should complete files). So as a starting point, our example looks like this:

```
_chown() {
  if (( COMP_CWORD == 1 )); then
    # complete users[.groups]
  else
    # complete filenames
  fi
}
```

Table 15-1. *bash Special Completion Variables*

Variable	zsh Equivalent	Purpose
COMP_CWORD	CURRENT	Indicates the word at which the cursor is positioned
COMP_WORDS	words	An array containing the words on the command line
COMP_POINT	N/A*	The position within the current word at which the cursor is placed
COMP_LINE	BUFFER	The current command line in full
COMPREPLY	compadd built-in	An array containing the list of matches; set by the function and read by bash

* There is no direct equivalent in zsh but the same information is conveyed by the PREFIX and SUFFIX variables.

The next step is to generate some possible matches. Let's deal with filenames first. bash completion functions return the list of matches in an array named COMPREPLY. You could use something along the lines of COMPREPLY=(*), but there is a better way. We have seen that with the -f option to complete we can make bash handle filename completion internally. To use that from within a completion function, there is a compgen built-in. It takes many of the same options as complete and allows access to many internal structures that would be otherwise difficult to access. compgen doesn't automatically add matches when run; it produces the list of matches as standard output and so needs to be used with command substitution (see the section "Command Substitution" in Chapter 2).

Tip compgen is not only useful in a completion function. Want a list of groups? Just type compgen -g. A list of signals? That's compgen -A signal.

So with command substitution, you are probably now envisioning something along the lines of COMPREPLY=($(compgen -f)). This is not all, however. bash does not automatically match the values supplied in COMPREPLY against what is currently on the command line. By passing the current word as an extra argument to compgen, it will match against it and only return those words that start with the current word. The current word is retrieved with ${COMP_WORDS[COMP_CWORD]}. So we now have this:

```
_chown() {
  if (( COMP_CWORD == 1 )); then
    : complete users[:groups]
  else
    COMPREPLY=( $(compgen -f -- ${COMP_WORDS[COMP_CWORD]}) )
  fi
}
```

■**Note** If you followed the section "bash_completion" in Chapter 10 and are using the bash_completion project, you can save yourself a lot of this trouble. bash_completion includes a `_filedir` function that you can call to complete filenames.

Merely defining a function is not sufficient for bash to use it: bash needs to know what function to associate with which command. The `complete` built-in's -F option makes this possible:

```
complete -F _chown chown
```

If you try this function out, it should complete nothing in the first argument position but complete filenames in subsequent argument positions. If you try to complete a directory, however, you may notice that it doesn't add a trailing slash. Adding a slash to directory names is a feature of bash's internal filename completion, but bash needs to know that it is completing filenames if it is going to enable such features. However, bash doesn't know that it is completing filenames here. To tell it, you need to specify the `filenames` completion option to the `complete` built-in. So the command becomes

```
complete -F _chown -o filenames chown
```

Now on to completion of the first argument. First we need to decide whether we want to complete users or groups. We can do this by checking to see if the current word already contains a dot. This is straightforward to do using pattern matching. So we need an `if` statement using `[[ ${COMP_WORDS[COMP_CWORD]} = *.* ]]` as the condition.

To complete usernames, we can use `compgen -u`. However, it would also be useful to add a dot after the username ready for the group to be specified. The `compgen` command's -S option allows a suffix like this to be specified. Unfortunately it also adds a space. You can prevent this with the -o `nospace` option to `complete`, but it would then apply when completing filenames too, which would be annoying. At this point, we have

```
_chown() {
  if (( COMP_CWORD == 1 )); then
    if [[ ${COMP_WORDS[COMP_CWORD]} = *.* ]]; then
      : complete groups
    else
      COMPREPLY=( $(compgen -S . -u -- $cur) )
    fi
  else
    COMPREPLY=( $(compgen -f -- ${COMP_WORDS[COMP_CWORD]}) )
  fi
}
```

Now finally, we need to complete group names. The hard part of this task is that it needs to cope with the user part already being there at the beginning of the word. We do this by extracting the user part from the current word and passing that to `compgen` as a prefix (with the -P option). We're using the current word a lot, so it helps matters if we copy it into a local variable (`local cur=${COMP_WORDS[COMP_CWORD]}`). To extract the user part of the current word, we need to cut off anything following the dot. For this we can use the `${...%%...}` pattern operator with a pattern that matches any non-dot characters. The expansion ${cur%%*([^.])} produces the user part of the word. We now indicate to compgen that this should be ignored. So this would give us this for completing groups:

```
COMPREPLY=( $(compgen -P ${cur%%*([^.])} -g -- ${cur##*.}) )
```

If you put this into the function and give it a try, it should now work. If not, make sure you have the extglob option set. The compgen -g option is actually quite a new addition, so if you don't have a recent version of bash, you may get an error message. To cope with that situation, we are going to generate our own list of groups. For most things that you will want to complete, bash doesn't have a handy compgen option, so it is useful to be able to do this yourself.

The list of groups on a system can usually be found in the file /etc/group. If you look at the file, you will see that it is a colon-delimited file where each line contains not just the name of a group but also an optional encrypted password and the list of users who are members of that group. We don't need all that extra information so we want to filter it out. The cut command can do this job for us: cut -d : -f 1 outputs just the first field in a colon-delimited file. Though we could use grep, it would be nice to still have compgen's ability to match the words against the current word. The -W option to compgen or complete allows a list of words to be supplied, so we can use that. bash first applies word splitting to the argument supplied with -W and then expands each resulting word. So the -g can be replaced in the function with -W '$(cut -d: -f1 /etc/group)'. Our final function looks like this:

```
_chown() {
  local user
  local cur=${COMP_WORDS[COMP_CWORD]}

  if (( COMP_CWORD == 1 )); then
    if [[ $cur = *.* ]]; then
      COMPREPLY=(
        $(compgen -P ${cur%%*([^.])} -W '$(cut -d: -f1 /etc/group)' -- ${cur##*.})
      )
    else
      COMPREPLY=( $(compgen -S . -u -- $cur) )
    fi
  else
    COMPREPLY=( $(compgen -f -- $cur) )
  fi
}
complete -F _chown -o filenames chown
```

Using an option to the complete built-in you can control what happens if no matches are generated by the function. Normally, nothing will be completed, but there are a few further options. By specifying -o default, bash will revert to filename completion, and by specifying -o dirnames, it will revert to completing directories. For a command such as chown where we want to complete all files, we can therefore leave the explicit filename completion out of the function and instead pass -o default to complete. This wouldn't help if we wanted to limit filename completion to only some filenames, image files perhaps. bash 3 adds a -o bashdefault option. This enables all the default completions. This includes filename completion but also covers such things as completing usernames after a tilde and variables after a dollar sign. You will find that it is useful to specify this for most commands.

zsh Example

As you'll see, the equivalent zsh function is no more complicated than the preceding bash example. Where it does become more complicated in zsh is when we make use of powerful extra features that are lacking in bash.

The first difference is that zsh uses different names for the special variables. Table 15-1 offers the zsh equivalents for the bash special variables, but all the variables used for ordinary zle widgets are also valid (see the section "Special Variables in zle" in Chapter 14) along with a number of variables for handling prefixes and suffixes (listed in Table 15-3). There is also a compstate associative array containing further information. The basic outline of the function looks very similar to that for bash:

```
_chown() {
  if (( CURRENT == 2 )); then
    # complete users[.groups]
  else
    # complete filenames
  fi
}
```

Note that because zsh indexes arrays from one instead of zero, words on the command line are also counted from one. So there is a slight difference from bash in that regard.

Completing filenames is a simple matter of calling the _files function. It handles everything to do with filename completion for you. Later on, we will show you the direct way to add matches without relying on preexisting functions, but for this function, let's keep matters simple and just use _files.

In zsh, we have complete control over what parts of the current word are considered for completion and what parts are ignored. So if we want to complete groups ignoring everything preceding the colon or dot in the current word, we can do that. The compset command allows you to specify parts of the current word to be ignored for the purposes of completion. We want to ignore everything in the word up to the first dot. The command to do this is compset -P '*.'. The -P option specifies a prefix to be ignored. Its return status indicates whether or not it was able the remove the specified pattern. So for completing users and groups, we can do this:

```
if compset -P '*.'; then
  _groups
else
  _users
fi
```

As you can see, completing usernames or groups is simply a matter of calling the existing functions. We now have a function for zsh that works at least as well as the bash example. However, there are still other things we can do to improve it. First, zsh does not have bash's limitations with respect to colons, so we can handle colons by changing the pattern to '*[.:]'. Next we want to add a suffix after completing users. zsh handles this in a similar way to bash:

we just pass the option -S '.' to _users. There are many common options like this that you can pass to other completion functions.

You may remember from the section "Prefix Completion" in Chapter 10 that with the complete_in_word option set, zsh looks at the word on both sides of the cursor when deciding what matches. For this to work properly, we want it to ignore anything after a dot when completing usernames. This way, if you go back to edit the username, you can use completion and the group is ignored. To specify a suffix to be ignored when completion does matching, compset supports an -S option similar to -P. So before calling _users, we will run compset -S '[.:]*'. In addition, we need to make the dot suffix when completing usernames conditional on whether this removed a suffix: if a dot is already there, we don't want to add another one. Our final function looks like this:

```
_chown() {
  if (( CURRENT == 2 )); then
    if compset -P '*[.:]'; then
      _groups
    else
      if compset -S '[.:]*'; then
        _users
      else
        _users -S '.'
      fi
    fi
  else
    _files
  fi
}
```

There is a further essential step we need to take before we can use this function: we must associate the function with the command whose arguments it completes. We have already seen how to do this: either run compdef _chown chown or make the function autoloadable and put a special tag on its first line:

```
#compdef chown
```

You might want to have a look now at the completion functions for chown that come with zsh and bash_completion. They do a number of more complicated things. The bash function handles colons and completes options for GNU chown. The zsh function is even clever enough to restrict the completed files to those for which the chown command would make sense. So if you complete after chown root, any files that are already owned by root will not be completed. You will also see that the same function additionally handles chgrp.

Another thing you may notice in the completion function zsh includes for chown is that it assumes some things about its environment. In particular, it relies on the extended_glob option for some of the patterns used. This is possible because the completion system sets up some aspects of the environment. The list of options it sets are listed in the _comp_options variable. These won't otherwise affect your interactive environment because the options are only set locally using local_options as we described in the section "Porting Scripts" in Chapter 13.

Adding Matches Directly

In the previous section, we used functions such as _groups to add matches in zsh. These functions are convenient, but for many things that you will want to complete, there won't already be an appropriate function you can call. In this section we'll explain how you can generate your own set of matches.

As an example of how to add matches directly, we'll look at how the _groups function itself works. Unlike bash, zsh does not use a shell variable similar to COMPREPLY for returning matches. Instead, a built-in named compadd is used. This has the distinct advantage that more information about the matches can be supplied with them. This avoids the problems we had with bash where the -o nospace option would have been useful for user completion but was better left out because it would have been a nuisance for group and filename completion.

Using the compadd built-in is a simple matter of passing it your list of matches. When writing the bash function, we showed how to get a list of groups using the cut program and the /etc/group file. So a working _groups function need contain no more than this:

```
compadd $(cut -d : -f 1 /etc/group)
```

PARAMETER MODULE

In order to be able to complete internal properties of the shell, some mechanism needs to be provided. In bash, that mechanism is the compgen built-in, an idea that was actually taken from early development stages of zsh's new completion system. In zsh, it was, however, deemed preferable to have functions for completing these properties, so we have _options, _parameters, _jobs, _aliases, etc. This makes things much more consistent.

But these functions still need to access the underlying information. The information was therefore made available in a number of shell variables. These variables are provided by the zsh/parameter and zsh/zleparameter modules. They are useful in many situations outside of completion.

For example, there is a commands associative array that acts as an interface to the internal hash table that maps commands to their location. So when the names of commands need to be completed, the list of keys in this associative array is used. It can also be useful if you want to check if a certain command exists. Instead of writing if whence -p *command* >/dev/null; then, you can write if (($+commands[*command*])); then.

To complete usernames, the _users function could do something akin to this but using the /etc/passwd file. However, zsh already keeps track of the list of users along with their home directories in order to support the tilde expansion feature for expanding user home directories. The zsh/parameter module, described in the sidebar "Parameter Module," includes a variable named userdirs that allows us to get at this information. It is an associative array mapping usernames to home directories. We're only interested in the usernames: the keys of this associative array. We could expand them using ${(k)userdirs} but compadd has a -k option for just this situation. So we can execute

```
compadd -k userdirs
```

There is also a similar -a option for taking the values of an array (or indeed of several arrays).

If we want functions like _users and _groups to be autoloadable, we still want compinit to be able to pick them up even though they aren't used directly for any commands.[2] To achieve this, instead of using the #compdef special tag on the first line of the file, we use #autoload instead.

Return Status

A well-behaved zsh completion function returns true if it successfully added matches or false if it failed. This is not vital in a function like _chown but in a function like _groups that is going to be called from other completion functions, it can be important. Typically the return status is used to facilitate fallbacks where completion for one thing is tried and, if it fails to add any matches, something else is tried. The conventional way to get the return status right is to have a local variable named ret initialized to 1. Whenever another completion function is called, zero is assigned to ret if matches were added. The double ampersand notation we saw in the section "Condition Tests" in Chapter 13 comes in useful for doing that. At the end of the function, the ret variable is then used for the return status. If you don't specify a return status in a shell function, the return status of the last command called is reused. So the _groups and _users functions consisting of just a call to compadd do not need any change. To demonstrate this scheme here, we'll modify our _chown function:

```
#compdef chown

local ret=1
local -a suf

if (( CURRENT == 2 )); then
  if compset -P '*[.:]'; then
    _groups && ret=0
  else
    compset -S '[.:]*' || suf=( -S . )
    _users "$suf[@]" && ret=0
  fi
else
  _files && ret=0
fi

return ret
```

We've also made use of a variable for the suffix here because this shorter way of handling compset -S is common.

---

2. In actuality if you look at the _groups and _users functions that come with zsh you will see that they are defined to be used directly for many commands such as groupdel and chsh. There are other functions, however, for which this is not so; _signals for example.

Debugging Completion Functions

Because completion is interactive in nature, it can be quite hard to debug. Turning the xtrace option on or putting print statements in the function is not ideal because all the output gets mixed up on the terminal.

To solve the problem for xtrace output, there is a widget in zsh named _complete_debug. It is normally bound to the key combination Ctrl-x ?. You use it where you would have otherwise pressed Tab, and it captures the trace output in a temporary file. A command to view this temporary file is then placed in your shell history, from which it can quickly be retrieved using the Up Arrow key. That just leaves you with the problem of going through the output and working out what the problem is. It will include trace information for all the helper functions you call along with the completers.

For simple debug information, you can just use _message, which is described later on, or zle -M, which we saw in the section "Outputting Messages" in Chapter 14. These have their limits, however, and are not an option from bash. The most effective solution is to redirect your debug output into a different terminal window. This is easy enough to do: just open up a new terminal window and run the tty command (or look in the TTY shell variable) to see the name of the device corresponding to the terminal. You can then redirect your debug output to this other terminal with a line similar to this:

```
print "words: $words" > /dev/pts/3
```

Since it is common to want to see the special completion variables, you might choose to create a function to print them out. For instance, the following function prints a breakdown of the current word using variables, which we will come to in the section "Prefixes and Suffixes" later in this chapter. We have chosen these because they are often useful to see. The -c option to print used here causes the arguments to be listed in columns:

```
compstatus() {
  print -c \
    "PREFIX: <$PREFIX>" \
    "SUFFIX: <$SUFFIX>" \
    "IPREFIX: <$IPREFIX>" \
    "ISUFFIX: <$ISUFFIX>"
}
```

Helper Functions

The functions we have looked at so far fall into two categories. There are functions like _telnet and _chown that handle a particular command, and there are functions like _groups and _users that complete words of a particular type and are designed to be called from other functions. Yet there is a third category, known as helper functions. They are used to solve common problems by abstracting out common constructs. In this section, we'll introduce some of the more useful helper functions provided by zsh, and show you how to use them.

Multiple Parts

To start, we'll examine one of the simpler helper functions. When completing filenames, rather than add every filename on your system including the full path to them as matches, only files and directories in the current directory are completed. If a directory name is completed (or typed), further completion will generate matches from the contents of that directory. Sometimes, when completing something else, you will want completion to work in the same way. This occurs wherever you have a lot of possible words arranged in a hierarchy with a common separator between each level in the hierarchy. Examples of this include the names of newsgroups and the kernel parameters modified with `sysctl` on Linux and BSD.

As an example, we'll look at completing files from a tar archive as arguments to the `tar` command. This is done for completion after, for example, `tar xvf foo.tar`. If the name of the archive file is in the second argument (`$words[3]`), we can get this list of files in the archive by running `tar tf $words[3]`. Having retrieved the list of files, we then have the complicated task of handling completion of the files one directory at a time. To simplify this task, we can use the `_multi_parts` function. To use `_multi_parts`, we first need to put the list of files in an array. `_multi_parts` can then be passed this array and the separator character as arguments, and it does everything else for you.

```
files=( $(tar tf $words[3]) )
_multi_parts / files
```

■**Caution** The example above won't work if you have files with spaces in their names. That's not a limitation of `_multi_parts` but of our method of creating the files array. We'll show how to deal with this situation in the next section.

Completing Options

Virtually all Unix commands take a whole raft of options as arguments. Some options take arguments themselves. Some commands allow single-letter options to be clumped together, so for example, `-abc` can be used instead of `-a -b -c`. Some options are incompatible with others and they can't be used together. On top of all these complications, code needs to be written to ensure the function honors any user preferences that have been configured using styles. The `prefix-needed` style introduced in the section "Requiring Prefixes" in Chapter 10 is an example of a style that affects completion of options. Coping with all of this can be quite messy, so to make things easier there is a helpful function—`_arguments`—that does a lot of the hard work for you.

To demonstrate `_arguments`, we'll use another example. For this we'll write a function to handle the NEdit text editor. If you've not heard of it, NEdit is a powerful yet easy-to-use editor with a graphical interface. It is available from `http://www.nedit.org/`. We've chosen it for this example because many of the common issues that come up when completing options arise for its options.

To use _arguments, you need to pass it a series of specifications each detailing an option. At their simplest, these specifications can be just the name of the options:

_arguments -create -display -geometry -read -tags -wrap *and so on ...*

The -display and -geometry options are common to all X programs, so there is an _x_arguments function that is a wrapper around _arguments. Because it adds these two options for you, we'll use it here.

In the section "Per-match Descriptions" in Chapter 10, we saw how descriptions can be associated with matches. _arguments makes it easy to specify these. Just follow each option with its description in brackets:

```
_x_arguments \
  '-read[open file read only]' \
  "-create[create file if it doesn't already exist]" \
  and so on ...
```

Many of the options take an argument. For example, there is a -line option that should be followed by the line number within the file to go to. It doesn't make much sense to complete line numbers, but it is useful for the completion system to prompt users if they try completion after -line. We can do this with the following option specification:

'-line[go to specified line number]:line number'

For other options, it does make sense to complete something for the argument. For example, there is a -background option that allows a background color to be specified. There is already a function for completing those color names understood by X: _x_color. We just need to call it. The specification for this is

'-background[specify background color]:background color:_x_color'

As things currently stand, we have option names being completed but not filenames. We could just call _files after _x_arguments, but this would have some associated problems. For example, it would not know not to complete files after options like -line and -background that take arguments. _arguments has an extra specification form that allows nonoption arguments to be specified. In this case, it is

'*:file:_files'

Instead of the asterisk (*), you could use a number. If we extended our chown completion to complete options, we could use a specification starting with 1 for completing the new owner instead of the ((CURRENT == 2)) test. The number would be 1 and not 2 because _arguments only deals with completion of command arguments: the CURRENT variable is designed to allow for when the cursor is on the first word of the command line, one position before the first command argument. _arguments also ignores any options when deciding if we are on the second word, so using an _arguments specification that starts with a number is not quite the same as checking the CURRENT variable.

Calling another function is not the only way to specify what is completed in a specification. You can just list some words in parentheses. For an example, we'll examine NEdit's -lm option.

It takes the name of a programming language as an argument, allowing NEdit to select the right rules for features like color syntax highlighting. We can specify the languages to complete like this:

```
'-lm[specify language mode]:language mode:(Ada C Fortran NEdit\ Macro)'
```

You can even specify descriptions for each match:

```
'-lm: :((CSS\:Cascading\ style\ sheets HTML\:Hypertext\ Markup\ Language))'
```

This is a more useful thing in other situations, but the example should demonstrate the point. The other description has been removed so as to fit this on a line; _arguments specifications can become quite long. Note how the colons have to be quoted with a backslash to avoid them being interpreted as the start of another argument (some options take more than one argument). Spaces in descriptions also needed quoting.

States

For completing the list of languages supported by NEdit, a hardcoded list is not ideal: support for new languages can be added, either with new versions of NEdit or by the user. It is better to generate the list of languages automatically.

We could write another completion function for this, but there is another way. For instance, you specify the name of a state in the _arguments specification. For -lm, it would look like this:

```
'-lm[specify language mode]:language mode:->languages'
```

Then, when _arguments returns, it sets a number of variables:

state—An array containing the list of states that need to be completed.

context—An array containing the zstyle context associated with each state.

line—A contracted version of the words array from which all options and their arguments have been removed.

opt_args—An associative array mapping options to their arguments.

In the vast majority of cases (and including this one), only one state can ever be completed at a time. You need to have something like optional arguments to options before you need to worry about handling several states. This allows us to simplify things a little: if we pass the -C option to _arguments, then the context array is not used and it will just put the zstyle context in the standard curcontext variable. This variable carries around the current context for zstyle throughout the completion system. Because we are now modifying all these variables, we need to declare them as being local at the top of our function. For curcontext, we also need to copy its existing value into it. So the upper part of our function now looks like this:

```
local curcontext="$curcontext" state line
declare -A opt_args

_x_arguments -C \
  '-lm[specify language mode]:language mode:->languages' \
  ...
```

NESTED EXPANSIONS

zsh allows expansions (`${...}` or `$(...)`) to be embedded inside another expansion. We haven't covered the full gory details of these nested expansions. Although these are very useful, complicated expressions can easily become ugly and unreadable. They also don't achieve much that can't be done with more standard Unix tools like `sed`, `awk`, and even `cut`. They are, however, used a lot in completion functions for parsing the output of commands because they run faster than the equivalent pipeline of Unix commands. To read them, the first thing to keep in mind is that you need to start from the inside and work your way outwards.

For completion, the same basic constructs tend to be used. The following list relates these basic constructs to their standard Unix equivalents.

- In most cases, begin with `${(f)"$(command)"}`, which turns the command output into an array of lines.

- Where you would use `grep`, you can use `${(M)...:#pattern}`. The `(M)` modifier can be removed to achieve the effect of `grep -v`.

- Where you want to select specific lines such as with `head` and `tail` or `sed`'s d and p (with -n) commands, you can use array indexing. So just add something like `[(r) *,-1]` on the end.

- For `sed`'s s command you can use the `${.../...}` and `${...//...}` forms or the `:s` modifier. If the `sed` regular expression uses "^" or "$" as an anchor, then the `${...%...}`, `${...#...}`, `${...%%...}` and `${...##...}` forms will be sufficient.

To give you an idea of the types of things you can do and an appreciation for what we mean by complicated expressions becoming ugly and unreadable, the following is an example:

```
print -l ${${${(@f)"$(</etc/passwd)"}#*:*:*:*:}%%[,:]*}
```

That takes the password file and removes chunks from the start and end of each line to leave just the real names. More specifically, this selects the fifth field on each line of `/etc/passwd`. To achieve this we use a pattern that alternately matches the field separator (a colon) and the contents of a field. By taking the shortest possible matches using the single # operator instead of ## we avoid the stars (*) ever matching a colon. This is a common way to select fields as you might otherwise do with `cut` or `awk`. You might think that we could use word splitting to separate the delimited fields. The difficulty in this example is that we have already split the input at line breaks and we want to pick the fifth field on every line. After word splitting, you would have one long array and taking the fifth element would return only the fifth field of the first line.

Certainly don't feel you have to use nested expansions for parsing. The speed difference isn't so great and there are other tricks you can use to speed up Unix pipelines. Often one instance of `sed` can replace a series of simpler commands like `grep` and `cut`.

Next we need to deal with actually handling the state. If you have more than one possible state, you will need a case statement at this point. We can get away with just checking if the `state` variable is set. Unfortunately, NEdit doesn't have an option that lists the available languages so we have to look inside the user's `.nedit` configuration file. The format of this file is similar to that of an X resources file. Languages are listed starting from a line beginning with "`nedit.languageModes:`".

The next line starting with "nedit." marks their end. So we can filter the file down to just these lines with sed:

```
sed -n '/^nedit.language/,/^nedit/ p' ~/.nedit
```

The name of each language is surrounded by other information, but there is a tab character on the left and a colon on the right. By piping the output of sed above to cut we can strip this down:

```
sed -n '/^nedit.language/,/^nedit/ p' ~/.nedit | cut -d $'\t' -f 2 | cut -d : -f 1
```

This command now gives us a list of languages. Passing the list on to compadd is not quite as simple as just using a command substitution. Some of the languages such as "NEdit Macro" contain a space and this needs to be quoted. Using the (f) variable expansion flag, which was introduced in the section "Expansion Flags" in Chapter 12, we can split it into an array at newlines. So the bottom of our function looks like this:

```
if [[ -n $state && -f ~/.nedit ]]; then
  compadd - ${(f)"$(sed -n '/^nedit.language/,/^nedit/ p' ~/.nedit |
      cut -d $'\t' -f 2 | cut -d : -f 1)"} && ret=0
fi

return ret
```

The (f) flag is used a lot in completion functions like this. Often, the whole expression is written as a nested substitution instead of using commands like sed. The result may run quicker but tends to be harder to read. The sidebar "Nested Expansions" has more information about these.

Exclusion Lists

Completion is more effective when it only generates pertinent matches. So _arguments doesn't complete options that have already been specified on the command line. Usually, it doesn't make sense to provide the same option twice to a command. Sometimes, however, an option can be used more than once. An example of this is the -xrm option, which NEdit, as well as many other X programs, take. It allows an X resource value to be set. Such options can be specified by preceding the option specification with an asterisk (*). So the specification for the -xrm option is

```
'*-xrm[specify X resource value]:resource:_x_resource'
```

Furthermore, in some situations certain options are mutually exclusive: they can't be used together. For example, NEdit has four options that select how line wrapping should work: -wrap, -nowrap, -autowrap, and -noautowrap. It only makes sense to use one of these options. Exclusion lists can be used to specify those options that contradict or are incompatible with each other. They are listed in parentheses at the beginning of an option specification. For example, for -wrap we would use

```
'(-nowrap -autowrap -noautowrap)-wrap[use continuous wrap mode]'
```

What this actually specifies is that the listed options cannot follow -wrap on the command line so it is also necessary to specify -wrap in the exclusion list of the other three options. Occasionally, you may come across a command where the order in which options are specified is significant and so you won't want to reciprocate the exclusions in that manner.

If you have an option that can only be used alone, you can specify "-" in the exclusion list for it to exclude all other options. For example, the specification for NEdit's -version option is

```
'(- *)-version[display version information]'
```

The asterisk in the exclusion list here also prevents files from being completed after -version.

Tip If you want to see the full NEdit function, then you can execute less $^fpath/_nedit(N). The (N) is a glob qualifier and has the effect of turning on filename generation to remove any expansions that don't resolve to an existing file. If you have the rc_expand_param option enabled in your setup (see the section "Array Expansions" in Chapter 12), you can omit the caret (^) from the expansion. The real completion function is further complicated by the fact that it additionally handles NEdit's client program.

That's about all there is to our completion for NEdit. However, there are a few more useful things you can do with _arguments. We mentioned at the beginning of the section that some commands allow single-letter options to be clumped together. If you pass the -s option to _arguments it will allow for that. Some commands such as grep use the argument "--" to specify the end of options and that no subsequent arguments should be treated as an option. Pass -S to _arguments and it will handle this. Other commands only allow options to precede their normal arguments. This you can specify with -A "-*". It needs to know what constitutes an option argument, hence the pattern.

The -s, -S, and -A options should come first before any specifications of options to be completed. The same applies to other options to _arguments such as the -C option, which we saw earlier. If you want to specify one of these as an option to be completed, you have a few choices: either rearrange your option specifications so that they appear last, give them a description, or add a single argument containing a colon to mark the end of options to _arguments.

Another thing that _arguments can do is automatically complete long options for commands that support the --help option. To make use of this, "--" should be given as an argument.

You'll have to read the manual for details, but there are yet more things _arguments can do.

Specifying Descriptions

To specify descriptions for completion match listings, the compadd built-in has a couple of options: -d specifies the per-match descriptions and -X prints the explanations above groups of matches. You will find, however, that you never need to use the latter directly because the headings are all handled as part of the tag system covered in the section "Tags, Labels, and Descriptions" later in this chapter. It is also quite rare to need to use the -d option directly. The reason for this is that there are helper functions that make the task simpler.

One such helper function is _describe. It is useful when all you want to do is complete a list of values, each with its own description. An example of such a situation is when completing subcommands for the xauth command. xauth allows you to manipulate authorization information used when connecting to X servers.

_describe takes two arguments. The first is the description for all the group of matches. The second argument is a little bit like the last (action) component of an _arguments specification. It is a list of matches and their corresponding descriptions with a colon separating matches from descriptions. So for xauth subcommands, it would look something like this:

```
_describe 'xauth command' '(
  add:add\ entry
  generate:use\ server\ to\ generate\ entry
  extract:extract\ entries\ into\ file
  nextract:numerically\ extract\ entries
)'
```

xauth actually has a few more subcommands than that, but in the interests of brevity we have left them out. Note how the list is contained within parentheses. Without them, the second argument is taken to be the name of an array. The array contains the list of matches, again with their descriptions. So the following is equivalent to the above:

```
cmds=(
  'add:add entry'
  'generate:use server to generate entry'
  'extract:extract entries into file'
  'nextract:numerically extract entries'
)
_describe 'xauth command' cmds
```

A step up in complexity from _describe is _values. It is useful where you are trying to complete the same set of values in a list. It is actually very similar to _arguments and supports many of the same features such as exclusion lists, parameters to values, and states. It is useful for commands like dd that take options of the form *name=value*.

_values can be useful where you just need a list where matches for each item in the list are taken from the same set of values. An example of this occurs in the completion for iptables, the Linux command for configuring firewall rules. The iptables completion uses the following to complete TCP flags:

```
_values -s , 'tcp flag' SYN ACK FIN RST URG PSH NONE ALL
```

The -s option specifies the separator character to use between items in the list. The first argument before the list of matches is then a description. A more complex example is in the completion for filesystem options in the _mount function. This function handles completion for mount, the Unix command for attaching a filesystem at a particular directory. The filesystem options are specified as a comma-separated list, and some of them take an argument after an equals sign. There are many possible options, and which are applicable depends on the type of filesystem. The following snippet containing some of the options for the Network File System (NFS) should give you some idea of the sort of things you can do with _values. You will probably also notice the resemblance to _arguments:

```
_values -s , 'file system option' \
  '(rw)ro[mount file system read-only]' \
  '(ro)rw[mount file system read-write]' \
  '(nolock)lock[use locking]' \
  "(lock)nolock[don't use locking]" \
  'rsize[specify read buffer size]:read buffer size' \
  'proto[specify protocol]:protocol:(udp tcp)'
```

Messages and Guards

Sometimes, it isn't useful or possible to complete anything but it can still be handy if the completion system prompts users to let them know what they are expected to type. We saw this in the NEdit example for completion after `-line` where it prompts the user with "line number". For printing such prompts, there is a helper function named _message, and using it is easy. For example:

```
_message 'line number'
```

Note You may see `_message` used with a `-e` option and a tag. This is an extension in version 4.2 of zsh that allows it to work with matches added using the `fake` style mentioned in the section "Defining Different Words to Complete" in Chapter 10.

One issue that occasionally arises with these messages is that if they are used at the same time as completing something else, the message actually blocks completion from being unambiguous. An example of this occurs in the completion for the pine e-mail program. There is a `-c` option that takes a numeric argument immediately after it, but there are also other options beginning with a "c" such as `-conf`. If you don't have pine itself installed, its completion won't work too well so try the following function to demonstrate the problem:

```
#compdef pine

_arguments \
  '-c+[specify context to apply to -f arg]:number' \
  '-conf[print out fresh global configuration]'
```

Note The plus sign after the `-c` is something we haven't come across before. It specifies that the argument to `-c` can appear either immediately after "`-c`" or in the following word. In this position, you can also use a minus sign if the argument must be in the same word. An equals sign is also valid and specifies that the argument can be in the following word or the same word if there is an intervening equals sign (e.g., `--from=file`). Finally, there is `=-`, which restricts the argument to just this equals form.

Now try to complete the -conf option using this function. Here, we set the format style first because the descriptions help to illustrate what is happening:

```
% zstyle ':completion:*:descriptions' format %B%d%b
% pine -co<tab>
number
option
-conf        -- print out fresh global configuration
```

It doesn't complete because more than one type of thing is considered a candidate for completion: numbers and options. The helper function _guard works around this problem. It takes two arguments: the first specifies a pattern to match against what has been typed so far and the second specifies a message to display if the pattern matches. So for pine, we use the following specification:

```
"-c+[specify context to apply to -f arg]: :_guard '[0-9]#' number"
```

Now, once the letter "o" of the -conf option has been typed, the pattern won't match, thus allowing the option to be unambiguously completed.

Running External Commands

When the completion system calls external commands to generate completion matches, it can sometimes be very useful for the user to be able to intercept this and have a different command run or the same command run but with different arguments. The possible uses for this are wide ranging. An option to the command may apply a filter, restricting or expanding the number of matches. It may be that the command's output format can be changed, affecting the descriptions given to matches. Perhaps a command such as ssh is used to access a remote system but the remote system doesn't run an ssh server, so it is useful to substitute the rsh command.

As an example, consider completion of process IDs. For this, matches are generated by running the ps command without any arguments. On its own, ps typically only lists those processes associated with the current terminal. This is often not very many. However, it is possible to configure this with the command style:

```
zstyle ':completion:*:processes' command 'ps -e'
```

This will cause every process on the system to be matched. As another example, the following changes the output format but only applies when completing process IDs for the kill command:

```
zstyle ':completion:*:kill:*:processes' command 'ps -o pid,s,nice,stime,args'
```

The _call_program helper function does the job of looking up this style. It acts as a simple wrapper around any call to an external program. So if you look inside _pids, the function that completes process IDs, you will see this line:

```
out=( "${(@f)$(_call_program processes ps 2>/dev/null)}" )
```

Similarly, for our tar completion example in the section "Multiple Parts" earlier in this chapter, we might use the following when extracting the list of files in an archive:

```
files=( $(_call_program files tar tf $words[3]) )
```

The first argument to _call_program is a tag: this is the last component of the zstyle context when the command style is looked up. Subsequent arguments specify the default command to run when the style isn't set.

Handling Styles

With more sophisticated completion functions, you may want to allow aspects of the function's behavior to be configurable using zstyle. As we saw in the last section, many helper functions look up styles for you so your function will react to many styles without your function having to do anything in particular. To get an idea of the styles looked up in a particular situation, invoke the _complete_help function with a numeric argument. Normally, you can do this by pressing Esc 2 followed by Ctrl-x h. This is primarily useful when configuring completion because it allows you to see what styles are looked up and the associated context. In this section, we'll look at how you can make your functions directly look up styles.

Looking Up Styles Directly

When we introduced the zstyle command in the sidebar "Configuring Completion Using Styles" in Chapter 10, we said that it allows styles to be defined. In addition, the zstyle command can be used to find out the value of a style. The usage is also similar: the familiar context and style name are there. The main difference is that an option is used to specify what type the value should be interpreted as. Table 15-2 lists the most useful of the available options.

Table 15-2. *Options to zstyle for Looking Up Styles*

-t	boolean (default *false*)
-T	boolean (default *true*)
-s	scalar (string)
-a	array

With the -s and -a options, an additional argument specifies a variable into which the style's value is put. To see this in action try running the following directly from the command line, which will return a list of the completers you use unless you rely on the defaults:

```
% zstyle -a :completion::::: completer arr
% print $arr
```

When looking up styles from a completion function, you need to know the appropriate context to use. As we mentioned when discussing states and the _arguments function, the current context is passed around in the curcontext variable. To illustrate the use of this, let's take an example. The completions for scp and rcp look up the remote-access style to check if it is okay for them to use ssh or rsh to connect to the remote system to obtain a list of files there. What they do is roughly as follows:

```
if zstyle -T ":completion:${curcontext}:" remote-access; then
  compadd $(rsh $host ls -1d $PREFIX\*)
else
  _message 'remote file'
fi
```

We are only interested in a true or false value here, so we can simply use the exit status of zstyle. Our use of -T instead of -t indicates that the value true is assumed by default. If it is true, the first branch of the if statement will execute and rsh will be used to get a list of files on the remote system to complete. If it is false, it will instead just display a prompt. Note that the curcontext variable doesn't include the initial :completion: prefix, so we need to specify that explicitly.

Where the style can have more values than just true or false, we need to specify the variable name. The return status will still indicate if the style is unset, allowing a default to be selected. For example, the _pids function contains the following line:

```
zstyle -s ":completion:${curcontext}:processes" insert-ids out || out=menu
```

Here, if the insert-ids style has not been set, it will default to the value menu. Note how the processes tag is added to the end of the context to indicate that we are completing process IDs. The tag is not carried around in the curcontext variable.

Keeping Track of the Context

The creation and updating of the curcontext variable is not the exclusive domain of the completion internals. Normally, when a completion function starts it will contain just the name of the completer and the command. The idea is that as more is determined about the current context, more information is filled in. It may be useful at this stage to recall that the zstyle context has the following form:

```
completion:function:completer:command:argument:tag
```

_arguments and _values fill in the argument field. This is why you need to be careful with the handling of the context when using states with _arguments. This argument field allows styles specific to an option argument to be set. To see the effect of this, we can use the _complete_help widget (usually bound to Ctrl-x h):

```
% set -o <ctrl-x><h>
tags in context :completion::complete:set::
    others-option-o-1  (_arguments _set)
tags in context :completion::complete:set:others-option-o-1:
    zsh-options  (_options _arguments _set)
```

Here we can see the contexts used when completing the argument to the -o option. The context's argument field contains others-option-o-1. This indicates that we are completing the first argument to the -o option in the others option set.[3] Given this, we could define a style that would apply when completing after the -o option but not after the +o option. The tag in both situations is the same, so the argument field is the only place the context differs.

Try experimenting with _complete_help to see some of the other values that appear in the argument field. For example, you may see values such as argument-1 and argument-rest, which are used when _arguments is completing nonoption arguments.

One common situation where you may want to modify curcontext is if you write a completion for a command that has subcommands. This seems to be popular with source-code control programs like CVS, SCCS, and Perforce, but you may also have seen it elsewhere, such as with Debian's apt-get command. The convention when completing for these commands is to include the name of the subcommand in the command field of the context. This allows styles to be set specific to a subcommand. For example, this style applies for the add subcommand of cvs:

```
zstyle ':completion::*:cvs-add:*' ignore-line true
```

Whenever you modify curcontext in a function, it should be declared local so that changes do not propagate up to the calling functions:

```
local curcontext="$curcontext"
```

The first thing you will want to do is complete the subcommands. _describe is generally appropriate for this job. The subsection "Specifying Descriptions"earlier in this chapter demonstrates _describe using xauth subcommands. If the main command can take options before the subcommand, _arguments can be used but finish with an _arguments specification that looks like the following:

```
'*::command:->subcmd'
```

An unusual characteristic of this specification is the use of two colons after the star (*). This causes _arguments to update the words special array and CURRENT special variable subsequent calls to _arguments to behave as expected, finding the name of a command in the first element of words and options thereafter. If you don't have options to deal with, you can also do this step manually like so:

```
shift words
(( CURRENT-- ))
```

Note You can modify all the special completion variables in this way. They don't even need to be explicitly declared local: their values are automatically saved and restored when entering and leaving a function.

---

3. Option sets are an unusual feature of _arguments, which are beyond the scope of this book. Have a look at the completion function for set to see how they are introduced.

Having taken this step, the name of the subcommand will be in the first element of the words array. We can now modify curcontext as follows:

```
curcontext="${curcontext%:*}-${words[1]}:"
```

This chops off the argument field of the context that generally is going to be empty. The subcommand is then added with a trailing colon to delimit the end of the command field. Everything is now ready to complete for each of the subcommands. So following this tends to be a case statement or separate functions are called for each subcommand.

Putting this all together with the xauth example we used in the section "Specifying Descriptions" earlier in this chapter, we have a function that looks like this:

```
#compdef xauth

local curcontext="$curcontext" ret=1
local subcmd

if (( CURRENT == 2 )); then
  _describe 'xauth command' '(
    add:add\ entry
    generate:use\ server\ to\ generate\ entry
    extract:extract\ entries\ into\ file
    nextract:numerically\ extract\ entries
  )' && ret=0
else
  shift words
  (( CURRENT-- ))
  subcmd="$words[1]"
  curcontext="${curcontext%:*}-${subcmd}:"

  case $subcmd in
    add)
      # complete for add subcommand
    ;;
    # and so on for all the other subcommands
  esac
fi

return ret
```

If you look at the xauth completion function distributed with zsh, you'll see that it doesn't bother to shift the words array. This is because it doesn't need to use _arguments when completing for any of the subcommands.

Making Full Use of Tags

This section takes us back to the subject of configuring completions. We have seen tags used to identify what type of thing is being completed. So far, we have only really seen them used in the zstyle context to allow style settings to take account of them. They are also useful in grouping similar matches in completion lists, and as we'll now see, they specify the order in which different types of matches are completed. We also meet tag labels, which allow completion for a particular tag to be subdivided. This provides scope for some very powerful things to be achieved with just zstyle. The next section will then go on to deal with the necessary things completion functions need to do to support this functionality.

Tag Ordering

Using the tag-order style it is possible to specify the order in which tags are completed. The resulting behavior is similar to using the ignored-patterns style and relying on _ignored to complete the ignored matches. tag-order can also be used to restrict the matches being completed to those for a particular tag. All the example uses of tag-order in Chapter 10 do that.

One example use for this is when completing in array subscripts. Try the following to see why:

```
% cd $path[<tab>
```

It nicely completes the array indices with descriptions for each element but also completes variables. The variables are there because math evaluation is used within array subscripts. The general policy is for all valid things to be completed with the onus being on users to restrict this where they find it inconvenient. In this case, it would be nice to get the variables out of the way. Using the tag-order style, this is as follows:

```
zstyle ':completion:*:*:-subscript-:*' tag-order indexes parameters
```

Now, if you try the same completion again, just the array indexes will be completed first. If you want variables to be completed, you have two choices. Either you type the beginning of your variable so that no array index will match or you use the _next_tags widget. _next_tags is normally bound to Ctrl-x n. Using _next_tags with a tag-order style can be a good way of managing situations where there are many matches of different types. See the section "Ordering with File Completion" later in this chapter for example use of _next_tags.

Note that after trying completion for all the tags you list, completion for any tags not listed is then tried. You can disable this by including a single hyphen in the value of the style. So if you want variables to never be completed inside array subscripts, you can do this:

```
zstyle ':completion:*:*:-subscript-:*' tag-order indexes -
```

Tag Labels

Tag labels provide a way of performing completion for a particular tag more than once. Typically it is used in conjunction with the ignored-patterns style to break up matches for a style into subgroups. As an example, let's consider completion of options to the configure scripts that come with the source to many programs. Often they allow you to enable or disable various features via options with names starting --enable or --disable. For example, zsh's configure script has a --enable-maildir-support option that enables support for maildir mailboxes— an alternative way to store e-mail messages—for the MAIL variable we saw in Chapter 7. For every --enable option there is always a corresponding --disable option, so listing both is not entirely useful. What we can do is arrange for the --disable options to be tried only after completion for other options has been tried. The fourth component of the zstyle context contains the name of the command whose arguments are being completed, so we can restrict this to completion for configure:

```
zstyle ':completion:*:*:configure:*' tag-order 'options:-other' options
zstyle ':completion:*:options-other' ignored-patterns '--disable-*'
```

The options:-other value in the tag order says that completion should be tried for the options tag but with the other label added to the context. This means that whenever a style is looked up as part of the option completion, the label will appear in the context. That label is therefore included in the context for the ignored-patterns style above. It isn't necessary to restrict the ignored-patterns style to the configure command because restricting the tag to options-other should be sufficient, provided you don't use the same tag label with options for another command.

Using tag labels here isn't actually necessary: we could just as easily have relied on the _ignored completer to pick up the --disable options. To do that, we would need to specify the ignored-patterns style with a context that selects the configure command:

```
zstyle ':completion:*:*:configure:*:options' ignored-patterns '--disable-*'
```

What makes tag labels more powerful is that they allow matches to be divided into more than two groups. Furthermore, if some style other than ignored-patterns has the effect of limiting matches, it could be used when separating matches into groups.

If more than one tag is listed in the same word in the value of the tag-order style, matches for both tags (or labels) are completed together. It is also possible to specify different descriptions for each tag label. So for configure, we can do this:

```
zstyle ':completion:*:*:configure:*' tag-order \
  'options:-enable:enable\ options options:-other:other\ options' \
  'options:-disable:disable\ options'
zstyle ':completion:*:options-enable' ignored-patterns '^--enable-*'
zstyle ':completion:*:options-disable' ignored-patterns '^--disable-*'
zstyle ':completion:*:options-other' ignored-patterns '--(en|dis)able-*'
```

This now has three separate descriptions for the different sets of options. By putting the specification for enable options together in the same word as other options, they are still completed together.

Often, configure scripts also have similar --with and --without options. We can do the same trick for them. We need ignored-patterns styles for each of them and to extend the pattern for the other options:

```
zstyle ':completion:*:options-with' ignored-patterns '^--with-*'
zstyle ':completion:*:options-without' ignored-patterns '^--without-*'
zstyle ':completion:*:options-other' ignored-patterns \
  '--((en|dis)able|with(|out))-*'
```

We also need to replace our tag-order style with one that includes the two new labels. I'll leave the descriptions out this time.

```
zstyle ':completion:*:*:configure:*' tag-order \
  'options:-enable options:-with options:-other' \
  'options:-disable options:-without'
```

If you set up your group-name style as suggested in the section "Grouping Related Matches" in Chapter 10, you will now have separate groups for each type of option. This is because it is including the label in the group name. We can, however, override this by specifying the name for the group explicitly. The following style puts all the configure options back into the same group so that they are listed together:

```
zstyle ':completion:*:*:configure:*:options-*' group-name options
```

■**Tip** Another thing you may want to try instead of completing --without and --disable options later is to use the hidden style. It allows matches to be completed but to be left out of completion listings.

Ordering with File Completion

For filename completion, there is somewhat separate handling for ordering different types of matches. This is controlled by the file-patterns style. Handling this style is actually all that _files does. Everything else is done in a function named _path_files. If you ever need to exert more direct control over filename completion in a function, you can call _path_files directly.

In the section "A Brief Tour of Programmable Completion" in Chapter 10, we said that completion after gunzip would fall back and try to match all files if no .gz files match. This is actually controlled by the file-patterns style. file-patterns acts like tag-order but allows you to associate glob patterns with tags. By default, files are divided up by three separate tags: globbed-files, directories, and all-files. Completion for them is tried in that order.

It is common to want directories and files to be completed together—so common, in fact, that this has been made the default in zsh 4.2. You can do this with the following style:

```
zstyle ':completion:*' file-patterns \
    '%p:globbed-files *(-/):directories' '*:all-files'
```

This is very similar to the tag-order style except that instead of needing to use ignored-patterns, a glob pattern is specified here directly. The %p is expanded to the glob pattern specified with the -g option to _files.

You can use this to handle additional filename extensions for a command. In fact you can even use it in lieu of a completion function if all you want to do is restrict the types of file completed for a particular command.

The following example causes OpenOffice.org files to be completed in addition to other zip files after unzip: they are actually zip files so this could be useful if you routinely want to poke around inside them.

```
zstyle ':completion:*:unzip:*' file-patterns \
    '*.sxw(-.):ooffice-files %p:globbed-files *(/):directories' '*:all-files'
```

Note how we have used the `(-.)` glob qualifier that we used with `_files'` `-g` option. This ensures that no directories are matched. Sometimes the globbed files may include directories. If you want all nondirectories to be completed first, and only then directories, you would need to use this:

```
zstyle ':completion:*' file-patterns \
    '%p(^-/):globbed-files' '*(-/):directories' '*:all-files'
```

This adds a glob qualifier to any pattern specified by the completion function to restrict matched files to those that are not directories.

The `all-files` fallback is useful because every now and then, files don't have the right suffix. The fallback is used if no matches are produced for the preceding tags, but you can also get to it with the `_next_tags` widget introduced in the section "Tag Ordering" earlier in this chapter. For example:

```
% ls
attachment  initrd.tgz  picture.png  zsh-4.0.9.tar.gz
% zcat <tab>
initrd.tgz       zsh-4.0.9.tar.gz
% zcat <ctrl-x><n>
attachment       initrd.tgz       picture.png       zsh-4.0.9.tar.gz
```

Trying Completers More Than Once

Labels can also be used in the completer list. This allows the same completer to be tried twice with different styles. For example, you might want to try correction with one error allowed, then another completer like `_approximate` or `_prefix` and then `_correct` again but with a more generous number of errors:

```
zstyle ':completion:*:::::' completer _complete \
    _correct:-first _approximate _correct:-second
zstyle ':completion:*:correct-first:::' max-errors 1
zstyle ':completion:*:approximate:::' max-errors 2
zstyle ':completion:*:correct-second:::' max-errors 5
```

Unlike the `tag-order` style, you cannot list more than one completer in the same word to have them tried together. If necessary you can get around this by having a wrapper function that calls another completer and then returns 1. The return status of a completer is used to decide if the next completer should be run.

Ordering Matches for Menu Completion

If you use menu completion, you are possibly more concerned with the order in which matches are cycled through. This is quite a different thing from the ordering you get with tag orders and the list of completers. With those, each tag or completer is tried in turn until one of them succeeds in matching, so anything further down the order is not tried at all. The order in which matches are cycled through for menu completion instead corresponds with the order in which they are listed.

To configure ordering for menu completion, you can make use of the group-order style. Going back to our example for configure scripts we can use

```
zstyle ':completion:*:*:configure:*' group-order \
  options-other options-enable options-with options-disable options-without
zstyle ':completion:*:*:configure:*' tag-order \
  'options:-enable options:-other options:-with options:-without options:-disable'
zstyle ':completion:*:*:configure:*:options-*' group-name ''
```

This will need the same ignored-patterns styles too. With these styles in place, menu completion will now only cycle through to options with the common prefixes after it has gone through all the other options. We have seen the group-name style before. Without it, all matches would go in a group named -default-. The group-order style is also useful if you don't use menu completion but want to change the order in which groups of matches are listed.

For filename completion, there is a file-sort style that changes the ordering of matches for listing and menu completion. We show a use for it in the section "Stand-alone Completion Widgets" later in this chapter.

Tags, Labels, and Descriptions

In this section, we show how to enable the use of tag ordering from your own functions.

Descriptions

Two types of descriptions are associated with matches in completion listings. The first type are those associated with a single match and, if enabled, appear to the right of the matches. The second type of description, which we will be considering in this section, are associated with a group of matches. They appear as headings within the lists of matches.

To associate a description with a particular tag, there is a helper function, _description. Normally, it is called from other helper functions, but you may want to use it directly if you are only interested in completing one type of thing. Usage is straightforward; you pass it a tag, the name of an array variable to put the necessary compadd options in, and a description. For example, if you just want to complete PostScript files, you might do this:

```
local expl

_description files expl 'PostScript file'
_files "$expl[@]" -g '*.ps(-.)'
```

The expl variable is conventionally used for description options. Note that it needs to be declared local if you use it. _description is used to handle a number of styles that are looked up, per tag, at this stage. These styles include format, ignored-patterns, ignore-line, and matcher. _description doesn't deal with the tag-order style, however. For that we need a loop over all the possible tags so that they can be completed in the correct order.

Tag Loops

Tag loops enable the tag-order style to work. When you see the full form of a tag loop, its workings will become clearer, but there are a number of helper functions that make it simpler by factoring out common constructs.

At the simplest level, the _wanted function implements an entire tag loop for you; however, it is restricted to completing one type of thing. For example, the following is similar to the example for _description:

```
local expl
_wanted files expl 'PostScript file' _files -g '*.ps(-.)'
```

The difference functionally between this and _description is that the tag-order style can be used to either disable completion in this context or to separate it out for several labels. You will see _wanted used quite a lot in existing completion functions. You would generally use _description when calling a function like _users that already contains its own tag loop for the same single tag but where you want a different description from the default.

As with all the functions mentioned here, _wanted defaults to passing the compadd options for the description as the first argument to the command it is given (_files in the previous example). However, when you write your own completion function, descriptions passed to your function should take precedence. A single hyphen can be used to indicate where _wanted should put the description options. So in this case, you would instead use

```
local expl
_wanted files expl 'PostScript file' _files "$@" - -g '*.ps(-.)'
```

If you need to complete more than one type of thing, you will need to construct the tag loop yourself. To do this, you first need to initialize the list of tags with a single call to the _tags function, passing it a list of the possible tags. Then you need a while loop that runs _tags without arguments for its condition. Inside the tag loop, you can use the _requested function in exactly the same way as _wanted. For example:

```
local expl ret=1

_tags bookmarks users hosts

while _tags; do
  _requested bookmarks expl bookmark compadd - foo bar && ret=0
  _requested users && _users && ret=0
  _requested hosts && _hosts && ret=0

  (( ret )) || break   # leave the loop if matches were added
done

return ret
```

Both _users and _hosts have their own tag loops and a suitable default description, so we don't need to run them directly from _requested. This skips the unnecessary label loop, which we'll see in the next section.

In a situation like this where you don't need several lines of code to complete one of the things, you can use the _alternative function instead. It takes _arguments like specifications. The equivalent, using it, would be

```
_alternative \
  'bookmarks:bookmark:(foo bar)' \
  'users: _users' \
  'hosts: _hosts'
```

Labels

The tag-order style allows tags to be further subdivided using labels, so another loop is used to handle each label. If you need to call compadd more than once or call more than one function when generating matches for one of the tags, you need to worry about this looping over tag labels. For labels, a second inner loop is used, which makes things simpler but does actually limit what you can do with the tag-order style: labels only work relative to other labels for the same tag and not relative to other tags. Label loops are implemented using the _next_labels function. This example uses two calls to _path_files for each of files and directories:

```
if _requested files; then
  while _next_label files expl 'local file'; do
    _path_files "$expl[@]" && ret=0
    _path_files -S/ -r '/' "$expl[@]" -/ && ret=0
  done
fi
```

That would go inside the tag loop. You can actually omit the _requested test if you are only completing for the one tag in the whole tag loop.

The final function in this family is _all_labels. It does for label loops what _wanted does for tag loops: wrapping it up into a single command.

_all_labels is useful where you only need one call to compadd or other completion function but want additional lines of code inside the _requested test. Normally such code is put outside the tag loop entirely and run regardless of whether the particular tag is to be completed. In some situations, though, you might not want to do that. For example, this code appears in the completion function for w3m:

```
if _requested w3mhistory && [[ -s ~/.w3m/history ]]; then
  w3mhistory=( ${(f)"$(<~/.w3m/history)"} )
  _all_labels w3mhistory expl 'url from history' compadd -a w3mhistory
fi
```

It would be quite valid to build the w3mhistory array outside the tag loop and just use _requested here, but it would then attempt to read the user's ~/.w3m/history file even if they had disabled completion for this tag. Obviously putting code outside the whole tag loop can have a performance benefit because it is not run for every loop iteration. So you need to think about where you put such code.

There are a number of options that are common to this family of functions. The most useful is the -V option, which prevents the matches from being sorted. This is mainly useful when completing a range of numbers because the sorting is not done numerically. It can be combined with -1 or -2 to control removal of duplicates.

▉Caution Sometimes you will want to nest tag loops. This commonly occurs as a result of calling completion functions that contain their own tag loop and in such cases no problems occur. You need to be careful if you try to nest tag loops within a single function. On exiting the inner tag loop, you will need to reinitialize the tags mechanism by calling _tags with the list of possible tags. This information is currently stored once for each function in the call stack and so is lost when initializing the inner loop. If in doubt use a second function.

Prefixes and Suffixes

When performing matching, the completion system needs to know what is before and after the cursor and what parts of this it should consider. In addition to the special completion variables we have seen so far are a number of further variables which hold this information. They are listed in Table 15-3.

Table 15-3. *Special Completion Variables*

Before the Cursor	After the Cursor	Purpose
PREFIX	SUFFIX	The part of the current word to be used in matching
IPREFIX	ISUFFIX	Those parts of the current word to be ignored for the purposes of matching
QIPREFIX	QISUFFIX	The quoted string outside of the word being completed

When completion starts out, PREFIX and SUFFIX hold the current word between them while IPREFIX and ISUFFIX will be empty. By transferring a string from the beginning of PREFIX to the end of IPREFIX, completion can be restricted to just a part of the current word. For instance:

```
IPREFIX="${IPREFIX}${PREFIX%%/*}/"
PREFIX="${PREFIX#*/}"
```

This might be used in filename completion to allow an initial directory portion of the current word to be ignored. This is exactly the same as the following:

```
compset -P '*/'
```

After completion, the final word will begin with whatever was in IPREFIX when the match was added. That will be followed by any prefix specified with the -P option to compadd. Next appears the match itself. The end of the word after the match follows the same structure in reverse using suffixes instead of prefixes.

■Tip You can actually put what you like in these special variables before calling compadd. If you're writing a completer or stand-alone completion widget, this can be useful in producing some unusual effects. Also useful in these situations is compadd's -U option, which disables the internal matching. Both of these things are beyond the scope of this book.

Hidden Prefixes

The compadd command also has a -p option, which specifies a prefix that is considered as part of the text to be matched. To help you understand the difference between -p and -P try the following with each. You'll need to put this line in a function and use compdef to associate the function with a command name.

```
compadd -M 'r:|.=* r:|=*' -p 'pre.' one two three
```

With -p, this will complete p.o to pre.one. Change the -p to a -P and it won't.

To understand why a hidden prefix is so named, it may be easier if you compare this use of -p with the following:

```
compadd -M 'r:|.=* r:|=*' pre.one pre.two pre.three
```

The difference is that when -p was used, the prefix didn't appear in the list of matches. If you want a prefix to be visible, you have to include it as part of all the matches like this. If you use -P, the prefix isn't part of the match, so it is also hidden. Note that if you use both -P and -p, then the prefix specified with -P will appear first in the resulting word.

As you might expect, there are also hidden suffixes; the compadd option for them is -s.

Removable Suffixes

In the section "Automatically Added Suffixes" in Chapter 10, you learned how zsh can remove suffixes added by a previous completion if the next key you type indicates that you most probably didn't want the suffix. The most common example of this is removing the slash after a completed directory if the next key you press is Return.

In the early part of this chapter, where we wrote a completion function for the chown command, we used a suffix to add the dot separator after completing users to leave the command line ready for adding a group:

```
_users -S '.'
```

It would be quite nice if this suffix could be removed if the user doesn't go on to type the name of a group. Though the chown command doesn't seem to balk at a superfluous dot, you will almost certainly come across commands that don't like extra separator characters at the end of a word.

The most common cases are handled by the -q option to compadd. This ensures that the suffix is removed if the next key typed inserts a blank or inserts nothing. That will include keys like Space and Return. In this case, because our suffix is only one character long, it will also remove the suffix if the next key typed is the same as the suffix. That means if the user presses . the command line will not include two consecutive dots as a result of the keypress. So for our chown example, we can now use

```
_users -q -S '.'
```

Sometimes, you may want more control over which following characters cause the suffix to be removed. There are two further options that allow this: -r and -R. With the -r option, you can give a list of the characters, and with -R you give a function that is run to make the decision. It isn't actually that common to need to use these; the manual has more details, if you want to learn more.

Stand-alone Completion Widgets

We have seen a few situations where a key other than Tab is used for completion. This was commonly used in bash, before it had programmable completion. As you might expect, such keys can be configured in zsh. You can either have the different key complete a different set of words, such as words from the history, or you can make it perform normal completion but with changes to the behavior. You may, for example, want to use a different key for approximate completion or have a key for case-sensitive completion.

Defining Completion Widgets

Just as zle -N can be used to create editor widgets, you can create completion widgets with zle -C. How they differ is that you also need to specify which built-in editor command's behavior you want (complete-word, menu-complete, etc.) and the name of your function is required instead of being optional. The manual gives this as an example:

```
zle -C complete complete-word complete-files
bindkey '^X\t' complete
complete-files() { compadd - * }
```

If you try to write widgets like this you will soon find that they won't work together with regular completion functions and many other things like tag loops. In the next section, we will show how you can write widgets that do interact well with the rest of the completion system.

If you look at the zsh manual, you will see that there are two separate manpages covering the newer, function-based, completion mechanism. The first—zshcompwid—covers the low-level features such as compadd and zle -C. The second manpage—zshcompsys—is about the set of shell functions (collectively referred to as just *compsys*) that use this. In this book we have talked about aspects of the two parts interchangeably.

As in the example above, it is quite possible to use completion widgets on their own without using compsys. But why might you want to? Back in the section "Asking the User for Input" in Chapter 13 we showed how you can use the vared command to read a line of input from the user with all the features of the zsh line editor (completion included) enabled. Suppose that you write a shell script that uses vared. Not using compsys means that your script doesn't need to run compinit to load the entire completion system. For example, you might have a script for editing e-mail that prompts you for each of the header fields before running your normal text editor. This couldn't be a written as a shell function if it is to be run by your e-mail program.

If you are using `vared` from a shell function instead of a script, the situation is simpler. A shell function runs directly in an interactive shell. This means that the completion system may already be enabled. The completion system includes a hook allowing you to easily define what is completed within `vared`. To use it, just set the `compcontext` variable to a string in the same form as those passed to `_arguments`. For example, a function that reads a hostname might look like this:

```
gethost() {
  local compcontext='hosts:host:_hosts'
  vared -c -p 'Enter hostname: ' host
}
```

Using a Different Completer

It is possible to have the functionality of a completer available on another key besides Tab. Common candidates for this are `_correct`, `_match`, and `_expand`. This is especially useful with any completer that isn't listed in your default `completer` style and, therefore, isn't already invoked by Tab. There is also an `_all_matches` completer that is useful to have bound to a key. It inserts all possible matches generated by another completer.

The `compinit` function binds your Tab key to a function named `_main_complete`, which sets up all the fundamental parts of compsys. Using a function named `_generic`, you can have this set up from your own widgets. `_generic` puts the name of your widget at the beginning of the zstyle context and calls `_main_complete`.

As an example, we'll take the `_match` completer. First we'll create our widget, associate it with `_generic`, and bind a key to it:

```
zle -C match-word complete-word _generic
bindkey '\e*' match-word
```

Now we need to specify which completer to use. The name of our widget, in this case `match-word`, gets added to the current context by `_generic` so we can restrict the style by that:

```
zstyle ':completion:match-word::::' completer _match
```

That, in essence, is all there is to it. Remember that you aren't limited to just one completer here. You might want to list `_all_matches` before `_match` and perhaps `_ignored` after it, for instance.

There may be other styles you may want to use to fine-tune the behavior of this widget. For instance, the `_match` completer looks up the `match-original` style to control whether it should place a * at the cursor position when generating matches.

Completing Different Words

`zsh` comes with a couple of custom completion widgets that do other things. We have already seen the one for history word completion, and there is also one, generally bound to Ctrl-x m, that completes to the most recently modified file. Both of these can be implemented with `_generic` and a few style settings.

For the `most-recent-file` widget, what we basically want is menu completion where files are completed in order of how recently modified they are. To enable menu completion, you can specify `menu-complete` instead of `complete-word` to `zle -C` like this:

```
zle -C most-recent-file menu-complete _generic
```

If you have menu selection enabled, it will now be invoked for the widget, which is not what we want. You could adjust your `select` style's context to skip this widget, but a better way is to use the `_menu` completer at the beginning of the list of completers. It forces later completers to use menu completion, disabling menu selection in the process. The `_menu` completer even overrides the behavior selected with `zle -C`, so whether we use `complete-word` or `menu-complete` there is immaterial.

For our main completer, all we need to do is use `_files`. We'll follow it with `_match` so that you can specify a glob pattern to restrict the types of files that will be matches. So we have this style:

```
zstyle ':completion:most-recent-file:::' completer _menu _files _match
```

This has now got us menu completion of files in alphabetical order, but we want the most recently modified file to appear first. Fortunately, `_files` looks up a `file-sort` style to specify how files should be sorted. Given the value `modification`, it will sort files by their last modified times. Other sort criteria such as file size or change and access times are also available. So we just add this style to handle the ordering:

```
zstyle ':completion:most-recent-file:*' file-sort modification
```

In typical usage, this widget is invoked once, and if the filename that appears is not the right one, it is tried again until the right one does appear. Therefore, listing possible matches is not particularly useful. Setting the `hidden` style to true hides the list. That leaves the description, which can be removed by setting the `hidden` style to `all`:

```
zstyle ':completion:most-recent-file:*' hidden all
```

A further change you may or may not want to do is to restrict the files matched to normal files. The `file-patterns` style we saw earlier allows that to be done:

```
zstyle ':completion:most-recent-file:*' file-patterns '*(.):normal\ files'
```

Don't forget to bind it to a key at the end of all this:

```
bindkey '^Xm' most-recent-file
```

To give you another example, here is one way to configure history word completion work:

```
zle -C history-complete complete-word _generic
zstyle ':completion:history-complete:::' completer _history
zstyle ':completion:history-complete:*' remove-all-dups true
zstyle ':completion:history-complete:*' sort true
bindkey '\e/' history-complete
```

Summary

Once you are used to the power of the shell's completion, it can be quite frustrating to discover that completion definitions are lacking for a command you use. Armed with the knowledge picked up in this chapter, you are now in a position to remedy that situation yourself. By using shell functions to define completions, both bash and zsh allow you to make use of many of the features we described earlier in the book. The result is a very powerful mechanism for configuring exactly how the shell handles completion for a particular command.

In this chapter, in addition to showing you how to generate completion matches, we have explained the many other features that are handled as part of the shells', and particularly zsh's, completion systems. We have shown you how to add descriptions to matches and group similar matches so that they can be listed together with a descriptive heading. We have demystified the tag loops system, which is behind the shell's ability to group matches and control the order in which matches are completed. We have also explained the details of zsh's _arguments function, enabling you to make use of its ability to complete command options, taking into account the many varying forms that command options take. Finally, we have shown that completion is not limited to your Tab key by demonstrating how different capabilities of the shell's completion system can be attached to another key.

And Finally...

That brings us to the end of this book. We hope that you've enjoyed learning about shells. Remember that bash and zsh are still being developed so many new and interesting features are being added all the time. We suggest you check out the latest versions. We've listed the web addresses in Appendix B along with links to other useful Internet resources.

■■■

Unix Programs

This appendix describes some of the hundreds of standard Unix programs available on a command line. These are also called Unix *utilities*.

We generally don't include commands that are built in (see the section "Where the Commands Are Located" in Chapter 1) to the shell. We also don't describe many programs. To see some of the others, use ls to list the directories /bin and /usr/bin. Also check out /opt and /usr/local/bin. (In Chapter 2 we developed an easier way to do this.)

To learn more about a program named (for example) xyz, type man xyz or info xyz.

Program	Description
awk	A programming language useful for processing text as either strings or numbers. See also sed (smaller and faster for text-only work) and Perl (larger and more sophisticated).
bzip2	Compresses files to save disk space. The bunzip2 program uncompresses permanently and bzcat makes an uncompressed copy on the standard output (the section "Writing Output to Files: Redirection" in Chapter 2 explains *stdout*). ("Zip" is a term for compressing files.) See also gzip.
cal	Shows a calendar for any month or year. There's an example in the section "Command Lines" in Chapter 1.
cat	This simple program reads the files named in its command-line arguments and outputs their contents, one after another, without stopping. (See also the less pager program, which shows files screen by screen.) Stands for "catenate" or "concatenate." Useful options: cat -t -v -e is a safe way to look at unknown files that might have "nonprinting" characters, which can mess up your terminal; the -e puts a $ character at the end of each line of the file so you can easily see trailing spaces.
chmod	Changes the access permission for files and directories so you can either share your files with other users or protect them. Stands for "change mode."
chown	Changes the owner and/or group of a file or directory. There's also a related command named chgrp that changes just group ownership.
chsh	Edits the system file /etc/passwd (or similar) to change the shell that runs when a user logs in.
clear	Erases your terminal screen. (May not erase any "scroll-back buffer" that shows what was on your screen before.) You may be able to achieve the same effect by pressing Ctrl-l (the letter "l").

Program	Description
column	Makes text into columns. (If your system doesn't have column, try paste—or a command like pr -t -l1 -*n*, where *n* is the number of columns you want.)
cp	Makes copies (duplicates) of one or more files. If the final command-line argument is a directory, all file(s) are copied to that directory. Warning: cp will overwrite an existing file without asking! To be asked, add the -i (interactive) option. See also ln.
cut	Removes some of each line of text: by column, by field, etc. (If your system doesn't have cut, try colrm or a programming language like awk or Perl.) See also paste. There's an example in the section "Editing Data, Continuing Command Lines" in Chapter 2.
CVS	The Concurrent Versions System (CVS) lets you recover previous versions of one file or a set of files. Similar systems include RCS, SCCS, and Subversion.
date	Shows the date and time in your current time zone (or another time zone if you set the TZ environment variable). There's an example in the section "Simple Commands" in Chapter 1. date can also be used to set the time and date on your system.
dd	Copies a file or standard input, converting and formatting the text. Often used for operations with magnetic tape but handy for other text processing too.
df	Displays information about the filesystem. Useful option: -h or -k (depending on your system) displays in an easier-to-read format. Useful argument: the pathname of a directory (like . for the current directory) shows information about the disk where that directory is stored.
diff	Compares two text files and shows the differences in your choice of several formats. Can also compare two directory trees file by file. Similar programs include cmp and comm.
du	Shows how much disk space is used by a file, a directory, or a directory tree. Useful option on some systems is -k, which shows file sizes in kilobytes (kb) instead of the default on those systems of 512 bytes (half a kilobyte).
echo	Outputs its command-line arguments. This is useful for programming and to show the shell expansion of arguments, like echo $SHELL or echo f*. There are examples throughout the book, including the sections "Where the Commands Are Located" and "Expansion and Substitution" in Chapter 1, and the sections "Writing Output to Files: Redirection," "Command Substitution," and "Programs and the Path" in Chapter 2.
Emacs	Powerful text editor. (Stands for "editor macros.")
env	Displays a list of environment variables set in the current process (typically, your shell). Can also run a program in a modified environment. We explain environment variables in the section "Passing Info to Processes with Environment Variables" in Chapter 3. Also see printenv.
file	Guesses what sort of content is in a file. (In general, Unix doesn't require filename "extensions," like .*txt* for text files, though they're often used.)
find	Searches a directory tree for files, directories, etc. with particular names or other characteristics.
gimp	Powerful editor for photos and other graphics. Requires a graphical display and a mouse. (Stands for GNU Image Manipulation Program.)

Program	Description
gnumeric	Spreadsheet. Requires a graphical display and a mouse.
grep	Searches through file(s) or its standard input (the section "Writing Output to Files: Redirection" in Chapter 2 explains *stdin*) for words or for a pattern called a *regular expression*. Stands for "globally search for a regular expression and print."
gzip	Compresses files to save disk space. The gunzip program uncompresses permanently and zcat makes an uncompressed copy on the standard output (the section "Writing Output to Files: Redirection" in Chapter 2 explains *stdout*). (The name is from GNU zip program, where "zip" is a term for compressing files.) See also bzip2.
head	Outputs just the first few lines from one or more text files. By default, the first 10 lines are output, but you can use an option to specify a different number (for example, -20 for the first 20 lines). It is often used as a filter as part of a pipeline. There is an example in the section "Here-Documents and Here-Strings" in Chapter 8. There is also a tail command that prints just the last lines.
kill	Sends a signal to a process. See the section "Starting and Stopping Processes: Signals, Job Control" in Chapter 3.
less	A *pager* program that displays files page-by-page (one terminal screenful at a time). Many handy features for searching, display, and much more. If your system doesn't have less, look for the related programs named more or pg.
ln	Creates a hard or symbolic link to a file, like a "shortcut" in Microsoft Windows. This makes the file accessible from another directory, and/or with a different filename, without making a separate copy. See the examples in the section "Links" in Chapter 8. See also cp and mv.
locate	Searches a database of the names of files on your filesystems. (Note: the database may not list all files, and it may be far out of date. Ask your system staff.)
look	Searches a sorted file. (By default, searches a list of dictionary words, which is a handy way to check spelling.)
lpr	Prints file(s) or standard input (the section "Writing Output to Files: Redirection" in Chapter 2 explains *stdin*). Your system may have the lp program instead. (Stands for "line printer.") Note: if the file has graphics in it, or was created by a graphical program such as a word processor, you should probably print by using the program that created the file.
ls	Lists the contents of directories and/or files. One of the many examples is in the section "The Filesystem: Directories, Pathnames" in Chapter 1.
make	Reads instructions from a file describing how to produce one or more output files from their input files. It checks which of the input files have changed and runs only those commands needed to update the output files. Typically it is used when compiling a software program.
man	Describes a program. You may also need the info program, which does a similar thing. There's an example in the section "Command Lines" in Chapter 1.
mesg	Controls whether other users can write (send messages) to your terminal with a utility such as write or talk.

Program	Description
mkdir	Creates one or more directories. The arguments are one or more pathnames—relative or absolute. For instance, mkdir papers makes a subdirectory named *papers* under the current directory, and mkdir /usr/local/foo makes a directory with that absolute pathname. Useful option: -p creates multiple layers of subdirectories if needed. (Stands for "make directory.") An example is in the section "Programs and the Path" in Chapter 2.
Mozilla	Graphical web browser available on many systems. Your system may also have other browsers such as *Netscape* or *Konqueror*.
mv	Renames files or directories, or moves them into different directories. (Stands for "move.") If the final command-line argument is a directory, all file(s) are moved into that directory. Caution: mv will overwrite an existing file without asking! To be asked, add the -i ("interactive") option.
passwd	Changes your login password. (Your system may use a different program. Check with your system staff.)
paste	Pastes text into columns. See also cut, column, and pr.
Perl	Sophisticated programming language with many uses. Terse syntax makes it powerful but code can be difficult to understand at first. Smaller languages include sed and awk.
pico	Easy-to-use text editor. Useful option (for editing shell setup files like .bashrc): -w tells Pico not to "wrap" (break) lines that are wider than your screen. A similar program named nano also exists.
pr	Makes text into columns, numbered pages with titles, and more. (Stands for "print," which made sense on the original teletype terminals where the output was printed onto a roll of paper!)
printenv	Displays a list of environment variables set in the current process (typically, your shell). We explain environment variables in the section "Passing Info to Processes with Environment Variables" in Chapter 3. Also see env.
ps	Shows information about processes. (Stands for "process status.") There are examples in the section "Command Lines" in Chapter 1 and the section "Starting and Stopping Processes: Signals, Job Control" in Chapter 3.
pwd	Shows the absolute pathname of your current directory. (Stands for "print working directory.") There's an example in the section "Relative Pathnames and Your Current Directory" in Chapter 1.
rm	Removes the files you list on its command line. Useful options: -i asks before removing each file, and -r removes a directory and all of its files.
rmdir	Removes directories named on the command line. Directories must be empty (use rm to remove any files in them first, or use rm -r to remove the directory *and* its files).
scp	Copies files to or from other computers using ssh. (Stands for "secure copy.") It is similar to the older, and relatively less secure, rcp (remote copy) command.
sed	The stream editor, sed, reads text from its standard input, applies one or more editing commands to the text, and writes the result to its standard output. The most-used sed command is probably s, which substitutes new text in place of existing text.
sort	Reads files or standard input (the section "Writing Output to Files: Redirection" in Chapter 2 explains *stdin*) and sorts their lines.

Program	Description
ssh	Runs programs on other computers or logs you into other computers. (Stands for "secure shell.") Two similar (but insecure) programs are rlogin and telnet.
strings	Extracts ASCII strings from binary files. This allows many other Unix commands that only work with plain text to be used on the result. So, for example, when used with grep it is possible to search the contents of a binary file.
tar	Archiving program that can write multiple directories and files into a single file, to a pipe, or (tar's original use) to magnetic tape. (The name stands for "tape archiver.") Your version of tar may be able to compress the archive file to save space; otherwise you can pipe tar's output through a compression program like gzip.
tee	Writes text from its standard input to its standard output and also to one or more files named on its command line. There's an example (as well as a zsh replacement for tee) in the section "Multiple Redirections in zsh" in Chapter 8.
touch	Creates empty files and changes the "timestamp" (last-modified date) of existing files. For an example, see the section "Building Pathnames by Completion" in Chapter 1.
tr	Translates characters. See the section "Command Substitution" in Chapter 2 for an example.
uniq	Compares each line of text with the next line, either showing duplicate lines or eliminating them. Often used with sort (though see sort -u, which runs uniq for you).
vi	Powerful text editor. (Stands for "visual." Originally, editors showed only one line of a file at a time.)
w	Detailed information about users logged in to your computer. See also who.
wc	Counts the number of lines, words, and characters in file(s) or standard input (the section "Writing Output to Files: Redirection" in Chapter 2 explains *stdin*).
wget	Gets files from Internet web and FTP sites.
which	Shows the absolute pathname of a program's file. (Also try type.)
who	Lists the users who are logged in to your computer. See also w.
xargs	Executes a command repeatedly with sets of arguments taken from its (xargs') standard input. Often used to process a list of arguments so long that they won't all fit on a single command line (as indicated by an error message like zsh: arg list too long: grep). Arguments containing spaces can cause errors; you can work around this with the -0 (zero) option on many versions.
xkill	Aborts graphical programs by closing their connection to the X display server. For killing graphical programs, this can be much more convenient than using the kill command because the window to kill is selected interactively using the mouse.
xterm	Creates a terminal window where you can use a shell. See the section "Opening a Terminal, Choosing the Shell" in Chapter 4.

External Resources

bash

- Free Software Foundation's web page: http://www.gnu.org/software/bash/bash.html

  In addition to a brief summary of bash, this page contains links to an online version of the manual and download locations.

- The author's web page: http://cnswww.cns.cwru.edu/~chet/bash/bashtop.html

  Chet Ramey, who coordinates the development of bash, maintains this web page. It contains a good deal more information than the Free Software Foundation page.

- Frequently Asked Questions (FAQ): ftp://ftp.cwru.edu/pub/bash/FAQ

- Mailing list: bug-bash@gnu.org

  There is only this one list and, though primarily intended for reporting bugs, it sometimes contains discussion of new features or behavior changes; it is also available as a Usenet newsgroup, gnu.bash.bug.

- bash debugger: http://bashdb.sourceforge.net/

  This is the web site for bashdb, which is covered in the section "The bash Debugger" in Chapter 13.

- bash_completion: http://www.caliban.org/bash/index.shtml#completion

  To get the most out of programmable completion in bash, install this. See the section "bash_completion" in Chapter 10 for more details.

zsh

- zsh home page: http://www.zsh.org/

  This serves as a jumping-off point to the main web pages and the various distribution sites from which you can download the source code. The mailing-list archives are also hosted here.

- zsh master site: `http://zsh.sunsite.dk/`

  This is the master site for the main zsh web pages. There are also mirrors of this site elsewhere. You can find news along with web versions of the manual, user guide, and FAQ here as well as all the other types of information you would expect to find on any open source project's web site.

- Users' mailing lists: `zsh-users@sunsite.dk`

  If you have any questions or problems with zsh, this is the place to ask. Topics discussed range in complexity from simple to highly advanced. There is also a `zsh-workers` mailing list used to coordinate further development of zsh.

- Distribution site: `ftp://ftp.zsh.org/pub/`

  This is the master site if you want to download the zsh source code. There are, however, many mirror sites, so we would recommend going to the zsh home page and picking the nearest one.

- zsh Wiki: `http://zshwiki.org/`

  This unofficial site allows you to share tips and tricks with other users.

General

- `comp.unix.shell`

  This Usenet newsgroup has lively shell-related discussion. It is probably also the best place to go if you have bash-related questions.

- KornShell: `http://www.kornshell.com/`

  Web pages for ksh are here. Binaries and source code for the 1993 version of ksh are available for download.

- tcsh web pages: `http://www.tcsh.org/`

- rc shell Unix implementation: `http://www.star.le.ac.uk/~tjg/rc/`

- Cygwin: `http://sources.redhat.com/cygwin/`

  Cygwin is a Unix emulation layer that runs on top of Windows. With it, you can run any of the Unix shells on Windows.

- MKS: `http://www.mks.com/`

  MKS sells Unix-like software, including shells, for Microsoft Windows.

- Linux Extended Attributes and ACLs: `http://acl.bestbits.at/`

  In the section "Accessing Extended Filesystem Attributes" in Chapter 13 we show ways of using filesystem *extended attributes* from the shell. This site has information about extended attribute support in the Linux kernel along with relevant patches.

Glossary

argument	These are the strings you type after a program name. Sometimes people distinguish between arguments and *options* (in the first sense of the two meanings of *option* that we describe in the glossary) to a program.
array	A type of shell *variable* that contains an ordered list of string values, called *elements* of the array. The shell provides syntax for you to extract or edit the individual elements.
associative array	A type of shell *variable* that contains a set of *key* and *value* pairs, both of which are strings. Using the key, you can extract the corresponding value from the associative array.
binding	See *key binding*.
buffer	Any area of computer memory used for temporary storage. In particular, the *line editor buffer* is the space where the shell stores the command line you are editing. In zsh *editor widgets*, you can refer to this using the variable BUFFER.
comment	A note in a *shell script* or *shell function* for humans to read but which the shell ignores. In shells, comments start with a # character and continue to the end of the line.
completion	The process whereby the shell examines a partial word typed by the user, usually a command name or command-line argument, as the basis for a guess about what the user is attempting to type. The shell then uses that guess to provide the missing part of the word. In the simplest case, you just press Tab. The most common type of argument to complete is a filename.
completion widget	A *shell function* with the special purpose of telling the shell how to complete parts of a command line, and perhaps also how to process the *matches*.
cursor	The place on the command line where you are editing; the point at which characters you type will be placed. A cursor is usually denoted by a solid block of color or a reversed, underlined, or flashing character.
Cygwin	A set of programs that make Microsoft Windows look more like Unix. This is the recommended way of running bash or zsh under Windows.

directory

A container for files, which may include other directories. The same as *folder*. Executing ls displays the contents of the current directory.

directory stack

A means for remembering the directories you've used most recently so you can refer to them or change back to them again without retyping the full name.

editor

A program for altering a file interactively. Common Unix editors include Emacs and vi, but there are many others. This term can also refer to the *line editor*, which is part of the shell.

editor widget

Also "editing widget." In zsh, a function written to add a new ability to the line editor or completion; see also *widget*.

environment

Every program, even if it isn't a shell, has a set of names, each with a string value, associated with it. These are collectively called the "environment"; the name of an individual element of the environment is an "environment variable." This looks to the shell like any shell *variable*. The variables *exported* by the shell form the environment of any program started from the shell. The environment can be altered by the program itself. Different programs use different environment variables; you'll need to consult the program's documentation to find out what they are. The most important environment variable is PATH, which tells the shell and other programs where to look for commands. Sometimes we use the word "environment" more generally to refer to the entire state of the shell, including its working directory.

escape

The term *escape* is widely used, but we are mostly concerned with two meanings:
1. The *escape key* is the key probably marked Esc in the top left-hand corner of your keyboard. In the shell's *line editor* you often press Esc before another key. The two keys form a *key sequence*.
2. In a string to be output with some form of special formatting, an *escape sequence* is a special set of characters used as shorthand for a special effect. Sometimes this is called an *escape* for short. A *prompt escape* is an example that is commonplace in shells.

exec

In Unix and similar systems, to *exec* a program is to replace the currently running program with another whose name and arguments are passed to the exec function. This procedure is the second part of starting a new program; see *fork*. exec is also the name of a shell built-in command.

expansion

Taking a command line and turning patterns, variables, and so on into arguments to pass down to the program; for example, turning the pattern *.txt into the argument list chapter1.txt chapter2.txt. This is used interchangeably with the term *substitution*. There is no real difference between the two terms though some types of expansion are always associated with one or other term (e.g., *process substitution*). Where the expansion can result in more than one word, the term *expansion* is normally favored.

export

To tell the shell to make a variable available in the *environment* of programs. For example, export PAGER=less allows other programs to see the variable PAGER with the value less.

filesystem	The complete set of files and directories on your system. Anything you can specify using names in the form `/usr/bin/zsh`.
folder	A common name in Windows and other GUIs for a *directory*.
fork	Forking creates a new *process* by making a copy of the current process (with some small differences). Often, the newly forked process will start doing a completely different task by *execing* another program. This is the normal way of starting a new program in Unix.
function	See *shell function*.
function keys	The set of keys marked *F1*, *F2*, and so on, at the top of the keyboard. You can use these for *key bindings*. You can also use many other special keys such as the ones marked Insert, Home, and so on.
glob qualifier	In `zsh`, an expression in parentheses after a filename pattern that tells the shell to restrict the files matched to certain types of file.
globbing	*Unix* slang for expanding patterns on the command line into filenames. The most common globbing pattern is the *wildcard* *.
GNU	Recursive acronym for GNU's Not Unix, and a commonly used term when referring to the Free Software Foundation's GNU Project. GNU software includes free tools provided by the Free Software Foundation, covering almost all the features you need to perform basic tasks. The tools are often supplied with *Linux*, but are also available for Windows (as the *Cygwin* tools) and, despite the name, for many *Unix variants*, too.
grep	A search program that is so often used in *Unix* that it has become a verb meaning "to search a set of file files for a matching pattern." grep originally came from "global regular expression print."
GUI	Graphical user interface, a means of executing commands with the mouse and menus. The primary alternative to the command line.
hard link	If you create a hard link to a file, you are effectively giving it another name; the original name and the hard link behave in exactly the same way.
history	The set of previously executed commands. The shell remembers these and their order for you to execute or edit them again.
interactive	An *interactive shell* is one that shows you a *prompt* and reads your commands, in contrast to a shell that is executing a *script*.
job	A task as the shell sees it: a set of programs running together which can be manipulated in one go using *job control* commands such as `kill`, `bg`, and `fg`. A job may be a simple process, or a pipeline. Compare *pipeline* and *process*.
key binding	Associating a set of keys or *keystrokes* with an editor command. For example, the left cursor key is usually bound to an editor command to move one character to the left on the command line. Some keys are bound by default, but you can customize the bindings.

keystroke	A set of keys you press at once for a particular effect. For example, holding down the Ctrl key and pressing a gives the keystroke Ctrl-a.
kill	*Unix* jargon: to terminate a program before it has finished running. `kill` is also a shell command that can send any *signal* to a program.
line editor	A modern shell gives you a lot of ways to move around and change the command line with *keystrokes*. Taken together, these capabilities form the *line editor*. Often, this behaves a bit like an *editor* program, but it is part of the shell.
link	An entry in a the filesystem that refers to another file. Either a *hard link* or a *soft link*.
Linux	A free version of the Unix operating system. Most Linux systems are based on *GNU* programs.
matches	In the context of completion, the generated words that are offered as possible completions.
modifier	A special key that is usually pressed and held down while another key is pressed. The Shift and Ctrl keys are examples of modifiers. When discussing the shell, we use the word to describe a way of altering command line arguments (for example, removing the directory part of a filename) that is described in Chapter 6.
operating system	The software responsible for the control of hardware and system resources such as the CPU, memory, and disk storage. It provides various core services to application programs.
option	The term *option* has two meanings: 1. A special argument to a command to change its behavior. In Unix, these options often begin with a hyphen. For example, in `ls -l`, `-l` is an option to the command `ls`. 2. A shell *option* is a way of altering the shell's behavior. Shell options don't have values, unlike *variables*, but are either on or off.
pager	A program such as `pg`, `more`, or `less` that can be used to view a file or the output of another command one screen (or *page*) at a time.
parameter	The word "parameter" is often used to refer to what we have called *variables* in this book. The `bash` and `zsh` manuals in particular use this term. In this book, we have limited the word to use in the context of the positional parameters (those accessed with $1, $2, $3, ...).
pipe	A way of allowing one process to send its output to the input of another process. In the shell, you create pipes between commands by putting the character | between them.
pipeline	A set of processes connected by a pipe, the output of one process feeding into the input of a next. This gives a very flexible way of massaging output. You can recognize a pipeline by a list of commands, each separated by the character |. Because of the name, people sometimes refer to a set of processes involving pipelines as "plumbing."

process	An instance of a single program with its own number (process ID, or PID); the fundamental unit of resources such as memory. Complicated programs may actually consist of multiple interacting processes performing slightly different tasks. Any program can generate new processes, which are called *child processes*. Compare *job*.
prompt	The characters that appear at the start of the line when you're about to type a command. In zsh, you can also make a prompt appear on the right-hand side. Prompts can contain *prompt escapes*.
prompt escape	Shorthand for making some special text appear in a *prompt*. For example, \u in bash and %n in zsh are prompt escapes that make the name of the user appear in the prompt.
quote	You *quote* text to prevent special characters such as white space, star, or question mark from being interpreted by the shell. The normal quotation characters are " and ' for blocks of text and \ for single characters. The backquote symbol ` has a special effect. See the main text for more explanation.
readline	The GNU library that supplies the *line editor* used in many programs, but in this book most notably in bash. You can configure it from within the shell.
redirection	Making the input of a command come from a specified source, or the output of a command go to a specified destination. If you are editing at a *terminal*, redirection is often used to make input come from a file or output go to a file for a single command. For example, echo MESSAGE >msg outputs the word MESSAGE and a newline to the file msg.
root	See *superuser*.
root directory	The top directory of the *filesystem*. All other directories are subdirectories of it. You can refer to it with a single forward slash (/).
scalar	The simplest type of data handled by the shell. A scalar is either a number (such as 7) or a character string (such as "hello"). A *scalar variable* can be used to hold a scalar value.
script	See *shell script*.
shell function	Often just called a "function," if that is unambiguous. A (usually) short program written in shell programming language. Unlike a script, it runs in the current shell, so it can change the environment of the shell itself. A simple function definition looks like fn() { echo I am a function; }. You execute it by typing the name, fn.
shell script	A program written in the shell programming language. A new shell is started to run every script. Compare *shell function*. Scripts can be written in many interpreted languages other than shells, such as Perl, Python, and TCL. "Interpreted" means the program is read and executed directly from the script, instead of being compiled into another form first.

signal
: A simple way of communicating from one program to another, or from the *operating system* to a program, to tell it that something has happened, such as a child program has finished, or to tell it to do something, such as exit immediately. If the program is a shell, it may run a *trap* at that point. Counterintuitively, you send a signal from the shell to another program using the kill command, even if you are not *killing* the program.

soft link
: A pointer to a file or directory. A soft link is an entry in a directory that only contains a note saying where the real file is. However, the *operating system* knows about this feature: most commands that read or write the soft link will read or write what the link points to.

source
: When used as a verb, this refers to executing the source or dot (.) built-in to run the commands that are contained in a file as if they were typed by the user.

spawn
: Another word for *fork* when used to start a new program.

startup file
: One of various files that the shell reads when the shell begins running. The shell then executes the commands in the file. You use startup files to customize the shell.

style
: In zsh, the style mechanism is a flexible way of configuring shell add-ons that use functions, such as the completion system and editor widgets. Unlike variables they can be different in different contexts and unlike shell options they can take values. The mechanism is based on the command zstyle.

subdirectory
: A *directory* inside another directory. When you run ls -F, subdirectories are the files marked with a /.

subscript
: With array references, an index appears inside brackets after the name of the array. What appears inside these brackets, which can be more than a single index, is often referred to as an array subscript.

subshell
: A child process (see *process*) of the shell. More specifically, it is a copy of the shell created by *forking* it. This is used to run code which doesn't affect the parent shell. You can start a subshell by putting a command in parentheses.

substitution
: See *expansion*.

superuser
: Every *Unix* computer has a special user called root who has extra powers. The superuser can read all files on the system, no matter the permissions. Many tasks performed by the *operating system* must be done by the superuser, but it is generally dangerous to do normal work as the superuser because it's much easier to damage important files or *kill* important programs.

suspend
: Stop a program temporarily from executing. The usual way of doing this is to press Ctrl-z when a program is running, or from the shell kill -STOP *pid*, where *pid* is the *process* ID.

terminal
: The area of the computer screen where you type commands and where the replies appear. On modern computers, this is nearly always a window on a graphical windowing system called a *terminal emulator*. In Unix-speak, people sometimes talk about a *tty*, for teletype, the forerunner of the terminal. In Windows-speak, people often talk about a *command prompt* window.

trap
: A shell command or a list of shell commands that you set up and which is run when something special happens in the shell, for example a shell is about to exit, or it detects that the size of the *terminal* window has changed. Most traps are associated with a *signal*; you can also use a trap to tell the shell to ignore some signals.

Unix
: A powerful family of *operating systems*. Very often used to refer to the set of programs normally supplied with the operating system, too, as in "ls is a Unix command." There are lots of slightly different versions of Unix; some of the most common are BSD (including FreeBSD and NetBSD), Solaris (or SunOS), AIX, HP-UX, IRIX, and Digital Unix. Unix inspired *Linux*, though it was actually written separately; in this book, we are often lax and refer to Unix when we mean anything similar.

variable
: A named object used to remember a value. The command name='Greg Arious' sets the variable name to the string Greg Arious. Later, you can use the form $name to insert the string Greg Arious into a command line.

widget
: Used fairly widely for a some element of a user interface composed out of smaller parts. In zsh, and more widely in this book, a shell function that implements a feature for the line editor or for completion, allowing you to add new commands of your own.

wildcard
: Sometimes used to refer to the character * when used as a pattern to match all characters and the character ? when used as a pattern to match any single character.

zle
: The zsh *line editor*, the part of the shell that allows you to edit the command line with keystrokes. It corresponds to *readline* in bash.

Index